Human Resource Management in the Health Care Sector

Recent Titles from Quorum Books

Innovation Through Technical and Scientific Information: Government and Industry Cooperation
Science and Public Policy Program, University of Oklahoma: Steven Ballard, Thomas E. James, Jr., Timothy I. Adams, Michael D. Devine, Lani L. Malysa, and Mark Meo

Transformations in French Business: Political, Economic, and Cultural Changes from 1981 to 1987
Judith Frommer and Janice McCormick, editors

Economics and Antitrust Policy
Robert J. Larner and James W. Meehan, Jr., editors

A Legal Guide to EDP Management
Michael C. Gemignani

U.S. Commercial Opportunities in the Soviet Union: Marketing, Production, and Strategic Planning Perspectives
Chris C. Carvounis and Brinda Z. Carvounis

An Analysis of the New Financial Institutions: Changing Technologies, Financial Structures, Distribution Systems, and Deregulation
Alan Gart

The Commercialization of Outer Space: Opportunities and Obstacles for American Business
Jonathan N. Goodrich

Computer Power and Legal Language: The Use of Computational Linguistics, Artificial Intelligence, and Expert Systems in the Law
Charles Walter, editor

The Ethics of Organizational Transformation: Mergers, Takeovers, and Corporate Restructuring
W. Michael Hoffman, Robert Frederick, and Edward S. Petry, Jr., editors

Cable TV Advertising: In Search of the Right Formula
Rajeev Batra and Rashi Glazer, editors

The Marketer's Guide to Selling Products Abroad
Robert E. Weber

Corporate Social Responsibility: Guidelines for Top Management
Jerry W. Anderson, Jr.

Product Life Cycles and Product Management
Sak Onkvisit and John J. Shaw

Human Resource Management in the Health Care Sector

A GUIDE FOR ADMINISTRATORS AND PROFESSIONALS

EDITED BY
Amarjit S. Sethi
AND
Randall S. Schuler

Q

QUORUM BOOKS
New York • Westport, Connecticut • London

Library of Congress Cataloging-in-Publication Data

Human resource management in the health care sector
    Includes index.
    1. Health facilities—Personnel management.
2. Health services administration. I. Sethi, Amarjit
Singh. II. Schuler, Randall S.
RA971.35.H86 1989   362.1′1′0683   88-18313
ISBN 0–89930–201–7 (lib. bdg.: alk. paper)

British Library Cataloguing in Publication Data is available.

Copyright © 1989 by Amarjit S. Sethi and Randall S. Schuler

All rights reserved. No portion of this book may be reproduced, by any process or technique, without the express written consent of the publisher.

Library of Congress Catalog Card Number: 88-18313
ISBN: 0-89930-201-7

First published in 1989 by Quorum Books

Greenwood Press, Inc.
88 Post Road West, Westport, Connecticut 06881

Printed in the United States of America

The paper used in this book complies with the Permanent Paper Standard issued by the National Information Standards Organization (Z39.48-1984).

10 9 8 7 6 5 4 3 2 1

Contents

EXHIBITS	vii
INTRODUCTION	ix

1. **Human Resource Management: A Strategic Choice Model**
   Amarjit S. Sethi and Randall S. Schuler — 1

2. **Strategic Human Resource Planning**
   Kirk C. Harlow and Joseph K. Taylor — 15

3. **The Role of Job Design and Job Analysis in the Strategic Human Resource Management Model**
   Amarjit S. Sethi, Patricia L. Birkwood, and Randall S. Schuler — 41

4. **Recruitment Strategies**
   Donna L. Gellatly — 75

5. **Performance Appraisal as a Strategic Choice for the Health Care Manager**
   Robert Boissoneau, Debrah J. Gaulding, and David N. Calvert — 95

6. **Performance-Based Pay Systems in Health Care**
   Eugene P. Buccini — 127

7. **Designing a Compensation System in the Strategic Human Resource Management Model**
   Lois Friss — 147

Contents

8. **The Role of Quality of Worklife in the Strategic Human Resource Management Model**
   Paula L. Stamps and Thomas E. Duston — 177

9. **Strategic Management of Quality of Worklife in the Home Care Industry**
   Penny Hollander Feldman and Alice M. Sapienza — 197

10. **The Role of Organizational Development in the Strategic Human Resource Management Model**
    Ruth B. Welborn — 221

11. **Occupational Safety and Health Strategies**
    James Hill — 235

12. **Employee Rights Strategies**
    John Bernat — 247

13. **Collective Bargaining and Legislation: Implications for Strategic Human Resource Management**
    Howard M. Leftwich — 275

14. **The Technostress Challenge: Implications for Strategic Human Resource Management**
    Amarjit S. Sethi and Denis H.J. Caro — 301

INDEX — 337

ABOUT THE EDITORS AND CONTRIBUTORS — 353

Exhibits

1.1	An Integrated Human Resource System	4
1.2	Strategic Management and Environmental Pressures	5
1.3	A Strategic Choice Model of Human Resource Management	7
1.4	Labor Force Age Group Distribution Percentages	9
1.5	Occupational Makeup of the Civilian Labor Force	10
1.6	Industries with the Greatest Number of New Jobs by 1995	11
1.7	Information Technologies: Functions and Applications	12
2.1	Integrated Human Resource Planning Model	18
2.2	Example of Staffing Level Estimation Using Workload Measures	22
2.3	Plot of Nursing Staff by Year and Linear Regression Time-Series Equation	24
2.4	Markov Analysis of Staffing Levels	28
2.5	An Example of Movement Analysis Using Expected Transition Estimates	29
2.6	Employee Replacement Chart for a 250-Bed Hospital	31
3.1	Central Elements and Activities in Health Care Human Resource Management	42
3.2	Job Design and Job Analysis Relationships	45
3.3	Job Characteristics Model of Work Motivation	49
3.4	A Model of Employee Reactions to Their Jobs	51
3.5	Principles for Changing Jobs	56

3.6	Predicted Relationships among Organizational Design, Job Design, and Employee Characteristics	58
3.7	Relationship between Job Design Changes and Elements of Technology and Modes of Control	60
3.8	The Problem-Solving Cycle	61
3.9	Working Styles of Identifying Employee Skills and Managerial Roles	62
3.10	Optimum Utilization of Human Resources	65
4.1	Personnel Requisition	78
4.2	Newspaper Box Ad	83
5.1	Performance Appraisals Rulings	98
5.2	Benefits Researchers Associate with the Development of an Effective System of Performance Appraisal	101
5.3	Characteristics of a Democratic Manager	109
5.4	Suggested Methods to Help Set the Tone in the Appraisal Interview	112
6.1	Barnes Hospital Incentive Plan	134
6.2	Checklist for Developing a Performance-Based Pay System	137
6.3	Organizational Readiness Questionnaire	142
6.4	Building Success into a Pay-for-Performance System	143
7.1	Hay Plan Compensable Factors	153
7.2	Job Evaluation Systems	156
7.3	Comparison of Salaries and Points for Selected Sex-Segregated Positions, State of Washington	167
7.4	Selected Results of Point-Factor Job Evaluation Pilot Study for the Illinois Commission on the Status of Women	168
9.1	Life Expectancies in OECD Nations	199
9.2	The Squaring of the Pyramid: Japan	200
9.3	Cost of Hospitalization and Health Care	200
14.1	Technostress: A Working Model	303
14.2	Dimensions of Technostress	306
14.3	A Strategic Choice Model of Technostress Management	308
14.4	Phases in Strategic Technological Planning	313
14.5	A Technostress Human Resource Monitoring System	315
14.6	Cultural Matrix	320

Introduction

Our objectives in preparing this book were to (1) bring together the contributions of outstanding scholars in human resource management in health care; (2) provide a guide for practitioners to use in applying various concepts and tools discussed in the book; (3) provide a textbook for university classes in health, business, science, nursing, physical education, and general education; (4) assemble a reference source for other human resource management scholars and practitioners; and (5) provide in a single volume a set of practical strategies for planning and managing human resource strategies suited to health care environments.

Chapter 1, which gives an overview of the purposes of strategic human resource management (SHRM), also provides an integrated human resource system and outlines theoretical perspectives underlying a strategic choice model. It discusses strategy and strategic choice and their relevance to human resource management (HRM), the impact of internal and external environments on HRM, and the roles of demographics, economy, technology, government, and values regarding HRM.

In Chapter 2, Harlow and Taylor present a strategic human resource planning model. The health care industry is undergoing numerous changes that are affecting the management of human resources: increased competition, technological advances, new roles for physicians, restructured delivery systems, changing worker values, and altered demographics. Because of these and other changes, the need for a strategic HRM planning framework is emphasized. Of the three major planning approaches ("muddling through," "rational planning," and "systems planning"), the authors prefer the use of a systems approach in developing a health care HRM planning model. This approach is also in accord with strategic choice model presented in Chapter 1 (see Exhibit 1.3). The model and process are presented in a step-by-step fashion for ease of discussion, but the reader is asked to keep in mind the interactive nature of the model.

In Chapter 3, Sethi, Birkwood, and Schuler discuss the importance of job design and job analysis for SHRM. Both theoretical perspectives and practical tools are provided in designing health care jobs in a manner so that both performance (or effectiveness) and quality of worklife are obtained. The authors discuss contemporary challenges health administrators face in job design and job analysis. Following the strategic choice model presented in Chapter 2, they examine the relationship of job design and job analysis with internal and external environments of health care organization: health care goals and technological change, union-management relationships, recruitment and selection, appraising performance, training and promoting, and compensation and legal considerations in job design and job analysis. A model of employee response to health care job design is presented that emphasizes employee perceptions, job qualities, job redesign, and organizational mission.

In Chapter 4, Gellatly examines strategic perspectives on recruitment strategies, including sources and methods for obtaining a competent health care workforce. Specific guidelines for administrators and professionals are provided to put these methods into practice.

In Chapter 5, Boissoneau, Gaulding, and Calvert explain the growing importance of performance appraisal systems as a strategic choice in SHRM and examine the legal considerations practitioners need in designing such systems. They discuss broad criteria for establishing systems and provide tools for setting them up. The authors explain the nature of a democratically oriented manager and discuss vehicles, such as quality circles, that managers can use to solicit from employees work-related suggestions for improvements. In a detailed analysis of performance appraisal process, they provide guidelines that practitioners can use in planning and implementing an effective performance appraisal system.

In Chapter 6, Buccini analyzes performance-based pay systems and the relevance and use of incentive pay plans in the health sector. He provides detailed guidelines for establishing and implementing pay-for-performance systems in health care organizations. He stresses the principle that the compensation system must be integrated with all other organizational choices related to quality control, job design, performance appraisal, and fringe benefits.

In Chapter 7, Friss discusses the nature, process, and objectives of compensation system for a health care organization. After examining trends in compensation, the author analyzes alternative methodologies for job evaluation, as well as scope, purpose, and philosophy of a pay system in an organization. In line with the strategic choice model presented in Chapter 1, the author analyzes both internal and external enviromental factors that influence compensation, emphasizing the need for establishing internal and external equity. Criteria for assessing the effectiveness of a compensation system are examined. The chapter analyzes special issues in compensation, including physician compensation, executive compensation, employee involvement and acceptance, pay satisfaction,

Introduction

and pay equity and comparable worth. In addition to comparable worth, the author recommends several alternate strategies for employers to avoid lawsuits and, more important, to remain competitive for competent health care workers of both sexes. The chapter provides detailed guidelines in planning and implementing a pay system for a health care organization.

In Chapter 8, Stamps and Duston analyze methods for improving the quality of worklife in the health fields. The authors discuss the nature of the quality of worklife (QWL) movement and its relationship to the critical issue of productivity. In accord with the strategic human resource management model used in this book, the authors regard QWL as a process that integrates recruitment selection and retention, job satisfaction, career development, job redesign, alternative patterns of work, and participative management. A model for an integrated QWL program is presented with practical guidelines and cautions in implementing this model in health care organizations.

In Chapter 9, Feldman and Sapienza focus on the jobs of more than 300,000 homemakers—home health aides in the United States. This chapter aims to put the job of the home aide in context, familiarize readers with the U.S. home care industry, provide some insights into the work from the perspective of the worker, and examine current practices to improve QWL for this group of workers. The chapter provides guidelines for practitioners and researchers to plan and develop QWL strategies for the health care industry in the United States.

In Chapter 10, Welborn examines another long-term strategic choice facing health care organizations: strategies for managing change. Organizational development (OD) is presented as a central strategy for coping with multiple and rapid changes in the health care sector, including accelerated growth of information technologies, numerous ethical and policy dilemmas, the reallocation of financial resources, and the shift from a patient-centered way of thinking to a bottom-line perspective by health care administrators and professionals. After reviewing OD theory and trends, the author examines the process and techniques of OD and how these can be planned, implemented, and monitored in the health care sector. The role of training in OD is also covered. The chapter provides guidelines for administrators and professionals in understanding the potential use of OD as a strategy for managing change, as well as classifying practical steps that health care organizations need to take in administering OD programs. The author claims that the failure of OD health care projects is more attributable to the lack of knowledge and skill on the part of the OD practitioner than to the uniqueness of the health care setting. The chapter fills this need by analyzing the concepts and tools of OD and its potential benefits for the organization and its administrators and health care professionals.

In Chapter 11, Hill describes the approaches and strategies for management of the safety and health of the work environment. A detailed analysis of legal considerations, employee rights in safety and health, worker compensation, and impact of technology on occupational safety and health are covered. Practical guidelines for administrators and professionals are provided.

In Chapter 12, Bernat emphasizes the role of employee rights in strategic human resource management. He examines the historical and current legal framework of employee rights. Special issues discussed include the Fair Labor Standards Act, Equal Pay Act, Title VII of the 1964 Civil Rights Act, affirmative action, ADEA, pregnancy, issues of control, relationships among professions in the workplace, predominance of women in nursing and other health occupations, comparable worth, and future trends in employee rights.

In Chapter 13, Leftwich examines the process of collective bargaining and the legal framework within which it takes place. The author discusses the implications of collective bargaining for strategic human resource management, which is changing a system of unilateral determination by management of terms and conditions of employment to one of joint determination by management and union. The author recommends guidelines for practitioners in understanding the legal framework for collective bargaining in health care organizations, preparing for bargaining, and understanding and utilizing the bargaining process.

In Chapter 14, Sethi and Caro examine the challenge posed by the emerging information technology and its implications for strategic human resource management. They introduce the concept of technostress, defined as perceived uncertainty resulting from the introduction and maintenance of information technology in health care organizations. Technostress can be utilized constructively, and proactive strategies can be employed by administrators and professionals to prevent stress and burnout in the workplace. A number of individual and organizational strategies are presented, including technological policy, strategic planning, organizational development, technological stress audit at the organizational level, and self-development strategies (among them training, nutrition, biofeedback, meditation, physical exercise, and time management at the individual level). The authors predict that managing information technology will become a strategic function of future health care organizations and will be one of the key strategic choices in the planning and implementation of human resource management systems.

Human Resource Management in the Health Care Sector

1
Human Resource Management: A Strategic Choice Model

*Amarjit S. Sethi
and Randall S. Schuler*

Strategic human resource management (SHRM) is the process of deciding on the strategic aims of a human resource system and making decisions to achieve those aims. Embedded in this process is the concept of a clear set of choices, aims, and performance indicators matched up with organizational personnel needs and perspectives of a health care organization. In this approach the emphasis is on making strategic decisions to ensure that a health care organization has the appropriate culture, as well as the right numbers and kinds of people working effectively to fulfill individual and organizational objectives. SHRM is thus directly connected to the overall mission, strategy, and structure of the organization.

The strategic management of human resources is a critical issue because of the numerous changes affecting health care organizations. This book explores the relevance and usefulness of selected strategic choices that can be used as human resource strategies at the organizational level to cope with the impacts of technological, medical, legal, economic, and sociopolitical changes in current and future health care organizations.

Each chapter contains at the end a set of guidelines to assist practitioners in applying various human resource management concepts and tools discussed in this book.

CHANGES AFFECTING HUMAN RESOURCE MANAGEMENT

Four major changes are influencing the formulation and implementation of a strategic human resources management system in a health care organization:

- Health care organizations are currently engaged in competitive activities, implying major changes in their organizational structure, including human resources (Webber, 1982; Flexner, Berkowitz, and Brown, 1981).
- We have entered an age of discontinuity, future shock, economic and social crises, and unprecedented rapid technological change. At the same time, international interdependence has increased, with consequent increases in unpredictability in forecasting future personnel requirements (Drucker, 1969; Toffler, 1970; Ansoff, 1978).
- There is an increasing trend to favor multisystem development among health care organizations, not only in hospitals but in long-term care, ambulatory care, diagnostic laboratories, and other areas of the health care field. This model stresses market penetration, market development, product development, and diversification involving geographic or purely volume expansion. The human resource planning function has become complex because of these developments.
- The health care industry has some unique characteristics that human resource planners need to consider: (1) The technology of patient care generates a high level of "technostress," or actual and perceived uncertainty. This uncertainty is increased by clinical characteristics associated with diagnosing and solving patient problems. (2) There is a need to establish and maintain an infrastructure to cope with pressures generated at the local level from physician appointments, physician referral patterns, supporting laboratory and other technical capability, and the needs of nurse staffing and other allied health care personnel. (3) There is an increase in competition among hospitals, between hospitals and physician groups, and between hospitals and insurance carriers. The health care industry is constantly struggling to redefine its traditional mission of community-oriented care, using new business-like patterns of expansion, economy, and efficiency in a multiunit health system (Luke and Kurowski, 1983).

Because of these generic and health industry–specific changes, the importance of human resource management has increased. Increasingly jobs in both small- and large-scale health care organizations are being redesigned to incorporate information technology. Workers must be able to function when they lack knowledge about how to perform a task and about what to do when in exceptional circumstances.

PURPOSES OF STRATEGIC HUMAN RESOURCE MANAGEMENT

SHRM is intended to accomplish the following aims:

1. Provide a systems approach to human resource planning, oriented toward the future and its management

Human Resource Management

2. Integrate human resource planning with corporate planning
3. Provide a foundation for employee career development
4. Be socially responsive to equity laws and affirmative action programs in identifying specific skills and future growth plans
5. Reduce personnel cost by helping health administrators to anticipate shortages or surpluses of health personnel and to correct these imbalances before they become dysfunctional
6. Be responsive to impacts of information technology on individuals, tasks, and the health care delivery system
7. Provide a methodology for evaluating the effect of alternate human resource strategies

Developments in information technology—the convergence of supercomputers and telecommunications, and national and international networking—permit the maintenance of a human resource information system. This technology allows vast job-related records to be maintained on each employee, including information on employee job preferences, work experience, and performance evaluations. Moreover, the information technology allows access to macrodata, both within the organization and outside, thus facilitating the realization of purposes of human resource management in the interests of health care organizations.

AN INTEGRATED HUMAN RESOURCE SYSTEM

In the health care industry, SHRM is necessary for effectively linking strategy to structure in various types of health care institutions. We recommend an integrated system connecting organization and job analysis, job design, succession planning, recruitment, assessment, training, performance appraisal, and career performance planning. Exhibit 1.1 depicts a basic human resource system, designed to chart strategically information flows concerning the planning and management of human resources in health care institutions.

This model combines organizational and personnel variables. Traditionally health care organizations have paid attention to the components depicted in circles. Now it is important for personnel departments to pay greater attention to the organizational and delivery systems, depicted in boxes. An integration of the various components shown in the figure provides a basis for a health care human system. The arrows indicate the information requirements needed for health care organizations to meet patient care quality and employee satisfaction.

For example, in Exhibit 1.1, should the health care organization's (HCO's) strategic plan call for expansion into new health services, medical technology, or markets, this information can be used to forecast the staff needed to meet those goals. These personnel forecasts can be used to develop other personnel functions, such as recruitment, assessment, job design, and job analysis. Succession planning should be considered while assigning health care workers to jobs, positions, and training. As a whole, the short-term and long-term personnel

Exhibit 1.1
An Integrated Human Resource System

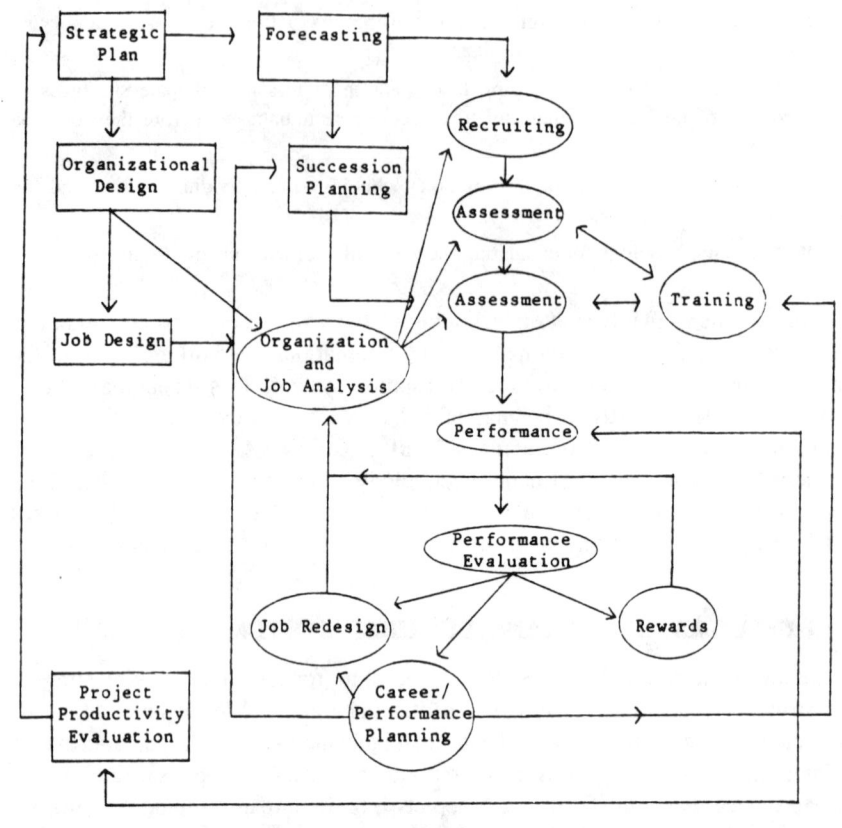

Source: M.A.V. Glinow, M.J. Driver, K. Brousseau, and J.B. Prince, "The Design of a Career Oriented Human Resource System," *Academy of Management Review* (1983). Reprinted by permission.

forecasts should be linked with organizational design and job design. "A fully integrated HR system considers these components and information linkages, not based on individual concerns solely, but because effective and efficient systems must be informed at the organizational level as well" (Glinow et al., 1983: 483).

Assessment, training, and performance evaluation are interlinked in an integrated human resource system, as Glinow et al. explain:

Once assessed, the individual should be assigned to a particular job classification or sent to *training* to develop, upgrade, or learn new skills.... Performance is the key criterion in this system affected by assignment of individuals to jobs.... Of crucial importance here are linkages to job analysis and individual assessment.... The *rewards* function should derive from as well as influence the performance evaluation.... Performance evaluation should activate a *career planning* function, as well as a performance planning

Exhibit 1.2
Strategic Management and Environmental Pressures

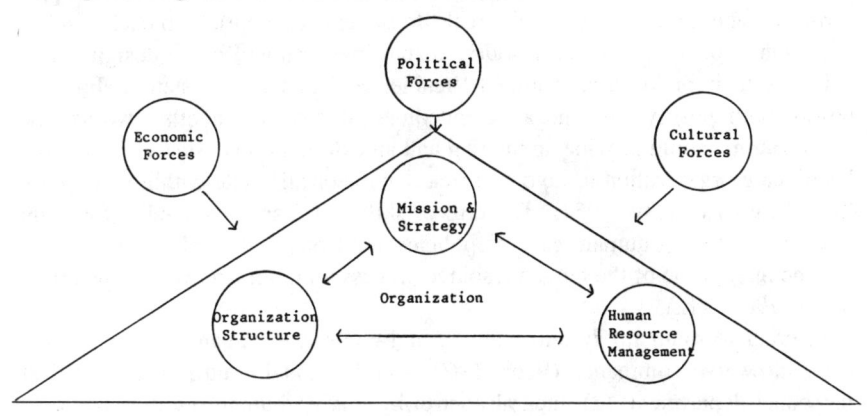

[Diagram: A triangle showing external forces (Political Forces at top, Economic Forces at left, Cultural Forces at right) pointing inward to an Organization composed of three interconnected circles: Mission & Strategy, Organization Structure, and Human Resource Management.]

Source: Adapted from N.M. Tichy, C.J. Fombrun, and M.A. Devanna, "Strategic Human Resource Management," *Sloan Management Review* (Winter 1982): 48, by permission of the publisher. Copyright © 1982 by the Sloan Management Review Association. All rights reserved.

function; consistent with maximizing individual potential and organizational objectives. (483–84).

THEORETICAL PERSPECTIVES

To understand the significance of SHRM, it is desirable to examine the two comparable models of human resource managing: the mechanistic model and the systems model. In a mechanistic model, management is a process that develops plans to meet specific goals. Goal setting is thus distinguished from planning. The external environment is left traditionally out of the management process. In a systems model, we must deal with the whole organization. In this perspective, human resource management is an open system that interacts with both internal and external environments. Exhibit 1.2 illustrates this interactional process in which management is future oriented and incorporates sociopolitical values that may guide human resource utilization. These values are changed by the system in order to place emphasis on norms that satisfy quality and performance to meet health care objectives. Human resource management becomes a creative exercise that can bring ideal values of high patient care quality and optimum employee performance into reality. This implies conceptualizing a human resource system that brings changes in the organization's design and culture, its technology, relationship, coalitions, evaluation system, reward structure, and economic and political realities of the external health care environment—thus providing a systems approach to the modification of contemporary human resource experience in health care organizations (Van Gigch, 1978).

Beer (1975) regards a systems view of human resource management as a viable survival strategy of cybernetics, conceptualizing the human resource as an interactive system of feedback, and a communications network that can perform "a cybernetic analysis of the real-life systems appropriate to each level of recursion" (p. 427). Human resource management should be so designed that it is able to improve organizational "resilience," that is, a system's ability to absorb both positive and negative outcomes of change. In other words, the organization should provide an internal and an external homeostasis to allow the health care organization to hold to a steady homeostatic state within its psychological limits (Ashby, 1954). The critical skill that managers need is foresight to oversee existing human resource policies and "map out viable strategies" to test the integration of the human resource process with human resource practices (Beer, 1969: 412).

In order to maintain system viability and control, a human resource system can follow five commands (Beer, 1969): (1) divisional control at the level of personnel department; (2) integral control by linking human resource planning to other personnel functions such as recruiting, training, and promotion; (3) internal homeostasis, by optimizing the organization's performance in relation to overall objectives; (4) external homeostasis, by creatively responding to external economic, political, and patient pressures; and (5) foresight, by formulating and testing human resource policies against a combination of possible futures.

A STRATEGIC CHOICE MODEL OF HUMAN RESOURCE MANAGEMENT

In Exhibit 1.3, the various elements of a strategic choice model of a human resource system are provided. The key elements are: (1) strategy and strategic choices; (2) internal and external environments; and (3) overall outcomes.

Strategy and Strategic Choices

The word *strategy* is used in a broad sense to encompass strategy formulation and its implementation. For us strategy is a pattern of action operationalized through rational policies and plans, as well as internal values for achieving ends in relation to human resources utilization. This definition is in accord with the one provided by Chandler (1962: 13) who defined strategy as "the determination of the basic goals . . . of an enterprise and the adoption of courses of action and the allocation of resources necessary for carrying out these goals." We have expanded the definition of strategy to include both rational (goal setting and implementing) and intuitive and incremental behaviors and values (Mintzberg, 1979: 25–26).

Strategic choice can be defined as the aim(s) (sometimes broadly conceived) of a dominant coalition. These are shaped by a coalition's internalized values and perceptions of power and mediated by transactions between it and the environment. Strategic decisions are part of a process in which a dominant coalition

Exhibit 1.3
A Strategic Choice Model of Human Resource Management

```
┌─────────────────────────┐
│ Internal Environment    │
│                         │
│ . Mission               │
│ . Organizational Structure │
│ . Organizational Culture│
└─────────────────────────┘
           │
           │
┌─────────────────────────┐         ┌──────────────────────┐
│ External Environment    │         │ Designing a          │
│                         │────────▶│ Human Resource       │
│ . Demographics          │         │ System               │
│ . Job Preferences       │         │                      │
│ . General Economic      │         │ Aims, Perceptions    │
│   Conditions            │         │ and Assumptions      │
│ . Information Technology│         └──────────────────────┘
│ . Values toward work    │                   ↕
│ . Values toward mobility│         ┌──────────────────────┐
│ . Values toward health  │         │ Moderated by         │
│   system                │         │                      │
│ . Government            │         │ Organizational Size, │
│   Intervention          │         │ Locus of Control     │
└─────────────────────────┘         │ Cost, Politics, Laws,│
                                    │ Values and Culture   │
                                    └──────────────────────┘
```

```
┌──────────────────────────────┐      ┌──────────────────────┐
│ Strategic Choices            │      │ General Outcomes     │
│                              │      │                      │
│ . Strategic Human            │      │ . Ensure match       │
│   Resource Planning          │─────▶│   between HRM        │
│ . Job design and analysis    │      │   strategies and     │
│ . Recruitment                │      │   Corporate          │
│ . Performance Appraisal      │      │   Strategies         │
│ . Compensation               │      │ . Organizational     │
│ . Organization Development   │      │   Effectiveness      │
│ . QWL                        │      │ . Competitive        │
│ . Occupational Health        │      │   gains              │
│   and Safety                 │      └──────────────────────┘
│ . Technostress               │
│ . Employee Rights            │
│ . Industrial Relation        │
│   – Collective Bargaining    │
│   – Dispute Resolution       │
│   – Contract Administration  │
└──────────────────────────────┘
```

proceeds to plan, shape, and/or exploit (either systematically or opportunistically) circumstances or events within the environment in ways that it perceives will bring it nearer to its aims. The element of choice lies in determining what circumstances or events to exploit. The purpose of a concept such as dominant coalition is to distinguish those who normally have the power to take initiative on matters such as the design of a human resources system from others who must respond to decisions. The concept relates to pragmatic acceptance by lower-level participants of power-holding roles and of decisions emanating from them (Dimmock and Sethi, 1986).

The perception of internal and external environments is moderated by organizational size, locus of control, cost-containment policies, and sociopolitical systems. The approach that we have taken is that it is not environment alone (e.g., technology) that causes productivity increases (or decreases) or better (or lower) quality of worklife but new values emerging from the impact of internal and external environments and how they are perceived.

The key human resources management (HRM) choices are strategic human resource planning, job design and job analysis, recruitment, performance appraisal, compensation (direct and indirect), organization development and training, quality of worklife, occupational health and safety, technostress, employee rights, and industrial relations. The chapters in this book examine these strategies in detail and provide guidelines for practitioners in developing an integrated human resource management system for their organizations.

Internal and External Environments

Internal Environment

There are three important relationships that HRM has with the internal environment:

1. *HCO's mission.* The systems approach links HRM with organizational mission (and its overall strategy to achieve that mission). This facilitates planning and also helps employees to cope with workforce reductions.
2. *Organizational structure.* This is the designed structure that provides legitimacy for people to carry out their tasks.
3. *Organizational culture.* Culture is the value system of a health organization expressed through its people and how they behave with each other and with patients.

External Environment

Many aspects of the external environment influence the evolution of human resource management in a health care organization. The first of these is demographics.

One of the significant factors influencing health manpower is the shrinking supply of young workers. After more than two decades of growth, the nation's

Exhibit 1.4
Labor Force Age Group Distribution Percentages

	Actual			Projected	
	1975	1979	1985	1990	1995
Age Group					
16-24	24.1	24.5	21.3	18.8	17.2
16-19	9.4	5.1	7.5	6.9	6.7
20-24	14.5	14.8	13.8	11.7	10.5
25-54	60.7	61.6	65.8	70.2	72.4
25-34	24.1	26.1	28.4	28.5	25.9
35-44	18.2	28.9	22.5	25.7	27.7
45-54	18.3	16.3	14.8	15.9	18.9
55 and over	15.2	13.9	12.9	10.9	10.2
55-64	12.2	11.3	10.3	8.7	8.3
65 and over	3.2	2.4	2.7	2.4	1.9

Source: H.N. Fullerton, "The 1995 Labor Force: A First Look," *Monthly Labor Review* 103 (December 1980): 15.

population between 16 and 24 has peaked. The number of young workers peaked in 1980 at 37 million and will drop to 24 million by 1990. It is estimated that by 1990, young workers will comprise only 16 percent of the workforce, down from 24 percent in 1979 (Schuler, 1984).

As shown in Exhibit 1.4, the 16 to 24 age group will continue to decline as a percentage of the total labor force and of the population. In the meantime, the 25–54 (especially the 35–44 segment) age group will continue to rise. The 35–44 age group is expected to increase to 42 percent between 1980 and 1990, from 25.4 million to 36.1 million. This will cause bottlenecks in the promotion paths for that age group for the next several years because the number of middle manager jobs for the 35–44 age group is expected to increase only 19.1 percent, from 8.8 million to 10.5 million. The consequences of bottlenecks may be increased dissatisfaction among employees, but greater selection opportunities for them as well. The expansion of health care facilities into multichain corporations and diversified products and services will pose new challenges for employers. The quality of worklife issues will center on the redefinition of job and its upward mobility. The value system of employees may change, perhaps with a greater focus on family life, thus necessitating a redefinition of success. New information technology may modify working patterns, with a significant number of employees working at home. The psychology of work itself may be transformed, with a renewed interest on the part of women who dominate the health care field, by focusing on their special needs, such as maternity pay, promotion equity, and career development paths.

A number of other demographic trends will influence health manpower supply:

1. Diminishing number of men in the labor force and increasing number of blacks and women

Exhibit 1.5
Occupational Makeup of the Civilian Labor Force

Occupational Group	Percentage of Total Labor Force	Percentage of Male Workers	Percentage of Female Workers
Professional and technical	14	14	16
Managerial and administrative	11	14	7
Sales	6	6	7
Clerical	18	6	34
Craftworkers	14	21	2
Operatives	15	17	11
Laborers	6	9	1
Service workers	14	10	21
Farmworkers	2	3	1

Source: Adapted from U.S. Department of Labor, Bureau of Labor Statistics, *Employment and Earnings* 27 (3) (Washington, D.C.: Government Printing Office, March 1980).

2. Increase in life expectancy for men (from 69.5 years in 1978 to over 70 years) and women (from 77.2 years in 1978 to 80 years)

3. Continued movement of the population to the southern and western portions of the United States

4. International migration adding almost 1 million people a year to the U.S. population.

5. Increasing proportion of workforce will be older. Between 2000 and 2010, it is projected that there will be a 42 percent increase in the 55–64 category. The population of persons aged 45–64 age is expected to increase from 43.6 million in 1980 to 72.9 million in 2010, and the population aged 65 and over is expected to increase from 24.5 million in 1980 to 42.8 million in 2020. (Schuler, 1984)

All of these population trends—both national and health care—are expected to pose major challenges for human resources management strategies.

Job preference is another aspect of the external environment. In the national economy as a whole, and also in the health care sector, higher percentages of women than men occupy clerical positions, and higher percentages of men than women are in managerial jobs. A majority of female workers are in service, clerical (secretarial), nursing, and teaching jobs (see Exhibit 1.5). The majority of men are in semiskilled (operative), skilled (craftworkers), managerial, and professional jobs. (The health care labor market and its demographic characteristics are examined in Chapter 2.) The social impact of job preference needs to

Exhibit 1.6
Industries with the Greatest Number of New Jobs by 1995

Industry	Number of new jobs	Percent of all new jobs
Retail trade	3,089,000	12.2
Business services	2,440,000	9.7
New construction	1,976,000	7.8
Eating and drinking places	1,583,000	6.3
Hospitals	1,461,000	5.8
Wholesale trade	1,149,000	4.6
Other medical services	1,024,000	4.1
Professional services	857,000	3.4
Education services (private)	514,000	2.0
Doctors and dentists services	502,000	2.0

Source: V.A. Personick, "Industry Output and Employment: BLS Projects to 1990," *Monthly Labor Review* (April 1983).

be analyzed. Future human resources management will need to examine the design of new programs that will help employees to cope with nontraditional jobs.

Moreover, it is estimated that by 1995, 23.4 million to 28.6 million new wage and salary jobs will be created (Personick, 1979; Rumberger, 1981). Of these, between 1.0 million and 4.6 million will be in high-technology industries. A substantial number (between 9 and 10 percent) will be in hospitals and health-related industries. The industries with the greatest number of new jobs by 1995 are noted in Exhibit 1.6.

The nature of economic conditions—inflation, productivity, wage settlements, international competition, and workforce utilization—is an important external factor to consider. The introduction of new information and medical technologies is one of the main influencing factors in manpower utilization, generating several conflicts in man-machine interface, raising ergonomic issues for health care managers.

The revolution in information technologies represents a turning point in Western economies, focusing on convergence in microelectronics, telecommunications, and artifical intelligence. The development of robots and fifth-generation computers will affect the health industry, as well as almost all other significant sectors of the economy. Exhibit 1.7 presents the scope and its impact on planning new products and services.

The use of information technology raises the issue of technological uncertainty (or *technostress*) in the delivery of health care, generating new levels of supervision, work redesign, social support, and social change strategies. Human re-

Exhibit 1.7
Information Technologies: Functions and Applications[a]

Data Collection	Weather Prediction	Radar, Infra-Red Object Detection Equipment, Radiometers
	Medical Diagnosis	CAT-Scanners, Ultrasonic Cameras
Data Input	Word Processing	Keyboards, Touch-Screens
	Factory Automation	Voice Recognizers (particularly for Quality Control)
	Mail Sorting	Optical Character Readers
Storage	Archives	Magnetic Bubble Devices, Magnetic Tape
	Accounting Systems	Floppy Disks
	Scientific Computation	Wafer-Scale Semiconductors (Still in Research Phase), Very-High-Speed Magnetic Cores
	Ecological Mapping	Charge-Coupled Semiconductor Devices, Video Disks
	Libraries	Hard Disks
Information Processing	Social Security Payments	General Purpose "Mainframe" Computers, COBOL Programs
	Traffic Control	Minicomputers
	Distributed Inventory Control	Multi-User Super-Micros, Application Software Packages
		"Expert" Systems
		Spreadsheet Application Packages, Microcomputers
	Medical Diagnoses	Super computers: Multiple Instruction-Multiple Data
	Engineering Design	(MIMD) Processors, Vector Processors, Data
	Scientific Computation	Drive Processors, FORTRAN Programs
		Array Processors, Associative Processors
	Ecological Mapping	Robotics, Artificial Intelligence
	Factory Automation	
Communications	Office Systems	Local Area Networks, Private Branch Exchanges (PBX) Editor Applications Packages
	Teleconferencing	Communications Satellites, Fiber Optics
	Rescue Vehicle Dispatch	Cellular Mobile Radios
	International Financial	Transport Protocols, Data Encryption,
	Transactions	Integrated Services Digital Networks (ISDN)
Data Output and Presentation	Word Processing	Personal Computers, Printers (Impact, Ink Jet, (Xerographic)
	Management Information	Cathode Ray Tubes, Computer Graphics
	Pedestrian Traffic Control	Voice Synthesizers

[a] This list is not exhaustive; any given technology may also be used for some of the other applications mentioned.

Source: Robert Arndt and L. Chapman, *Potential Office Hazards and Control* (Washington, D.C.: Office of Technology Assessment, 1984), p. 39.

source planners face a tremendous challenge in meeting technostress at work in order to raise productivity and quality of worklife (Sethi et al., 1987).

Value systems will have an impact. A value system is a process of organizing conceptions about things and interests that persons (or groups) consider desirable. The three key areas where value changes may affect human resources planning are work, mobility, and health systems.

Two key ingredients in values toward work involve the work ethic and challenge in jobs in various health care organizations. The work ethic has been transformed, although it has not disappeared. Job enrichment has become a central issue in quality of worklife programs, and job redesign is an important segment of coping with new work values arising out of new patterns of work stemming from new technology. Organizational executives will have to increase their sensitivity to culture and values in management to ensure well-satisfied employees, which in turn will result in better patient care.

Employees' values toward mobility will have a significant impact on human resources management in the health sector, especially in recruiting, training, promoting, and motivating managers and professionals.

Values toward health systems are in constant flux. There is a greater emphasis on providing a community-oriented, equitable health care delivery system while stressing business-like efficiency values of economies of scale, expansion, and innovation.

The increasing role of government is the most pervasive factor in human resources management. Government regulations impose requirements for the protection of workers from injury, pollution, hazard, and labor-management relations. The various legal considerations governing health care delivery systems are an important component of strategic human resources management.

In summary, the changes in these four major areas—demographics, the economy, social and health care values, and government regulations—are likely to have a significant impact on how human resources choices are made in managing health care delivery systems.

Overall Outcomes

The values that emerge from the interplay of the environment and persons in that environment require strategies directed not only at changing the person or the environment but toward developing new aims, perceptions, and assumptions about how HRM is to be integrated into the working environment. The nature of strategic HRM decisions will generate outcomes that include: (1) matching HRM strategies with overall corporate strategy; (2) organizational effectiveness, which includes efficient performance, quality of worklife, and patient satisfaction; and (3) competitive gains in expanding and innovating health care organizations.

REFERENCES

Ansoff, H. I. (1978). Planned management of turbulent change. In *Encyclopedia of Professional Management*. New York: McGraw-Hill.

Ashby, W. R. (1954). *Design for a Brain*. London: Chapman & Hall.

Beer, S. (1969). The aborting corporate plan: A cybernetic account of the interface between planning and action. In E. Jantsch (Ed.), *Perspectives in Planning*, 397–422. Paris: Organization for Economic Cooperation and Development.

———. (1975). *Platform for Change*. New York: John Wiley.

Chandler, A. D., Jr. (1962). *Strategy and Structure*. Cambridge, Mass.: MIT Press.

Dimmock, S. J., and Sethi, A. S. (1986). The role of ideology and power in systems theory: Some fundamental shortcomings. *Industrial Relations* 41:738–55.

Drucker, P. F. (1969). *The Age of Discontinuity: Guidelines to Our Changing Society*. New York: Harper & Row.

Flexner, W. A., Berkowitz, E. N., and Brown, M. (1981). *Strategic Planning in Health Care Management*. Rockville, Md.: Aspen Systems.

Fombrun, C. J., Tichy, N. M., and Devanna M. A. (1984). *Strategic Human Resource Management*. New York: John Wiley.

Glinow, M. A. V., Driver, M. J., Brousseau, K., and Prince, J. B. (1983). The design of a career oriented human resources system. In S. Levey and N. P. Loomba (Eds.), *Health Care Administration: A Managerial Perspective*, 479–92. Philadelphia: J.B. Lippincott.

Luke, R. D., and Kurowski, B. (1983). Strategic management. In S. M. Shortell and D. Kaluzny (Eds.), *Health Care Management*, 461–82. New York: John Wiley.

Mintzberg, H. (1979). *The Structuring of Organizations*. Englewood Cliffs, N.J.: Prentice-Hall.

Personick. V. A. (1983, April). Industry output and employment: BLS projects to 1990. *Monthly Labor Review*.

Rumberger, R. W. (1981, July). The changing skill requirements of jobs in the U.S. economy. *Industrial and Labor Relations Review*, 578–90.

Sethi, A. S., Caro, D., and Schuler, R. S. (Eds.), (1987). *Strategic Management of Technostress in an Information Society*. Toronto: Hogrefe International.

Schuler, R. S. (1984). *Personnel and Human Resource Management*. St. Paul, Minn.: West Publishing Co.

Toffler, A. (1970). *Future Shock*. New York: Bantam.

Van Gigch, J. P. (1978). *Applied General Systems Theory*. New York: Harper & Row.

Webber, J. B. (1982). Ideas outspace reality of hospital strategic planning, but do they pinpoint the future? *Hospitals* 56: 68–71.

2
Strategic Human Resource Planning

*Kirk C. Harlow
and Joseph K. Taylor*

The health care industry is experiencing numerous changes affecting the management of human resources, among them increased competition, technological advances, new roles for physicians, restructured delivery systems, changing worker values, and altered demographics (Eisenberg, 1986; Neudeck, 1985). In addition to operating in a dynamic external environment, the internal composition of the health care industry is also one of the most complex. A typical 300-bed hospital is comprised of an extraordinarily diverse workforce represented by over 200 job titles ranging from dietitian to phlebotomist (U.S. Department of Labor, 1970). To be effective, the health care institution must be able to attract and retain an appropriate mix of employees to carry out current operations and adapt to the changing environment. As Eisenberg (1986) notes, the impact of this dynamic and complex system "demands that each facility be prepared to develop a human resources strategic plan" (p. 154). In this chapter we discuss the process of strategic human resource planning for health care institutions.

THE CONCEPT OF PLANNING

Planning in its general form is determining what actions will be undertaken to bring about some identified future state. A variety of orientations have been proposed within this broad context. One common form is the "muddling-through" approach described by Lindblom (1959). This approach, also known as incrementalism, characterizes planning as a process of making small adjustments to current activities without a clear delineation of future objectives. A typical manifestation of this process would be an annual increase of 10 percent in the nurse recruitment budget regardless of whether nurse recruitment is the most effective way to ensure adequate nursing staff. This planning orientation is rarely held up as ideal but is often an accurate description of how planning is done in many organizations.

A second form is rational planning. Rational planning (called mechanistic planning in Chapter 1) involves the identification of specific objectives and the determination of the most effective activities to achieve those objectives. Inherent in the rational approach is the collection and analysis of *all* relevant data from which to make the best decision. One of the primary criticisms of this approach is that it is impossible to collect and analyze all the necessary data to choose the best set of activities to reach an objective. Even more important is the assumption that planning is being done in a perfectly certain world. Faludi (1973: chap. 7) has aptly called this orientation "blueprint" planning since it is only after the plan has been fully implemented that an evaluation is done to determine if the objectives were met.

A third orientation is the systemic view. In this approach, planning is not a step-by-step process but a process of interrelated steps. Although the steps are often similar to those of rational planning, including identification of objectives and actions to achieve them, the process provides for feedback at a variety of points, which may result in ongoing revision. Thus the formation of objectives may be influenced by knowledge of activities that can be implemented feasibly. In addition, this view of planning incorporates the concept of equifinality (Katz and Kahn, 1978: chap. 2). The premise of this concept is that a system can move toward a final state from different initial conditions and in a variety of ways. In other words, it is not assumed that there is one best way to achieve what is desired.

The human resource planning approach presented in this chapter incorporates the systems orientation. The process is presented in a step-by-step fashion for ease of discussion, but readers should keep in mind the interactive nature of the process. Williams and Manzo (1983: chap. 2) suggest that a plan be put in a looseleaf notebook to accommodate updates. In this vein, the view of planning we offer is not one of a completed document but of an ongoing process incorporating new inputs and modifications as needed.

HUMAN RESOURCE PLANNING

Human resource planning may be defined as an interactive process of determining policies and programs necessary to ensure that the right people with the right training and motivation are in the right place to perform the work necessary for the organization to reach its objectives (Burack and Mathys, 1979: chap. 1; Cook, 1984: chap. 2). As this general definition suggests, human resource planning is a core activity of strategic human resource management. It is a link

Strategic Human Resource Planning

between the various components of the human resource management system. Organizational structure and job design are primary inputs guiding the identification of the right people. Recruitment and selection activities are guided by the information developed through human resource planning. Compensation policies affect the organization's ability to obtain and retain adequate human resources. Thus human resource planning influences and is influenced by all aspects of strategic human resource management.

A MODEL OF HUMAN RESOURCE PLANNING

A general model presenting six phases of human resource planning is provided in Exhibit 2.1. Each of the phases is discussed in detail in the remainder of this chapter. There are, however, several general aspects of the model meriting discussion.

First, the model should not be interpreted as a step-by-step approach to human resource planning. Because the process is systemic, with feedback occurring on an ongoing basis, this model should be viewed as a set of interactive components comprising an ongoing planning process. For example, information about the possible introduction of new technology may alter estimates of productivity that are used in estimating employment demand. Or the revision of the promotion policy may affect projections regarding staffing levels.

Second, human resource planning continuously cycles through this process at various levels of detail. For example, the organization might begin the process by simply discussing each phase in a qualitative fashion during a management meeting in order to determine what information is available and to develop an understanding of current activities. The next cycle may include adding new information leading to specific planning outputs. In addition, gaps in information may be identified with the third cycle, accommodating this new information.

The third important aspect of this model is that human resource planning (HRP) has been divided into two interrelated levels, operating and strategic. The operating level represents human resource planning with an annual time horizon; planning is done for the workforce needs in the next twelve months. The primary intent of HRP at the operating level is to project staffing requirements throughout the year and determine how these requirements will be met. The strategic level addresses the long-term time horizon. In this case the focus of planning is on more general issues, such as future labor force composition, new technology, and changing business strategy, as well as the development of overall human resource policies.

The fourth important feature of this model is the relationship of HRP to business planning. Numerous authors have noted the important link between human resource planning and business planning (Alpander, 1982: chap. 2; Burack and Mathys, 1979: chap. 1; Cherrington, 1983: chap. 4; Smith, 1983). Logic suggests that business plans should influence human resource plans, but also relevant human resource information such as labor force availability should

Exhibit 2.1
Integrated Human Resource Planning Model

Operating Level	Strategic Level

Business Plan

Operating Plan	Strategic Plan
Phase 1: Estimate Employment Demands	
Forecast Next Year's Level of Operation	Determine Relationship of Long Term Strategy to Human Resources
Measure Workload/Productivity	Forecast Long Term Employment Needs
Forecast Employment Needs	
Phase 2: Estimate Internal Supply	
Develop Transition data	Develop Replacement Charts/Succession Plans
Forecast Supply	Forecast Long Term Transitions and Supply
Phase 3: Reconcile Demand and Supply	
Identify Short Term Employment Needs	Identify Long Term Employment Needs
Phase 4: Assess External Environment	
Assess Workforce Availability	Environmental Scan

Strategic Human Resource Planning

Exhibit 2.1 (continued)

Phase 5:
Establish Policies,
Goals, and Programs

Set Productivity
Objectives

Set Manpower
Objectives

Specify Action
Plans

Establish Long
Human Resource
Policies

Specify Programs
to Achieve Policies

Phase 6: Monitor
and Evaluate

Monitor
Implementation

Review and
Revise Action
Plans

Assess
Performance

Monitor
Implementation

Review information
and Update Plans

Evaluate Policy
and Program Effects

influence the development of business plans. Nonetheless, the integration of HRP with business planning is not a common practice in many organizations (Craft, 1980; Rowland and Summers, 1981).

WHO SHOULD BE INVOLVED IN HUMAN RESOURCE PLANNING?

There is no perfect mix of individuals to participate in the health care organization's human resource planning. HRP will involve a broad array of people within the organization who will provide necessary information and be affected by the recommendations developed in the plan. In general, the most common arrangement for HRP is for it to be part of the personnel department (Burack and Mathys, 1979: chap. 2). We suggest, however, that a planning team be comprised of relevant organizational representatives from finance, marketing, operations, legal, and personnel. Effective HRP requires information from and has an effect on each of these organizational components. Primary staffing of the team should be the responsibility of personnel. In addition, the governing board should be involved in considerations of broad human resource policy. Laliberty (1984) has pointed out that human resources comprise a major part of the health care organization's assets and merit the same attention that the governing board gives to capital assets.

PHASES OF HUMAN RESOURCE PLANNING

The foundation of effectively carrying out any phase of HRP is the availability of information in the appropriate form. A cornerstone is a well-defined job classification system. The typical health care institution with 2,000 employees may have more than 200 different jobs (USDL, 1970). Each job type represents a core unit of analysis for human resource planning, although as Cherrington (1983) suggests, planning for each of these jobs can be difficult and time-consuming. One solution to this problem is to collapse specific jobs into broader categories applying specific criteria (Cherrington, 1983: 29):

1. The specific skill preparation and educational requirements needed to perform the job
2. The degree of responsibility and location of the job in the organizational hierarchy
3. The nature of the activities performed

Such an approach might lead to a general category of staff nurse as the focus of planning. The aggregation of jobs into broader categories, however, should be done with great caution. The current level of specialization in the health care field often requires employees with a very specific mix of training and experience. (A more detailed discussion of job analysis methods is provided in Chapter 3.)

Phase 1: Determine Future Employment Demand

The first phase of human resource planning is to determine the organization's expected human resource demand or, more specifically, to estimate future employment levels by job or broader job category and to develop information about the types of jobs that will comprise the organization in the future. The discussion that follows first presents approaches for determining short-term demand and then approaches for determining long-term demand.

Short-term demand

Forecasting short-term demand is the process of determining expected staffing levels in the next year. This process consists of two general steps: (1) determining expected service levels in the next year and (2) relating staffing levels to estimated service levels.

Expected service levels

The determination of expected service levels is essential to estimating the future staffing needs of the health care organization. It is at this point that the interface between HRP and business planning is particularly evident. The most common measure of service levels in health care is the utilization rate, often in terms of occupied beds or patient days. Patient visits, procedures, tests, or direct contact hours are usual measures of service in allied health services and outpatient settings.

Typically short-term forecasts of service levels are prepared as part of the business planning process, and these forecasts will be an input for HRP. There are two important issues that should be noted with respect to service forecasts in health care organizations. First, most health care organizations experience seasonal variations in utilization. A point estimate of expected utilization for the next year will be helpful in estimating general staffing levels, but it is also useful to estimate utilization levels at various points in the cycle to provide for the anticipation of potential variation in staffing levels (Bracken et al., 1985).

Second, the assumptions underlying the forecasts of expected service levels should be considered carefully. At the most basic level, one assumption is that utilization next year will be similar to that in the current year. However, changes in medical practice or the external environment such as an increase or decrease in population, a new industry in the community, an economic downturn, or the entry of new competitors can have dramatic effects on utilization rates. For example, the high rate of layoffs in Houston, Texas, during 1986 resulted in declines in utilization as people left the area or deferred elective or less acute admissions. In addition, internal business decisions may affect utilization. For example, a decision to undertake a more aggressive marketing campaign may result in increased utilization.

The forecast of future service levels is an essential element of estimating future staffing needs. Health care institutions today operate in a rapidly changing environment that makes accurate forecasting difficult. Nonetheless, as Cherrington (1983) writes:

Employment forecasting does not have to produce accurate estimates of future employment needs in order to be useful. The forecasting process itself, apart from the numbers that result, facilitates the planning process. Requiring managers to think about the future and to anticipate the kinds of events that might occur is a useful process even though the events that do occur may be quite different than those anticipated. (135)

Relating staffing levels to expected service levels

The estimation of the effect of changes in service on staffing levels requires developing the relationship between service and workload, the measurement of workload per full-time-equivalent (FTE) employee, and the estimation of changes in productivity.

First, workloads are tied directly to the service level measures. For example, workloads of many for the jobs in a hospital are generally tied to patient days. In nursing, the workload unit often is defined as hours of nursing care. In radiology, it might be defined as procedures.

Once workload has been defined, it is necessary to determine the amount of workload per service unit. For example, for medical and surgical nursing, the number of nursing care hours per patient day is usually between four and five. For radiology, we might determine that there is .686 procedure per patient day.

Exhibit 2.2
Example of Staffing Level Estimation Using Workload Measures

Estimated patient days in next year based on 170 beds at .67 occupancy	41,574
Estimated number of procedures per patient day	.686
Total estimated procedures	28,520
Estimated standard time per procedure (includes vacation, holidays, sick time and PF&D)	.95
Estimated total hours	27,094
Annual paid hours per FTE	2,080
Estimated paid FTEs	13

Conversion of nursing care to total nursing care hours can be determined by multiplying the estimated number of patient days by nursing care hours per patient day and then dividing that total by the number of hours worked per FTE to arrive at an estimate of nursing staff level needed.

An example of this process for radiology is presented in Exhibit 2.2. This process requires an additional step to convert procedures into work hours. In addition, the standard time is increased to correct for eighty hours of vacation, fifty-six hours of holidays, forty hours of sick time, and 10 percent for personal time, fatigue, and delay (PF&D).

Exhibit 2.1 represents the most basic approach to workload measurement and paid staff required.[1] More sophisticated management engineering approaches can be applied. Such approaches develop detailed time and motion analyses to arrive at standard times for elements of jobs (Bradley, 1982; Gerner, 1982; Pochter, 1982). The elements of a specific position can be aggregated to arrive at a standard time per service unit for a given job. For example, the standard time for a radiology procedure in Exhibit 2.1 is .95 hour. (It should be noted that the number of procedures per patient day and the standard time varies from institution to institution.)

An important consideration when measuring workload is the estimation of future productivity. In the examples above, it was assumed that productivity in the forecast year would be the same as that in the standard year. Employee productivity, however, is subject to a variety of factors, including improved work methods, training, and the introduction of equipment. It is not uncommon to underestimate the short-term productivity loss associated with bringing a new administrative computer on line. Time-absorbing factors such as training and

Strategic Human Resource Planning

operating parallel systems frequently are not taken into account, resulting in unanticipated overtime or staff additions. Although difficult to predict, possible changes in productivity should be considered in the process of estimating staff demands.

Long-term demand

The forecast of long-term demand is the estimation of workforce needs using a two- to ten-year time horizon. These forecasts are intimately tied to the long-term strategy of the health care organization and should take into consideration changes in current service levels and strategies that may lead to changes in service mix or the type of services offered. For instance, more and more hospitals are shifting from predominantly acute care inpatient services to an increased emphasis on ambulatory care and mental health services. These strategic shifts have had dramatic affects on staffing levels and workforce composition.

Once the implications of long-term strategy have been considered, a variety of quantitative and qualitative forecasting approaches can be applied. Among these are workload estimation, time-series and regression techniques, and delphi analysis. These particular methods, selected because of their relative feasibility of implementation, are discussed below.

Workload estimation

The workload estimation approach to forecasting is an extension of the short-term approach. It involves extending short-term forecasts into the future based on estimated service levels in future years. For instance, inpatient nursing demand in five years would be estimated using the fifth-year forecast of daily census in the hospital.

This approach is clearly dependent on the accuracy of the projections of future workload levels. In addition, as the target year of the projections extends further into the future, it becomes increasingly difficult to assess changes in productivity that may affect workloads. Finally, this approach is only suitable if the design of jobs remains constant in the future. The introduction of new technology, the addition or elimination of services, changes in case mix, or demographic changes such as the aging of the population are factors that may result in a change in job design.

Time-series and regression projections

Of the variety of quantitative statistical approaches for forecasting future staffing demands, two variations are time series and regression. The time-series approach to projection uses trends over time in the past to estimate the future. One of the key assumptions of this approach is that the past is an accurate predictor of the future. An example of a linear trend time-series analysis for a multi-institutional system or a large hospital is provided in Exhibit 2.3. In this example, nursing staff levels are being estimated based on data from the past ten years. Using time-series analysis, an equation that represents the trend line

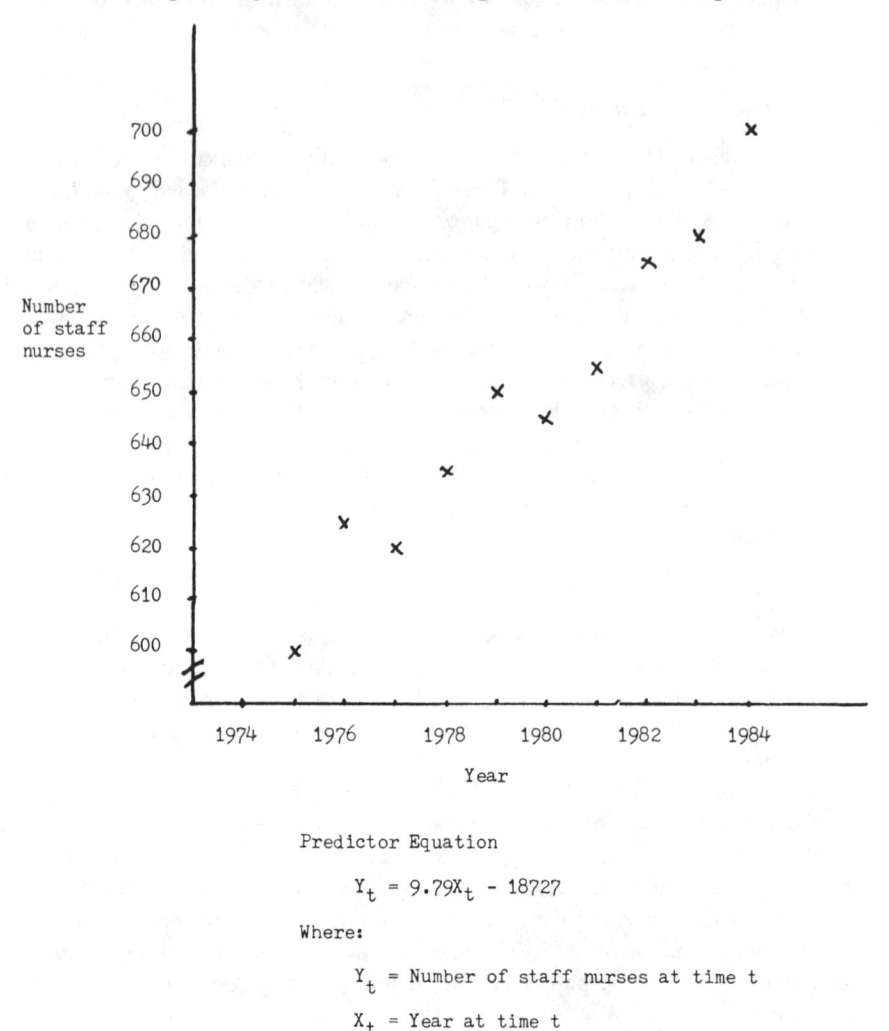

Exhibit 2.3
Plot of Nursing Staff by Year and Linear Regression Time-Series Equation

Predictor Equation

$$Y_t = 9.79X_t - 18727$$

Where:

Y_t = Number of staff nurses at time t

X_t = Year at time t

is determined and can be used to estimate staff needs in the future. In this case, the estimate for the next year would be a medical-surgical nursing staff level of 706. In addition, a prediction interval may be determined for this estimate to account for the variability of the estimate (Kleinbaum and Kupper, 1978: chap. 5).

One advantage of this approach is that it is relatively easy to assemble the necessary data and the calculations are quite straightforward. In addition, human resource forecasts are not dependent on information about expected service levels, which may not be forthcoming. The approach, however, assumes a stable environment experiencing linear change and does not account for possible changes in internal practices, technology, or environmental conditions.

A second form of quantitative projection is linear regression analysis. Analytically similar to time-series analysis, regression analysis assumes a relationship between one or more independent variables and a dependent variable. For example, it is logical to assume that a hospital's annual level of patient days is a good predictor of nursing staff levels. Hence, through the development of a statistical relationship between patient days and nursing staff levels, an estimate of future nursing staff levels may be determined based on projected patient days. Like time-series analysis, an equation is developed from which future staffing levels can be derived.

The similarity between regression and time-series analysis results in the common advantage of ease of data collection and calculation. One additional advantage is that the prediction is tied directly to business activity and thereby accounts for expected changes in business activity. This relationship, however, leads to several disadvantages. First, staffing estimation is dependent on the availability of forecasts of future service levels. In addition, the accuracy of the human resource forecast will be dependent on the accuracy of the service level forecast. Third, there is the questionable assumption that the variables are linearly related. Finally, this method assumes future experience may be based on historical values.

A number of other time-series and regressive approaches address factors such as nonlinearity and multiple independent variables (see Hanke and Reitsch, 1981; Kleinbaum and Kupper, 1978). Shapiro and Glandon (1984) have presented an example of a multivariate quantitative approach specific to medical staff that goes beyond the medical staff-to-bed ratios and applies a forecasting model that incorporates variables related to physician demographics, service area, hospital characteristics, and the local health care market.

Regardless of which approach is used, there are two important caveats. First, it is obvious that these approaches operate on a variety of assumptions regarding the relationship of variables and the stability of the future. As Burack and Mathys (1979: chap. 5) suggest, no forecast should be provided without a full delineation of the assumptions upon which it is based. The confidence placed in a forecast should reflect a complete understanding of these assumptions. Second, the forecast is only as good as the data upon which it is based. Craft (1980) notes that the data used in human resource projections are often collected informally and can be incomplete and inaccurate. He adds that it is common to attribute unjustified precision to a forecast since the term itself tends to connote conclusiveness. Quantitative forecasts should serve as one informational input into the HRP process, but the information should be given the appropriate weight in light of the forecast's validity.

Delphi

The delphi approach to planning is a qualitative method to bring about a group decision (Delbecq, Van de Ven, and Gustafson, 1975). Rather than bringing group members together face to face, group opinions are solicited through a series of questionnaires. Burack and Mathys (1979: 148) outline the procedure as follows:

1. Define a problem or question
2. Check for form, clarity of terms, and feasibility (i.e., answerability of the question)
3. Identify, select, and orient panel of "experts"
4. Issue first-found questionnaire
5. Facilitator receives first-round responses and analyzes and summarizes them
6. Facilitator sends out questionnaire (modified, if necessary) and first-round summary of relevant information to benefit panel members
7. Facilitator receives second-round responses and analyzes and determines degree of convergence. Possible results of this analysis might be to set up a face-to-face meeting with the panel members to reconcile differences or initiate another round

The application of this approach to estimating long-term staffing levels may involve obtaining answers to questions such as, "What changes do you see in the types of patients served by this hospital in the next five years?" and "How do you see these changes affecting the current composition of the hospital staff?" Hospitals today face numerous environmental demands requiring adaptation that may lead to changes in service and workforce composition. The delphi technique is an important approach to assist in the anticipation of those changes and identification of effects on hospital staffing. It lacks the specificity of the quantitative approaches, but that specificity may be somewhat illusory.

Putting long-term forecasts together

Health care institutions operate in a complex and changing environment. One way to address this type of environment in forecasting is to use a what-if approach. In this approach, forecasts are prepared on the basis of a number of possible conditions. For example, a forecast based on three different estimates of patient days may be developed, or the delphi questionnaire might be designed to solicit responses based on different scenarios. Use of this approach provides an upper and lower bound regarding future staff levels.[2]

The quality of long-term forecasts can be enhanced by using more than one approach and examining the convergence of the results. A strong combination is to use both linear regression with three estimates and the delphi technique to forecast expected staffing levels in the future.

Phase 2: Assess Internal Supply

The next phase in the process of human resource planning is to determine what the expected internal supply of personnel will be in the future. Changes in internal supply are a function of a number of factors that result in employees exiting the organization, among them, retirement, voluntary and involuntary termination, and employee layoffs. Changes within specific job categories occur as a result of promotions, demotions, and transfers. Future suppy can be estimated by assessing the impact of these transitions on staffing levels. This work will also develop an understanding of why particular transitional patterns occur within the organization. Finally, it will provide knowledge of the skills and job potential of current employees.

Short-term analysis

Short-term analysis of internal supply has two components: (1) determining transition rates and estimating future supply based on those rates and (2) developing an assessment of the cause of employee transitions.

One basic approach to estimating future supply is to determine a rate for resignations and terminations for a given job or job category and to apply that rate to current staff levels. For example, if the turnover rate for orderlies is .40 and the current number of orderlies employed is 100, then expected number of orderlies rema'ning in the coming year will be sixty. Although this approach is quite rudimentary, it does require that accurate and complete data be available regarding turnover. Cherrington (1983: chap. 4) suggests that the previous year's turnover rate may be the best predictor of the next year's rate, although the assessment of historical turnover patterns can provide useful information regarding the stability of the rates, as well as possible explanations for changes in rates.

One of the shortcomings of this approach is that it does not account for promotions, demotions, and transfers within the organization. Another approach for estimating future staff levels using both internal transition and turnover data is Markov analysis (Bleau, 1981; Cherrington, 1983: chap. 4; Hooper and Catalanello, 1981). An example of Markov analysis is provided in Exhibit 2.4. In this example, a matrix of three sequential job categories—staff nurse, charge nurse, and nursing administration—is created, with initial staffing levels presented across the top. Transition probabilities representing movement between positions and turnover rates are then applied to obtain expected staff levels. Sixty-eight percent of the staff nurses remain in that position, 2 percent are promoted to charge nurse, and 30 percent exit. Completing the matrix results in the staffing levels at the end of the year being presented along the right side.

Both methods described apply transition probabilities, therefore assuming historical stability of transitions. In addition, transition probabilities based on job categories with fewer than thirty to fifty employees may have substantial standard errors. Thus, these approaches are best applied in health care organizations with

Exhibit 2.4
Markov Analysis of Staffing Levels

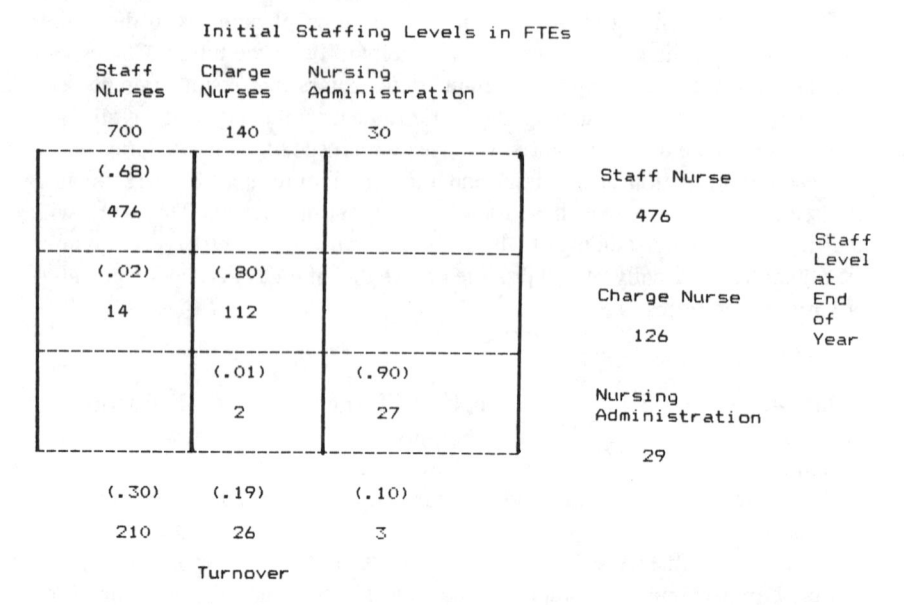

Initial Staffing Levels in FTEs

Staff Nurses	Charge Nurses	Nursing Administration		
700	140	30		
(.68) 476			Staff Nurse 476	Staff Level at End of Year
(.02) 14	(.80) 112		Charge Nurse 126	
	(.01) 2	(.90) 27	Nursing Administration 29	
(.30) 210	(.19) 26	(.10) 3		

Turnover

large numbers of employees in a given job category, such as large hospitals or multi-institutional systems.

In smaller health care organizations or when planning for job categories with fewer employees, it is possible to use movement analysis (Burack and Mathys, 1979). This method, as presented in Exhibit 2.5, creates a table in which the first column is the current staffing level for a variety of positions. Additional columns are set up to represent factors that will reflect position-specific increases or decreases in staff levels. The last column provides an estimate of expected staff levels at the end of the year. The difference between this approach and approaches using transition probabilities is that the figures represent estimates of expected real changes and are not derived from historical probabilities.

To obtain the data for movement analysis requires that the human resource planner involve unit-level administrators in the planning process. Judgments of administrators coupled with historical patterns serve as the basis for estimates. The advantage of this participation is that it may result in a greater commitment to HRP among the administrative staff. The primary disadvantage is that it adds paperwork to administrative jobs and can lead to corresponding resistance. Ideally this approach is tied to the annual department budget process, reducing possible duplication of effort.

In a later section of this chapter we discuss the development of human resource policies to assist in meeting the goals of the plan. It is important to recognize, however, that policies shape transitions within the organization and consequently affect internal supply. For example, affirmative action goals may require outside

Strategic Human Resource Planning

Exhibit 2.5
An Example of Movement Analysis Using Expected Transition Estimates

Position	C1 Staff level beginning year	− C2 Retirements	− C3 Terminations	− C4 Resignations	− C5 Promotions out	+ C6 Promotions in	= C7 Staff Level end of year
RN-CCU	67	1	3	24	1	0	38
RN-ER	18	0	1	3	0	0	14
RN-CPU	24	0	0	6	1	0	17
SUPERVISOR CCU	3	0	0	0	1	1	3
SUPERVISOR ER	2	0	0	0	0	0	2
SUPERVISOR CPU	3	0	1	0	0	1	3

recruitment to fill open positions if the pool within does not provide appropriate candidates. Similarly, policies regarding internal promotion, retirement, and termination affect movements within the health care organization that modify internal supply. As a result, estimates of internal supply should be conducted in the light of different policy assumptions.

Long-term estimation

There are three components of long-term supply estimation: trend evaluation, replacement planning, and estimation for changing operations.

Trend evaluation

Trend evaluation is the examination of various transition and vacancy patterns to develop an understanding of causes and the extent to which these patterns can be expected to continue in the future. High turnover rates, for example, may point to a problem in the management of human resources (Farrell and Rusbult, 1985; Price, 1977; Roseman, 1981). Although short-term estimates can be made to determine the effect of turnover on staff levels, understanding the causes of turnover is important to developing longer-term approaches to maintaining appropriate staffing levels.

The evaluation and management of turnover should take into consideration two distinctions: functional versus dysfunctional and controllable versus uncontrollable (Abelson, 1986). Although turnover may be costly to the organization in terms of increased recruitment, lost time due to interviewing and selection, training, and lost productivity (Hall, 1981), turnover also may have benefits. Wage and benefit costs may be reduced by replacing senior employees with new employees; or, somewhat less tangibly, benefits may be derived from the ideas brought to the organization by new employees (Abelson, 1986). A further benefit may be the productivity gains associated with the replacement of dissatisfied employees or poor performers. Thus, turnover is not inherently negative and should be evaluated on the basis of relative costs and benefits.

A second distinction is to differentiate between controllable and uncontrollable turnover. Turnover resulting from retirement or moving with a spouse cannot be controlled. Alpander (1982: chap. 7) has pointed out that turnover rates tend to vary with the age of employees and their point in the career cycle. Turnover rates among younger employees are quite high. Rates also tend to pick up during both mid- and late-career stages. An understanding of the composition of the organization's workforce can be useful in anticipating the degree to which the internal supply of personnel can be expectd to change. The organization with predominantly mid- and late-career workers can anticipate higher turnover in the future, which has implications for recruiting, training, and productivity. (Equal employment opportunity regulations, of course, limit the organization's ability to control the age of the workforce through employment practices.)

Replacement planning

An important component of long-term supply analysis is replacement planning. Typically replacement planning is done through the development of a replacement chart (Exhibit 2.6). This chart is a piece of the organizational hierarchy that contains information about the current job incumbent and possible internal replacements for that individual. Ratings indicating the individual's current performance and potential for advancement are presented. Based on the chart in Exhibit 2.6, the senior vice-president of operations would be the most likely candidate to replace the chief executive officer. The replacement chart, however, is only a summary tool for planning. Underlying the chart is detailed information about the individual, including managerial skills, human relations abilities, problem-solving skills, and other relevant competencies (Whiston-Fox and Mitchell, 1984). Replacement planning is useful not only for responding to turnover but is an important part of the organization's career planning process.

Changing operations

Most health care organizations are venturing into increasing diversification of services as part of their long-term strategy. Some of the emergent services may include outpatient physical therapy units, alcohol and drug treatment programs, ambulatory surgery units, and home health care. At the same time, other services are being pared back or eliminated. A significant part of planning for these programs is ensuring that the appropriate staff is available.

A short-term perspective on changes in options usually involves some combination of workforce reductions and recruitment. A longer-term perspective may add retraining or cross-training existing staff into the list of program options.

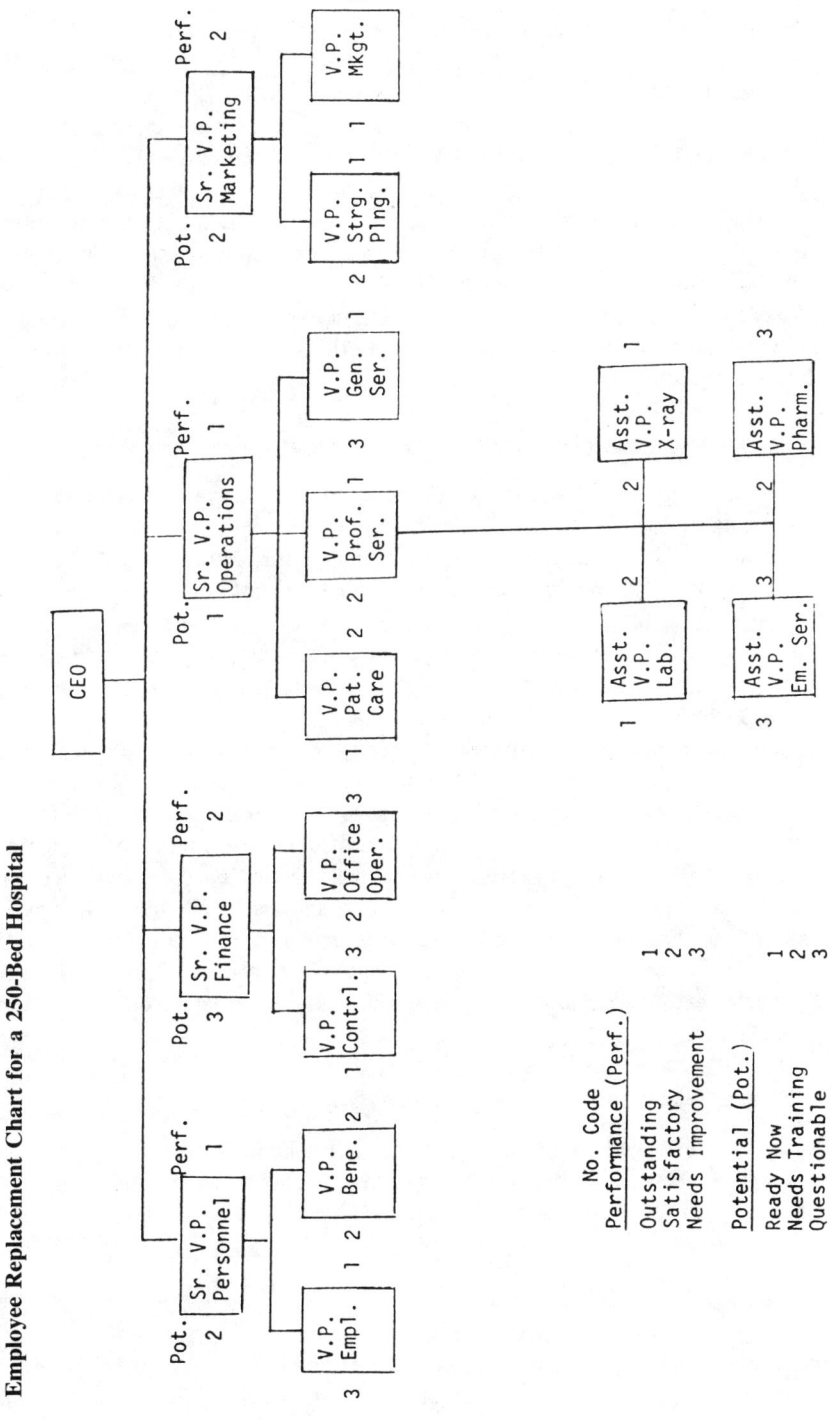

Exhibit 2.6
Employee Replacement Chart for a 250-Bed Hospital

```
                                              CEO
                                               |
     ┌─────────────────────────┬───────────────┴──────────────────┬──────────────────────┐
     │                         │                                  │                      │
  Pot.│Sr. V.P.    Perf.    Pot.│Sr. V.P.   Perf.              Pot.│Sr. V.P.   Perf.   Pot.│Sr. V.P.   Perf.
   2 │Personnel    1       3  │Finance     2                  1  │Operations  1      2  │Marketing   2
     │                        │                                  │                      │
  ┌──┴──┐                 ┌───┴───┐                  ┌───────────┼───────────┐       ┌──┴──────┐
  │     │                 │       │                  │           │           │       │         │
Pot.│V.P.    V.P.│Pot.  Pot.│V.P.   V.P.│Pot.    V.P.│   V.P.│     V.P.│    V.P.│   V.P.│
 1,2│Empl.   Bene.│ 2    3  │Contrl. Office│ 3    Pat.│   Prof.│    Gen.│   Strg. │  Mkgt. │
  3 │                  1    │        Oper. │      Care│   Ser. │    Ser.│   Plng. │        │
                                                2,2       1,3      1,1    1,1      1,3

                   ┌─────────┬─────────┬─────────┐
                   │         │         │         │
                Asst.     Asst.     Asst.     Asst.
                V.P.      V.P.      V.P.      V.P.
                Lab       X-ray     Em. Ser.  Pharm.
                1,2       2,1       3,3       2,3
```

No. Code
Performance (Perf.)

Outstanding   1
Satisfactory   2
Needs Improvement 3

Potential (Pot.)

Ready Now   1
Needs Training   2
Questionable   3

Although we are somewhat ahead of ourselves in discussing strategy at this point, it is in anticipation of these strategies that we suggest a skills inventory as part of the long-term supply analysis.

A skills inventory is an assessment of the knowledge, experience, education, and abilities of current employees. Established in a computer data-base, it is possible to examine the skills inventory to find employees who may have appropriate training and experience to fill new positions. In addition, information about the lack of appropriate skills among existing employees is important to formulating long-term strategies to meet future staffing needs. This, of course, is substantially more elaborate than posting new positions as they are created. It is, however, in line with the purpose of HRP to anticipate staffing needs of the organization.

Phase 3: Reconcile Supply and Demand

The reconciliation of staffing supply and demand is an obvious step in determining staffing needs. It is at this point in the analysis that surpluses or deficits in staffing levels are determined given estimated demand and internal supply. For example, the regression estimate of demand for staff nurses discussed above indicated a forecasted need of 706 FTE positions next year. The Markov analysis suggested that 476 staff nurses will be in place next year based on expected employee transitions. The result of these two analyses indicates that demand exceeds supply by 230 FTE positions.

The longer-term perspective will generally be more qualitative and provide general conclusions about future staffing patterns. For example, a forecast may indicate a 10 percent decrease in the demand for medical-surgical unit staff nurses over the next three years. In addition, the analysis of turnover rates might indicate slow attrition among this nursing staff. Based on these two pieces of information, it is possible to conclude that a surplus in nursing staff may be expected in the future. Data from the skills inventory can be generated to determine if the existing nursing staff can be used in other services provided by the health care organization or in new services to be established such as ambulatory care.

Phase 4: Assess the External Environment

Developing a working knowledge of the external environment is an important element of effective HRP. The development of both short- and long-term strategies to meet the organization's staffing needs is a direct function of the environment.

Short-term analysis

The primary focus of environmental assessments with a short-term planning horizon is to develop information about the external labor supply and the extent to which adequate labor may be obtained to meet anticipated needs. It is at this point that HRP and recruitment clearly interface. The ability to obtain an adequate labor force is a function of the current labor pool and of the organization's ability to recruit from that pool. Since recruitment is addressed in detail in Chapter 4, we will not discuss it at this point. Suffice it to say that current labor market information and recruitment data including yield ratios are essential inputs for strategy development.

Long-term analysis

The scope of long-term analysis goes beyond the estimation of the extent to which an adequate labor supply will be available in the future. Often called environmental scanning, this component of future human resource availability relates to planning the impact of a variety of environmental factors on the organization's human resources. Included among these factors are demographic patterns, political and legal developments, emerging social values, scientific and technological advances, and economic patterns.

A full discussion of the effect of each of these on health care human resources goes well beyond the limits of this chapter. Several patterns are briefly discussed, however, to show the kinds of issues that might be examined in an environmental scan.

The examination of demographic patterns may include a general assessment of future workforce composition by age, race, and sex. In addition, data might be collected about the projected supply of persons in particular health care specialties. For example, according to data provided in the *Fifth Report to the President and Congress on the Status of Health Personnel in the United States* (Health Resources and Services Administration, 1986), the proportion of female physicians will increase from 12 percent in 1981 to 20.6 percent in 2000. Similar increases are expected among podiatrists, dentists, optometrists, and pharmacists (Friedman, McTernan, and Leiken, 1985; Salmon and Culbertson, 1985; Savage, 1985). The entry of women into these more powerful health care professions may reduce the availability of traditional nursing staff and require policies regarding day care and maternity leave, as well as a review of compensation equity.

Over the years, political and legal changes have had dramatic effects on the management of health care human resources. The elimination in a few states of certificate of need reviews and the entry of prospective payment are two recent changes. An issue on the immediate horizon is unionization. One of the only industries in which unions are currently experiencing growth is health care (McCormick, 1986). Whereas foreign competition has reduced union effectiveness in industrial settings, the health care industry is not affected by foreign competition. The introduction of collective bargaining has many effects on planning for human resources, including reduced flexibility in restructuring jobs to meet an organization's needs.

One of the most commonly noted changes in social values is employees' increasing expectation to participate in managerial decisions. As a result, management development programs have placed a greater emphasis on participatory management. Technology too will have substantial effects on future human resources in health care. The introduction of new technologies will require continued retraining of existing personnel, with skills becoming obsolete at an increasing rate. Scientific advances such as the introduction of the drug lovastatin, which may reduce blood cholesterol levels (Waldholz, 1986), could result in a reduced demand for cardiovascular care, with the concomitant reduction in personnel with this specialty.

Finally, future economic patterns will have a variety of effects. Cost-containment and utilization review will continue to require health care institutions to improve efficiency and employee productivity. In addition, a weak economy may increase the competition for jobs, resulting in a larger employee pool from which to recruit.

These are only a small number of possible changes that will affect the planning for health care human resources in the future. The similarity between this process and environmental scanning in strategic planning is obvious. An integration of both activities is clearly the most efficient way to use the organization's resources.

Phase 5: Establish Policies, Goals, and Programs

The first four phases of the HRP process have described a process of gathering, assembling, and interpreting a variety of data about the present and future state of human resources. This phase focuses on determining what actions will be taken in the light of this information. Three interrelated areas are discussed: (1) policy development specifying general guidelines for human resource management; (2) goal setting to identify results to be achieved; and (3) programming to develop specific activities to be undertaken.

Human resource policies

An organization's human resource policies shape both short- and long-term goals and programs. Policy is defined in *Webster's Third New International Dictionary* as "a definite course or method of action selected from among alternatives and in light of given conditions to guide and determine present and future decisions." In the context of HRP, policies represent the general guidelines regarding management of human resources. These policies should reflect the organization's philosophy and mission and provide guidance in the shaping of goals and programs.

A number of common areas of policy development in the health care organization that have a direct impact on goal development and programming are affirmative action, reduction in force, discipline and termination, training, and compensation. An aggressive affirmative action policy, for instance, influences choices regarding management succession, recruitment, termination, and a variety of other activities related to organizational staffing. A compensation policy, written or unwritten, that creates a compensation system resulting in paying the

Strategic Human Resource Planning

lowest possible wages will lead to higher turnover rates and recruitment difficulties.

Prior to establishing goals and programs, various organizational policies should be reviewed and evaluated. A policy need not be written but may simply be the modus operandi of the organization. Failure to consider implicit policies may result in rejection of a strategy or inadequate implementation.

Goal setting

To avoid confusion, we use *goal* and *objective* interchangeably as the statement of a result to be achieved in the future. Results can be either ends or means. An example of a goal stated as an end would be, "To recruit and employ fifteen registered nurses in the next three months." A means goal might be presented as, "To conduct six management training programs in the next year." Ideally each means goal has some specifc result goal to which it is directed. The goal-setting component of the HRP process involves development of ends goals. Means goals are developed as part of the programming process.

Ends goals emerge directly from information that has been developed in previous phases of the planning process and reflect both long- and short-term horizons. Although the information will lead to specific conclusions about job categories, these conclusions will fall into two general areas:

1. The relationship of internal supply to future demand. Internal supply will be greater than, less than, or equal to expected demand.
2. The relationship of external supply to staffing needs. The availability of appropriate personnel in the external environment will be adequate or inadequate to meet the needs of the organization.

There is often a tendency in the goal-setting process to state goals in a manner that immediately limits the means for attaining them. For example, a common goal statement emerging from a projected nursing staff shortage would be, "To increase nursing staff by 10 percent." The options for achieving this goal are limited to nurse recruitment. An alternative way of stating this objective might be, "To eliminate the projected staffing shortage of ten full-time-equivalent nurses within the next three months." Although nurse recruitment is a possible option for achieving this goal, this statement opens up additional possibilities that emphasize improved productivity.

Programming

There is a fine distinction between programming and goal setting. We will define programming as specifying the means for achieving the ends goals. The output of the programming process is a statement of means goals. Programming generally has two steps. First is unconstrained development of options to achieve ends objectives. This might be accomplished through brainstorming or some other form of creative thinking (see Ulschak, Nathanson, and Gillan, 1981). The second part is the identification of feasible alternatives in the light of constraints. Organizational policies, laws, and budgets are common constraints that limit potential activities. For example, equal employment opportunity guidelines prohibit programs that discriminate against protected groups.

The most common programs to meet short-term staffing shortages will be recruitment, productivity improvement, or a combination of the two. Many health care organizations also use temporary employees, contract employees, and float pools (Bracken et al., 1985) to meet seasonal demands. Programs to address long-term shortages may include recruitment and productivity improvement and interventions to increase or enhance the labor supply. One of the authors, for instance, met with administrators of local vocational schools and encouraged them to develop training programs to prepare local unskilled people for vocational and technical jobs in the hospital. Health care organizations today may need to take a more active role in ensuring that local schools, colleges, and universities are providing students with the basic skills necessary to become productive future professional employees.

There are also several common approaches for meeting projected staff surpluses: layoffs, hiring freezes, early retirement programs, voluntary resignation programs, job reclassification, and part-time or reduced hours (Cherrington, 1983: chap. 4; Lehr and Middlebrooks, 1984; Robinson, 1985). Regardless of the approach, effectively planning for organizational downsizing is essential in the health care industry today (Lehr and Middlebrooks, 1984; Swanberg, Margolis, and Knutson, 1983; Van Sumeren, 1986).

Two primary areas to consider when planning for a reduction in force are employee relations and organizational operating structure. Employee relations covers the full range of issues, from the approach to be used to reduce staff levels to maintaining employee morale. Questions such as whether work hours should be reduced to spread the reduced workload among all employees or whether full-time employees should be cut to limit the effect to a few must be considered (Swanberg et al., 1983). In addition, one consequence of a reduction in force is that the morale of the remaining workers generally declines. It may be necessary to have "grief management" programs to assist employees in adjusting to the change.

Organizational structure issues must also be considered. Van Sumeren (1986) notes that the 200-bed hospital has widely different organizational requirements from the 300-bed hospital. As a result, new staffing plans must be developed. This may lead to actions including collapsing two jobs into one, cross-training, and job enlargement (Robinson, 1985). In addition, it is necessary to determine the best approach to a reduction in force, across-the-board reductions, shifting more employees to part time, or the elimination of specific programs.

Phase 6: Implementation, Monitoring, and Evaluation

Once programs to achieve goals have been identified, it is necessary to begin implementation. The actual implementation of most programs falls outside the

Strategic Human Resource Planning

purview of HRP, with most programs being undertaken as components of other aspects of institutional human resource management. For example, obtaining new employees falls in the area of recruitment, developing management skills falls in the area of training, and handling employee morale problems may be part of organizational development. HRP outputs become inputs for these processes.

An often overlooked part of HRP is monitoring and evaluating to evaluate whether goals were achieved and show why (or why not). Monitoring is used here as an ongoing assessment of implementation of programs. The focus is on whether what is being done is consistent with what was planned. It also involves ongoing determination of the degree to which projections matched actual occurrences.

Evaluation is the determination of the extent to which goals were achieved. For example, was the ten-nurse staffing shortage reduced in the allotted three months? Evaluation and monitoring data are essential to determine why the HRP goals were or were not accomplished. Monitoring examines the process of achieving goals, and evaluation assesses whether they were achieved. Together they provide feedback regarding what needs to be done in the future and how to go about achieving new goals.

IMPLEMENTING THE HUMAN RESOURCE SYSTEM IN HEALTH CARE

An overview of a six-phase process of HRP for health care organizations has been provided in this chapter. As a conclusion, we offer a brief discussion of some roadblocks to implementing this system and ways to clear the path.

Roadblocks to Planning

There are several important roadblocks to effective HRP that should be considered as the system is implemented. The first of these is management resistance. Most management will support HRP activities until those activities begin to require management time. Unfortunately, HRP does require management time to provide needed information, including business planning information.

A second, and related, roadblock is the extensive amount of information necessary to carry out the planning process. Transition rates, employee demographics, staffing levels, and labor supply are just a few of the types of information needed. A third issue is that planning requires time and effort for which the payoff may not occur until well into the future. Reacting to a manager's demand for more staff to carry on today's work results in immediate feedback and reward. The results of effective planning may not be realized for five or more years; setting aside time for this work is often difficult when coping with today's crises.

Clearing the Path

Reducing management resistance to HRP is not easy. Resistance is not only a result of limited time but is also rooted in conflict between staff and line management. Several steps can be taken to reduce this resistance. First, commitment from top management is essential. This commitment must go beyond the symbolic, such as a supportive memorandum, to a more concrete action, such as involvement of a member of the HRP team on the strategic planning team. Second, every effort should be made to tie HRP activities together with other management planning activities, such as programming and budgeting. Finally, those responsible for HRP should educate management about the planning process—what is to be done and how the information is to be used. Management should be given the opportunity to participate in all aspects of HRP.

The development of a human resource information system is the primary means of reducing time and effort associated with obtaining information for HRP. It should be noted that a system set up solely for HRP would not have much benefit. Integrated systems tying strategic business planning information and human resource information together offer an efficient use of resources. There are substantial data common to accounting, compensation, budgeting, training, performance management, quality assurance, benefits management, and HRP.

The last roadblock to remove—resistance to planning in general—may be the most difficult to overcome since it requires setting aside planning time when the planning activity may conflict with more immediate demands on time. For some health care organizations, planning will be a clear priority, and setting aside time will not be difficult. For organizations new to planning or for which there has been difficulty implementing planning, several steps can be taken. First, start with small steps. Break the overall HRP process into pieces and begin slowly, giving the process time to evolve. Second, start with a part of the organization that appears to be most interested and in which HRP may demonstrate success. Finally, it may be useful to get outside assistance from a corporate staff member or external consultant to get the process underway.

NOTES

1. For an alternative approach applied to laboratory personnel, see Rubenstein (1984).
2. Nutt (1984) has provided an interesting discussion of decision modeling methods to develop a decision support system for staffing.

REFERENCES

Abelson, A. A. (1986). c management of turnover: A model for the health service administrator. *Health Care Management Review* 11 (2): 61–71.

Alpander, G. G. (1982). *Human Resources Management Planning*. New York: AMACOM.

Bleau, B. L. (1981). The academic flow model: A Markov-chain model for faculty planning. *Decision Science* 12: 294–309.
Bracken, J., Calkin, J., Sanders, J., and Thesen, A. (1985). A strategy for adaptive staffing of hospitals under varying environmental conditions. *Health Care Management Review* 10 (4) 43–53.
Bradley, C. M. (1982). Work measurement by time study. In H. E. Smalley (Ed.), *Hospital Management Engineering: A Guide to Hospital Management Systems.* Englewood Cliffs, N.J.: Prentice-Hall.
Burack, E. H., and Mathys, N. J. (1979). *Human Resources Planning: A Pragmatic Approach to Manpower Staffing and Development.* Lake Forest, Ill.: Brace-Park Press.
Cherrington, D. J. *Personnel Management: The Management of Human Resources.* Dubuque, Iowa: Wm. C. Brown.
Cook, Mary F. (1984). *Human Resources Director's Handbook.* Englewood Cliffs, N.J.: Prentice-Hall.
Craft, J. A. (1980). A critical perspective on human resource planning. *Human Resource Planning* 3 (2): 39–52.
Delbecq. A. L. Van de Ven, A. H., and Gustafson, D. H. (1975). *Group Techniques for Program Planning.* Glenview, Ill.: Scott, Foresman.
Eisenberg, B. (1986). Strategic human resource plans help providers survive changing conditions. *Modern Healthcare* 16 (7): 154–56.
Faludi, A. (1973). *Planning Theory.* Oxford, Eng.: Pergamon Press.
Farrell, D., and Rusbut, C. (1985). Understanding the retention function: A model of the causes of exit, voice, loyalty, and neglect behaviors. *Personnel Administrator.* 30 (4): 129–40.
Friedman, E., McTernan, E. J., and Leiken, A. (1985). A historiography of a model statewide allied health manpower supply/demand study. *Journal of Allied Health* 14: 129–39.
Gerner, E. J. (1982). Methods-time measurement analysis of outpatient department paperwork. In H. E. Smalley (Ed.), *Hospital Management Engineering: A Guide to Hospital Management Systems.* Englewood Cliffs, N.J.: Prentice-Hall.
Gove, P. B. (ed.) (1971). *Webster's Third New International Dictionary of the English Language Unabridged.* Springfield, Mass.: Merriam.
Hall, T. F. (1981). How to estimate employee turnover costs. *Personnel* 58 (4): 43–52.
Hanke, J. E., and Reitsch, A. G. (1981). *Business Forecasting.* Boston: Allyn and Bacon.
Health Resources and Services Administration. (1986). *Fifth Report to the President and Congress on the Status of Health Personnel in the United States.* DHHS publication no. HRS-P-OD-86-1. Washington, D.C.: Government Printing Office.
Hooper, J. A., and Catalanello, R. F. (1981). Markov analysis applied to forecasting technical personnel. *Human Resource Planning* 4 (2): 41–52.
Katz, D., and Kahn, R. (1978). *The Social Psychology of Organizations.* 2d ed. New York: Wiley.
Kleinbaum, D. G., and Kupper, L. L. (1978). *Applied Regression Analysis and Other Multivariable Methods.* North Scituate, Mass.: Duxbury Press.
Laliberty, R. (1984). Health care governing boards need to be more involved in human resource planning. *Health Matrix* 2: 38–39.
Lehr, R. I., and Middlebrooks, D. J. (1984). Work force reduction: Staff cuts are often an unpleasant and a legal liability. *Personnel Journal* 63 (10): 50–55.

Lindbloom, C. E. (1959). The science of muddling through. *Public Administration Review* 19: 79–88.
McCormick, Brian. (1986, December 5). Union activity on the rise, new AHA report states. *Hospitals* 60 (23): 73.
Neudeck, M. M. (1985). Trends affecting hospital's human resources. *Hospital and Health Services Administration* 30 (3): 82–93.
Nutt, P. C. (1984). Decision-modeling methods used to design decision support systems for staffing. *Medical Care* 22: 1002–13.
Pochter, R. T. (1982). Work performance in medical records. In H. E. Smalley (Ed.), *Hospital Management Engineering: A Guide to Hospital Management Systems.* Englewood Cliffs, N.J.: Prentice-Hall.
Price, J. L. *The Study of Turnover.* Ames: Iowa State University Press.
Robinson, M. L. (1985). The changing hospital labor force. *HealthSpan* 2 (9): 14–18.
Roseman, E. (1981). *Managing Employee Turnover: A Positive Approach.* New York: AMACOM.
Rowland, K. M., and Summers, S. L. (1981). Human resource planning: A second look. *Personnel Administrator* 26 (12): 73–80.
Rubenstein, N. M. (1984). Realistic staffing via workload recording. *Medical Laboratory Observer* 16: 58–64.
Salmon, M. E., and Culbertson, R. A. (1985). Health manpower oversupply: Implications for physicians, nurse practitioners and physician assistants. *Hospital and Health Service Administration* 30 (1): 100–115.
Savage, R. A. (1985). Manpower needs in 1990: A mildly rosy point of view. *Pathologist* 39 (2): 56–61.
Shapiro, R. J., and Glandon, G. L. (1984). Medical staff planning: An approach to managing critical hospital assets. *Health Care Management Review* 9 (1): 27–40.
Smith, E. C. (1983). How to tie human resource planning to strategic business planning. *Managerial Planning* 32 (2): 29–34.
Swanberg, G., Margolis, L., and Knutson, K. (1983). Planning now for the possibility of layoffs can temper turmoil, trauma. *Modern Healthcare* 13 (10): 150–54.
Ulschak, F. L., Nathanson, L., and Gillan, P. G. (1981). *Small Group Problem Solving: An Aid to Organizational Effectiveness.* Reading, Mass.: Addison-Wesley.
U.S. Department of Labor (1970). *Job Descriptions and Organizational Analysis for Hospitals and Related Health Services.* Washington, D.C.: Government Printing Office.
Van Sumeren, M. A. (1986). Organizational downsizing: Streamlining the healthcare organization. *Healthcare Financial Management* 40 (1): 35–39.
Waldholz, M. (1986, December 23). New cholesterol drug enhances Merck's role as a leader in research. *Wall Street Journal*, 1–12.
Whiston-Fox, S., and Mitchell, R. J. (1984). Management succession plan prepares for change. *Hospital Manager* 14 (2): 3–4.
Williams, E. E., and Manzo, S. E. (1983). *Business Planning for the Entrepreneur: How to Write and Execute a Business Plan.* New York: Van Nostrand Reinhold.

3
The Role of Job Design and Job Analysis in the Strategic Human Resource Management Model

Amarjit S. Sethi,
Patricia L. Birkwood,
and Randall S. Schuler

Job design and job analysis are important elements of the process of human and personnel management. In this chapter we will discusss the theoretical aspects of these processes and examine how these processes are performed in the health care area of the public sector.

The links between how jobs in a health care institution are designed and their impact on productivity and quality of patient service are well established in the human resource management literature. Middlemist, Hitt, and Greer (1983), for example, show how jobs, people, and organizations are logically interrelated (see Exhibit 3.1). The nature of the jobs in a health care organization (HCO) influences the ability of administrators, doctors, nurses, and other employees to achieve both organizational and patient-related goals. As a result of their central importance, the manner in which jobs are designed is crucial to patient care services and to employee satisfaction.

CONTEMPORARY CHALLENGES IN JOB DESIGN AND JOB ANALYSIS

In the design and analysis of jobs there are several critical contemporary challenges for HCOs:

Exhibit 3.1
Central Elements and Activities in Health Care Human Resource Management

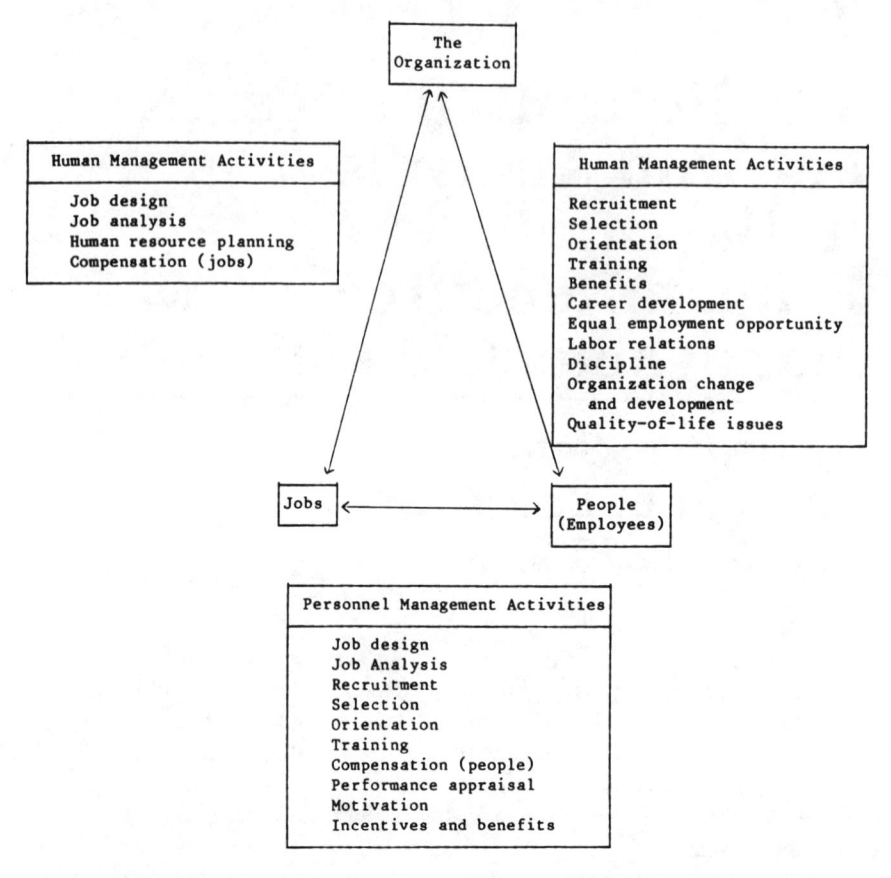

```
                        ┌──────────────┐
                        │     The      │
                        │ Organization │
                        └──────────────┘
                              ↑ ↑
                             /   \
┌─────────────────────────┐ /     \ ┌─────────────────────────────────┐
│ Human Management         │       │ Human Management Activities      │
│ Activities               │       │                                  │
│ Job design               │       │ Recruitment                      │
│ Job analysis             │       │ Selection                        │
│ Human resource planning  │       │ Orientation                      │
│ Compensation (jobs)      │       │ Training                         │
└─────────────────────────┘        │ Benefits                         │
                                   │ Career development               │
                                   │ Equal employment opportunity     │
                                   │ Labor relations                  │
                                   │ Discipline                       │
                                   │ Organization change              │
                                   │   and development                │
                                   │ Quality-of-life issues           │
                                   └─────────────────────────────────┘
         ↓                                       ↓
   ┌─────────┐                            ┌──────────────┐
   │  Jobs   │ ←─────────────────────────→│    People    │
   └─────────┘                            │  (Employees) │
                                          └──────────────┘

              ┌─────────────────────────────────┐
              │ Personnel Management Activities │
              │                                 │
              │ Job design                      │
              │ Job Analysis                    │
              │ Recruitment                     │
              │ Selection                       │
              │ Orientation                     │
              │ Training                        │
              │ Compensation (people)           │
              │ Performance appraisal           │
              │ Motivation                      │
              │ Incentives and benefits         │
              └─────────────────────────────────┘
```

Source: Adapted from R.D. Middlemist, M.A. Hitt, and C.R. Greer, *Personnel Management* (Englewood Cliffs, N.J.: Prentice-Hall, 1983).

- What critical characteristics should HCOs consider in the design of jobs?
- How can HCOs determine which individuals are likely to respond most favorably to different job designs?
- What are alternate ways of designing jobs?
- How does job analysis relate to selection, performance appraisal, and training?
- How can job design and job analysis help improve organizational effectiveness?
- How can different perspectives on job design and job analysis be used to promote morale and productivity? For example, in many HCOs, professionals generally determine for themselves what work to do and how to do it, whereas technicians' jobs are highly structured. How can organizational needs be matched with those of the individual?

Jobs, people, and organizations are logically interrelated, with jobs serving as the vital link between organizations and employees (Middlemist et al., 1983) (see Exhibit 3.1). The nature of the jobs in an organization influences the ability of both the organization and its employees to achieve certain goals. As a result of their pivotal position, the manner in which jobs are designed is crucial to the productivity level of a health care organization and to the satisfaction level of its employees.

JOB DESIGN AND JOB ANALYSIS AS STRATEGIC CHOICES

In line with the strategic choice model presented in Chapter 1, job design and job analysis are highly significant for strategic human resource management (SHRM).

Job design refers to the arrangement of task content so as to satisfy organizational and human requirements. Job design produces a set of purposes, task characteristics, and task duties in a particular organizational setting, based on a set of unique organizational and personnel qualities (Middlemist et al., 1983). Hand in hand with job design is job "redesign," which is the restructuring of a job's characteristics, duties, and purposes so as to improve an employee's satisfaction with the job, quality of worklife, and often productivity (Hackman, 1983).

Job design and redesign not only influence levels of employee motivation, productivity, and quality of worklife but can also serve as an alternative to promotion and can allow all employees to participate in a wide range of jobs, an especially important factor due to the legal necessity for equal opportunity employment (Schuler, 1984).

In order for jobs to be designed properly, their essence must be determined through careful analysis. Job analysis is a systematic process for gathering information about a job. Such information is used to produce job descriptions and specifications. Job descriptions contain the duties, characteristics, conditions, purposes, and standards of jobs. Job specifications list the skills, knowledge, and abilities needed to perform the job duties under specified conditions, as well as individual preferences, interests, and personalities that may be most suitable to the job (Schuler, 1984).

Job analysis is required for job classification, evaluation, design and redesign, recruitment, selection, placement, performance appraisal, worker training, career development, workforce planning, fulfillment of legal requirements related to equal opportunity or occupational health and safety regulations, providing justification for the existence of a job, and for delineating the place of a job in an organization.

RELATIONSHIPS BETWEEN JOB DESIGN AND JOB ANALYSIS

One of the premises of strategic choice model is that various HRM activities are interrelated and transactional. The extensive relationships between job design and analysis, with other personnel and HRM activities, and with various facets of an organization are described below (see Exhibit 3.2).

Health Care Goals and Technology

The design of jobs in an HCO reflects the organization's design, technology, and goals. Jobs in fact reflect the organization's perception of the most appropriate means by which to accomplish its goals, which serve to establish the purpose of jobs, the nature of the organization's expectations from workers, and the legitimacy of job demands. An organization's technology frequently places constraints on job design as a result of the costs that would occur if design or redesign required technological changes and/or due to the limits of the state of the art technology.

Union-Management Relations

The relationship of job design and redesign to job classification has implications for wages and benefits; consequently an organization requires union support prior to any design or redesign. In some cases, bargaining with a union must occur prior to acceptance of management's desired job changes. Unions can also support certain job change programs for the purpose of saving jobs and/or for improving quality of worklife.

Recruitment and Selection

Job design is important in these areas due to the changing workforce composition (i.e., increasing numbers of women and elderly persons) and also due to an increased need for expansion of jobs as an alternative to promotion. Job analysis is used to specify the types of job applicants required and where they are required. These factors influence productivity levels and serve to validate selection procedures and decisions.

Appraising Performance

In order to evaluate personnel in terms of job-related dimensions, the appraisal method must reflect accurately the duties of the job, as detailed in the job analysis. Lack of proper job analysis may lead to questions regarding the validity and objectivity of the appraisal.

Exhibit 3.2
Job Design and Job Analysis Relationships

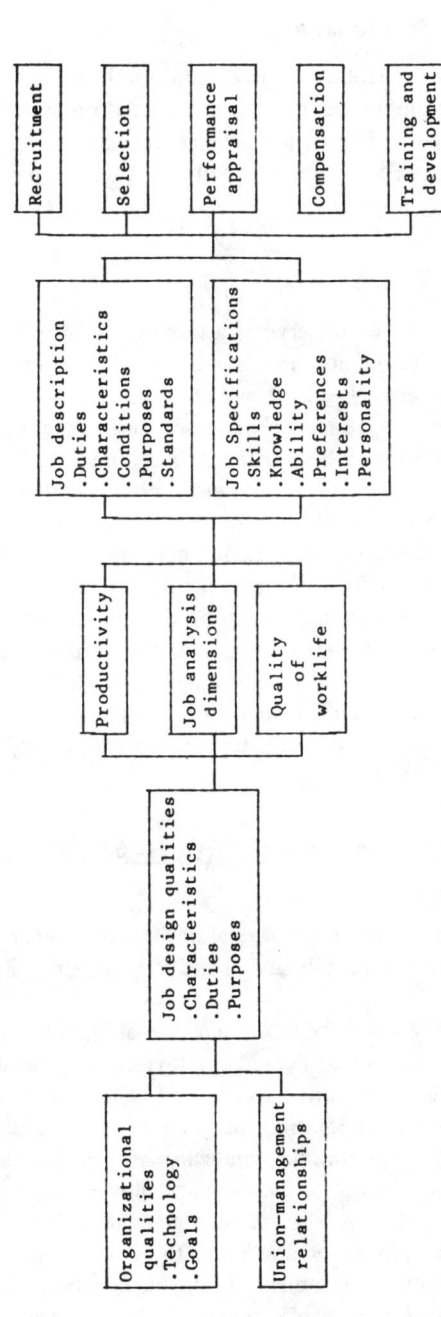

```
Organizational
qualities
.Technology
.Goals                Job design qualities        Productivity
                      .Characteristics                              Job description
                      .Duties                    Job analysis       .Duties                    Recruitment
                      .Purposes                  dimensions         .Characteristics
Union-management                                                    .Conditions                Selection
relationships                                    Quality            .Purposes
                                                 of                 .Standards                 Performance
                                                 worklife                                      appraisal
                                                                    Job Specifications
                                                                    .Skills                    Compensation
                                                                    .Knowledge
                                                                    .Ability                   Training and
                                                                    .Preferences               development
                                                                    .Interests
                                                                    .Personality
```

Source: R.S. Schuler, *Personnel and Human Resource Management* (St. Paul, Minn.: West Publishing, 1984).

Training and Promoting

Job specifications must be used to examine skills required for a particular job so that health care employees may be trained and promoted in accordance with human resource needs. Use of job analysis reveals areas for improvement and often leads to increased efficiency and effectiveness of patient care and performance.

Compensation

Job analysis is required to serve as a framework for job evaluation and classification, which in turn determines level of pay. The organization must ensure that internal and external levels of pay are fair.

Since job design and job analysis interact with so many aspects of personnel management, the responsibility for these procedures lies with many individuals in the organization. Top management must support and understand the job design program, including redesign, because the organization's goals will affect the selection of a job design strategy. Health care administrators must also provide authority to the personnel manager to facilitate his or her effort to obtain the cooperation of the other managers during design and redesign. The personnel department and other managers must ensure that the design and redesign of jobs reflect the HCO's goals, patient care goals, and the employees' needs. The personnel department is usually responsible for job analysis to ensure that uniform standards and methods are applied. Line managers provide information for job analysis (Schuler, 1984).

LEGAL CONSIDERATIONS IN JOB DESIGN AND JOB ANALYSIS

In addition to an extensive set of relationships with other HRM activities and aspects of the organization, job design and job analysis are influenced by legal considerations.[1]

In 1973 Congress passed the Vocational Rehabilitation Act stating that handicapped individuals cannot be denied employment or educational opportunities by sole reason of their disability. Section 503 of the act mandates organizations with federal contracts over $50,000 and employees over the age of 50 to prepare affirmative action plans to hire the handicapped in each of their plants or offices (Peterson, 1981). Regardless of contract size, however, all employers with federal contracts must make "reasonable accommodation" to the physical or mental limitations of an employee or applicant; to comply, employers may have to design jobs and work environments to enable handicapped persons to work. Although the needs of one disabled person are not necessarily reflective of those of another, it appears as if the cost of accommodation requires relatively minimal expense (Strom and Ferris, 1982).

Job design is of concern to employers not just because of the Vocational Rehabilitation Act. Health care employers must also accommodate employees and applicants in order to comply with consent decrees and affirmative action programs for protected group members.

Job design, particularly job redesign, also faces legal concerns imposed by the National Labor Relations Board, created by the National Labor Relations Act (NLRA) of 1935 to provide a basic framework for labor relations in the United States (Fasman, 1982). Part of that framework holds that employers must not become, or act as, a labor organization on behalf of the employees. By engaging in certain changes in the work environment such as job design changes, employers may be found in violation of the act, although the chances of this appear minimal (cf. General Foods Corp., 231 NLRB 1232 [1977]). Nevertheless, employers must be aware of possible charges of unfair labor practices when making alterations in the work environment and in the nature of the jobs (Fasman, 1982). Employers must consider job design changes as they affect job classification and union-management contract provisions.

Several legal considerations and constraints also face job analysis, largely because it serves as the basis for selection decisions, performance appraisal, and training determinations (Thompson and Thompson, 1982). These considerations and constraints have been articulated in the Uniform Guidelines (of 1978) and several court decisions. For example, section 14.C.2 of the Uniform Guidelines states: "There shall be a job analysis which includes an analysis of the important work behaviors required for successful performance. . . . Any job analysis should focus on work behavior(s) and the tasks as associated with them" (Schuler, 1984: 95). Where job analysis has not been performed, the validity of selection instruments has been successfully challenged (*Kirkland* v. *New York Department of Correctional Services*, 1974; *Albermarle Paper Company* v. *Moody*, 1975). Numerous court decisions regarding job analysis and promotion and performance appraisal also exist. For example, in *Brito* v. *Zia Company* (1973), the court stated that the performance appraisal system of an organization is a selection procedure and therefore must be validated—that is, it must be anchored in job analysis. And in *Rowe* v. *General Motors* (1972), it was ruled that to prevent discriminatory practices in promotion decisions, a company should have written objective standards for promotion. These objective standards can be determined through job analysis. In *U.S.A.* v. *City of Chicago* (1978), the court stated that, in addition to having objective standards for promotion, the standards should describe the job to which the person is being considered for promotion.

The Uniform Guidelines acknowledge some of the several different purposes of job analysis and consequently establish requirements for job analysis. For example, when an empirical relationship between a selection instrument and job performance is being determined, the job performance measure must be anchored in job analysis that identifies the important job "elements," "work behavior(s)," "duties," or "work outcomes." When a content relationship between the selection instrument and the content of the job is being sought, the content of the job can be determined by a job analysis that identifies the work behaviors or the observed work products. When a construct relationship is being determined (between the selection instrument and the job), the analysis must clearly describe the constructs believed to underlie successful performance. Keep in mind that according to the Uniform Guidelines (section 14A), "Any method of job analysis may be used if it provides the information required for the specific validation strategy used" (Schuler, 1984: 96).

In Canada, there is an increased awareness of legal considerations resulting from the application of the Charter of Rights, specifically section 15. These refer to alternatives and experiences of redress for equal pay for work of equal value in the health care industry. The legal structure includes human rights legislation, the Canadian Human Rights Code, the Employment Equity Act of 1986, the Pay Equity Act in Ontario, and the Canada Labor Code. The impact of pay equity legislation on job analysis is significant and is considered an important reform in human resource management in both private and public sectors. Pay equity legislation has raised two key questions:

- Will pay legislation be the panacea for employment inequities, or will it threaten the very groups it seeks to benefit?
- What types of reforms are required, and will they be financially viable as well as socially acceptable?

Early managerial approaches to job design focused primarily on attempts to simplify employees' tasks so as to increase production efficiency. Taylor and other scientific management theorists, believing that workers were largely economically motivated, advocated the reduction of tasks to their simplest forms in combination with financial rewards on a piecework basis. In doing so, both the goals of the organization and the employees would be satisfied. This approach to simplified job design reached its peak from a technological view in assembly line production techniques (Steers and Porter, 1983).

Only in recent years have organizational psychologists and practicing managers studied undesirable behaviors in connection with task performance. These investigations have resulted in increased attention to job design and redesign and their effects on motivation, performance, and satisfaction. Operationalization of this new focus has in some cases improved job satisfaction, productivity, and the quality of products but has been costly in terms of training time and associated expenses (Hackman, 1983).

THEORETICAL PERSPECTIVES ON JOB DESIGN

The two most influential theoretical views on job design have been the job characteristics approach and the sociotechnical systems approach (Cordery and Wall, 1985).

The job characteristics approach emphasizes work properties and their role as

Exhibit 3.3
Job Characteristics Model of Work Motivation

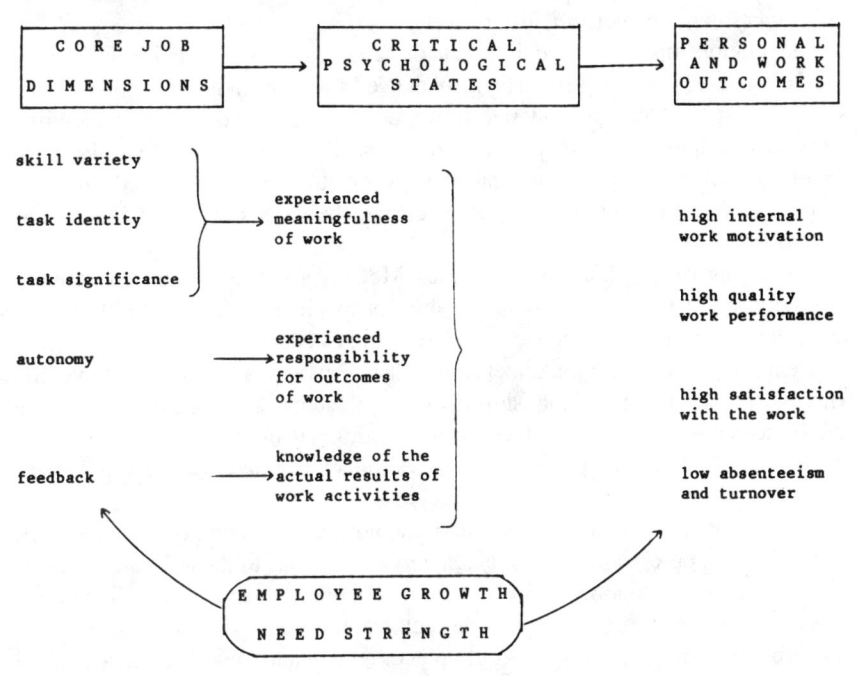

| CORE JOB DIMENSIONS | → | CRITICAL PSYCHOLOGICAL STATES | → | PERSONAL AND WORK OUTCOMES |

skill variety
task identity   → experienced meaningfulness of work
task significance

autonomy   → experienced responsibility for outcomes of work

feedback   → knowledge of the actual results of work activities

high internal work motivation

high quality work performance

high satisfaction with the work

low absenteeism and turnover

EMPLOYEE GROWTH NEED STRENGTH

Source: J.R. Hackman, "Work Design," in J.R. Hackman and J.L. Suttle, *Improving Life at Work*. Copyright © 1977 by Scott, Foresman and Co. Reprinted by permission of J.R. Hackman.

determinants of attitudinal and behavioral outcomes. One of the best representations of this approach is the Job Characteristics Model (Hackman and Oldham, 1976) (see Exhibit 3.3). 274 This model specifies five core job dimensions as defining the salient properties of work: skill variety (range of skills and talents used), task identity (degree to which the job involves completion of a product from beginning to end), task significance (with respect to people in the internal and external environment), autonomy (degree of freedom, independence, and discretion in work scheduling and procedures), and feedback (degree to which activities provide clear and direct information about performance effectiveness). These job characteristics supposedly act to determine three critical psychological states, which affect a person's motivation for and satisfaction with the job. Skill variety, task identification, and task significance are said to enhance experienced meaningfulness (i.e., the employee experiences the work as generally important, valuable, and worthwhile); autonomy is said to enhance experienced responsibility (i.e., the employee feels personally responsible and accountable for the results of the work performed); and feedback is said to lead to knowledge of results (i.e., understanding on a fairly regular basis of how effectively he or she is performing a job) (Cordery and Wall, 1985). These three critical psychological states are held to determine personal and work outcomes such as internal work motivation, quality work performance, satisfaction with work, and attendance behavior (low absenteeism and turnover).

The relationships across the three sets of variables are moderated by individual needs, especially as represented by growth need strength. Individual growth need strength is postulated to moderate how people react to complex, challenging work. The authors propose that high-growth-need individuals are more likely to experience a critical psychological state when their job is enriched and will respond more positively to a psychological state than will low-growth individuals (Hackman, 1983).

Extensions of the Job Characteristics Model have been proposed recently through introduction of additional variables or by changing relationships among component variables. Other workers have suggested inclusion of task interdependence as another core job dimension; role clarity and challenge as intervening variables; a curvilinear relationship between job scope (a composite of the core job dimensions) and job satisfaction; and additional moderators such as work context satisfaction, job longevity, and need of achievement (Cordery and Wall, 1985).

The sociotechnological approach uses the notion of autonomous work groups and a description of salient work characteristics similar to those in the previous model, although autonomy is deemed the most important component. In contrast to the previous approach, however, the sociotechnological perspective recognizes that job change requires simultaneous and complementary modification to several aspects of the total work situation, among which the supervisor is prominent (Cordery and Wall, 1985).

Cordery and Wall (1985) suggest that an even greater emphasis be placed on supervisory behavior in the redesign of jobs because research has demonstrated that enrichment of employee jobs often strains the relationship with the supervisor due to the transfer of autonomy, decision-making responsibility, discretion, and quality control. Having a supervisor's cooperation in redesign is critical; her or his behavior largely determines how much support and encouragement is received from the rest of management. Further, the supervisor must provide employees with clear boundaries as to the limits of their new discretion, ensure that employees have or can acquire the skills and knowledge needed to exercise discretion, provide structure to those aspects of the work situation over which the group has limited control, and provide feedback.

HOW HEALTH CARE EMPLOYEES REACT TO JOBS: A MODEL

Many researchers have noted the distinction between the objective set of activities that comprise a job and the job incumbent's perceptions of those activities. Aldag and Brief (1979) have devised a model to depict how health care employees react to their jobs (see Exhibit 3.4). The model proposes that in

Exhibit 3.4
A Model of Employee Reactions to Their Jobs

The Job	Employee Perceptions	Employee Attributes	Motivational State	Employee Reactions

Actual Task Activities Which Comprise the Job → Task Attributes (Variety, Autonomy, Task Identity, Task Significance and Feedback) → Self-Perception of Job Behavior Caused by the Task Attributes → Intrinsic Motivation (Employee Feels Freely Vested in the Job) → Positive Affect Toward Job (High Satisfaction and Attachment) → Low Turnover and Absenteeism

→ High Effort → High Performance

[Valence of Task Attributes] [Instrumentality of Task Attributes]

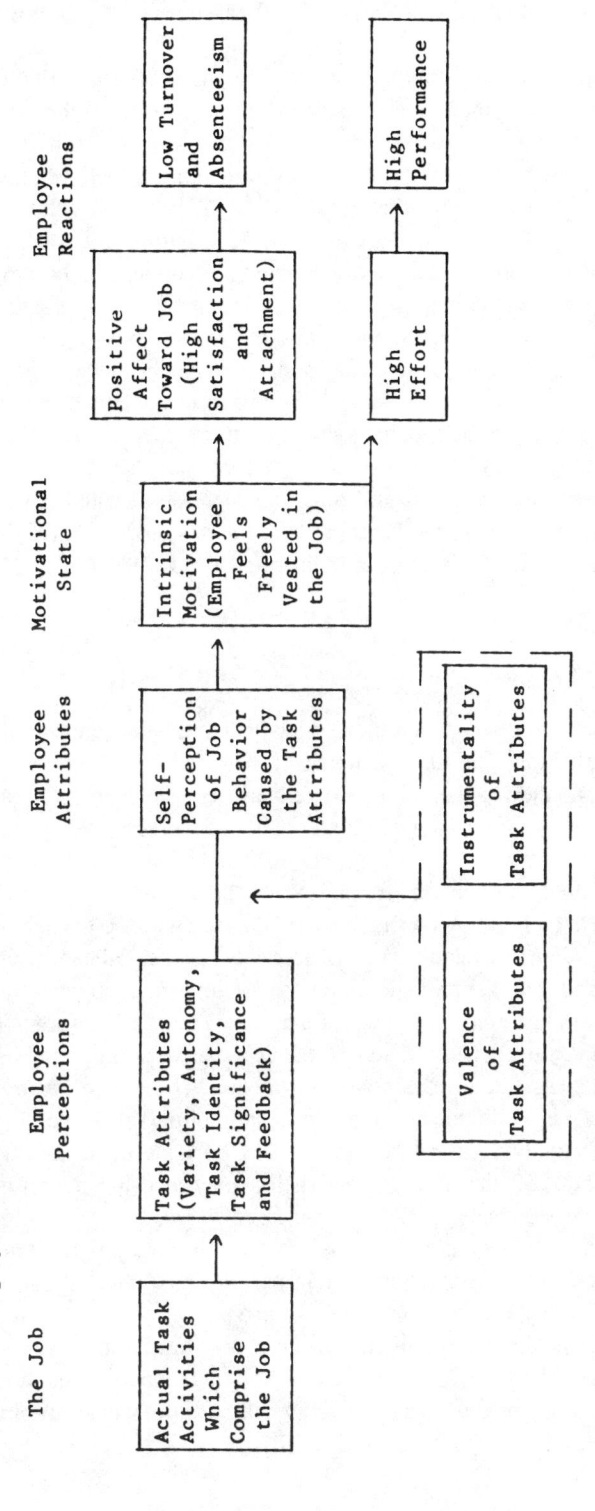

Source: From *Task Design and Employee Motivation* by Ramon J. Aldag and Arthur P. Brief. Copyright © 1979 by Scott, Foresman and Co. Reprinted by permission.

addition to the importance of employees' perceptions of task attributes, valences (i.e., anticipation of increased satisfaction by experiencing the attributes) and instrumentality (i.e., the perceived likelihood that task performance will lead to experiencing attributes) are also critical. If an employee believes task attributes to be positively valent, he or she will associate job behavior with task attributes, which leads to a state of intrinsic motivation regarding the job. This state of intrinsic motivation influences the employee's reactions. If the employee perceives task attributes as being present in a job and as being positively valent, then he or she will react positively toward the job in terms of experiencing high satisfaction and strong attachment to and involvement in the job. This should result in reduced tardiness, absenteeism, and turnover and increased task persistence. If the employee perceives the task attributes as being present in a job, positively valent, and contingent upon performance, he or she will react by increasing performance effort and thus will increase the quality or quantity of work. Careful attention to the ideas presented in this model can facilitate suitable job design and redesign initiatives (Aldag and Brief, 1979).

JOB QUALITIES

Job design involves consideration of job characteristics, duties, and purposes. Employers must have an understanding of these job qualities in order to design jobs that will allow an employee to experience achievement, responsibility, challenge, and meaning such that both quality of worklife and productivity may increase.

Schuler (1984) provides a description of the job qualities. He lists ten job characteristics by building on the five core characteristics proposed by Hackman and Oldham (1976). In addition to task variety, task significance, task identity, autonomy, and feedback, Schuler notes the importance of cognitive job elements (such as communicating, decision making, analyzing, and information processing); physical job elements (such as lifting, speed, positioning, lighting, and sound); quantitative and qualitative job overload (having too many duties and insufficient time, or requiring more skills and abilities than the employee possesses, respectively); and role underload (the opposite of overload). In combination, several of the ten characteristics may act to influence employee motivation, performance, turnover, and absenteeism.

Job duties are the specific activities that comprise a job and are in fact the behaviors performed by the employee in order to do a job. "Purposes" refer to the reasons for a job's creation and existence.

Job design is influenced by the desired end result of the organization as determined by its goals. Careful attention to all three job qualities should increase the likelihood that job design and redesign will be optimal in terms of maximizing productivity and quality of worklife.

JOB REDESIGN

Hand in hand with the concept of job design is that of job redesign—the restructuring of a job's characteristics, duties, and purposes so as to improve an employee's quality of worklife and increase productivity.

Prior to the undertaking of a redesign effort, the HCO must determine if a meaningful change is feasible given the jobs being considered, the people who will be involved, and the social organizational, and cultural environment in which the work is performed. It is necessary to select jobs for redesign carefully; to recognize the limitations of the technology being used; to consider the employees' readiness and desire for change; to consider whether management is prepared to handle potential problems that may result from the redesign; and to recognize the need for top- and middle-management commitment to the redesign project (Aldag and Brief, 1979).

Aldag and Brief (1979) suggest that a redesign task force should contain representatives from management, labor, and technical specialties. This task force could proceed using a series of logical steps.

First, data must be obtained regarding the task activities that comprise the target jobs, as well as other jobs that could be affected. Second, the relationships between the activities identified through job analysis and the perceived presence of salient task attributes must be explored using questionnaires and interviews. Third, a specific redesign intervention must be formulated, tackling one task attribute at a time. Fourth, activities that should increase the employee's perceptions of the attributes must be identified. The task force must ensure that the activities are technically feasible, that incumbents want to and can perform these activities, that the current performers of the activities are willing to forfeit them, and that the activities are made contingent upon some performance level so both the effect and effort of the incumbents are enhanced. Fifth, a number of incumbents must be selected for use in a trial intervention. During the trial consideration must be given to the impact of the redesign intervention in terms of satisfaction, performance, and costs and benefits. Sixth, the physical aspects of the work environment must be redesigned, if necessary, and trial incumbents must be trained for their new activities. Finally, if the intervention appears successful, the remaining employees must be trained for their new tasks, Throughout the entire redesign process, the task force must be aware that a comprehensive effort requires time to implement and that the intervention will affect not only the redesigned jobs but interrelated jobs as well (Aldag and Brief, 1979).

During redesign Hackman (1983) suggests keeping a focus on the desired change by basing redesign activities on an appropriate theory so that jobs are actually changed and not merely changed on paper. It is also necessary to prepare for unexpected problems related to the intervention and to develop contingency plans. The advantages of such an approach are twofold: employees, managers, and consultants will be made aware that problems may emerge elsewhere in the work system, and all parties will be better able to cope with them.

The effects of the redesign intervention must be evaluated continuously in order to determine if the effort was worthwhile in terms of satisfaction, productivity, costs, absenteeism, and other factors. Further, those responsible for the intervention should encourage an organizational climate that views evaluation as a learning experience rather than just an assessment. Such an outlook will minimize discouragement if the intervention is not immediately successful. Hackman suggests that difficulties be confronted early in the redesign process to avoid unpleasant surprises later. The task force must be aware of the nature and commitment of management and union leaders to the intervention and the criteria against which the project will ultimately be evaluated (Hackman, 1983).

The redesign process must be constructed such that it fits with the organization's change objectives. The use of a participatory approach is particularly useful in HCOs because employees will feel less threatened if they have an opportunity to be involved in the process, the quality of the data obtained tends to be high as employees realize that their jobs will be affected by their comments, and the widespread expectation of change may lessen resistance (Cordery and Wall, 1985).

APPROACHES TO JOB DESIGN AND REDESIGN

There are four major approaches for the process of job design: scientific (traditional), individual contemporary, team contemporary, and ergonomic. Other approaches exist but tend to be subsets or combinations of these four.

1. *The Scientific Approach.* In this approach, popular in industrial engineering circuits, jobs are designed such that tasks do not exceed the abilities of the employees. Work is frequently divided into small, simple segments and employees are constrained to repetitive performance of a narrow range of activities. Quality underload is common. Such an approach is well suited to motion time studies and to the use of incentive pay. The basic philosophy of the scientific approach rests on the premise that workers dislike work and are motivated only by economic rewards. Jobs designed using the scientific approach tend to lack variety, significance, autonomy, feedback, and identity and consequently lead to low employee motivation (Schuler, 1984).

2. *The Individual Contemporary Approach.* This approach frequently achieves high productivity levels without neglect of the human aspect of work as in the scientific approach. Among the most common individual contemporary approaches are job rotation, enlargement, enrichment, specialization, and simplification.

Job rotation refers to increasing the number of duties that an employee performs over a period of time by having him or her move from one job to another in some prearranged, logical sequence. The contents of specific jobs remain unchanged, however. Such an approach provides new job skills, changes work and social relationships on the job, provides relief from boredom, increases the sense of identity and purpose, and allows sharing of repetitive tasks. Job rotation may be useful only in the short run unless some of the jobs are meaningful and challenging. This approach is most useful when some jobs have been simplified and others have been enriched (Middlemist et al., 1983).

Job enlargement refers to the addition of more duties to a specific job and may be used to combat excess specialization. The number of tasks required for a job is increased by adding tasks similar in complexity to those currently performed but that require different skills. This approach can help employees to develop new skills or use a wider variety of existing skills, may increase independence by allowing employees to determine their own methods and pace of work, and may increase feelings of accomplishment by increasing levels of responsibility (Middlemist et al., 1983).

Job specialization may seem like an application of the scientific method in that it requires breaking down the work process into a series of smaller, more specialized tasks. In fact, this approach is necessary to some types of work, such as in the case of computer programmers, analysts, and operators. In such jobs, the complexity of the technological skills required in one job area provides for a variety of challenges (Middlemist et al., 1983).

Job simplification refers to the deletion of those elements of a job that are least demanding and are not required for task accomplishment. The objective of this method is to improve satisfaction and productivity by allowing employees to spend more time performing challenging, complex, and important tasks. Such an approach requires careful analysis of all task elements of a job and is most successful when implemented with another job change strategy such as job enrichment (Middlemist et al., 1983).

Job enrichment refers to the addition of more complex and challenging tasks so as to add different job characteristics to a job (vertical loading). Such a process allows employees more discretion over their work and greater involvement in planning, decision making, and control. Enrichment attempts to increase motivation, and thus satisfaction and productivity, by providing for more challenging tasks and increased discretion (Schuler, 1984).

Hackman (1983) suggests five principles for enriching jobs so as to lead to improvement in each of the five core job dimensions (see Exhibit 3.5). Natural work units may be formed such that basic work items are identified and grouped into natural and meaningful categories. This approach increases task identity and significance. Tasks may be combined such that several fractionalized tasks are put back together to yield a large module of work. This approach increases skill variety and task identity. Client relationships may be established to allow for contact between the worker and the use of his or her products. Jobs may be vertically loaded so as to increase autonomy through increased responsibility and freedom in time accomplishment. The objective of this method is to improve satisfaction and productivity by allowing employees to spend more time performing challenging, complex, and important tasks. Such an approach requires

Exhibit 3.5
Principles for Changing Jobs

CHANGE PRINCIPLES	CORE JOB DIMENSIONS
combining tasks	skill variety
forming natural work units	task identity
establish client relationships	task significance
vertical loading	autonomy
opening feedback channels	feedback

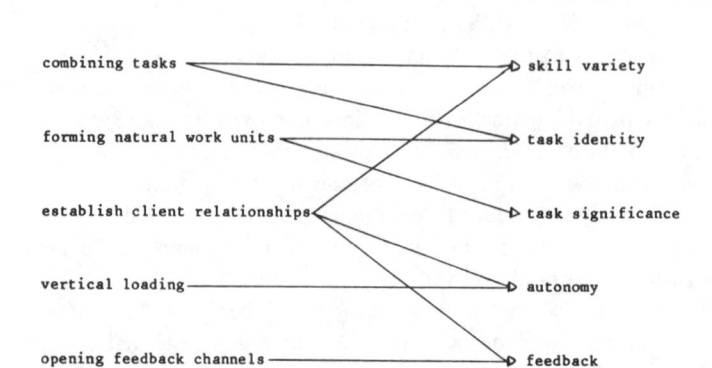

Source: J.R. Hackman, "Work Design," in J.R. Hackman and J.L. Suttle, *Improving Life at Work*. Copyright © 1977 by Scott, Foresman and Co. Reprinted by permission.

careful analysis of all task elements of a job, and management, and to encourage troubleshooting. Finally, feedback channels may be opened to increase the feedback dimension.

3. *The Team Contemporary Approach*. This approach involves the design of jobs for teams of employees in an attempt to consider both social and technical aspects of interrelated jobs. Often autonomous work teams are formed. These teams are groups of employees assigned to perform a natural unit of work and are often given responsibility to manage their own work, acquire necessary materials, set the timing of tasks, assign tasks, and control employee efforts. The groups are allowed discretion as long as output meets organizational requirements. Often group gain sharing and participation in decision making are used. The use of autonomous work teams has developed in response to increasing dissatisfaction with lower-level jobs and to changing employee values (Schuler, 1984).

4. *The Ergonomic Approach*. This approach attempts to design jobs such that they are suited to the characteristics and physical abilities of employees so as to enhance the ease and comfort of performance. For example, employees who make extensive use of computer terminals may be provided with a working environment that minimizes eyestrain and muscle fatigue through the use of proper lighting, ventilation, provision of adjustable chairs, and provision of table tops at heights that increase the comfort of typing. Frequently the ergonomic approach is used to create equal opportunity employment and to help an organization meet its legal requirements for employment and safety, to utilize human resources more effectively, and to increase productivity (Schuler, 1984).

ASSESSMENT OF JOB DESIGN AND REDESIGN APPROACHES

Individual Factors

HCOs must be aware of individual employee's skills, knowledge, and abilities by making use of written tests and/or interviews. The employer must also be familiar with the personality, interest, and preferences of the individual in question, especially regarding the strength of the higher-order needs. Individuals with a strong growth need are more likely to exhibit a positive response to job change than are those with a weak growth need. Questionnaires may also be employed to determine employee's perceptions of task characteristics, as these influence the response to task characteristics. In certain instances, physical abilities and physiological responses may also be of significance (Aldag and Brief, 1979).

Situational Factors

In certain situations, attempts to redesign jobs yield few or negative results. Such situations include those in which certain job characteristics are already present at such a high level that the employee's desire for them is already satisfied; where lower-order needs remain unsatisfied, such as level of pay and relations with coworkers or supervisors; and where other factors in the environment impair an employee's ability to respond to the enrichment provided by job redesign. Individuals charged with the responsibility of redesign efforts must be aware of such situations so as to correct undesirable elements and/or to avoid wasting the organization's financial resources (Aldag and Brief, 1979).

Organizational Factors

Several factors inherent in the organization itself necessarily affect job design and redesign strategies: organizational design, personnel and human resource policies and practices, the existence of control systems, and technology.

Organizational Design

HCOs tend to be designed either mechanistically (designed to maximize efficiency) or organically (capable of flexibility and adaptability). There is no optimal organizational design in terms of guaranteeing the success of job design or redesign efforts; rather, an organization must be appropriately designed so as to meet the demands of its environment. The mechanistic approach tends to be more suitable to stable, predictable environments, while the organic approach tends to be better suited to uncertain environments (Aldag and Brief, 1979).

A critical factor in the success of job change efforts is the degree to which the orientation of the tasks and the organizational design are congruent. Aldag

Exhibit 3.6
Predicted Relationships among Organizational Design, Job Design, and Employee Characteristics

Simple Routine Jobs	"Enlarged" Job

High-Growth Need Employees The individual feels under-utilized and overcontrolled. Predict high frustration, dissatisfaction, and turnover. (1)	**High-Growth Need Employees** Predict that the individual responds to the cues in his job, and chafes at the perceived overcontrol by the organization. (3)
Congruence is the "classical" mode. Predict effective performance, adequate levels of satisfaction, and adequate attendance levels. (2) Low-Growth Need Employees	Predict that the individual responds to cues from the organization, and that he does not deal effectively with his job. (4) Low Growth Need Employees
High Growth Need Employees Predict that the individual responds to the cues in the organization, and that he chafes at the restrictiveness of his job. Predict he will try and succeed in having the job changed, or resign. (5)	**High-Growth Need Employees** Congruence in the "flexible" mode. Predict very high quality performance, high satisfaction, good attendance, and low turnover. (7)
Predict that the individual responds to the cues in his job and that he performs reasonably adequately but that he is constantly uneasy and anxious about the perceived unpredictability of organizational management. (6) Low-Growth Need Employees	The individual is overwhelmed by organizational and job demands. Predict psychological withdrawal from the job or overt hostility and inadequate job performance. A person killer. (8) Low-Growth Need Employees

Source: From L.W. Porter, E.E. Lawler III, and J.R. Hackman, *Behavior in Organizations* (New York: McGraw-Hill, 1975).

and brief (1979) have proposed a model for task-organization fit (see Exhibit 3.6). The model suggests that employees receive cues from the overall organization and the job and that the strength of the individual's growth needs, the extent to which jobs are enriched, and the degree to which the organization is organic are determinants of whether there is proper individual-task-organization congruence. The higher the congruence is, the higher the level of employee satisfaction and productivity is. Complete congruence occurs when a high-growth-need individual works in an enriched job in an organic environment and when a low-growth-need individual works in a routine job in a mechanistic environment with a bureaucratic orientation. Bureaucratic orientation is a measure of the extent to which an individual desires a restricted, formalized work structure. While strength of higher-order needs influences the response to task characteristics, bureaucratic orientation affects the reactions to the degree of overall structure (Aldag and Brief, 1979).

Personnel and Human Resource Policies and Practices

The extensive interaction of job design and job descriptions with various personnel functions implies the need for cooperation of several individuals so that a job design and redesign technology will be effective (Schuler, 1984).

Existence of Control Systems

An emphasis on accountability, procedures, and authority, as expressed through dependence on such tools as production and quality control reports, attendance reports, and the use of close supervision, is frequently necessary to reduce the complexity of jobs and to delineate the responsibilities of workers. However, the use of such tools erects impersonal boundaries that influence how employees behave and what they are and are not willing to do. Consequently such systems are often not conducive to job design and redesign interventions. Individuals attempting to institute such changes must be aware of the potential impact of such tools on the success of the job change efforts (Schuler, 1984).

Technology

This term refers to the machines, methods, and materials used by an HCO to produce patient care and related services. Optimal organizational design is a function of medical and other technology. Technology may constrain redesign effort due to the costs associated with changing the technology or due to the limits of the best available technology. Technology affects the extent to which employees follow a product from beginning to end and the amount of discretion afforded employees. Consequently models of task organization design should incorporate the effects of technology (Slocum and Sims, 1980).

Schuler (1977) argues that there must be a three-way fit between the technology of an organization, the task required, and the organizational structure; otherwise employees receive conflicting messages about their expected behavior (role conflict) and fail to have a clear understanding of the outcomes expected as a result of performing their roles (role ambiguity). Stress results.

Slocum and Sims (1980) proposed a model to integrate technology, job design, and organizational characteristics (see Exhibit 3.7). These authors discussed the relation of the elements of technology (workflow uncertainty, task uncertainty,

Exhibit 3.7
Relationship between Job Design Changes and Elements of Technology and Modes of Control

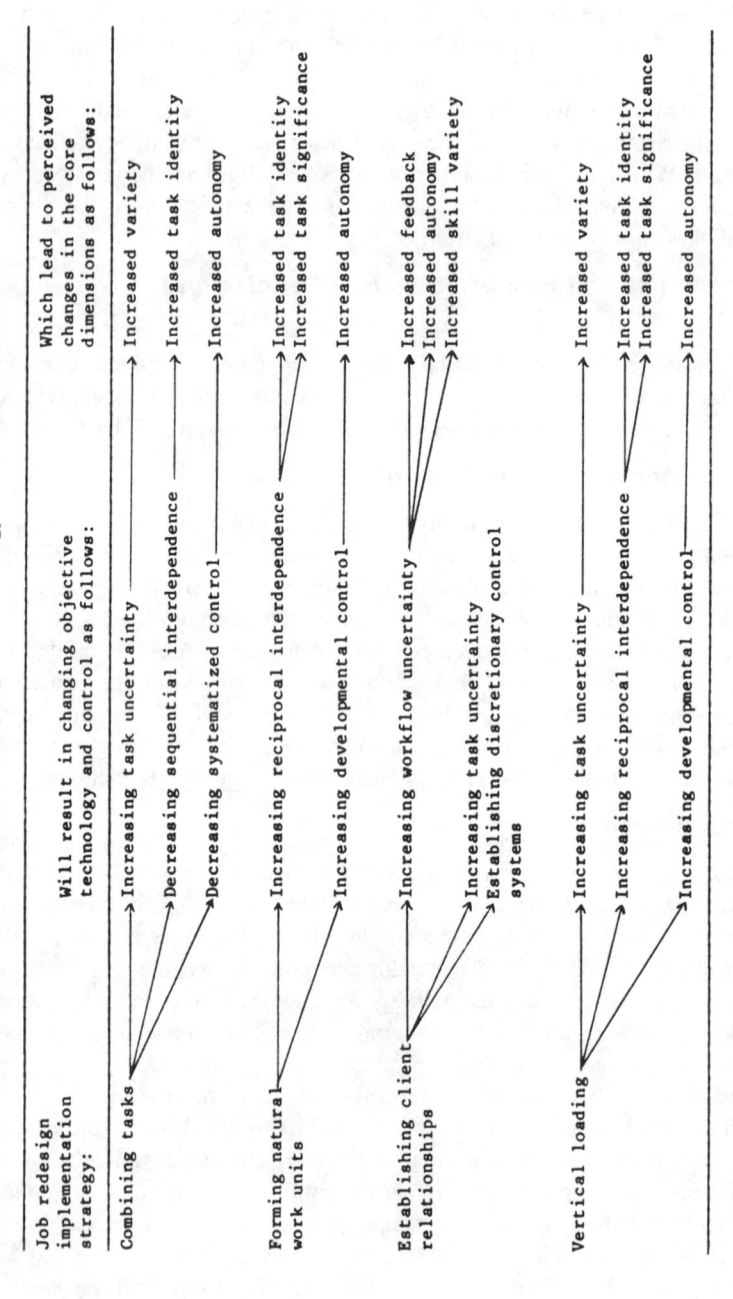

Job redesign implementation strategy:	Will result in changing objective technology and control as follows:	Which lead to perceived changes in the core dimensions as follows:
Combining tasks	→ Increasing task uncertainty → Decreasing sequential interdependence → Decreasing systematized control	→ Increased variety → Increased task identity → Increased autonomy
Forming natural work units	→ Increasing reciprocal interdependence → Increasing developmental control	→ Increased task identity → Increased task significance → Increased autonomy
Establishing client relationships	→ Increasing workflow uncertainty → Increasing task uncertainty Establishing discretionary control systems	→ Increased feedback → Increased autonomy → Increased skill variety
Vertical loading	→ Increasing task uncertainty → Increasing reciprocal interdependence → Increasing developmental control	→ Increased variety → Increased task identity → Increased task significance → Increased autonomy

Source: J.W. Slocum and H.P. Sims, "A Typology for Integrating Technology, Organization, and Job Design," *Human Relations* 33 (3) (1980): 205.

Exhibit 3.8
The Problem-Solving Cycle

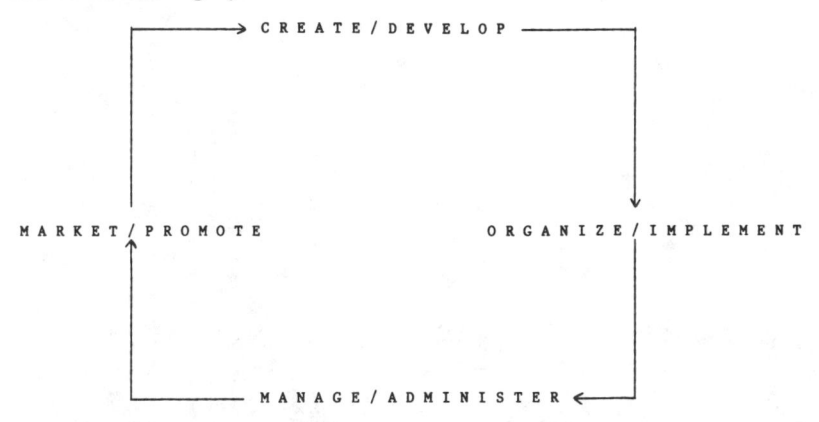

```
        ┌──────→ CREATE/DEVELOP ──────────┐
        │                                  │
        │                                  ↓
MARKET/PROMOTE                    ORGANIZE/IMPLEMENT
        ↑                                  │
        │                                  │
        └────────── MANAGE/ADMINISTER ←────┘
```

Source: From A. Coil, "Job Matching Brings Out the Best in Employee," *Personnel Journal* (January 1984): 56. Reprinted with permission of *Personnel Journal*, Costa Mesa, California; all rights reserved.

job interdependence) with modes of control (type of interdependence, managerial control, level of self-regulation). They also examined the effect of job redesign implementation strategies, such as combining tasks, forming natural work units, vertical loading, and establishing client contacts on these elements of technology and control, and examined the resultant change in perception of the core dimensions of the job.

JOB MATCHING: FINDING THE RIGHT PERSON FOR THE JOB

An HCO that spends considerable time and thought in job design indicates its desire to match the job with an employee such that both productivity and quality of worklife are high. This is especially true in the cases of jobs that require more than a repetitive performance of routine tasks.

Research has indicated that the most satisfied and productive employees are those who are carefully matched to their new jobs (Coil, 1984). An appropriate match means that the primary tasks of the job allow the employee to use his or her strongest and preferred skills.

Although an employee may possess many skills, there are certain skills that each individual prefers to use over others. Such skills come most naturally to the individual and help the person to achieve his or her most satisfying and successful accomplishments. Often individuals tend to gravitate toward tasks and situations that allow them to utilize their preferred skills to their fullest (Coil, 1984).

Employees who are permitted to exercise their strongest and preferred skills

Exhibit 3.9
Working Styles of Identifying Employee Skills and Managerial Roles

CREATORS/DEVELOPERS

Creators/Developers are innovative people who generally:

- need a degree of quiet time in which to create and think
- prefer longer periods of time to develop their ideas
- like to work with a small group of other stimulating people in brainstorming and creative sessions
- have a vision of the future, the end product, or the project
- become restless and bored in apposition that requires maintenance of a project, goal, etc.
- tend to think long term and are more concerned with the future and less concerned with day to day details
- dislike detail work, except when analyzing the abstract creative details that compose a part of the creative plan
- prefer to work with someone who likes to implement and will help the creator with the coordination of details
- have many interest and, therefore, find it difficult to concentrate on any one project or activity for extended periods of time (months and years)
- derive satisfaction from fantasizing, thinking, and reflecting
- tend to be somewhat idealistic and abstract

Possible Limitations

- coming up with more ideas than can be implemented
- creating ideas that others of dissimilar thinking and working styles cannot understand, assimilate, or implement
- spending too much time on creating and reflecting, and not enough time on actively implementing ideas

IMPLEMENTORS

Implementors are task-oriented individuals who generally:

- like a great deal of variety to their day
- like to keep active and busy physically as well as mentally
- like to move around and have flexibility
- prefer short term projects with tangible results and outcomes
- prefer to work with a Creator and Developer who establishes the general parameters of a project
- are most interested in the application and utility of an idea or project
- are more interested in the short-term results and day-to-day activities
- can work alone to implement a project or plan, although they may not prefer to
- enjoy attending to and following-up detail
- derive satisfaction from the organizing and ordering of tasks, materials, and details
- tend to be practical and pragmatic

Possible Limitations

- impulsively rushing to implement an idea without taking into consideration long-term ramifications
- being too shortsighted, focusing only on the immediate and day-to-day details without sufficient consideration for the whole picture
- focusing on the immediate and concrete results without sufficient regard for the intangible effects and outcomes, such as the emotions and politics that might surround a situation

62

MANAGERS

Managers are leaders who generally:

- need to have an impact on the direction and development of a group or organization
- like variety and flexibility in their work
- work well, and even thrive, under time and environmental pressure
- are skilled at juggling many activities at one time
- prefer to delegate details to others
- see the whole picture
- need to work with others and are sensitive to the needs of others
- can work with people at all levels of the organization

Possible Limitations

- theoretically, an effective manager would not suffer from extremes of preferred skills or working style
- the primary responsibility of a manager is to orchestrate the organization's people and activities in such a way as to maintain a balance between possible extremes in goals, functions, working styles, roles, and activities according to the organization's needs

MARKETERS/PROMOTERS

Marketers/Promoters are goal-oriented people who generally:

- prefer to have a high degree of interaction with people
- like variety and flexibility in their tasks and responsibilities
- prefer a relatively unstructured environment
- become restless and dissatisfied when expectations and end results are vague and intangible
- are more interested in the utility and practicality of an idea or project because it makes it easier to sell
- deal well with or can withstand rejection
- adjust easily to a variety of situations and people
- are most comfortable working toward specific goals
- are task oriented

Possible Limitations

- being so goal-oriented that they neglect subtle steps and consequences leading to the goal
- keeping so intent on the selling that they give insufficient attention to the creation and development of new ideas, plans, and projects
- promoting and selling a concept before it has been sufficiently thought out and proven to be viable
- going ahead with a concept before the mechanisms are in place to deliver the product, service, idea, or project

63

are most valuable to the organization. Such individuals are often highly productive, exhibit good attendance behavior, and tend to remain with the organization (Coil, 1984).

Coil (1984) has proposed a model designed to assist managers in identifying an employee's specific and preferred skills (Exhibit 3.8). The model is in essence a problem-solving cycle; each category represents a group of related skills that must be performed if a problem is to be solved, a task completed, or a new project developed successfully. When these categories are applied to individuals, they depict four distinct working styles that define the various roles an individual plays: the creator/developer; the implementor; the manager; and the marketing/promoter. Descriptions of each of these four working styles are provided in Exhibit 3.9. Application of such a model can assist the manager in writing and interpreting job descriptions, recruiting and hiring, delegating, forming work teams, and determining career paths.

Scott (1983) has developed the theme of job matching by following the hiring process through to orientation of the new employee, job clarification, goal setting, and performance appraisal (Exhibit 3.10).

JOB ANALYSIS

The process of analyzing job tasks and requirements and establishing adequate guidelines for a job design has been promoted by both legal regulation and the social and political necessity of rendering work conditions more humane (Middlemist et al., 1983). Several methods of job analysis have been developed over the last several years to address the increased interest in these areas.

Job analysis is an important process because of its multiple uses. This section will provide a discussion of two immediate applications of job analysis information, the job description and the job specification, some common methods of obtaining information for job analysis, and will examine and briefly evaluate several techniques for job analysis.

Job Descriptions

Although the specific format and content of a job description should reflect the unique management needs of an organization, there are several guidelines for writing job descriptions. According to Jones (1984), a job description should contain the following sections:

1. Identification and documentation: Provides information needed for general administration, record keeping, and legal functions. Contains job title, location of the job, resource of information, name of the analyst, data and wage categories, and job code.

2. Job summary: Gives the reader a synopsis and clear picture of the nature of the job and lines of supervision. Contains job title, title of immediate supervisor, and statements of major activities required.

Exhibit 3.10
Optimum Utilization of Human Resources

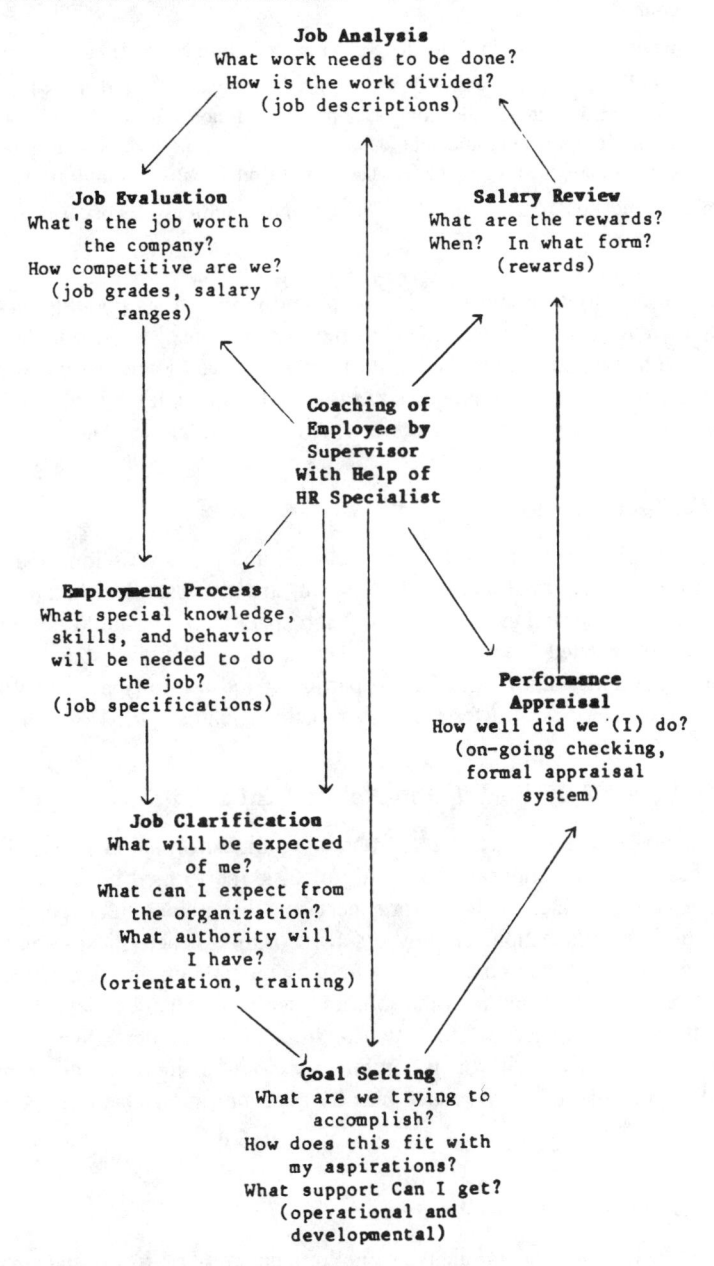

Job Analysis
What work needs to be done?
How is the work divided?
(job descriptions)

Job Evaluation
What's the job worth to the company?
How competitive are we?
(job grades, salary ranges)

Salary Review
What are the rewards?
When? In what form?
(rewards)

Coaching of Employee by Supervisor With Help of HR Specialist

Employment Process
What special knowledge, skills, and behavior will be needed to do the job?
(job specifications)

Performance Appraisal
How well did we (I) do?
(on-going checking, formal appraisal system)

Job Clarification
What will be expected of me?
What can I expect from the organization?
What authority will I have?
(orientation, training)

Goal Setting
What are we trying to accomplish?
How does this fit with my aspirations?
What support Can I get?
(operational and developmental)

Source: From S. Scott, "Finding the 'Right Person,'" *Personnel Journal* (November 1983): 896. Reprinted with permission of *Personnel Journal*, Costa Mesa, California; all rights reserved.

3. Job duties and responsibilities: Provides a thorough description of what is done, how it is done, and why it is done, using a series of statements describing major duties that comprise the job.
4. Job requirements: Lists the knowledge, skills, and abilities needed to perform the job.
5. Minimum qualifications: States qualifications using relatively crude pass-fail selection standards. Minimum qualifications are a prime focal point for investigation into equal opportunity employment and should be stated in terms of specific educational level, training, or equivalent experiences according to preestablished, uniform standards.
6. Job specifications: Statements about the job and conditions of work used to establish job difficulty or worth.

Job descriptions should be as accurate and complete as possible and should be written in a terse, direct style, in the present tense. Each sentence should begin with an active verb and reflect an objective. Unnecessary words and ambiguities should be eliminated so as to avoid confusion. Descriptions of tasks should reflect assigned work and worker traits (Schuler, 1984).

Job Specifications

Job specifications are based on job analysis and job descriptions and are used primarily to select qualified employees, but are also useful in human resource planning and in training. Consequently job specifications should be precise, as well as job related. Care must be taken to show that the stated education, experience, and skills required for a particular job are truly necessary in order to avoid accusations of discriminatory practice (Schuler, 1984).

Methods of Gathering Job-Related Information

The most common methods for obtaining the information required for job analyses are observation and recording of tasks performed by incumbents; interviews with the incumbent and/or supervisor; discussion with experts, familiar with the jobs in question, employee self-recording of activities; completion of a questionnaire (structured or unstructured) by incumbents and/or by supervisors, peers, or others familiar with the job; and use of mechanical devices (for production line jobs) such as stopwatches, films, and counters. Such techniques may be used individually or in combination so as to increase the volume and detail of information or to reduce bias by obtaining more than one perspective (Schuler, 1984).

Techniques for Job Analysis

Most techniques for job analysis employ standardized forms and procedures to obtain information. Such structured techniques may focus on aspects of the job (job focused) or on the characteristics of the individual (person focused).

The Role of Job Design and Job Analysis

Job-focused techniques include functional job analysis, the management position description questionnaire, the Hay plan, methods analysis, Task Inventory CODAP, the job inventory approach, and threshold traits analysis. Person-focused techniques include the position analysis questionnaire, physical abilities analysis, the critical incident technique (and its extended form), guidelines-oriented job analysis, the job element method, ability requirement scales, the domain sampling approach, and AET.

Job-Focused Techniques

Functional job analysis (FJA) was developed by the U.S. Department of Labor to describe the nature of jobs in terms of people, data, and things, for the purpose of developing job summaries, job descriptions, and employee specifications. FJA serves as a conceptual system for defining the dimensions of worker activity and as a method of measuring activity levels. The fundamental premises of FJA are the following:

1. A fundamental distinction must be made regarding what gets done (tasks) and what workers do to get things done (behaviors).
2. All jobs involve people, data, and things; consequently, workers draw on interpersonal, mental, and physical resources, respectively.
3. All jobs to some extent require the employee to relate to people, data, and things.
4. Although the behavior of workers or tasks they perform can be described in an infinite number of ways, there are only a few definitive functions involved. Only a narrow and specific range of worker characteristics and qualities is required for each function.
5. There is a hierarchical and ordinal relationship of functions appropriate to dealing with people, data, and things, proceeding from complex to simple. When at any level, the employee is expected to perform any functions required for lower levels.

FJA uses a set of functions associated with people, data, and things as a basis for describing over 30,000 job titles in the *Dictionary of Occupational Titles*. While FJA is a comprehensive technique, it is largely narrative in nature and requires highly trained personnel for proper implementation (Schuler, 1984).

The Management Position Description Questionnaire (MPDQ) utilizes a checklist to examine thirteen job factors containing 197 items related to managerial work. The job factors are product, market, and financial planning; coordination of organizational units and personnel; internal business control; responsibility for products and services; public and customer relations; advanced consulting; level of autonomy; approval of financial commitments; staff service; supervision; complexity and stress; advanced financial responsibility; and broad personnel responsibility. MPDQ is especially useful to determine the training needs of employees moving into managerial jobs, evaluation of managerial jobs, compensation, and development of selection procedures, and performance appraisal forms (Schuler, 1984).

With the Hay plan, the analyst uses interviews with job incumbents to gather the required information regarding job objectives (why it exists and why it is paid), dimensions (extent of responsibility, impact of actions), accountability (regarding the organization, strategic planning, tactical planning, executing and directing the attainment of objectives, and review and control), and nature and scope of position (how the position fits into the organization, general composition of supporting staff, general nature of technical, managerial, and human relations knowledge required, nature of problem solving required, and nature and source of control or freedom to act). The skill of the interviewer is critical in obtaining the required information (Schuler, 1984).

Methods analysis or motion study originated in the field of industrial engineering. Its purpose is to describe how to do a job as efficiently and effectively as possible. It is usually performed in nonmanagerial jobs in which individual activity units can be identified more readily. Methods analysis attempts to determine the optimal position of hands, tools, and mechanical devices such that work efficiency is increased and that there exists economy of motion. Some common forms of methods analyses are work measurement and work sampling. In the former, standard times for all units of work activity in a job are determined so as to produce a standard time for the entire job. These times are used for wage incentive plans, cost determination, cost estimates for new products, and balancing of production lines and work crews. Work sampling involves taking instantaneous samples of work activities of individuals or groups. Activities are timed and classified into predetermined categories. The result is a description of activities by classification of a job and the percentage of time for each activity (Schuler, 1984).

Task Inventory CODAP utilizes subject matter experts to create a list of tasks and then to rate each according to the relative amount of time spent on it. These ratings are analyzed by a computer program called CODAP and then converted into job dimensions. This technique is best suited to labor-oriented jobs (Wright and Wexley, 1985).

In the job inventory approach, jobs are categorized, such as those of nurses, physicians, physician assistants, and dentists. Kane and Jacoby (1973), for example, demonstrated that physician assistants could do certain jobs currently performed by physicians, and physicians' jobs may be expanded to include patient counseling and preventive medicine (Charns, 1983; Nelson, Jacobs, and Breer, 1985; Braun, Howard, and Pondy, 1972).

Threshold traits analysis is composed of three parts. First, demand and task analysis is done using subject matter experts to create a list of job tasks and the conditions under which they are performed. Tasks are then rated and organized under twenty-one standardized job dimensions. Second, experts determine the level of each of thirty-three standardized job traits required to reach acceptable performance on the job. Finally, technical competence analysis is used to determine any other knowledge or skill necessary for successful performance (Wright and Wexley, 1985).

Person-Focused Techniques

The Position Analysis Questionnaire (PAQ) is a structured questionnaire divided into six sections, each with some of 187 job elements. PAQ also contains seven additional items related to amount of pay (used for research purposes). The six divisions are information input, mental processes, work output, relationships with other people, job context, and other job characteristics. Each of the 187 elements is rated on one of six rating scales: extent of use, importance to the job, amount of time required, possibility of occurrence, applicability, and other. On the basis of the six divisions and the six rating scales, the nature of the job is determined in terms of communication, decision making, and social responsibilities; performance of skilled activities; physical activity and related environmental conditions; operation of equipment and vehicles; and processing of information. Formation of job clusters using this information is useful for staffing decisions and development of job descriptions and specifications (Schuler, 1984).

Physical abilities analysis (PAA) utilizes nine ability categories to analyze the physical requirements of tasks. These cateogries include dynamic, trunk, static, and explosive strength; extent and dynamic flexibility; gross body coordination and equilibrium; and stamina. In addition, seven-point scales are used to determine the extent to which each job requires each of the nine abilities. PAA in combination with appropriate job design is useful to accommodate workers to jobs (Schuler, 1984).

In the critical incident technique (CIT), individuals familiar with a job describe the critical job events (those that they have observed in the last six to twelve months and that represent effective and ineffective performance) to a job analyst. In addition, interviewees must describe the events preceding the incidents, consequences of the incident behavior, and whether the behavior was under the incumbent's control. The critical incidents are then rated on the basis of their frequency of occurrence, importance, and extent of ability required. Finally, the critical incidents and their characteristics are clustered into job dimensions and used to describe jobs, to develop performance appraisal forms, to carry out performance appraisals, and to identify training needs. One problem with CIT is its tendency to reveal only extremes of performance (Schuler, 1984).

Extended CIT overcomes the shortcomings of the previous technique by obtaining examples of good, bad, and average performance. Incumbents identify job domains or umbrellas under which many specific tasks may be included. Following identification and definition of the domains, the job analyst lists task statements that represent each domain. Such information is provided by the incumbents, who record scenarios that reflect the three different levels of performance for each domain. Following construction of the task statements, a different group of incumbents indicates whether they actually perform these tasks, their frequency, the difficulty in task performance, and the relative importance of a task. Such information can be used for job descriptions. Extended CIT can be used to develop performance appraisal forms if incumbents indicate the level of performance each task statement represents and place it in one of the domains initially identified. Incumbents then describe the physical and mental abilities necessary to perform the tasks in each domain. This process is useful to develop selection procedures and job specifications (Schuler, 1984).

Guidelines-oriented job analysis (GOJA) begins by having incumbents list their names, length of time in a job, experience, and location of the current job. This is followed by a series of steps. First, incumbents list their job domains. Second, they list important or critical duties typically performed during successful job performance in each domain. Third, they indicate duty frequency. Fourth, they determine the skills and knowledge required to perform each duty. Fifth, required physical characteristics are listed. Finally, incumbents describe other characteristics necessary to perform the job. The result is a job description, a set of individual skills, knowledge, and attributes needed to perform the job, and a basis for developing job-related selection procedures and performance appraisal forms (Schuler, 1984).

In the job element method, standardized forms are used to allow people familiar with a job to identify its related job elements (knowledge, skills, attributes, and required personal traits). Each of the elements is then rated on four scales: barely acceptable (the percentage of barely acceptable employees who exhibit this element); superior (the percentage of superior employees who exhibit this element); trouble likely (the probability of trouble occurring if an employee does not possess this element); and practical (the practicality of expecting to find people with this element). These scales are designed to identify which skills employees should have when starting a new job and which skills may be acquired through training. Although the scales create a degree of uniformity, the information that is gathered is different for each job (Wright and Wexley, 1985).

Ability requirements scales are similar to the job element method, but they do not use a standardized format. They use a set of behaviorally based scales to measure how much each of thirty-seven abilities is needed to perform a job (Wright and Wexley, 1985).

The domain sampling approach uses subject matter experts to make lists of tasks, which are used to define a set of knowledge, skills, and attributes necessary, in their estimation, for effective performance of a job. Each of the knowledge, skill, and attributes traits is then rated in terms of importance and time spent using the trait in the job (Wright and Wexley, 1985).

AET (an acronym for the German phrase meaning ergonomic job analysis) originated in West Germany in 1975 when the government ordered a study to investigate wage discrimination against working women. The study required a job analysis procedure that allowed for a detailed investigation of workload and strain within a given work environment. Since 1975 this technique has been continuously developed and applied to a variety of managerial and nonmanagerial jobs.

AET has a three-part structure (A, B, C) involving a work systems analysis, a task analysis, and a job demand analysis. In part A, the types and properties of work objects, the equipment to be used, and the physical, social, and organizational working environment are documented on numerical and nominal scales. Part B involves examination of the behavioral requirements of tasks. Tasks that are related to material work objects, abstract work objects, and other persons are rated on thirty-one numerically scaled items. Performance of a task (as rated in part A) under the conditions documented in part B leads to job demands that are evaluated in part C in terms of perceptions, decisions, and response-activity levels required. Each of the three parts of this analysis uses observations and interviews by trained analysts to gain information (Rohmert and Landau, 1983).

Assessing Job Analysis Techniques

As the potential utility of job-related information becomes increasingly apparent, personnel managers need to adopt a total organizational view when selecting a job analysis technique. Frequently the technique used is the only one with which the personnel manager is familiar (Midddlemist et al., 1983). Selection should be based on two primary factors: the ultimate uses of the information obtained and the most appropriate and practical technique for the particular organization (Ash and Levine, 1980).

The personnel manager must decide which of several potential purposes are relevant to the job analysis objective. These purposes may include job descriptions and specifications, job classification, evaluation, job design and redesign, recruitment and selection, performance appraisal, worker training, career development, efficiency and safety, workforce planning, and legal requirements (Schuler, 1984). Following this decision, the personnel manager must determine which of the techniques are not suitable to the expressed job analysis objectives. The appropriateness of a technique is reflected in the type and level of information it provides. For example, if the purpose of the analysis is training and development, the technique must allow for clear identification of behavioral examples of performance and skills and abilities required for performance (Ash and Levine, 1980).

In addition, certain practical factors must be considered. These include capability (is the method in operational form?); availability (is the methodology standard, or must it be tailored for each specific job?); occupational versatility and suitability (is the method suitable for analyzing a variety of jobs in the organization?); level of standardization (will the technique produce norms, which can be compared with data from different sources?); respondent-user acceptability; necessity for and availability of job analyst training (how many respondents or sources of information are needed to ensure that the data are dependable?); cost (including materials, training, consulting fees, salaries for the analyst, respondents, clerical support); quality of the outcome (relative to other techniques);

user understandability and involvement (extent to which those who are affected by the results are involved in data collection); reliability and validity (consistency of results and accuracy of information obtained); number of job objectives served; and utility (overall benefits versus cost) (Ash and Levine, 1980).

GUIDELINES FOR ADMINISTRATORS AND PROFESSIONALS

- Develop job design and analysis systems that serve many functions
- Use flexible versions of the individual contemporary and ergonomic approaches
- Redesign jobs in order to accommodate the needs of workers and the organization
- Utilize line managers, personnel officers, and senior management in job redesign and enforce their own working definitions for job analysis, descriptions, and specifications so as to ensure organization-wide uniformity and comparability
- Use job-focused techniques, particularly the Hay plan, and avoid the use of other structured job analysis techniques as a result of competing priorities for time and resources
- Use line managers to write job descriptions and specifications in cases of job redesign and utilize trained personnel officers or other experts for job analysis
- Initiate mechanisms for ongoing improvement of the current systems of job design and job analysis
- Pay greater attention to formalized techniques and their application in individual job design and job analysis situations

NOTE

1. Portions of this section are adopted from R. S. Schuler, *Personnel and Human Resources Management* (New York: West Publishing Co., 1984). Reprinted by permission.

REFERENCES

Aldag, R. J., and Brief, A. P. (1979). *Task Design and Employee Motivation*. Dallas: Scott, Foresman.
Ash, R. A., and Levine, E. L. (1980, November-December). A framework for evaluating job analysis methods. *Personnel*, 53–59.
Braun, J. A., Howard, D. R., and Pondy, L. R. (1972). The physician's associate: A task analysis. *Physician's Associates* 2 (3): 77–82.
Charns, M. P. (1983). Work design. In S. M. Shortell and A. D. Kaluzny (Eds.), *Health Care Management*, 207–23. New York: John Wiley.
Coil, A. (1984, January). Job matching brings out the best in employees. *Personnel Journal*, 54–60.
Cordery, J. L., and Wall, T. D. (1985). Work design and supervisory practice: A model. *Human Relations* 38 (5): 425–41.

Fasman, Z. D. (1982, Autumn). Legal obstacles to alternative work-force design. *Employee Relations Law Journal*, 256–81.
Hackman, J. R. (1983). Work design. In R. M. Steers and L. W. Porter (Eds), *Motivation and Work Behavior*, 490–516. New York: McGraw-Hill.
Hodes, B. (1983, June). Planning for recruitment advertising. *Personnel Journal*, 492–501.
Jones, M. A. (1984, May). Job description made easy. *Personnel Journal*, 31–34.
Kane, R., and Jacoby, L. (1973, November). Alterations in tasks in the physician office as a result of adding a medex. Paper presented at American Public Health Associates Meeting, San Francisco.
Middlemist, R. D., Hitt, M. A., and Greer, C. R. (1983). *Personnel Management*. Englewood Cliffs, N.J.: Prentice-Hall.
Miles, R. E., and C. C. Snow. (1983, January). Designing strategic human resource systems. *Orgnizational Dynamics*, 36–52.
Nelson, E., Jacobs, A., and Breer, D. (1975, February). A study of the validity of the task inventory method of job analysis. *Medical Care* 13 (2): 104–13.
Petersen, D. J. (1981, March-April). Paving the way for hiring the handicapped. *Personnel*, 43.
Rendero, T. (1981, January-February). Consensus—Job analysis practices. *Personnel*, 53–66.
Risher, H. (1984, January-February). Job evaluation: Problems and prospects. *Personnel*, 53–66.
Rohmert, W., and Landau, K. (1983). *A New Technique for Job Analysis*. London: Taylor and Francis.
Schuler, R. S. (1984). *Personnel and Human Resource Management*. St. Paul, Minn.: West Publishing.
Scott, S. (1983, November). Finding the "right person." *Personnel Journal*, 894–902.
Slocum, J. W., and Sims, H. P. (1983). A typology for integrating technology, organization, and job design. *Human Relations* 33 (3): 193–212.
Steers, R. M., and Porter, L. W. (Eds.) (1983). *Motivation and Work Behavior*. New York: McGraw-Hill.
Strom, L. J., and Ferris, G. R. (1982, August). Issues in hiring the handicapped: A positive outlook. *Personnel Administrator*, 75–81.
Thompson, D. E., and Thompson, T. A. (1982). Court standards for job analysis in test validation. *Personnel Psychology* 35: 865–74.
Wright, P. M., and Wexley, K. N. (1985, May). How to choose the kind of job analysis you really need. *Personnel*, 51–55.

4
Recruitment Strategies

Donna L. Gellatly

Recruitment is the human resource management activity that furnishes or replenishes the organization with a fresh supply of qualified potential employees. The process begins when the strategic decision is made to seek recruits and ends when their applications are submitted. A critical element of the recruiting process is the timing of this activity. A ready source of applicants must be available when the organization requires them. Therefore recruitment becomes an ongoing activity of the personnel department in terms of planning and monitoring the marketplace, staying current with wage and salary levels and benefit programs, and complying with the legal requirements that govern this process.

The many and diverse activities of the recruitment function include:

- Determining the present and future recruitment needs of the organization in conjunction with institutional planning
- Increasing the pool of job applicants at minimum cost
- Assisting the selection process by reducing the number of obviously underqualified or overqualified job applicants
- Reducing the probability that job applicants, once recruited and selected, will leave the organization after only a short period of time
- Meeting the organization's responsibility for affirmative action programs and other legal and social obligations regarding the composition of its workforce
- Identifying potential job applicants who would be appropriate candidates
- Evaluating the effectiveness of various recruiting techniques and sources.[1]

RECRUITMENT AND THE LAW

In the United States, a body of equal opportunity law that comprises legislation, executive orders, state human rights laws, and case law has developed over the past twenty-five years. Although these laws specifically apply to selection, promotions, raises, and other issues, they directly affect recruitment. Because they essentially help identify who will be selected, they also identify who should be recruited. (For a more detailed discussion of the provisions of these laws, refer to Chapter 5.)

- Title VII of the Civil Rights Act of 1964, as amended by the Equal Employment Opportunity Act of 1972, is the federal law that prohibits employment discrimination based on race, color, religion, sex, or national origin. It prohibits sexual harassment when the person must submit to such activity to be hired, receive a raise, or be promoted.
- In 1978, Title VII was amended to include the Pregnancy Discrimination Act, which requires employers to treat pregnancy and pregnancy-related medical conditions as any other medical disability.
- The Age Discrimination in Employment Act of 1967 protects workers aged 40 and over from arbitrary age discrimination in hiring, discharge, pay, promotions, fringe benefits, and other aspects of employment.
- In applying handicap discrimination protection under the Rehabilitation Act of 1973, handicapped status is assigned to any person with any physical or mental impairment that substantially limits one or more major life activities.
- The Vietnam Era Veterans Readjustment Act of 1974 provides preference in hiring for military veterans.

A number of states have enacted their own fair employment practices legislation. Many of these states have prohibitions against discrimination on the basis of age, marital status, arrest record, political affiliation, color blindness, unfavorable military discharge, or sickle cell trait. Legislation regulating the employment of aliens has also been enacted by some states.[2]

Canada has similar legislation. The Employment Equity Act of 1986 covers equity in employment. A proposed amendment, bill 154, has been introduced to modify and expand this legislation.

RESPONSIBILITY FOR RECRUITING

In hospitals, nurse recruiters may be assigned to the nursing administration or nursing education department; recruiters for nonnursing and nonphysician personnel usually are assigned to the human resource management (personnel) department. Individual department managers or supervisors may initiate the process or participate in seeking qualified candidates; however, the recruitment process is coordinated at the personnel department or nursing administration level. This coordination process is necessary to avoid duplication of effort, ensure

Recruitment Strategies

compliance with equal opportunity and affirmative action policies and goals, and expedite the recruiting process. Experienced personnel recruiters are aware of the best methods of recruiting certain classes of employees at the least possible cost.

Initiating the Process: The First Step

"Define the organization's needs first. When a vacancy occurs, take advantage of the opportunity to rethink the position and change it if necessary. In this way, you will ensure that the person being hired will become a valued member of the organization, rather than filling a box on an old organizational chart."[3]

Recruiting begins when a manager confirms the need to retain the position and initiates the personnel requisition (Exhibit 4.1). The personnel requisition is compared against the position control system, which controls the staffing in an institution. The system lists all authorized budgeted positions to be filled in each job category (for example, eight physical therapists). The typical system is divided into departments. Normally no one is hired unless a vacancy exists within a given job category.

Governmental position control systems assign a position control number to each budgeted position. Only one person may occupy this position. Therefore an existing employee must terminate employment before a replacement begins work. This process eliminates duplication of salaries but limits the ability to train new personnel by the person vacating the position.

Constraints on Recruitment

Recruiters usually identify job openings from specific requests made by department managers. Once a job opening is identified, recruiters review the job's requirements from job analysis or specification information and by interviewing the supervisor. Any changes are then incorporated into the written job description. It is important that the recruiter understand the job requirements because they will influence the recruiter's methods for locating satisfactory applicants. The recruitment process is not without its challenges. They may be constraints generated from within the organization, by the recruiter, or by the external environment.

The first potential source of constraints may be in the form of organizational policies. Policies seek to achieve uniformity, economies, and other organizational objectives that, although unrelated to recruitment, may affect the process. One common organizational policy is to promote from within so that current employees have the first opportunity for job openings.

Another constraint to the recruitment process is the affirmative action program. If an organization has such a plan, the plan may specify certain needs, such as a need for more women or minority representation. This will influence the recruiter's methods.

Exhibit 4.1
Personnel Requisition

TODAY'S DATE:	DEPARTMENT NAME:	COST CENTER NUMBER:
POSITION TITLE:		POSITION CLASS NUMBER: POSITION CONTROL NUMBER:
DATE REQUIRED:	SHIFT OR HOURS:	DAYS:
ON-CALL TIME:	OVERTIME:	CLASSIFICATION: ___ temporary ___ permanent ___ full-time ___ part-time
Brief Description of Position: (attach written job description)		
HOURLY RATE:	ANNUAL SALARY:	EXISTING POSITION ___ NEW POSITION ___
REASON FOR VACANCY: ___ new position ___ voluntary termination ___ promotion ___ transfer ___ involuntary ___ leave of absence ___ death ___ other ___ termination		
EMPLOYEE BEING REPLACED:		LAST DAY WILL WORK:
RECOMMENDED SOURCES FOR RECRUITING:		
OTHER COMMENTS AND INFORMATION WHICH MAY ASSIST IN THE RECRUITING PROCESS:		
HIRING SUPERVISOR:	DEPT.	EXT.	DAYS AND TIMES WILL INTERVIEW:
APPROVALS: Manager _____			Date: _____
Associate Administrator _____			Date: _____
Budget Approval _____			Date: _____

Recruitment Strategies

A recruiter may have his personal recruiting preferences—perhaps recruiting at his or her alma mater or having one method that has proved successful.

External conditions can strongly influence recruitment. Changes in the labor market, the unemployment rate, the pace of the economy, spot shortages, and the competition's recruiting activities affect the methods used in recruiting personnel.[4]

SOURCES AND METHODS FOR RECRUITING PERSONNEL

Internal Sources

Existing employees are an immediate source of recruits for vacancies. These vacancies may be filled through promotions or by reassignments of existing staff. Many institutions first recruit from within (sometimes called "checking your own backyard").[5] The process of posting vacancies is motivating for most employees even if they fail to win the position. The money saved on search and recruiting expenses can then be used for specialized training needed by an otherwise qualified current employee. The advantages of such a policy include increased employee morale and motivation, reduced expenses for recruitment and orientation training, and knowing the candidate's work habits and accomplishments. Disadvantages may include infighting and competition between employees over promotions, inbreeding of ideas that may stunt fresh perspectives, and the lengthy period required to fill and train the initial vacant position and the subsequent vacant positions that result from it.

Another problem with relying exclusively on internal recruitment is complying with equal employment opportunity and affirmative action policies. The organization's affirmative action plan may specify certain needs, such as greater representation of women or minorities, that cannot be satisfied with the current composition of the institution's workforce.

Finally, the Peter principle may come into play. If an employee has "reached his level of incompetency," who is to tell this person that he or she, though totally qualified for his or her current position, is not qualified for that next step in advancement? If the person is told, what does that do to his or her attitude? An organization may lose a capable employee due to the difficulty in diplomatically turning down his or her request for a new position within the organization.

Internal recruitment is usually accomplished through posting job vacancies and by establishing career planning programs. Job posting is accomplished by publicizing vacancies through notices to current employees. Some human resource managers include notices to employees' friends, former employees, and former applicants among the sources available for internal recruitment. For the purpose of this discussion, only current employees are considered internal recruits. All others are considered external candidates.

Career planning programs also relate to recruitment. Through career planning, employees are advised of job opportunities and may enter a formal training program to advance within the organization. Interested employees complete interest questionnaires and self-analysis profiles and then compare the results with specifications of the jobs in which they are interested. Employees are also given career counseling and informed about how they can obtain any additional training that they may need.[6] As part of its employee benefits program, an institution may subsidize or reimburse employees for additional educational courses or training that would assist in their current positions or make them eligible for future promotions.

Job posting may be used to emphasize that employees are considered first for lateral transfers, promotions, or applying for any available vacant position when one's own position is eliminated. The job posting system must be operationally feasible and accepted by those using it, and must meet the legal criteria for nondiscrimination. It is important that such a system be uniformly and fairly maintained. If the organization has an equal employment opportunity record that is less than satisfactory, care must be taken to ensure that minorities have the opportunity to apply for positions.[7] Job posting may also be required under a union collective bargaining agreement.

To be operationally feasible, the job posting system must make information available in a timely manner to the greatest number of employees. The most common method of announcing job openings is a bulletin board posting outside the human resource office or cafeteria, within the employees' locker rooms, or near common entrances to the institution. Other methods of giving notice include publishing the job openings in the employee in-house publication, sending position announcements to department supervisors, and including announcements in the employees' payroll check envelopes.

Eligibility criteria to apply for a new or vacant position within the institution should be established. Requirements may include a minimum amount of time employed by the institution, minimum time period in the present position, allowable number of bids a year or reporting period, and satisfactory performance ratings.

Timing and coordination of the internal recruitment effort must be carefully planned. The time interval between the posting of the notice and the application deadline may be one to two weeks. Once the deadline is past, applications should be reviewed and qualified employees called for interviews. All applicants should be notified of the final hiring decision prior to public announcement of the selected candidate. The time period between selecting the candidate and the candidate's actually assuming the new job may vary. Variations range from thirty days to six weeks, but the time period may be extended if the move would create a serious problem in the applicant's present department.

Should the present supervisor be notified of the employee's application for promotion or transfer? Opinions vary. Some organizations require the supervisor's signature on the bid itself. Another alternative is to require that the present

Recruitment Strategies

supervisor be notified only if the employee is a serious candidate for the opening. This alternative would prevent ill feeling or negative consequences between the employee who wants to leave a current position and the supervisor if he or she is not chosen for the new position and must remain in his or her present job. The final alternative is to inform the present supervisor after the employee has accepted the offer. In this case, however, the hiring supervisor would be prevented from gaining any potentially valuable information from the present supervisor prior to the hiring decision.[8]

External Recruiting

When a decision is made not to recruit from within the organization, many sources for recruiting external candidates are available. Developing an external recruiting strategy involves considering such elements as the position to be filled (accountant, nurse, radiology technician), the time available for recruiting, and the labor pool availability within the geographic areas.

One advantage of recruiting from outside the organization is that the applicant may bring a new perspective to the institution and is not aligned with current internal work groups. Additionally, the applicant labor pool is larger than the number of qualified applicants within the organization. Perhaps the major advantage of looking outside the organization in filling vacancies or newly created positions is not having to recruit or train two or more individuals. If a current employee is promoted or transferred, the transferred employee plus the replacement or replacements must be trained in their new duties and responsibilities as well.

There are also disadvantages of recruiting from external sources: the cost of recruiting, the lead time required between identifying the vacancy and filling it, dealing with the unknown new employee, and perhaps a morale problem with current employees who feel they are qualified to perform the job.

Robert Half, founder of a search firm, developed a hiring attitude study conducted by Burke Marketing Research. This study consisted of a 10 percent sampling of personnel directors and top management of the Fortune 1000 companies. The response indicated that the amount of time required to fill different positions varied by category of compensation. The most frequent period of time for positions under $25,000 annual compensation was two to four weeks. For positions being recruited within the $25,000 to $49,000 range, the period of time was one to two months. The amount of time for the $50,000 to $100,000 salary category as between two and four months. As the position's compensation level increased, the period of time required to fill the position increased proportionately.[9]

Selected external recruiting sources utilized by the health care industry include the following:

- Radio and television
- Newspaper advertisements

- Trade and professional journals
- General business journals
- Professional organizations and job referral services
- Union halls
- Public and private employment agencies
- Executive search firms
- Outplacement agencies
- High schools, trade, and technical schools
- Colleges and universities
- Internship and residency programs
- Foreign (alien) recruitment
- Recommendations and referrals
- Unsolicited walk-in or write-in applicants
- Local governments and community organizations
- Career fairs
- Minority candidate fairs and affirmative action employment programs

Radio and television advertising may be too expensive for recruiting individual positions. These media may be appropriate when a large number of positions are being recruited, such as for staffing a new facility. If the recruiting budget is adequate, advertising on television and radio shows that target the local community usually produces the best results. Indeed, one cable station, Cable Employment Network, is dedicated to the job openings function.

Newspapers and professional journals are the most common methods of recruiting external candidates. Major metropolitan area newspapers maintain separate sections for classified advertisements and management advertisements (sometimes called box ads). These management or professional job openings are usually found adjacent to or following the business section of the newspaper (see Exhibit 4.2). The Sunday edition normally carries the most employment advertising. However, local custom may prevail; the *Vancouver (B.C.) Sun* includes most of its employment advertising in the Friday edition. Some newspapers have special days for specialized industry advertising. The *Chicago Tribune* includes a "Health Care Opportunities" page in its "Living" section. This section is printed on Mondays and is adjacent to the weekly listing of Nursing Events.

Although most classified employment advertising sections alphabetize position openings, many newspapers have special sections devoted to specialized industries. Within these sections are all positions related to health care, aerospace, and so on. These positions may be cross-referenced within the general classified ads by referring readers to a larger advertisement in another category or classification.

Exhibit 4.2

> **DIRECTOR OF MARKET INFORMATION AND PLANNING**
>
> Mercy Center for Health Care Services, a 300+ acute care hospital serving the Fox River Valley and Chicago's western suburbs, seeks a highly motivated individual to manage its market information and planning activities including market research, market plans for new and existing services and C.O.N. development. The Director will work with hospital management and physicians in advising on new products, business diversification and the overall future direction of the organization. This is an exciting opportunity to inject new and innovative ideas to help achieve Mercy Center's aim of providing quality health services to the area.
>
> The right candidate will be a creative, results-oriented, skilled individual with at least 2 — 3 years of increasing marketing/planning responsibility, preferrably in the health care environment. An MBA or MHA is required. Please submit a resume with a cover letter (including salary requirements) designed to convince us you're the right person for the job to:
>
> Director of Human Resources
> **MERCY CENTER FOR HEALTH CARE SERVICES**
> 1325 N. Highland Av.
> Aurora, IL 60506
>
> equal opportunity employer m/f

Source: Reprinted with permission of Mercy Center for Health Care Services.

National newspaper advertising may be appropriate when there are few or no potential applicants within the local service area. The *Wall Street Journal*'s main day for classified employment advertising is Tuesday. This publication is produced for various geographic locations within the United States. Additionally, the *National Business Employment Weekly*, published by Dow Jones, contains all classified employment advertising that had been included in each geographic edition of the *Wall Street Journal* within the past week.

Trade publications, such as *Hospitals* and *Healthcare Financial Management*, have extensive classified employment ads, usually located in the back of each issue. This form of recruitment may be the most specifically targeted method for locating technical specialists. However, the long lead times necessary to prepare an issue for publication often extend the time period between identifying the vacant position and actually filling it.

Some institutions do not identify themselves in written employment ads; instead, applicants are instructed to respond to a box number. These blind ads may not produce the number and type of responses that the institution desires. Currently employed individuals may not want to respond to a blind ad because of the possibility that the ad was placed by their current employer or that their response could be forwarded to their employer. To counter this problem, some newspapers and other publications offer special confidential services. They will not forward a resume if the person responding indicates on the reply envelope that he or she already works for the advertiser. Publication personnel discard any response with the advertiser's name written on it.

Blind advertisements requesting responses to the publication's internal box numbers are usually kept in strict confidence. Box numbers to general post office boxes can be traced by asking the post office to identify the name of the person or institution that rents the box.

Robert Half of Robert Half International believes that companies deliberately choose to omit their names from advertisements for some of the following reasons:

- They are looking outside the company for personnel and don't want others in the company to find out about it
- The company has a bad reputation and its name is likely to discourage applicants
- They don't have a specific job in mind but are scouting to see who is available just in case
- The company doesn't want to tip off the fact that it is thinking of moving or it's developing a new product line[10]

Among the criteria of a creative recruitment ad, the advertising firm of Deutsch, Shea & Evans includes such items as those that will generate interest, present information, give viewpoints, instill believability, stress the uniqueness and human element, be visually functional and, most important, generate a response.[11] A good recruiting ad should serve at least three functions:

- The ad should generate qualified inquiries by targeting the most appropriate audience. A poorly written ad may generate many inappropriate job applications and, in fact, may generate no qualified applicants.
- It should create a favorable employer image. A well-produced ad will generate interest in the firm whether the reader is seriously seeking employment or is just generally perusing the classified employment section.
- The recruitment ads should have a positive effect on present employees. Phrases such as "join our dedicated workforce" or such statements as "the qualified clinician will discover a coordinated, dedicated staff and supportive peers..."[12] will enforce the positive image of the institution and its employment force.

Print advertisements should include such information as a general description of the job, the type of institution, general location of the company, salary or salary range, and required professional certifications or minimum education requirements. Institutions should be aware that their employment classifications or position titles may not be readily identifiable to outsiders. Instead of advertising for an RN II, the general responsibilities of the position should be described, as in the following advertisement:

> RN: AT LEAST TWO YEARS EXPERIENCE IN AN ACUTE CARE SETTING. BSN & ILLINOIS LICENSE REQUIRED. FOR INTERVIEW CALL RITA DARCY, SOUTHERN HOSPITAL, 555-1212.

The type of institution should be identified. Whether the advertiser is an acute care hospital, nursing home, or home health agency will influence the number of qualified respondents with the requisite experience and/or interest.

Even if the blind form of advertisement is used, it is appropriate to indicate the general vicinity of the institution such as the "northwest suburbs of Chicago" or "central metropolitan Chicago." Thus respondents can make their own decision as to whether they would be interested in commuting to this location. An institution may identify its preferred candidate only to have the offer turned down or a relocation allowance requested as a condition of employment when the commuting distance is considered by the applicant to be too long or inconvenient.

The phrase "competitive salary and benefits" may have various interpretations. A salary range based on education and experience will target applicants who would accept this range of compensation. Many institutions require applicants to indicate their salary history and then identify applicants whose current salaries fall within the position's range. By identifying the salary range in the advertisement, the applicant pool is restricted to those who are truly interested in the position.

If a license or certification is a condition of employment, it should be stated in the ad. Professional certifications such as certified public accountant, licensed practical nurse, or registered respiratory therapist may be found in health care employment ads.

Advertisers should take careful measures to avoid wording that may be construed as discriminatory based on sex, race, national origin, or handicapped. Many advertisers identify themselves as affirmative action/equal opportunity employers.

Many of the health care industry's trade and professional associations offer job referral services or job banks. They also have job boards or job books at their annual business meetings. The American Society of Hospital Marketing and Public Relations publishes a monthly newsletter as a benefit to its members. It acts as a clearinghouse for positions available and positions wanted in the areas of health care marketing, public relations, and communications. The job referral service is free to members and prospective employers. Other organizations maintain files of applicants and position openings that are available on request.

Trade unions maintain hiring halls or referral services for their building trade members. Electricians, plumbers, and mechanical engineers experienced in health care facilities are in great demand. If a health care facility is unionized, the collective bargaining agreement between the facility and union will detail the steps to be taken in recruiting trade personnel.

The Federal-State Employment Service consists of the U.S. Employment Service and its affiliated state employment services that make up the nation's public employment service system. During 1984, this service made 5.1 million placements, of which 4.7 million were in nonagricultural positions. To be eligible for unemployment insurance, U.S. workers must register with the state employment service. These workers and other voluntarily registered individuals receive counseling, testing and placement services. These services also provide special attention to handicapped workers and military veterans. The Job Training Partnership Act (JTPA) of 1984 replaced the Comprehensive Employment and Training Act (CETA). This program and the Work Incentive (WIN) Program for employable recipients of Aid to Families of Dependent Children train and place workers in clerical and semiskilled positions in private industry. Employment service personnel actively seek positions for its registrants. Employers who register with the service receive prescreened referrals of qualified applicants and may be eligible for tax credits or government-subsidized wages for an initial period of employment.[13]

Private employment agencies generally handle clients at either end of the employment spectrum: unskilled workers and professional and managerial personnel. Agencies handling unskilled workers prescreen clients by administering skill and aptitude tests and checking potential references before referring their clients to prospective employers. They normally charge two to four weeks of the applicant's salary as a placement fee. Professional and managerial worker placement fees run from one to three months' salary. Some states have specific legislation that bars employment agencies from charging the applicant for placement. In most cases, the placement fee is paid by the employer.

Executive search firms undertake candidate searches on behalf of employers. These firms, sometimes called head hunters, actively recruit employed individuals. They may recruit under their own name, stating in their advertisements, "We are recruiting for a vice-president of finance on behalf of our teaching hospital client." The search firm will present three or four prescreened candidates for their client's consideration. Executive search fees are based on time spent in the search process. They receive their consulting fee for submitting candidates; it does not matter if the search does not produce a placement.

A new development in the health care industry is the use of outplacement agencies as a method of recruiting needed personnel. One organization's problem may be another's solution. Qualified experienced personnel in many position classifications may be available due to reductions in workforce, layoffs, mergers, downsizing, or closure of surrounding institutions.

Recruitment Strategies

Educational institutions are excellent sources of recruiting entry-level personnel. Many of these institutions have placement services for their current students and alumni. Secondary schools can furnish clerical and unskilled employees. Trade and vocational schools can furnish building trade personnel and specialized applicants, such as radiology technicians, medical technicians, and nursing aides. Colleges and universities can furnish entry-level professional applicants.

Important criteria in developing a college recruiting program include evaluating accredited programs, the reputations of the program and institution, proximity to the organization, and personal management preference.[14] This personal management preference is sometimes called the "good old boys' network." Their alma mater is a known quantity. School loyalty, however, may limit the number of qualified candidates considered for the job and inadvertently violate equal employment opportunity requirements.

Accreditation may limit recruiting efforts. Most of the international accounting firms do not recruit at nonaccredited schools. The accrediting agency for health administration is the Accrediting Commission on Education for Health Services Administration (ACEHSA). Program accreditation affirms that the college and the program meet certain criteria. Through its evaluation by an external agency, curriculum, teaching facility, and library and research facilities are reviewed. The Robert Half survey response indicated that 77 percent of those surveyed stated that they took the reputation of candidates' colleges into consideration when selecting employees.[15]

Secondary schools and colleges may have cooperative work-study programs. The student works part time or in the summer while completing graduation requirements. Many health care technical and administrative programs have required internships or residencies that must be completed as part of the degree requirements. Accredited programs in health administration require students to complete an external field experience or residency. Students may work in acute care hospitals, nursing homes, or governmental agencies. At the end of these residencies, students write a paper summarizing their experience during the residency period. These types of work arrangements are excellent opportunities to evaluate potential employees on the basis of their actual work performance. These students are also sources who may be able to refer additional students to the institutions.

Although many hospitals in the United States are laying off employees due to a decline in inpatient census or reduced financing mechanisms, a growing shortage of specialized nurses exists. The U.S. Department of Health and Human Services predicts that two jobs will be available for every registered nurse graduating with a bachelor degree by 1990.[16] Of the 1.9 million registered nurses in the United States, only 78.7 percent of them are employed in nursing.[17] U.S. hospitals are recruiting nurses from Canada, the Philippines, England, and Ireland, according to the American Hospital Association. The association reports that 14 percent of all nursing positions are unfilled at 1,000 hospitals.[18] Hospitals are combining their efforts to recruit foreign personnel. Three hospitals in the suburban Chicago area are jointly underwriting the Great Britain recruiting trip of one of the administrators to recruit critical care nurses.

The Immigration and Naturalization Service and the U.S. Department of Labor cooperate in expediting immigration applications and granting visas for persons who have needed skills that are not currently available in the U.S. labor market. However, effective June 1, 1987, the United States began to enforce the provisions of the Immigration Reform and Control Act. An employer must review documents that show the identity and proof of U.S. citizenship or work authorization of every employee hired since November 4, 1986, and keep records of its documentation. Employees must be fully documented, or the institution will be fined.

Many institutions involve their employees in the recruitment process. Bonuses are sometimes awarded to employees for referring applicants who are subsequently hired. The quality of applicants referred by employees tends to be high because the employee will tend to be selective in referring applicants to his or her own institution since the applicant's success, or lack thereof, may reflect on the present employee. A major concern with employee referrals, however, is the potential for perpetuating the current composition of the workforce. While this may not impede affirmative action obligations, the potential exists.

Most community-based health care institutions attract walk-in or write-in applicants. Individuals simply walk into the personnel office or write a letter asking if a position is available. Such factors as corporate image, working conditions, relationships with labor, and participation in community activities influence the number of these applicants. The use of walk-ins as a method of recruiting is found in clerical and plant and service positions.

Even if a vacancy does not exist, most institutions have the job seeker fill out an employment application and will keep it on file from three to six months. When a vacancy does occur, the personnel director reviews the application file for possible candidates. This method of recruiting should not be used exclusively in filling vacant positions. If the workforce does not contain parity representation of protected class individuals in all categories of employment, this recruiting method may violate equal opportunity laws by perpetuating the composition of the workforce.

Firms involved in affirmative action recruiting may use community organizations, veterans' associations, the Urban League, the NAACP, and military bases. In fact, many central service managers and purchasing agents are former career military personnel who were trained in procurement and supplies control.

Qualified handicapped worker referrals may be made by occupational training programs from rehabilitative health care institutions and government training programs. Governor James Thompson of Illinois created the Jobs Now Program, which offers a toll-free telephone number for employers with positions to fill and plugs into a referral network of voational agencies throughout the state. Some community agencies specialize in certain disabilities. The Chicago Lighthouse for the Blind, the Chicago Hearing Society, and the Northern Illinois chapter of the Multiple Sclerosis Society offer support to the applicant and the employer in the interview and employment process.

Another source of recruiting is retirees. Retirees have become an excellent source of recruiting for part-time food service worker positions. They work a three- to four-hour shift in which they transport meals from the dietary department to the nursing units, deliver trays to patients under nursing supervision, and collect and return trays to the dietary department. Retirees are also used in the mailroom, reception areas, and file rooms.

The McDonald's Corporation recently conducted a nationwide recruitment campaign using television and radio advertising to encourage retirees to "un-retire" and work part time as counter and grill people in their fast-food restaurants. Results appear to be favorable.

In a survey conducted by Frank Sanders and Robin Galstad of Appleton Papers, 33.8 percent of the respondents said they maintained a pool of exempt and nonexempt company retirees for part-time or temporary work assignments; 45.2 percent use retirees on a contractual basis to perform various job duties.[19] By maintaining an as-needed pool of retired employees, an institution can handle special projects and surges in patient utilization without employing additional permanent staff, temporary help or consultants.

SPECIAL RECRUITING CONCERNS

Child Care

With more than 54 percent of women with children under 6 years of age in the paid labor market, the issue of child care directly influences the employment of working parents. A recent study, "Mothers in the Workplace," conducted by the National Council of Jewish Women's Center for the Child, revealed that 83 percent of the organizations surveyed did not provide employer-assisted day care.

Health care institutions have found that in-house child care services provide major recruiting and employee retention benefits. Commercial child care centers seldom care for children after 6 P.M. By offering in-house services from 6:30 A.M. until midnight, these facilities have been able to recruit needed second-shift personnel, reduce absenteeism due to the lack of child care, and increase the availability of employees to work overtime. This service benefits both the employee and the supervisor who is attempting to cover the needed extra hours.

Affordable child care is the issue of the 1980s. The average weekly rate for Chicago area hospital-based child care is $80 per child. Institutions have restructured their salary and benefit programs to offer subsidized child care services either in-house or through neighborhood nonprofit organizations that offer child services to the community. A comprehensive child care program may be able to lure needed professionals to the institution.

Dual Career Couples

Organizations are assisting spouses of new employees in the employment process. The trailing spouse is often the one who can make or break a relocation. Spousal job assistance may range from casual job tips to picking up the cost of spousal job assistance. Assistance may include resume writing, job counseling, and payment for extra job-finding trips for the spouse. As second incomes become more of a necessity than an option and career-minded women play a larger role in the permanent workforce, institutions are beginning to offer these services to hotly recruited key position candidates.

Handicapped

Federal and state employment laws normally do not require special space renovations to accommodate handicapped workers. However, many health care institutions have been able physically to accommodate handicapped workers with minimum effort since they already have to comply with the U.S. Rehabilitation Act and have designed their facilities to accommodate physically disabled patients. To restrict recruiting efforts to the able-bodied severely limits the potential for securing the best candidate for the job. Indeed, I have found that one of the most respected vice-presidents of finance in the midwestern United States is confined to a wheelchair. If this hospital had not employed him, it would have not benefited from his many years of experience and innovative financial management techniques.

ALTERNATIVES TO RECRUITING ADDITIONAL PERSONNEL

Recruiting is an expensive process. The time and expense of placing advertisements, travel expenses, and relocation allowances can add up. As Robert Burnson, project director of Evangelical Health Systems, notes, "A box advertisement can cost about the same as a compact automobile."

Alternatives to recruiting additional full-time personnel include subcontracting or staff leasing, retention of consultants or temporary help, covering the additional services through the use of overtime or on-call hours, and flextime or job sharing to cover needed hours.

Employment leasing has been used for many years in the health care industry. Frequently the dietary, housekeeping, or laundry departments are staffed with leased workers. Under this concept, the institution terminates its employees; the workers are then immediately rehired by the leasing company and leased back to the original employer to do their old jobs. Nothing much changes except that the original employer relinquishes to the independent leasing company the responsibilities of being an employer. That firm does the payroll, files the payroll taxes, recruits new workers, and terminates unsatisfactory ones. It may also

Recruitment Strategies

provide needed management services. In these service departments, employee turnover is high. The leased firm then becomes responsible for securing replacement workers. Additionally, service departments staffed on patient census or utilization can be expanded or reduced at will.

Another way to cover fluctuations in staff coverage is to establish an in-house registry of on-call or temporary personnel. When additional staff is required, these people are asked to work for a certain amount of hours or days. This practice eliminates the fixed overhead of a full-time employee who would be paid whether or not he or she is actually needed to provide patient care services. In some departments, such as admitting and dietary, workers are needed for only certain hours. There then appears a lull in the action until the workers' services are needed again later in the day. Flextime and job sharing have been successful in covering these fluctuations while keeping slack-time employment costs to a minimum.

EVALUATING RECRUITING METHODS

Which recruiting method is the best? Most results must be evaluated by both the number of successful hires and by the resultant costs. Although the use of an executive search firm may produce a substantial number of potential hires, its search fee may place a financial burden on a limited recruiting budget.

An applicant log should be maintained for at least three years. The log should record the race, sex, age, handicap, and veteran status of each applicant by date and position desired. The information may be recorded based on visual survey or by having the applicant complete a document containing this information, which would be retained separately from the application itself. Each applicant's data form should note the referral source of each applicant, recruiting method or technique, recruiting costs, the recruiter who reviewed the applicant's form or conducted the interview, and the disposition of the application. The disposition of the application may contain such categories as the following:

- Interviewed; no position available; no offer
- Interviewed; position available; no offer; reason for rejection
- Interviewed: offer extended but rejected
- Interviewed; offer extended and accepted
- Application reviewed but rejected; reason for rejection

This information will facilitate both the recruiting evluation process and the maintaining of affirmative action statistics. Data may be summarized into reporting statistics by source and method and may be used to compare results from period to period. Among the statistics used by human resource departments in evaluating recruiting efforts are number of applicants, by source and method; offers and hires, by source and method; recruiting cost per applicant; qualified applicants' ratio to total applicants; and applicants of protected groups' ratio to total applicants.[20]

GUIDELINES FOR ADMINISTRATORS AND PROFESSIONALS

What works best? It depends on the institution. However, some practical suggestions regarding the recruiting function can be surmised.

Affirmative Action

- Avoid recruiting primarily on the basis of employee referrals or walk-ins. This method tends to perpetuate the present composition of an institution's workforce. Excessive reliance on such recruiting methods has been interpreted by the U.S. courts to be a discriminatory practice.
- Train and use minority employees as recruiters and interviewers. Send minority employees to high schools, colleges, job fairs, and minority recruiting centers.
- Seek out minority group and female leaders in the community. Inform them of employment opportunities, and request their active assistance in referring qualified candidates for employment consideration.
- Encourage minority group employees and women to refer their friends and relatives for jobs.
- Where applicable, use community organizations for recruiting purposes.
- Establish and maintain contact with employment counselors in schools with large minority enrollments.

Methods, Techniques, and Evaluation

- Evaluate recruiting methods and techniques. Compare recruitment costs to time savings.
- Maintain ongoing recruitment activities. Develop and conduct annual wage and benefit surveys to monitor current market conditions.
- Determine reasons and frequency of applicants rejected without an interview. Revise recruiting practices accordingly.
- Follow up on employees hired. Keep records of method of recruitment, length of employment, and turnover for each position classification.

NOTES

1. M. A. Camuso, "The Employment Trip—Six Stages to Success," *Personnel Journal* 63 (1) (November 1984): 66.
2. *1986 Guidebook to Fair Employment Practices* (Chicago: Commerce Clearing House, 1986), pp. 14–15.

3. E. A. Kazemek and H. Greenberg, "Management Issues," *Health Care Financial Management* (December 1986): 104.

4. *Ideas and Trends in Personnel* (July 13, 1984), Chicago: Commerce Clearing House, p. 10.

5. Kazemek and Greenberg, "Management Issues," p. 104.

6. *Ideas and Trends in Personnel*, pp. 37–38.

7. L. S. Kielman and K. J. Clark, "Recruitment: An Effective Job Posting System," *Personnel Journal* (February 1948): 20–25.

8. Ibid., p. 25.

9. R. Half, *Robert Half on Hiring* (New York: Crown Publishers, 1985), pp. 212–13.

10. Ibid., p. 49.

11. *Creative Aspects of Recruitment Advertising: A Checklist* (New York: Deutsch, Shea & Evans, 1976).

12. "West Suburban Hospital Medical Center," *Chicago Tribune*, May 24, 1987, p. 19.

13. U.S. Department of Labor, *Employment and Training Administration* (Washington, D.C.: Government Printing Office, 1984).

14. J. Lindroth, "How to Beat the Coming Labor Shortage," *Personnel Journal* 61 (4) (April 1982): 268–72.

15. Half, *Robert Half on Hiring*, p. 12.

16. U.S. Department of Health and Human Services, *Fifth Report to the President and Congress on the Status of Health Personnel in the United States* (Washington, D.C.: Government Printing Office, 1986).

17. *American Nursing Association Survey* (1984).

18. C. Kleiman, "Nursing Profession Looks for Shot in Arm," *Chicago Tribune*, June 7, 1987, p. 1.

19. "Utilizing Retired Employees," *EMA Reporter*, 12 (8) (October 1986): 1–2.

20. W. E. Glueck, *Personnel: A Diagnostic Approach*, 3d ed. (Planto, Texas: Business Publications, 1982), p. 265.

5
Performance Appraisal as a Strategic Choice for the Health Care Manager

*Robert Boissoneau,
Debrah J. Gaulding,
and David N. Calvert*

Since the beginning of the 1980s, the health care industry has been undergoing a rapid metamorphosis as the pressure from price competition along with other economic incentives forces its managers to increase organizational productivity as their basic means of cost containment. The technical expertise of both staff and the technology that they use, when combined with the organizational need for interdependence, provides significant incentives for managers to explore any programs that offer the potential to increase employee productivity significantly. Increasingly, organizations have begun to look at the subject of employee performance review as an integral part of any organizational success that they might enjoy in the future. In a poll of 3,500 organizations, the primary human resource concern reported by management was their performance appraisal system (Gehrman, 1984).

GROWING CONCERN FOR THE STUDY OF PERFORMANCE APPRAISALS

In the last two decades, there has been a substantial increase in the amount of management research and literature on the subject of employee and managerial job performance. With the development of a healthier theoretical base, the practitioner can select from a number of publications information and strategies that can be helpful in the selection, development, and implementation of a system of performance review to match the idiosyncrasies of their individual environments (Bernardin and Klatt, 1985; Bernardin and Beatty, 1984; Carroll and Schneier, 1982; DeVries, Morrison, and Shullman, 1981; Henderson, 1980; Latham and Wexley, 1981). The rewards of this research were shown in a recent study of administrators. The study concluded that administrators of those programs that had characteristics recommended by research scholars consistently perceived their programs to be more effective (Bernardin and Klatt, 1985). The depth and the growth of this interest is further depicted by the number of comprehensive reviews performed in management journals over the past twenty years (Bernardin and Klatt, 1985; Landy and Farr, 1980; DeCotiss and Petit, 1978; Miner, 1977; Barrett, 1966).

LEGAL CONSIDERATIONS IN PERFORMANCE APPRAISALS

In the last few years, the judicial system has worked to protect the rights of the employee during and after the appraisal process (e.g., Barrett, 1966; DeCotiss and Petit, 1978; Landy and Farr, 1980; Miner, 1977; Bernardin and Klatt, 1985: 79). The courts are examining more closely performance appraisal systems under a range of federal and state civil rights laws that protect special classes of people from discrimination by employers. Falling generally under the rubric of employee selection, performance appraisal systems are labeled as discriminative if they have a disproportionately negative impact on classes of people specifically protected under civil rights legislation (Romberg, 1986; Gehrman, 1984). The courts have recently begun to examine performance appraisal systems from the perspective of a contractual obligation on the part of the employers. Although employers have no legal obligation initially to establish a formal system for appraising performance, the courts have stated that once an employer institutes a system, it has established a contract with its employees to use the system for the purpose for which it was established and in the manner in which it was described to employees (Romberg, 1986). Exhibit 5.1 offers a summary of the rulings that pertain to performance appraisal.

This pressure from the judicial system has caused some organizations to make significant changes to protect themselves from charges of discrimination. Tied to a desire to bring a wider range of input into the design of such systems, these systems of performance appraisals utilize input from compensation professionals, computer experts, industrial psychologists, job evaluations specialists, attorneys, and other staff specialists in their final design (Gehrman, 1984). To some managers of these organizations, the resulting increase in complexity of its performance appraisal systems has made it even more difficult to administer. They have expressed concern that this plethora of information has done nothing but provide additional obstacles (Gehrman, 1984).

Although quite a few companies are showing concern over the growing number of legal attacks on performance appraisal systems, results from another survey suggest that this concern is not shared by all participants. For example, fewer than half have a training program in the appraisal process, and 60.1 percent believe that the essay technique, which is subjective and often based on personal traits, is very or extremely important (Zippo and Miller, 1984).

Designing a Performance Appraisal System

Despite the prominent level of research and the belief of experts that the use of some form of performance appraisal (PA) is practiced by virtually all modern organizations, the extent of its use or its overall effectiveness is still debatable (Levine, 1986; Hobson and Gibson, 1984). Studies have suggested that although the incident of PA may have increased in the last decade, most of the problem exists because of the difficulty in designing a system that is effective for all levels of employees. One survey found that over half of the 588 companies sampled did not have a PA system that evaluated members of top management and that over one-third lacked programs to evaluate nonmanagement personnel (Zippo and Miller, 1984). Throughout the literature on the subject, researchers tell how these problems are consistently compounded by the inherent constraints that arise when individuals are placed in superior-subordinate relationship (Rice, 1985b). The underlying conclusion is summarized best by one survey that concludes that despite the proliferation of research and writing on the subject, the state of managerial performance appraisal is still rather primitive (Bernardin and Klatt, 1985). Some experts have even inferred that researchers themselves are to blame for any overall deficiency. Taylor and Zawacki (1984) concluded that people who study PA systems may be overly concerned about form rather than substance. They are accused of failing to realize that the real issue in developing any kind of system is to define goals and then to match those expectations with the appropriate tools and techniques. Taylor and Zawacki conclude that before an organization can implement an effective PA system, it must first build an awareness of the conflicts that often block the realization of any potential rewards. That examination begins by understanding the component parts that make up the process: (1) the reasons for their use, (2) how they are used by organizations, and (3) the nature of the conflicts that traditionally impede organizations from realizing the benefits and rewards available from the successful implementation of such a program. Such an awareness will facilitate any organization in designing, developing, and implementing a more effective system of performance appraisal.

Performance Defined

Employee performance is the perceived level of competence attained by an employee relative to some estalished standard. Ideally, acceptable performance is the level of performance exhibited by an employee when the employee understands and discharges all job duties and responsibilities effectively. Unfortunately, reality suggests that good performance is in the eyes of the beholder,

Exhibit 5.1
Performance Appraisals Rulings

THE FOLLOWING ARE REPRESENTATIVE OF RECENT RULINGS MADE IN THE JUDICIAL SYSTEM.

A. From a civil rights perspective an employer has little cause for concern unless it is shown that the performance appraisal system or other selection system has a disproportionately negative impact on a protected class (Segar vs Civiletti, D.D.C. 1981).

B. Instruments that have a disproportionately negative impact on a protected class are more likely to be supported by the courts if they are developed from a systematic analysis of a particular job. The more specific, objective, and behavior oriented the analysis, the more likely the system will be sustained (Greenspan vs Automobile Club of Michigan, E.D. Mich., 1980).

C. Systems that emphasize work behaviors rather than personal traits are more likely to be sustained. Assessing job performance in terms of personal appearance or subjective characteristics such as "helpful" or "loyal" are particularly difficult to support, unless they are supplemented with objective, behavior-oriented measures such as "gets assignments accomplished promptly" or "usually provides solutions rather than problems." (Statsny vs Southern Bell Telephone & Telegraph, M.D. N.C. 1978, Johnson vs Uncle Ben's, 5th Cir. 1980 Mosack vs Shell Chemical, D.C. Ala. 1981 and Grubb vs M.A. Foote Memorial Hospital 6th Cir. 1984).

98

D. Courts tend to look more favorably on appraisal systems that include communication and feedback as essential elements of the system. Communication should travel in several directions. Supervisors should tell their employees up front and clearly what the standards are against which they will be evaluated. Moreover, after employees have been performing the job, they should be given explicit feedback on how well they are doing in terms of those standards (Friend vs Leiditiger, E.D. Va. 1977 and Bay vs Goodyear Tire & Rubber Co. D.C. Tx. 1980).

E. Training supervisors to conduct proper appraisals and to avoid bias is an important consideration imposed by courts in evaluating appraisal systems that have a negative impact. Even better, the training should include written instructions to which supervisors can refer when conducting appraisals. Appraisal systems should be kept current. Job descriptions should be updated to ensure that performance is being measured against current expectations (Detroit Police Officers Association vs Young, E.D. Mich., 1978).

F. Appraisals should be written, documented, and retained, and personnel decisions should be consistent with the appraisals given (Bennett vs. Eggers, D.C. N.J. 1981, and EEOC vs Consolidated Edison of New York, S.D. N.Y. 1983).

G. Any employee should be informed of the penalty for poor performance during the appraisal interview if termination is pending. This is especially important with employees with a significant amount of service with the organization (Chamberlain vs Bissell Inc., Mich. E.D. 1983).

Sources: Martin, 1986; Romberg, 1986.

99

often an unwarranted victim of a supervisor's perception of circumstances, needs, and priorities. By itself this perception can influence the ultimate assessment of an individual's performance more than the actual performance itself.

Much of the challenge of developing a PA system comes from studies of human nature, which suggest that developing an effective system that can teach individuals to standardize their thought processes is not simple. Studies have shown that the process of forming judgments is a dynamic one, often shaped and molded by single incidents. Whether formal or informal, knowing or unconscious, evenhanded or biased, managers constantly hand out judgments about employees' job performance (Romberg, 1986). While many systems purport to appraise people on results, in practice, people are also appraised on how they do things, which is usually not formally described in setting employee objectives (Gehrman, 1984).

PURPOSE, OBJECTIVES, AND IMPORTANCE: WHY PERFORMANCE APPRAISALS ARE DONE

While the obvious function of a performance appraisal is to evaluate employee performance, it is generally agreed that a system of performance appraisal generally serves two fundamental broadly based needs in an organization: (1) It helps provide administrative control, which can subsequently improve organizational development and ultimately performance, (2) It helps facilitate individual development (Regal and Hollman, 1987; Rarick and Baxter, 1986; Hobson and Gibson, 1984). Although it is difficult to separate the individual benefits by category, collectively PAs can provide a wide range of benefits—from organization-wide improvements in employee motivation, productivity, and relations that increase the effectiveness of personnel planning to decisions about individuals relative to their pay, retention, and promotion (see Exhibit 5.2 for additional information). A 1984 survey of human resources managers reinforced the breadth of its application when researchers showed that organizations were using such systems to assist compensation, training, promotion, manpower planning, retention, and discharge and as a validation of their selection technique (Zippo and Miller, 1984). Although there continues to be debate among experts as to which purpose is most important, there seems to be a consensus that the development of a PA system is essential to the long-term success, growth, and survival of all organizations (Hobson and Gibson, 1984; Rarick and Baxter, 1986; Naffziger, 1985).

EFFECTIVENESS OF PERFORMANCE APPRAISAL SYSTEMS

One basis for judging the effectiveness of any system is how well it accomplishes its purpose(s) (Levine, 1986). Another good measure is how those who utilize the program perceive its fairness and accuracy (Gehrman, 1984). It has

Exhibit 5.2
Benefits Researchers Associate with the Development of an Effective System of Performance Appraisal

Administrative & Organizational Control - Provides a connection between organizational and individual objectives; Helps integrate people into an explicit and purposeful culture; Maximum utilization of resources achieved; The quality of product/service is improved; Provides evaluative information for use in making administrative decisions; Improves employee relations; Increases employee productivity.

Individual Development - Provides feedback to the employee about performance against established goals; Builds employee awareness; Identifies barriers to better performance; Helps assess the need for and the effectiveness of employee training and development including those necessary for promotion or improved job performance.

Individual Reward - Supports career-planning; Is the mechanism that is most effective for determining salary increases, bonuses, promotion; Can specify what job behaviors are appropriate and how these behaviors are related to the reward system; Ensures that rewards are distributed to those who most deserve them; Provides opportunities for recognized achievers.

Motivation - Employee's self worth, independence and creativity are enhanced in positive atmosphere; Moral & loyalty increased; Can stimulate employee growth and development; Builds commitment to established plans for individual development and training; Integrate people into an explicit and purposeful culture.

Personnel Planning - Can assist in the validation of the organization's selection system; Identifies performance deficiently for which training or dismissal is appropriate; Can define skill levels and staffing needs; Improves evaluation of performance and potential of individuals and departments; Provides a basis for determining salary increases, promotions, termination and other administrative decisions; Helps to clarify boundaries between individual responsibilities.

Communication - Can clarify goals and expectations of both superior and subordinate; Fosters constructive criticism, feedback and action plans; Leads to learning on the part of bosses, about what subordinates think and feel in relation to jobs and what affects motivation and performance; and on the part of subordinates what is needed to achieve favorable assessments of job performance.

Sources: Odiorne, 1987; Regal and Hollman, 1987; Mallinger and Cummings, 1986; Dorfman, Stephan, and Loveland, 1986; Gehrman, 1984; George, 1986; Levine, 1986; Martin, 1986; Rarick and Baxter, 1986; Romberg, 1986; Naffziger, 1985; Hobson and Gibson, 1984; Pajer, 1984; Zippo and Miller, 1984.

been argued that the establishment of clear relationships between desired behaviors and organizational rewards is a critical component of an effective control system. Thus it seems that in order for the PA system to lead to effective organizational control and eventually individual development, two conditions must be met: the system must provide reliable evaluative information about performance and establish clear relationships between desired performance behaviors and organizational rewards (Hobson and Gibson, 1984).

Under any of these criteria, the overall success of PA is rather suspect. Despite its apparent benefits, the idea of appraisal has not been well received by managers or subordinates, who typically view the process as ineffective (Grant, 1987; Gehrman, 1984). This statement is more a reflection of the quality of the operating systems rather than an objection to the idea of PAs in general. Employees in general prefer having some kind of appraisal system because it increases the likelihood of succeeding objectively and on merit (Romberg, 1986). Such communication also provides a legitimate avenue for employees to receive feedback from supervisors who might otherwise be uncomfortable about giving it. Although performance appraisal is a basic part of every manager's job, experts suggest that it is usually done poorly, frequently not done on a formal basis, and sometimes not done at all. The gravity of the latter two situations is that the employee is left to assume that no evaluation must mean that job performance is satisfactory, when frequently it is not the case (Odiorne, 1987; Cocheu, 1986).

Nature of the Conflict

Most of the problems with PA are the timeless result of human nature. George (1986) suggests that a quick recall helps to explain:

Why is it that so many managers, faced with the task of appraising a subordinate's performance, duck unpalatable issues and resist the honest exchange of opinions and feelings?

Why is it that managers frequently reject the suggestion that appraisals can help them manage better and that it represents a worthwhile investment of their time?

One clue is certainly in the nature of transactions between individuals involved in the appraisal. Ask yourself, With how many people do you freely share judgments and feelings about one another, openly and honestly, in a climate of trust and in which problems and differences are faced? For most people, such candor in life is rare, captured only once or twice in special treasured relationships. Developing such a rapport takes an immense amount of time, effort, and, eventually, trust. Unfortunately most organizations do not do enough to foster these kinds of exchanges (George, 1986). George (1986) argues that in setting up appraisal situations between people at work, organizations are expecting interactions of a nature and quality that are not part of most relationships; they expect people to exhibit a degree of openness that does not come naturally. The difference in status between the boss and subordinate hampers this kind of communication. Managers often feel uncomfortable with the review not only because they lack the necessary interpersonal skills to carry them off smoothly but often because they are not sure that they have accurately evaluated their employees. Subordinates afflicted with the same discomfort and not wanting to look bad in the eyes of the boss shy away from informing the boss of any difficulties they might be having so that they can defend themselves in the event they are given poor ratings. Consequently criticism by the boss is most often interpreted by the subordinate as a condemnation of the employee's work, and the appraisal interview is experienced as a deflating encounter to be avoided whenever possible (Odiorne, 1987; Grant, 1987; George, 1986; Mallinger and Cummings, 1986; Rice, 1985b; Pajer, 1984).

Frequency of Evaluations

According to a study by Levine (1986), most appraisals are conducted on an annual basis by an employee's immediate supervisor with the supervisor's supervisor looking over the results or possibly adding his or her views. Altany (1987) found that some 86 percent of respondents like the idea of annual or semiannual reviews. In that study, a significant percentage believed that the more frequently evaluations occurred, the better. Researchers have advocated that any increase in frequency will reduce the anxiety of the yearly review and as an ongoing communication tool can help balance the employee's need for supportive feedback with the organization's need to develop productive employees (Malinauskas and Clement, 1987). Although frequent evaluations would provide significant benefits, they would also require managers to have two face-to-face discussions with each subordinate for each appraisal period. Most managers complain about the amount of time required by PAs involving just one interview; the prospect of two interviews increases their resistance to the process (Wight, 1985).

Level of Satisfaction

One reason for the general dissatisfaction with PA systems is a general lack of agreement on their purpose. Should they merely evaluate performance or critique and improve it as well? Should they be used primarily to determine salaries and prospects for promotion or as a means of training and career development? Should they focus on how an employee does the job or the results achieved? Just who are they supposed to help: the employee or the supervisor? Although no performance review system can accomplish all these goals, confusion about conflicting purposes often undermines attempts to attain any of them (Rice, 1985b). One result is that few organizations are satisfied with their PA system and fewer still know why (Manuel, More, and Parkinson, 1987). Of those who even know a problem is present, most maintain that awareness only at an intuitive level, not based on fact (Manuel, More, and Parkinson, 1987; Phillips, 1987). For many employees and their supervisors, appraisal in practice tends to become a grand annual exercise, more of a bureaucratic nightmare than a means of ensuring continual development of people. To them the appraisal routine is a grinding chore, a major imposition rather than a major part of their jobs. It is to be dealt with as expeditiously as possible so that they can get back to real job priorities. Rarely do these people see the process as relating to recognition, succession planning, and promotion (Cocheu, 1986; George, 1987). In a 1987 study by Odiorne, 70 percent of employees surveyed reported that their boss did not give them a clear picture of what was expected of them, and only 20 percent said that their results were reviewed.

Critics like Douglas Gehrman (1984) suggest that much of this growing dissatisfaction arises from how PA systems are utilized. He suggests that part of the problem is that in most organizations, the annual exercise of documenting PAs is generally geared toward short-term goals related to satisfying the compensation system at the expense of long-term goals related to providing employees with effective developmental counseling.

Some studies have suggested that the situation could be getting worse. Managers, researchers, and employees have complained that recent changes in the environment have shifted the role of performance review from a collaborative systems approach (administrative control and individual development) that helps individuals grow and develop to an overemphasis on systems designed to withstand the scrutiny of governmental and legal challenges (Taylor and Zawacki, 1984). A survey of managers of Fortune 500 companies showed that they believed that their PA systems provided monetary rewards but little motivation. Furthermore, most believed that their systems were very limited in effectively adapting to any dramatic changes either in employee performance or in the business environment (Gehrman, 1984). Some respondents to another survey contended that if managers did their job properly, reviews would be unnecessary (Altany, 1987).

Although some surveys show that managers perceive the process as positive in the development of leadership, productivity, and efficiency (Zippo and Miller, 1984), other studies suggest that the actual appraisal procedures used provide little common ground for objective, factual discussion between bosses and subordinates, sometimes neglecting to compare achievements with expectations and often failing to recognize all of the factors that influence performance (George, 1986). At their worst, reviews have been accused of encouraging short-term performance, annihilating long-term planning, building fear, demolishing teamwork, and nourishing rivalry and politics. The aftereffects of some poorly administered reviews have left some people bitter, others despondent and dejected, and even some unfit for work for weeks after receipt of their rating, unable to comprehend why they are judged inferior (Altany, 1987). With such a plethora of bad marks, it is no wonder that managers and employees alike dread the process.

Consequences

No matter how perfect or potentially beneficial a program is, if the usage is not consistent with the system's objectives, the objectives will not be met. Many

PA systems suffer because management and employees view compensation-driven appraisal programs as an exercise sponsored by the compensation department staff to meet pay objectives and not as a vital part of the process of effectively managing and motivating people (Gehrman, 1984). The effect of such a viewpoint on the organization is significant. The absence of a viable appraisal system, even one that may be quite informal, reduces an employer's ability to improve the performance of employees. If employees do not clearly understand what they are expected to do or the standards for doing it and if supervisors do not make these expectations clear, employees are left to chance or intuition to bring their behavior in line with the supervisor's expectations. Further, without an appraisal system, there is no ready system through which an employer can easily document poor performance to support some kind of disciplinary action (Romberg, 1986). People are not motivated when they do not know what is expected of them and how well—or how poorly—they have done (Odiorne, 1987).

ESTABLISHING PERFORMANCE APPRAISAL STANDARDS

The development of individual performance standards by managers with their employees is a key element in any successful PA system (Phillips, 1987). Probably no other element of the PA process is as critical as ensuring that employees understand the job as management defines it, what the boss's priorities are, and the goals and the results they wish to achieve (Gehrman, 1984). Communication of this information is the hallmark of an effective communicator and, usually, an effective evaluator. Even jobs that at first glance appear to be quite similar can have subtle but significant differences because of the different work styles of supervisors, different priorities within a department, and so on. Often, when an appraisal system is not working, either no performance standards were established or the employees of each manager have the same standards (Phillips, 1987).

Employers should write a job description and establish performance standards for every job, even if the job fits within a family of jobs such as secretary or financial analyst. It is important to be sensitive to individual differences in job performance and provide a format for capitalizing on each person's unique pattern of strengths and weaknesses (Regal and Hollman, 1987; Romberg, 1986). Although job descriptions may have many similarities, unique job descriptions enable supervisors to describe the differences that may be important to the effective performance of a particular job (Romberg, 1986). Appraisal forms should have space for the supervisor to describe key job responsibilities. Preprinted forms that list broad skill areas are useful but should be supplemented with blank spaces for the supervisor to add or substitute skills and identify key job responsibilities. Each responsibility should be described in clear, specific language, and whenever possible, job goals should be defined in objective and measurable terms.

The PA system, like an organization, must be dynamic and systemizing if it is to succeed. It cannot be viewed as an isolated activity imposed on an already overworked supervisor. The step-by-step process must be designed and implemented in a coherent, valid, and thorough process. To be effective, a new appraisal system must fit in with existing programs and practices, produce positive results, and be acceptable to both employees and supervisors. Criteria for establishing PA appraisal systems include the following:

1. Identify needs and objectives
2. Identify jobs to cover
3. Develop job descriptions and job specifications
4. Choose appropriate appraisal instruments
5. Provide program guidance
6. Set standards of performance
7. Recognize other factors for success

Employee Involvement: The Importance of Communications

An appraisal program is not an isolated activity. When fully integrated into the organization, it will affect and be affected by many other programs and activities. A number of useful sources can be utilized:

- People
- Files and records
- Policy and procedure manuals
- Tables and organizational charts
- Executives, managers, and supervisors in appropriate areas
- Wage and salary surveys and programs
- Newsletters
- Benefit programs
- Consultants and management specialists

Need for Employee Participation

Input from employees not only helps in the design and development of the program but also improves the potential for its subsequent acceptance. The only effective personnel programs are those that line management understands, accepts, and implements (Gehrman, 1984). The more actively subordinates are involved in the evaluation process, the more likely they are to view the appraisal as an asset in their personal development. This collaborative style of appraisal is likely to reduce subordinates' stress during the interview because, as part of the decision-making process, they feel less helpless about the outcome (Mallinger and Cummings, 1986). It is important to utilize selected, knowledgeable, and skilled employees from different areas of expertise during the early development period and after the program has been developed but prior to formalization and operational. A wise employer will first use the newly developed instrument on an experimental basis to determine the overall effectiveness by obtaining feedback from supervisors and the employees. This feedback process should be ongoing. Suggestions and comments will lead to modifications and usually improvements in the system (Romberg, 1986).

Development and implementation of a successful PA program is time-consuming and demands thorough research to develop the system that will create the maximum results for the organization and its employees. The efforts put forth in the initial stage determine the benefits as the system is utilized. The growth and prosperity desired by the organization from the employees through the managers can be achieved only through carefully developed appraisal systems that are consistant and continually updated. Effective appraisal requires resources and time. Human resources managers often find they receive in proportion to what they invest in a PA system (Naffziger, 1985). Appraisal is not an additional luxury. To achieve real success, an organization must make PAs part of management (George, 1986).

Democratically Oriented Manager

Through the literature on performance appraisals, experts have recommended that managers exercise a supportive leadership style, characterized as a democratic manager. This approach provides a means of increasing the effectiveness of the PA interview. Also the democratic orientation is beneficial to the working relationship in general (Mallinger and Cummings, 1986). Although it is a definitive style of management, democratic management is more than anything else a way of thinking. It is an attitude that makes its managers work vigorously to construct an environment where workers feel comfortable in participating in work-related decisions. Experts have proposed that the quality of the relationship between the boss and subordinate goes a long way to reduce the tension during an interview (Mallinger and Cummings, 1986). Research shows that supportive bosses have the best relationships with their subordinates and that subordinates who work for supportive bosses have the most motivation (Odiorne, 1987).

In most institutions of higher learning, modern management education programs maintain the bulk of their emphasis on the teaching of quantitative knowledge and skills, at the expense of attitude development. This occurs because of the university's belief in the scientific approach, the ease in identifying the importance of knowledge and skills, and their relative lack of controversy. This attitude exacerbates many of the problems inherent in the PA process. For example, some practitioners and academics look with disfavor on the observation technique because of the great possibility of error due to bias. However, it is important to note the wide use of the observation technique by managers and to realize how much more helpful it would be to teach people observational skills rather than to decry the use of management observation. Despite its detractors, reality suggests that observational techniques will continue to play an important role in decision making (Boissoneau, 1984).

Democratic management is an outgrowth of the human relations school of management, tempered by systems analysis. It is distinguished from the school of human relations, whose advocates want happy employees. Democratic managers want an organizational environment in which employees become productve and satisfied. Using vehicles such as quality circles, democratic managers advocate communication to solicit employees' work-related suggestions for improvements. Exhibit 5.3 identifies characteristics of the democratic manager.

THE PERFORMANCE APPRAISAL PROCESS

Job performance is the culmination of three elements working together: (1) skill, the raw materials that an employee brings to the job (knowledge, abilities, interpersonal competencies, and technical competencies); (2) effort, the motivation an employee exerts toward getting the job done; and (3) the nature of external conditions, the degree to which they are favorable in facilitating an employee's productivity (Snell and Wexley, 1985). To be effective, a rating system must take into account all of these factors when evaluating employee performance. To achieve this effectiveness, the development of a system of performance appraisal is based on a four-step process:

1. Performance goals are established
2. Work standards are communicated
3. Job performance is monitored
4. Feedback on accomplishments and areas that need improvement is given (Martin, 1986)

Successful completion of each step depends on honest, clear, easily understood communications between supervisor and rated employee. Within the interview process itself, there are three major phases: preview, interview, and review.

Although the overriding objective of the preview phase is to set the stage for the discussion itself (Malinauskas and Clement, 1987), this process also provides a vehicle for a number of other purposes. Specifically it allows the manager to:

1. Reiterate the organization's philosophy of performance appraisal
2. Reach a mutual understanding of performance criteria
3. Give the employee a chance to prepare a self-assessment
4. Set the time, place, and agenda for the appraisal interview itself

Exhibit 5.3
Characteristics of a Democratic Manager

1. **Democratic managers foster an open environment.**

2. **Democratic managers think in terms of "all of us together."** They know that managers have the leadership responsibility of trying to meld individuals into a unified organization and that there will always be people who do not fit easily into the organization. They take the attitude of looking out for all people in the organization, including themselves.

3. **Democratic managers believe that problems affecting people in the organization should be handled directly.**

4. **Democratic managers consider personnel to be more important than other resources.** This point of view contends that other resources merely support the work that personnel performs with clients.

5. **Democratic managers put personal choices in perspective.** Knowledgeable managers understand that securing as much useful information as possible will ensure that the best decision is made. Also, concerned personnel need to know that their thinking on an issue is considered important. Furthermore, democratic managers realize the importance of consensus in service organizations and try to reach it when possible.

6. **Democratic managers give relatively high standing to individuality.** They know that people need to show their individuality.

7. **Democratic managers encourage personnel development.** Knowing that personnel are important, democratically oriented managers initiate programs to help employees develop new knowledge, skills and attitudes. In a similar vein, democratic managers see themselves as teachers.

8. **Democratic managers favor decentralized management.** This reflects the management style of supporting personnel by placing responsibility for decision making at as low level in the hierarchy as possible.

9. **Democratic managers believe that past management failings have been mostly human.** They believe that the great majority of management failures have been due to poor relationships with people.

Source: Boissoneau, 1984.

Supervisors can encourage openness and trust by giving the employee the rating form they will use ahead of the scheduled interview. This gives the employee the opportunity to fill out the form and then compare his or her answers to the actual appraisal (Denton, 1987). Experience with self-appraisal suggests that this practice is likely to yield a more realistic rating and a greater acceptance of the final rating by both subordinates and supervisors. Employees who engage in self-assessment before an interview usually rate themselves lower, perhaps because they know an unrealistic or self-serving rating could affect their manager's perception of them. Further, some managers have found that asking subordinates to perform an initial self-appraisal encourages an open and nondefensive discussion of performance (Malinauskas and Clement, 1987).

The environment in which the interview actually takes place is important. If the discussion is conducted in the manager's office, the employee may feel threatened. A neutral place that provides a more relaxed atmosphere will be less of a threat to most employees. A pleasant, well-lighted room might be appropriate. Ensuring the absence of interruption is also conducive to a more meaningful, focused discussion (Malinauskas and Clement, 1987).

To accomplish assessment objectives, the evaluator must plan what to say and to have specific good and bad points about each employee's performance. Evaluators need to anticipate reactions and provide constructive comments to those being evaluated. Showing patience is one of the best ways for the appraisal interview to function more smoothly. Employees should not feel obligated to talk during the entire interview. An employee pause may mean an attempt to comprehend the evaluator's comments. It would be a mistake to fill in the pauses with conversation. The evaluator must take the time to listen (Denton, 1987).

It is equally important for managers to prepare themselves for the interview by developing a positive frame of mind with respect to the performance review. Time should be taken to understand the evaluation instruments to be used to help ensure an accurate appraisal. Appraisals themselves should utilize specific examples of good and poor performance. Raters should review the rated employee's job functions, work standards, achievements, and qualifications for higher-level jobs in the organization in which formal or informal training would enhance the individual's potential and career (Odiorne, 1987; Martin, 1986; Mallinger and Cummings, 1986; Grant, 1987).

Managers must also prepare their employees for the interview. Employees should not be surprised by their job description, by the skills that the supervisor believes are necessary to do the job, or even by the supervisor's opinion about how well the employee is doing. By the time a formal appraisal is conducted, both the employee and the supervisor should have a pretty good idea of how things are going. Unfortunately, the opposite situation is often true (Romberg, 1986).

A manager should communicate to subordinates how the interview will be conducted, what will be discussed, and what the subordinate's role in the interview will be. Particularly important is letting the subordinate know what to expect during the review session. By telling employees beforehand that they will be discussing some positive and negative aspects of performance, a supervisor can set the stage for a more productive discussion (Grant, 1987).

Employees should be encouraged to compare job performance with previously established standards, assess career objectives both within the organization and in their career field, and draft work goals for the forthcoming period. If performance reviews are done quarterly or semiannually, the development of goals

Performance Appraisal

for the remainder of the rating period should be emphasized, with some discussion of the goals for the following rating period (Odiorne, 1987; Martin, 1986; Mallinger and Cummings, 1986). It is essential that managers convince their subordinates of the purpose and value of performance (Grant, 1987).

Finally, the manager should inform the employee well in advance of the time and place of the interview. The session should be held on company time and should not come when the employee is extremely busy with other functions (Grant, 1987). An agenda for the discussion should be prepared so that the process moves smoothly. The agenda can be dictated by performance issues on the appraisal form itself or by goals set in previous appraisal sessions. The agenda needs to be identified well in advance of the interview so that both participants can give careful thought to the items to be addressed. The manager might also identify specific objectives for what is to be accomplished. Once the preliminaries are taken care of, the interview itself can be conducted (Grant, 1987). Suggestions for conducting an appraisal interview are contained in Exhibit 5.4.

Need for Documentation

Although it is not possible to remember every aspect of an employee's performance, it is essential for a manager to keep some kind of record. Managers may balk at spending the time needed to document, but these records serve as the basis for fair and objective performance evaluations that employees expect. They also serve as the foundation for any future feedback (Smith, 1987). If at all possible, a rater should keep a journal on the rated employee's accomplishments during the period to be reviewed—or the rated employee can keep a journal to which both parties may refer during the PA. Recording accomplishments when they happen greatly increases the accuracy of the evaluation and reduces the possibility of rating employees on the basis of their most recent accomplishments (Martin, 1986; Mallinger and Cummings, 1986).

It has been documented that both positive and negative feedback can help motivate an employee to improve performance. When an employee hears that the work he or she is doing is noticed and appreciated, usually the individual will work harder to achieve even better results. In the case of poor performance, the employee may be unaware of the problem (Smith, 1987). Documentation should be such that a third party reading the record should be able to agree with the manager's conclusions. The reader will have reached these conclusions by reading descriptions of the employee's behavior, not the manager's opinion of the employee (Smith, 1987). Managers must be consistent, documenting the performance of every subordinate, not just those who are performing unsatisfactorily, so that they cannot be accused of inventing a case against any subordinate—something managers must be particularly cautious of, especially when protected-class employees are involved (Smith, 1987).

Exhibit 5.4
Suggested Methods to Help Set the Tone in the Appraisal Interview

SMALL TALK. Since the manager wants the employee to present his or her full views and insights relative to performance, the manager should try to set the employee at ease with some small talk about non-work-related subjects of mutual interest. It is best to address the subject of communications directly, explaining the importance of honest communications during the interview.

PRAISE. In the appraisal process it is wise to give praise. Praise will not spoil your employees, but can be a powerful motivator and keeps the conversation constructive.

CENTER THE DISCUSSION ON GOALS AND RESULTS. "These are the goals you set; now let's look at how the results came out" is an excellent starting point.

AVOID CASTING BLAME, OR FINDING FAULT. Don't focus on personal strengths or weaknesses or on personality and character.

CLARIFY. Ask a lot of questions to clarify what has been said. If the subordinate arrives at some insight, restate it. Keep the focus on the other person, not on you or your problems.

FOCUS ON FUTURE, NOT ON THE PAST. The purpose of a performance review is not simply to go over the past and find out what went wrong and why. Rather, it should review the past to find opportunities for future success. The key question isn't "Why did you fail?" but "How can we sew this up so we don't get caught again? or "How could you do an even better job next year?

MAKE NOTES DURING THE DISCUSSION. People usually are flattered that you're interested enough in what they have to say to make notes.

USE SUPPORTIVE QUESTIONS. One of the best ways to indicate that your are supportive and caring is to ask three questions near the end of the discussion: (1) What can I do to help you do an even better job?; (2) What could I do differently to help?; and (3) Is there anything I can refrain from doing to make it easier for you to do you job.

AVOID ABSOLUTES. Words like "always" and "never" are easy to refute. Share responsibility. The burden for the staffer's failure falls, in part, on the editor.

DISCUSS STRONG PERFORMANCE AREAS FIRST. Doing this first will make the employee more receptive to the negative criticism later on. Each of the areas in which the supervisor feels the employee has done well should be discussed separately. The manager should then try to get the employee's agreement on the precise level of performance. It is important that consensus be reached. Once agreement is reached on the ratings, the manager can issue any contingent rewards.

OFFER CONSTRUCTIVE ALTERNATIVES. The manager should provide specific data that subordinates can use to enhance their level of performance. Avoidance of criticism is critical. Moreover, by offering specific, non-critical information to improve performance the superior can help the subordinate perceive the interview process in a positive light.

Sources: Altany, 1987; Denton, 1987; Grant, 1987; Odiorne, 1987; Mallinger and Cummings, 1986; and Giles and Landauer, 1984.

The Interview

The interview is the face-to-face meeting between the manager and employee held primarily to exchange ideas. Neither party should actually conduct the interview; both need to experience it. The interview process can be a complex, potentially emotional interaction. Latent with the possibility for perceptual differences, defensiveness, and conflict, the interview can result in faulty listening, misunderstandings, and even hostility. Those who need development the most may learn the least (Malinauskas and Clement, 1987). The purpose of an appraisal interview is fourfold:

1. To make sure employees have a clear understanding of how the manager thinks they are performing.
2. To resolve any misunderstanding about what is expected from employees. This involves straightforward and honest discussions with ample time given for questions and answers.
3. To plan on establishing a program designed to improve employee performance.
4. To build confidence between managers and employees.

Thus the objectives should be to inform, encourage, and give recognition (Denton, 1987).

Closing the Session

Before the interview is over, the manager should have reviewed all aspects of the job. Tasks, task priorities, performance standards, and any contingent reward or penalty systems should be covered to build morale before ending the conversation. Employees should be clear on the nature of their jobs and any changes they should make. Knowledge of the reward-penalty system is also crucial. A few departing comments encouraging workers, reemphasizing their strong points, and letting them know that the organization is behind them and is willing to help them will serve to build morale. Workers should leave the meeting feeling trust in and respect for the manager. Without attention to these basics, future relations with subordinates and future performance reviews will suffer (Grant, 1987).

Following Up the Interview

Feedback is the most important factor in a successful performance evaluation. Providing feedback to managers about the quality of their PA ratings would seem to have several advantages:

1. It is relatively inexpensive
2. It is based on actual ratings made by each manager as part of the formal PA process

3. It can provide managers a basis upon which to compare their ratings to those made by other managers (Davis and Mount, 1984)

Each manager must provide subordinates with continuous feedback about results throughout the year. Timely information about how well people are performing their work is necessary if they are to grow. Too much feedback, however, could turn into a form of nagging or overly close supervision. Continuous review works best when people have clearly defined job objectives and a means of measuring their own performance on the job (Odiorne, 1987).

A review phase may be held on a more informal basis, perhaps as soon as a month after the appraisal interview, to reflect on the goals previously set. This meeting can be initiated by the manager or the worker, depending on their relationship (Malinauskas and Clement, 1987; Mallinger and Cummings, 1986). The concept of the review phase arises from the literature that suggests providing feedback or reinforcement for improved performance should be an ongoing rather than a more threatening, infrequent, periodic activity. Perhaps more important, frequent discussion of progress allows the two parties to stay in touch with regard to the goals set in the interview phase (Malinauskas and Clement, 1987).

The performance review is not finished with the interview. The manager must help to develop and implement any of the improvement strategies decided on during the interview by checking subordinate progress in pursuing these strategies. The manager should not wait until the next review to discuss progress made in overcoming deficiencies. Close, frequent monitoring of progress should occur. Further counseling or coaching may be required to bring the employee along. A performance review without such follow-up is a performance review without control (Grant, 1987).

Appendix 5A
Recommendations: Performance Appraisal Guidelines for Practitioners

A. BE CLEAR REGARDING THE PURPOSE OF APPRAISAL

- Requirements of the job.
- Necessary improvements and how to achieve them.
- Assistance and resources available.
- Employee strengths and weaknesses.
- Rewards and benefits vs risks and consequences.
- Importance of the job to the organization.

B. HOW PROGRAM IS TO BE USED

- Simplicity
- Suitability
- Validity
- Consistency
- Flexibility
- Practicality
- Reliability
- Ease to use
- Fairness

C. ESTABLISH PROGRAM OBJECTIVES

- Behavioral statements specifying particulars the program is designed to accomplish
- Out growths of and consistent with the statement of purpose.
- Build provisions for accomplishing each objective

D. DETERMINATION OF JOBS REQUIRING APPRAISALS

- Types of jobs
- Level of employee

E. DETERMINATION OF WHOM WILL BE THE APPRAISER

- Review by prior to processing
- Person with good, first hand knowledge of the duties being evaluated
- Direct supervisors

F. MINIMIZE PAPERWORK

- Streamline procedures constantly
- Allow adequate time
- Use Human Resources Department if available
- Utilize instruments that are valid & easy to complete
- Stagger dates to avoid overloading supervisors

Appendix 5A (continued)

G. ASSESS BENEFITS AND RISKS

- With inadequate benefits an organization may choose to postpone implementation until factors are balanced.
- Risk of employees manipulation or blame for organization problems

H. KNOW THE WORKFORCE

- Long service (majority/minority)
- Educational knowledge and skill level
- Low turnover
- Union and or civil service rules and regulations

I. IMPACT AND ACCEPTABILITY

- Report cards (negative feedback)
- Complicated system (time consuming)
- Unbalanced increase in compensation
- Appraisals completed, filed & forgotten
- Perceived unfairness

J. AVOID PROBLEMS

- Spend adequate time in development
- Ensure sufficient communication
- Obtain employee and supervisory acceptance
- Monitor and "de-bug" as required
- Avoid overreacting to criticism
- Do not make promises that cannot be kept
- Maintain accountability

- Do not rush implementation
- Obtain managements support
- Provide sufficient break-in time
- Address abuses and defects
- Avoid over promoting beyond realistic achievement
- Do not expect positive results too quickly
- Provide sufficient time for supervisor to do an effective appraisal

- Look for and recognize signs that program is achieving the desired objectives

APPENDIX 5B
FUTURE TRENDS: ENTERING THE WORLD OF INCENTIVE COMPENSATION

In the world outside the health care industry, the typical objectives for a compensation system will generally include the following:

1. To motivate employees, executives, and managers to achieve departmental and organizational goals
2. To attract, recruit, and retain top management talent
3. To maintain a competitive reward structure for all jobs
4. To be performance driven, with the best performers receiving the highest rewards (Egan, 1986; Gehrman, 1984)

Although most health care organizations share at least the first three of these, there has always been some hesitancy to include the fourth. Until recently, the significant part of management's compensation has been based on tenure or other factors rather than contributions to organizational performance (Schuster, 1986). Only within the last decade have incentives been introduced to alter the compensation formula. When the federal government and other large payers enacted several competitive payment schemes essentially in response to the growing concern over escalating health care costs, hospitals were offered significant incentives to lower health care costs by controlling the number of services they provide per case, the length of stay per case, and the unit cost of such service (Channon, 1986).

With the realization that failing to respond to these incentives will ultimately threaten the now financially exposed organization, CEOs and hospital boards have begun to take action to extend the cost-containment psychology. One interesting but controversial alternative has been to utilize incentive plans as a means of passing along the financial risks and incentives to personnel who control utilization (Egan, 1986; Channon, 1986). From an organizational standpoint, incentive compensation has several advantages. Financially, it reinforces the goals, objectives, and priorities of the organization (Channon, 1986). It stimulates performance by providing extra compensation for attaining goals, reinforcing the planning process, and driving improved profitability (Channon, 1986). When performance is crucial to continued success and managers are viewed as central to how well an organization does, it makes sense to tie the manager's financial fortune to that of the organization. When managers know their best interests and those of the organization are directly linked, they are more likely to be attentive to established performance priorities (Schuster, 1986). A recent survey of top health care facilities showed that hospitals that have incorporated incentives into their compensation system have been well rewarded for their efforts. The results showed a significant relationship between hospitals that were financially successful and those that link management's pay to the hospital's economic performance (Schuster, 1986).

Incentive Payments for Managers and Physicians

Although it is important to develop an effective incentive system for influencing management, the most significant incentives systems that hospitals must continue to develop are those that reward doctors who hold the line on costs. Effective design and implementation of a working system with the ability to pass along economic incentives to the physician for controlling costs is perceived by most experts to be the critical component in cost containment. Among the more commonly used approaches already developed is a deferred compensation plan in which physicians share in any cost savings a hospital realizes through their efforts. In this system, a hospital tracks each participating physician's costs performance on a case-by-case basis, the cost for each case compared with a target cost for the appropriate diagnosis related grouping (DRG). Each doctor accumulates credits and debits, depending on whether his or her performance is above or below the target. On a regular basis the savings are put in a tax-deferred annuity program. Although they are not put in the doctor's name, they are internally earmarked and payable upon the doctor's retirement, death, or disability (Riffer, 1986; Long, 1985).

Although developing a system to extend incentive payments in management is challenging, it does not face the number of obstacles or offer the rewards that developing a similar system for physicians does. Most facilities with religious affiliations have traditionally rejected the idea because they felt that such compensation was inconsistent with their nonprofit philosophy (Egan, 1986; Jordon and Wyatt, 1984). Other organizations have been apprehensive that the community might not understand or accept the need for incentives.

It has also been attacked from a medical standpoint. According to critics led by the American Medical Association (AMA), there are still questions about the potential problems that could result from economic affiliations between physicians and health care facilities. The AMA has been adamant that the incentive systems pose a threat to quality of care, putting physicians in a bad position by giving them financial benefits based purely on duration of stay. According to the AMA, that could be contradictory to good patient care (Riffer, 1986).

According to a group of researchers, there are also several leftovers from the cost-based system of reimbursement that significantly constrain hospitals from developing ties to their staff physicians (Cohen and Keane, 1983). The conflict comes from several rules instituted historically by Medicare to protect itself against unnecessary payment under a system in which most costs were reimbursed on a retrospective basis:

1. The anti-kickback rule: Generally forbidding the sharing of reimbursement with a third party, except under certain conditions

2. The prudent buyer rule: Limiting reimbursement to the level of costs that a prudent buyer in the community would have incurred

3. The related party rule: Limiting reimbursement for costs paid to a related party to the actual costs to that party (Averill et al., 1984)

According to Averill et al. (1984), "Residual application of these reimbursement rules may compromise the ultimate efficiency of the system in controlling health care costs" because they effectively limit hospitals from forming the kind of economic arrangements that other industries utilize. Despite some early rulings in favor of the idea of incentive compensation, the AMA has continually urged that the issue be extensively examined before it is formally adopted. Health Care Financing Administration (HCFA), with some assistance, is studying the situation (Rust, 1985).

Future of Incentive Payments

Incentive compensation for key hospital personnel, whether physician or managers, is still very much in the pioneering stage (Egan, 1986). Although internal and external pressures to resist such payment schemes are still preventing their spread, competitive pressures are compelling hospitals to overcome their apprehensions about sharing the savings that these managers bring. Despite questions about incentive systems with regard to Medicare fraud and abuse laws and a facility's loss of tax-exempt status, so far both the HCFA and the Internal Revenue Service have ruled favorably toward the development of such payments (Riffer, 1986). In all likelihood, the health care industry will continue the trend toward implementing compensation programs resembling those already in place in general industry (Egan, 1986).

REFERENCES

Altany, D. R. (1987, March 9). Valuable, but not fair. *Industry Week*, 16.
Averill, R. F., Kalison, M. J., Sparrow, D. A., and Owens, T. R. (1984, April). Part 4, Responding to PPS. The outside response. *Healthcare Financial Management*, 98.
Bannister, B. D. (1986). Performance outcome feedback and attributional feedback: Interactive effects on recipient responses. *Journal of Applied Psychology* 71 (2): 203–10.
Barrett, R. S. (1966). *Performance Rating*. Chicago: Science Research Associates.
Becker, B. E., and Cardy, R. L. (1986, November). Influence of halo error on appraisal effectiveness; A conceptual and empirical reconsideration. *Journal of Applied Psychology* 71 (4): 662–71.
Bedeian, A. (1971, Spring). Rater characteristics affecting the validity of performance appraisals. *Journal of Management* 6: 37–45.
Bernardin, H. J., and Beatty, R. (1984). *Performance Appraisal: Assessing Human Behavior at Work*. Boston: Kent.
Bernardin, H. J., and Klatt, L. A. (1985, November). Managerial appraisal systems: Has practice caught up to the state of the art? *Personnel Administrator*, 79–86.
Bernardin, H. J., and Pence, E. C. (1980). Effects of rater training: Creating new response sets and decreasing accuracy. *Journal of Applied Psychology* 65 (1): 60–66.
Boissoneau, R. A. (1984, August). The democratically oriented pharmacy manager. *Topics in Hospital Pharmacy Management*, 44–51.
Boissoneau, R. A., and Edwards, M. R. (1985, March-April). Multiple rate performance appraisals: Solutions for hospital personnel. *Hospital and Health Services Administration*, 54–66.
Borman, W. C. (1977, August 20). Individual difference correlates of rating accuracy using behavior scales. Presented at American Psychological Association, 86th Annual Convention, San Francisco.
——— (1979). Format and training effects of rating accuracy and rater errors. *Journal of Applied Pscyhology* 64 (2): 410–21.
——— (1975). Effects of instructions to avoid halo error on reliability and validity of performance evaluation rating. *Journal of Applied Psychology* 3: 556–60.

Bovbjerg, R. R. (1987, Winter). Incentives versus controls in health policy. *Journal of Policy Analysis and Management* 8: 265–70.
Carroll, S., and Schneier, C. (1982). *Performance Appraisal and Review Systems*. Glenview, Ill.: Scott Foresman.
Channon, B. (1986). Executive incentive plans for hospitals. *Topics in Health Care Financing* 12 (4): 27–38.
Cocheu, T. (1986, September). Performance appraisals: A case in points. *Personnel Journal*, 48–55.
Cohen, H. A., and Keane, J. C. (1983, Fall). The regulator's view of hospital costs. *Topics in Health Care Financing*, 84.
Davis, B. L., and Mount, M. K. (1984, March). Design and use of a performance appraisal feedback system. *Personnel Administrator*, 91–97.
DeCotiss, T. A., and Petit, A. (1978). The performance appraisal process: A model and some testable propositions. *Academy of Management Review* 3: 635–45.
Denton, D. (1987, February). How to conduct effective appraisal interviews. *Administrative Management*, 15–19.
DeVries, D. L., Morrison, A. M., and Shullman, S. L. (1981). *Peformance Appraisal on the Line*. New York: John Wiley.
Dobbins, G. H., and Russell, J. M. (1986). The biasing effects of subordinate likableness on leaders' responses to poor performers: A laboratory and a field study. *Personnel Psychology* 39: 759.
Dorfman, P. W., Stephan, W. G., and Loveland, J. (1986). Performance appraisal behaviors: Supervisor perceptions and subordinate reactions. *Personnel Psychology* 39: 579-97.
Egan, P. S. (1986, September 5). Executive paychecks to jump 4.9% in 86. *Hospitals*, 50.
Farh, J., and Werbel, J. D. (1986). Effects of purpose of the appraisal and expectation of validation on self-appraisal leniency. *Journal of Applied Psychology* 71 (3): 527–29.
Gehrman, D. B. (1984, March). Beyond today's compensation and performance appraisal systems. *Personnel Administrator*, 21–33.
George, J. (1986, May). Appraisal in the public sector: Dispensing with the big stick. *Personnel Management*, 32–35.
Giles, R., and Landauer, C. (1984, March). Setting specific standards for appraising creative staffs. *Personnel Administrator*, 35–47.
Grant, P. C. (1987, March). A better approach to performance reviews. *Management Solutions*, 11–16.
Greene, R. J. (1987, February). Effective compensation: The how and why. *Personnel Administrator*, 112–16.
Henderson, R. (1980). *Performance Appraisal: Theory to Practice*. Reston, Va.: Reston Press.
Heneman, R. L. (1986). The relationship between supervisory ratings and results-oriented measures of performance: A meta-analysis. *Personnel Psychology* 39: 811.
Hobson, C. J., and Gibson, F. W. (1984, March). Capturing supervisor rating policies: A way to improve performance appraisal effectiveness. *Personnel Administrator*, 59–68.
Hospitals more interested in incentives. (1986, April). *Hospitals*, 34–36.

Jordon, D. R., and Wyatt, C. J. (1984, July). Financial pressures force hospitals to take a second look at incentives. *Modern Healthcare*, 140.

Kane. J. S., and Freeman, K. A. (1986, December). MBO and performance appraisal: A mixture that's not a solution, part 1. *Personnel*, 26–36.

────── (1987, February). MBO and performance appraisal: A mixture that's not a solution, part 2. *Personnel*, 26–32.

Kleiman, L. S., and Durham, R. (1981). Performance appraisal: A critical review. *Personnel Psychology* 34: 103–21.

Knight, P. A., and Saal, F. E. (1986). Heroism is no substitute for success: Effects of strategy and outcome on perceptions of performance. *Journal of Occupational Psychology* 59: 81–92.

Landy, F. J., and Farr, J. L. (1980). Performance rating. *Psychological Bulletin* 87: 72–107.

Latham, C. P., and Wexley, K. N. (1981). *Increasing Productivity through Performance Appraisal*. Reading, Mass.: Addison-Wesley.

Lazer, R., and Wikstrom, W. (1977). *Appraising Managerial Performance*. The Conference Board.

Levine, H. Z. (1986, June). Performance appraisals at work. *Personnel*, 63–71.

Long, J. (1985, January 7). What will you be worth to your hospital under DRGs? *Medical Economics*, 142.

McMillan, J. D., and Biondi, C. G. (1986, November). Job evaluation: Generate the numbers. *Personnel Journal*, 56–63.

Malinauskas, B. K., and Clement, R. W. (1987, February). Performance appraisal interviewing for tangible results. *Training and Development Journal*, 74–79.

Mallinger, M. A., and Cummings, T. G. (1986, Spring). Improving the value of performance appraisals. *SAM Advanced Management Journal*, 19–21.

Manuel, P., More, J., and Parkinson, N. (1987, May). Does your appraisal system stack up? *Personnel Journal*, 82–87.

Martin, D. C. (1986, August). Performance appraisal, 2: Improving the rater's effectiveness. *Personnel*, 28–33.

Miner, J. B. (1977). Management appraisal: A review of procedures and practices. In W. Hammer and F. Schmidt (Eds.), *Contemporary Problems in Personnel*, pp. 228–38. Chicago: St. Clair Press.

Naffziger, D. W. (1985, August). BARS, RJPs and recruiting. *Personnel Administrator*, 85–96.

Napier, N. K., and Latham, G. P. (1986). Outcome expectancies of people who conduct performance appraisals. *Personnel Psychology*, 39: 827–37.

Odiorne, G. S. (1987, June). How am I doing? *Working Women*, 32–37.

Pajer, R. G. (1984, June). Performance appraisal: A new era for federal government managers. *Personnel Administrator*, 81–89.

Pearce, J. L., and Porter, L. W. (1986). Employee responses to formal performance appraisal feedback. *Journal of Applied Psychology* 71 (2): 211–18.

Phillips, K. R. (1987, March). Red flags in performance appraisal: How to discover if your performance appraisal system is working. *Training and Development Journal*, 80–82.

Posner, M., Jr. (1982). *Executive Essentials* 24, 231–53.

Rarick, C. A., and Baxter, G. (1986, Winter). Behaviorally anchored rating scales

(BARS): An effective performance appraisal approach. *SAM Advanced Management Journal*, 36–39.
Regal, R. W., and Hollman, R. W. (1987, June). Gauging performance objectively. *Personnel Administrator*, 74–78.
Rice, Berkeley. (1984, March). Reversing performance review. *Psychology Today*, 80.
——— (1985a, September). Performance review: The job nobody likes. *Psychology Today*, 30–36.
——— (1985b, December). Rating people: Performance review. *Current*, 9–13.
Riffer, J. (1986, March 5). Physician-incentive plans may be put on hold. *Hospitals*, 80.
Romberg, R. V. (1986, August). Performance appraisal, 1: Risks and rewards. *Personnel*, 20–26.
Rust, M. (1985, April 26). Changes in market seen restructuring physicians practices. *American Medical News*, 1.
Schmidt, F. L., Hunter, J. E., and Outerbridge, A. N. (1986). Impact of job experience and ability on job knowledge, work sample performance, and supervisory ratings of job performance. *Journal of Applied Psychology*, 71 (3): 432–39.
Schuster, J. R. (1986, March 16). Successful hospitals pay for performance. *Hospitals*, 86–88.
Smith, M. (1987, March). Putting their performance in writing. *Management Solutions*, 5–10.
Snell, S. A., and Wexley, K. N. (1985, April). Performance diagnosis: Identifying the causes of poor performance. *Personnel Administrtor*, 117–27.
Taylor, R. L., and Zawacki, R. A. (1984, March). Trends in performance appraisal: Guidelines for managers. *Personnel Administrator*, 71–80.
Teel, K. S. (1986, March). Are merit raises really based on merit? *Personnel Journal*, 88–95.
Timpe, A. D. (1986, September 5). Motivation of personnel, *Hospital*, 50–55.
Updata [Column] (1986, November). *Healthcare Financial Management*, 6.
——— (1986, December). *Healthcare Financial Management*, 6.
Verespej, M. A. (1987, February 23). Performance appraisals. Still the safest way to fire an employee. *Industry Week*, 5.
Wagel, W. H. (1987, February). Performance appraisal with a difference. *Personnel*, 4–6.
Wexley, K. N., and Snell, S. A. (1987). Managerial power: A neglected aspect of the performance appraisal process. *Journal of Business Resources* 15: 45–54.
Wight, D. T. (1985, May). The split role in performance appraisal. *Personnel Administrator*, 83–87.
Williams, K. J., DeNisi, A. S., Meglino, B. M., and Caffery, T. P. (1986). Initial decisions and subsequent performance ratings. *Journal of Applied Psychology* 71 (2): 189–95.
Zippo, M., and Miller, M. (1984, May–June). Performance appraisal: Current practices and techniques. *Personnel* 61: 57–59.

6
Performance-Based Pay Systems in Health Care

Eugene P. Buccini

Performance-based pay has been around for a long time. From ancient craftsmen who were paid based on the amount and quality of the goods they produced to the modern factory worker who is on an incentive pay program, the goal has always been the same: to base the rewards on the results achieved. Today one of the major changes taking place throughout the health services industry is the introduction of performance-based pay systems or, as Edward Lawler (1981) calls it, the "new pay."

Increases in pay are no longer seen as mainly a factor of completing another year of employment. Rather, with the increasingly competitive market and the focus on productivity, health care organizations more and more are basing pay on performance, thereby changing their organizational culture and values (Wallace, 1987). This chapter will examine performance-based pay systems, their advantages and disadvantages, the different types of systems, the present health care experience, and guidelines for administrators who are considering implementing pay-for-performance systems in their organizations.

PERFORMANCE-BASED PAY: THE SYSTEM

Definitions

In order to discuss the subject of performance-based pay, it is first necessary to have a common definition of terms used to describe the various elements of such systems:

Salary: The pay received by an employee for the services rendered for a certain period of time.

Bonus: An amount of money received over and above salary for achieving certain specified results. Bonuses are usually paid in a lump sum and do not become part of an employee's regular salary.

Merit pay: An amount of money received over and above salary for a job well done. Merit pay usually becomes part of an employee's regular salary.

Performance appraisal: An objective evaluation of an employee's work performance.

Incentive pay: A plan of payment that relates pay of employees to effort and output, either individually or as a group.

Objectives

The basic objectives of a performance-based pay system are to:

1. Directly reward the employee for his or her efforts and results achieved
2. Tie the individual and/or group's objectives to the objectives of management and/or the organization
3. Provide a system to motivate employees to increase their performance levels

In establishing a performance-based pay system, care should be given to ensure that the plan meets these basic objectives.

Development in Health Care

While performance-based pay has been used by business organizations for a number of years, only recently has this trend developed in health service organizations. In fact, the number of health care institutions with incentive plans increased from 40 percent to 62 percent between 1984 and 1986 (Jones, 1986). In a survey of 132 hospitals, 76 were using incentive–merit pay plans compared with 56 that indicated they were not (Sellentin, 1985). In another survey, Cole (1986) found that the number of health care executives who received bonuses increased to 1,106, representing 10.1 percent of the CEOs, 9.5 percent of associate administrators, and 9.6 percent of directors of nursing.

The cause of this increase is the change in health care environment itself. With the advent of the DRG system, cost controls, and increased government regulation, hospitals have had their own reimbursement tied to results. Hospitals are now rewarded on the basis of efficiency, and the money available to reward managers and employees must come from the results of this efficiency.

The second reason for the growth of performance-based pay systems in the health care sector is the increase in competitiveness in the health services arena. Hospitals are competing with other hospitals for the same patient base; hospital-based programs are competing with nursing home-based programs and with home care programs of various kinds. In some cases, health services organizations are competing with the same physicians who provide services to these organizations. As with any other competition, there are usually winners and there are losers, and to the victors go the spoils. Therefore the achievement of organizational goals becomes essential for survival and growth. In order to ensure such achievement, health service organizations are using systems that reward those who contribute to their success.

The move to the entrepreneurial approach also has fostered interest in pay for performance. Underlying the philosophy of entrepreneurship are the two pillars of risk and reward. By taking calculated risks, one can increase the opportunity for success. With this success comes reward. Therefore, if organizations wish to instill this entrepreneurial approach in their managers and employees, they must develop systems that encourage risk taking for greater rewards. This philosophy is the basis of pay-for-performance systems. Carner (1984) has noted the results of profit sharing in both profit and not-for-profit organizations, concluding that employees earn more, the organization profits more, and the client receives a better value.

PERFORMANCE-BASED PAY: THE EVIDENCE

Performance-based pay systems have distinct advantages and disadvantages. Whether an organization should adopt such a system therefore requires careful review of both the advantages and disadvantages in regard to the organization itself.

Advantages

Among the many advantages of performance-based pay systems are the following:

Pay is tied to results: the amount of money a person earns is directly tied to his or her contribution to the organization. Pay is based on results and not time in position, friendship, or political influence.

Productivity increases: Because people tend to work harder in order to maximize their pay, the amount paid is directly tied to what is accomplished, thus increasing individual or group productivity.

Potential for increased earnings: Performance-based pay systems provide the opportunity for employees to control their own pay levels. A person has the potential to increase his or her earnings based on his or her own individual (or group) performance.

Increased attention to organizational objectives: Since performance-based pay systems tie pay increases to organizational objectives, they have the advantage of focusing a manager's or an employee's attention on specific objectives that are considered organizationally important at the time.

Potential for increased satisfaction: Since employees now have direct input into determining their own pay, the potential exists for increasing employee satisfaction and morale.

Effective recruitment tool: Given the opportunity to be paid based on results usually appeals to achievement-oriented individuals. These are the same people who tend to be entrepreneurial in their approach to work. Thus, the organization that utilizes a pay-for-performance system will be better able to attract these types of individuals.

Disadvantages

Among the disadvantages are the following:

More disparate pay structure: Since each person receives a different level of increase (based on individual or group performance), the pay structure will become less and less structured, resulting in compression and equity issues.

Increased dissatisfaction: Just as there is the potential for increased employee satisfaction, there is also the potential for increased dissatisfaction. This may arise from perceived unfairness with the system, jealousy, frustration with continuous rewards that are less than others, or dissatisfaction with salary compression.

Administrative cost and complexity: Performance-based pay systems are considerably more complex than the simple across-the-board raise system. As a result, they tend to cost more in terms of time and resources needed for implementation.

Limited application: While performance-based pay systems can work with all levels of employees, they do not necessarily work under all conditions. For example, they usually do not work when there is a limited pool of money available for raises, when the market rate of jobs is increasing very rapidly, or when there is a critical shortage of supply of labor in a particular field (e.g., nursing). In this last case, large increases in salary, often in rapid succession, are usually necessary to attract and retain these employees. Therefore performance-based pay becomes less effective.

Necessity for greater communication: Utilizing a performance-based pay system requires a substantial amount of increased communication between administration and employees covered by such a system. Included are communications regarding organizational objectives, potential rewards, and interim assessments as to how well the employees are doing. Not all organizations are ready or willing to spend the extra time or resources required for this communication.

Money as the only motivator: Once a performance-based pay system is established, organizations may fail to recognize sources of motivation other than money, such as intrinsic job satisfaction, increasing levels of responsibility and authority, and high level of management-employee trust (Milkovich and Newman, 1984). Should the entire objective of one's job become the attainment of additional dollars, many who entered the health care field for reasons other than money may be turned off. In fact, managers and employees involved in direct patient care may see this emphasis on money as having an adverse effect on patient care (Browdy, 1985).

VARIATIONS IN SYSTEMS

There are numerous variations of the performance-based pay system, each meeting the specific needs of specific organizations.

Merit Pay Plans

Merit plans tie compensation increases to employee performance. In the health service industry, merit pay plans usually involve a merit increase to an employee's salary based on the results of a performance review. Such a review, which usually takes place over a one-year period (or more often), assesses the employee's performance based on the actual job the employee is performing, accomplishing defined objectives, and achievement of some other specified criteria. The concept of a merit pay plan is to provide salary increases based on merit rather than longevity, organizational membership, or some other nonperformance-related criteria.

Simple Incentive Plans

These plans are short-term incentive plans that are usually based on a piece-rate or hourly rate. Each is meant to reward employees for producing units of output above a preset level.

The piece-rate system is perhaps the oldest form of incentive compensation, going back to ancient craftsmen and currently having acceptance in factory or goods-producing jobs. The employee is paid a set amount for each unit of work produced (e.g., each laboratory test made or each X-ray taken) or is paid a premium for producing units of output above a certain number within a given period of time. In order to assess the proper levels at which to pay an incentive, careful job studies must be made. It is paramount to set rates at a fair standard for both the organization and the individual. Because of the complexity of health care, it is difficult and time-consuming to develop piece-rate standards for most jobs. Therefore this system is not widely used by health services organizations today.

The standard hour plan is a variation of piece-rate system is is especially suited for clerical employees. It is based on a calculation of units produced beyond the standard, at which the employee would receive incentive compensation based on his or her increase.

The advantage of simple incentive plans is that they are easy to administer. The disadvantage is that they have limited use in the health services industry.

Gain Sharing

Gain sharing is a compensation plan that rewards performance against goals. The focus is primarily on cost savings. Should an employee(s) reach the target set and this results in cost savings for the organization, the employee(s) then shares in the savings, usually in the form of a cash bonus. Gain sharing has become popular in industry and is now being applied to the health care environment.

Scanlon Plan

The Scanlon plan, originally developed in an effort to reduce costs in a steel mill, is a variation of gain sharing. It usually encompasses all employees, including management, and is geared to produce labor efficiently. The dollars saved through reduced labor costs are distributed to the employees (75 percent) and to the organization (25 percent). Because the plan includes all employees, it promotes teamwork.

Profit Sharing

Profit sharing refers to the practice of awarding employees a share, fixed in advance, of the profits earned by an organization. It usually serves to produce teamwork and act as a group incentive. Unfortunately, profit sharing in the past has been overly represented by one basic type—deferred compensation. Using this method, the employees do not actually share in the profits until they are ready to retire. This is little incentive for the worker today. More progressive profit-sharing plans provide for the profits to be paid out directly upon calculation of the project.

Bonus Plans

Bonus plans usually are based on specific accomplishments during a set period of time. Their unique feature is that they are granted on a one-time, lump-sum basis as opposed to a merit award, which becomes part of an employee's salary. Therefore an employee has to earn his or her bonus based on accomplishments each year.

Another advantage is that since the bonus is paid out on a lump-sum basis, the amount usually appears larger than what one would receive if it were paid out in partial payments on a weekly basis. Thus it has a far more significant effect in tying reward to results.

Skill-Based Pay

This is another name for pay-for-knowledge systems. The basis for this system is that a worker can gain additional dollars for learning new tasks. The more tasks an employee is able to perform, the higher is his or her pay. The highest rate is reached when all positions are learned.

In recent study, the U.S. Department of Labor found that pay-for-knowledge systems are used by about 8 percent of U.S. corporations listed on the American and New York stock exchanges, although primarily in manufacturing industries (Gupta, 1986). This has the advantage of increasing organizational effectiveness (by having workers who can do several tasks) and providing a motivation to learn as well. The one major negative to this system is that it requires a high investment in training on the part of the organization.

PERFORMANCE-BASED PAY IN HEALTH CARE

In 1986, the American Compensation Association and the American Productivity Center cooperated in a survey of 3,000 employees to determine the use of alternative compensation design (O'Dell, 1986). The percentages of those surveyed who were using alternative compensation designs are as follows:

Profit sharing, 32 percent

Lump-sum bonus, 30 percent

Individual incentives, 28 percent

Gain sharing, 13 percent

Small group incentives, 14 percent

All salaried workforce, 11 percent

Two-tier pay plan, 11 percent

Pay for knowledge, 5 percent

Earned time off, 6 percent

In addition, the survey provided data regarding the future. In fact, many of the firms not using alternative compensation designs plan to do so in the next five years. The increase in percentages of those planning new designs are as follows:

All salaried, 31 percent

Pay for knowledge, 75 percent

Gain sharing, 68 percent

Profit sharing, 20 percent

Small group incentives, 70 percent

Individual incentives, 31 percent

Lump-sum bonus, 29 percent

Two-tier pay plan, 33 percent

Earned time off, 36 percent

The study was not limited to health services organizations, but it does serve as a benchmark as to the coming changes in compensation practices, especially in performance-based pay.

Exhibit 6.1
Barnes Hospital Incentive Plan

Level	Components	Weight	% of Base Salary in bonus	Total Potential Bonus (as % of Salary)
President	Profit Sharing	50%	up to 15%	30%
	Formulation of Strategies	50%	up to 15%	
Executive Vice President	Profit Sharing	40%	up to 10%	
	Formulation * Implementation of Strategies	40%	up to 10%	25%
	Avg. of V.P. Productivity Improvement Payments	20%	up to 5%	
Department Head	Profit Sharing	33 1/3%	up to 5%	
	Implementation of Approved Dept. Goals	33 1/3%	up to 5%	15%
	Department Productivity Improvement	33 1/3%	up to 5%	
Manager	Profit Sharing	30%	up to 3%	
	Implementation of approved dept. goals	35%	up to 3.5%	10%
	Department productivity improvement	35%	up to 3.5%	
Staff	Profit Sharing	50%	up to 3%	6%
	Department productivity improvement	50%	up to 3%	

While industry has been developing and using performance-based pay systems at an increasing rate over the last five years, a number of hospitals have also begun their own systems. In each case, the system used was designed to meet the specific needs and culture of the particular hospital. In a major teleconference presentation, "Incentive Compensation in the Health Care Industry," the American Hospital Association illustrates the details of the performance-based systems of three such hospitals.

Barnes Hospital

The system at Barnes Hospital, St. Louis, Missouri, is primarily a bonus system that provides for different incentive opportunities based on the level of employee. At Barnes Hospital, all levels of staff have the opportunity to earn a bonus.

The key to the Barnes Hospital program is the different elements of the job that incentive is focused on for each level of employee. This recognizes that each level has different responsibilities for profitability, achieving specific objectives, and so on. The results of this program are encouraging: a profitability increase, as well as gains in productivity, morale, and the sense of ownership by employees.

San Pedro Peninsula

A different approach was used by San Pedro Peninsula Hospital in San Pedro, California. This program was limited to managers and was unique in that not only were managers able to earn more than their base salary but part of this base salary was put at risk as well. In this program, the market median rate is determined for a particular job. The base salary at San Pedro is then calculated at this rate less 5 percent. This 5 percent is considered the incentive threshold. Managers are encouraged to reach this threshold based on performance. The program was designed so that 90 percent of the managers could meet this threshold level. Beyond this threshold is the incentive target. This incentive target is up to an additional 5 percent above the threshold level.

Thus, a manager, based on performance, can earn only 95 percent of the median market rate for his or her job or up to 105 percent of this rate. Beyond this target level is a third category, the maximum level, based on truly exceptional service. Only a few managers are expected to achieve this level. This is another example of a performance-based pay system geared to rewarding managers for performance.

Planned Parenthood

A still different approach was used at Planned Parenthood in Schenectady, New York. The performance share system, which I developed, is based on the concept that each individual has a stake in the overall performance of the organization while being responsible for his or her own performance.

At the beginning of each year, a percentage of surplus is allocated to a performance pool. Management then determines a set number of organizational objectives. At the end of each year for each objective achieved, each employee receives one performance share. Each employee also can receive performance shares based on his or her individual performance as determined by the annual performance appraisal. At the end of the year, the total potential shares are divided into the allocated surplus in order to determine the value of each share. Each employee's earned shares are then multiplied by the share value to determine the total bonus available (which is given in a lump-sum payment). The advantage of this system is that both organizational performance and individual performance are rewarded.

Although a manager may want to maneuver to get the majority of resources available in order to achieve his or her personal objectives, this person may be denying himself or herself the opportunity to earn organizational performance shares had a more deserving department received these resources. The other benefit of such a plan is that the payout varies each year based on the surplus achieved and does not get built into the salary.

The literature on the use of performance pay systems in health services organizations is limited but growing. Shyavitz, Rosenbloom, and Conover (1985) list hospitals that have experimented with various types of incentive systems. What is especially noteworthy is the vast difference in plans implemented by different health services organizations. Clearly the culture and needs of an organization have a strong influence on what system is adopted.

GUIDELINES FOR ADMINISTRATORS

In establishing a performance-based pay system, administrators have many choices to make and pitfalls to avoid. Organizational changes that affect an individual's pay are an extremely volatile issue. Therefore it is essential that caution be taken to ensure the success of such a program. In addition, one cannot merely take a performance-based pay system used at one health care organization and use it in another hospital or nursing home. Such systems must be tied to the culture, goals, and staff of the organization in which it is to be implemented. Following are guidelines for administrators to consider for designing and implementing a performance-based pay system.

Key Criteria

In designing a performance-based system, a number of criteria are necessary for the success of such a system (see the checklist in Exhibit 6.2):

Competitive base salary: One of the most important criteria for success is that the organization have a competitive base salary before beginning a performance-based pay system (Doud and Kazemek, 1986). Otherwise, managers and employees alike will tend to manipulate the reward system in order to provide the basic external equity that they feel should have been in place all along.

Internal equity: An organization must have a pay system that is internally equitable in order to avoid the same type of manipulation that occurs when salaries are not competitive externally. The primary focus of the performance-based pay system must be rewarding performance, not correcting organizational pay inequities.

Criteria-based performance appraisal: Since the performance-based pay system is based on rewarding results, the measurement system must be valid and reliable. For merit-based pay systems and others, this means having a criteria-based performance appraisal system. This appraisal system must accurately and objectively measure the effectiveness and/or results of an employee's performance. This becomes even more essential when the amount of a person's pay will be based on this measurement system.

Trust in management: Because performance-based pay systems have a variable

Exhibit 6.2
Checklist for Developing a Performance-Based Pay System

Do you have competitive base salaries? ___
Is your current pay system internally equitable? ___
Do you have a criteria-based performance appraisal system? ___
Does a high level of trust in management exist? ___
Is there open communication? ___
Does your system provide potential for high earnings? ___
Is the potential award known ahead of time? ___
Is pay truly based on performance? ___
Does the employee have control over his or her performance? ___
Is the performance measurable? ___
Are the units of output identifiable? ___
Is the measurement quantifiable? ___
Do the employees covered understand the plan? ___
Do those covered perceive the plan to be equitable and fair? ___
Does management give the plan its proper attention? ___
Are your managers trained in effective management techniques? ___
Are all those covered by the plan trained to do their jobs? ___
Is training updated on a regular basis to keep pace with the changes in the health care environment? ___

pay-out, it is essential that those covered by such a system have a high degree of trust in management. Otherwise there will be a high degree of resentment toward management if one does not obtain the reward he or she was expecting (blaming the results on a management that was not trusted in the first place).

Open communication: management must maintain open communication with its employees during this process. Those covered by a performance-based pay plan must know how well they are performing and must have information available to them regarding the performance indicators used, such as the organization's profit, revenue, earnings, or market share.

Potential for high earnings: In order to be effective, a performance-based pay system must offer those covered by the plan the opportunity to make substantially higher earnings than they otherwise might have made to provide them with the necessary incentive to strive and stretch. In addition, the potential award must be specified so that the employee knows what he or she is striving for.

Pay based on performance: In order for a performance-based pay system to work, pay truly must be based on performance. This must be clearly spelled out in the plan, and it should be visible by the results obtained.

Employee control over performance: For this system to work, the employee must be able to exert direct control over his or her own performance. While some performance goals may be tied to overall organizational effectiveness, the employee's ability to influence this effectiveness must be tied to his or her own performance.

Performance and output must be measurable: The organization must be able to measure performance and output in a valid and reliable way. This pertains to the individual's own performance, as well as to the overall organizational performance. Such performance measures must be as objective as possible and should be quantifiable. The unit's output must also be easily identified, be measurable, and, where appropriate, be quantifiable.

Employee understanding: The employees covered by the plan should understand all of the elements of the plan, including what is expected of them, how the plan works, the measurement system that is used, and the pay-out that can be expected. In addition, the employees should perceive the system as equitable and fair to themselves, to their work group, and to the organization.

Management attention: For such a system to work, management must give it constant attention. There needs to be a regular assessment as to what is being accomplished and what is not. There must be continuous communication with those covered by the plan. There must also be continuous reinforcement of the importance of the results of the plan to the organization and to those employees covered.

Trained managers and employees: It is important to the success of such a plan that the managers and employees covered by it be fully trained in how to use the plan and how to perform their own roles. Managers must be effective as managers if they are to lead their employees to success. All individuals covered by the plan must be trained to do their own jobs if they are to accomplish their goals. This is especially true in today's ever-changing health care environment.

Involvement in the program: In designing a performance-based pay plan, two basic questions need to be answered: Who should be involved in the actual design of such a program, and who is to be covered by it? The first question has a more standard answer. The key players who must be involved include the chief executive officer, the chief operating officer, the heads of human resources, finance, planning, the general counsel, board of trustees, staff and line managers, and outside consultants. Each has a significant role to play in the process.

The chief executive officer is a key role in that the members of the organization have to see the CEO as solidly behind the pay-for-performance plan. It is the CEO who ultimately implements the organization's strategic plan. Therefore, when rewards are tied to the overall goals of the organization, the CEO has to be perceived as lending his or her support to both the goals and the rewards for achieving them.

The chief operating officer is in charge of the day-to-day affairs of the health care organization. It is he or she who is usually most aware of impediments and roadblocks that exist within the organization that could limit the effectiveness of a performance-based pay plan. As a result, he or she also has a key role to participate in the plan's design and implementation.

The chief planning officer is usually responsible for the strategic and long-range plans of the organization. Just as the chief human resource officer serves as the technical resource person for human resources, so does the chief planning officer serve as the technical resource person for planning. Thus, he or she serves in a key capacity when rewards are tied to achieving the strategic plans of the organization.

The chief financial officer's role is to ensure that any pay plan designed meets the fiscal needs of the organization, especially with regard to pay-outs, impact on financial stability, and cash flow. In addition, since many of the measures of performance for upper-level managers are key financial components such as revenue, earnings, and return on investment, it is imperative that the chief financial officer be involved in the design and implementation of the plan.

The general counsel is responsible to ensure that any performance-based pay plan meets the legal requirement of the Internal Revenue Service, especially with regard to not-for-profit health services organizations. He or she must ensure that the tax-exempt state of the organization is not threatened by the pay plan.

The board of trustees ultimately determines the strategic direction of the organization and must approve all policies, including those that involve pay and rewards. It is important that the board be involved in the design of the plan in order to ensure that it meets the goals and criteria determined by the board for the organization as a whole.

The managers themselves, who either are included in a performance-based pay plan and/or who manage employees who are, should be involved in the design of the plan. Their impact is invaluable; they are on the direct firing line and often have the best knowledge on pitfalls, obstacles, and opportunities regarding their employees.

Outside consultants are generally used by organizations without sufficient technical expertise in the area of performance-based pay systems. However, in addition to the obvious benefit of providing technical expertise, outside consultants can act as facilitators. They can help bridge differences between the various, often powerful managers who are designing the program and may also be in a better position to answer some of the hard questions, especially with regard to whether the organization has the necessary criteria in place in order for the pay plan to be successful.

The second question that needs to be answered is who should be covered by the performance-based pay plan. The possibilities include the chief executive officer, the chief operating officer, all officers of the organization, department heads, middle-level managers, supervisors, all employees or any combination of these. The level of inclusion in the performance-based pay plan depends on many variables. Browdy (1986) has suggested the following guidelines for determining the management level:

- Positions upon which the institution is absolutely dependent for growth and a competitive market position
- Actions and decisions that have an impact across organizational lives
- Direct responsibility for substantial fiscal, material, and human resources
- Direct responsibility for implementing board policies

Of course, an institution may want to include all employees in a performance-based pay plan. In fact, the organization may even use different types of plans for different groups of employees.

Measures of Performance

Perhaps nothing distinguishes one organization's performance-based pay plan from another's more than the measures of performance that are utilized. These vary from institution to institution and, in some cases, within the institution itself, based on actual management level. The most common measures of performance used are:

Market share
Revenue
Earnings
Return on investment
Productivity
Cost containment
Program development
Goal attainment
Quality of care

While each of these measures is different, all serve to focus the individual's or group's efforts. In fact, in determining what measures of performance to use, it is first necessary to determine at what levels performance objectives will be set in order to focus these measures. The targets are generally at one of four levels (or a combination of each):

Institutional goals: Goals that focus on overall institutional activities and performance
Departmental goals: Goals that focus on departmental activities and performance
Team toals: Goals that focus on a team's activities and performance
Individual goals: Goals that focus on departmental activities and performance

Each of these has different positive effects. For example, because institutional goals (e.g., overall patient satisfaction) are obtained on an institution-wide basis, everyone in the plan must work together to achieve this goal. Therefore teamwork, interdepartmental relations, and overall institutional communication are generally improved. Where the focus is in departmental goals, interdepartmental cooperation and teamwork are generally improved. Where the focus is on individual goals, the individual identifies the most with this goal, and there is a direct impact on the individual's performance. Overall achievement on the part of the individual is generally greater when the individual's goals are the focus.

Thus, each system must be geared to the specific goals and concomitant improvements the organization is serving. Each combination is different and has a different effect. In the Planned Parenthood of Schenectady's Performance Share Program, 70 percent of the potential performance shares were based on the attainment of institutional goals and 30 percent were based on individual goals. Clearly the emphasis of this program was on building teamwork and improved interdepartmental relations, as well as achievement. For some organizations, this is the right mix. For others, different combinations of goals will meet their particular needs.

Performance Pay-out

Just as there are many variations of the measures of performance, there are also a number of questions regarding how to pay out the reward, to whom it should go, and the level of managerial discretion.

Merit award versus bonus: The merit award involves rewarding the individual with a salary increase, usually in terms of a percentage. Merit awards usually vary with the level of achievement. The key characteristic is that it becomes part of an individual's regular salary. The bonus usually is a lump-sum payment that can be a percentage of salary or a flat dollar amount. It varies based on the level of achievement.

Individual versus group incentive: Decisions will have to be made whether to give out the award based on individual effort or a group effort. If a group effort is chosen (as in some salary plans), an overall award can be made to a group (or department), and it will divide it among its members.

Formula versus discretion: A decision will have to be made whether to have the award based strictly on a predetermined formula or whether to allow a manager discretion in giving monetary awards to those who report to him or her. While organizationally the formula-based systems are the most objective and most equitable, managers usually prefer to have some discretion in the size of the award. They feel that this is needed in order to provide for the intangibles (other goals that are not included in the plan) and for any changes or extenuating circumstances.

Full-time versus part-time: Decisions will have to be made on whether to apply the plan only to full-time employees or to provide it to part-timers as well.

Exhibit 6.3
Organizational Readiness Questionnaire

ENVIRONMENTAL ASSESSMENT

Would the key leaders in your organization be supportive of an incentive compensation system?
- ___ Chairman, Board of Trustees
- ___ Chief Executive Officer
- ___ Chief Operating Officer
- ___ Vice President, Finance
- ___ Vice President, Human Resources
- ___ Vice President, Nursing
- ___ Vice President, Medical Staff

Who should be included in development of an Incentive System?
- ___ Key Staff Departments
- ___ Key Line Managers

Will you need an outside consultant to assist in designing the incentive plan? If so, what firms do you want to invite to start a proposal?

Does your health care organization currently have a criteria-based performance planning and evaluation system?

What outcomes/results do you want to achieve as a result of an incentive compensation system?

Which health care system organizations can you contact that have already implemented an incentive compensation system? Can the AHA or your state or metropolitan health care association assist you in identifying outside resources?

Who will be involved in approving a plan to provide incentives?

PLAN DESIGN

Who should be eligible to receive incentives?
- ___ Corporate Management Staff
- ___ Executive Management
- ___ Middle Management
- ___ Supervisory Staff
- ___ All Employees
- ___ Medical Staff

At what level should performance objectives be set?
- ___ Corporation wide
- ___ Organization wide
- ___ Division or departmental
- ___ Team
- ___ Individual

Source: J.D. Browdy, "Incentive Compensation in the Health Care Sector," *Incentive Systems That Work: Rewarding High Performance*. Teleconference, Chicago, American Hospital Association, 1986.

Exhibit 6.4
Building Success into a Pay-for-Performance System

1. When you give an economic adjustment, do you raise your salaries proportionately?
2. What have you done to change your culture to an entrepreneurial, or at least, market-based, environment?
3. What do you plan to do?
4. To what extent does the average employee influence the overall success of the organization?
5. Do you currently have an open, trusting climate? On a scale of 1 to 100, how open and trusting is your environment?
6. Do you actively communicate with employees at least once per month? How?
7. Will the focus of making extra money available for raises be based on additional income or reduced costs?
8. How will you arrive at a total figure for a raise each year?
9. Will you still give economic adjustments? If not, how will you keep your entry level salaries competitive?
10. Is the productivity adjustment planned as an increase in salary or a bonus?
11. Do you plan to factor out poor executive decisions from the productivity increases due? If so, how?
12. How do you plan to rationalize to employees of a particular department - who have done extremely well in cutting costs- that there will be no productivity increase because two additional departments have exceeded their budgets?
13. Are you prepared to accept employee recommendations openly?
14. Are you prepared to spend the necessary time and money to train all staff so that you will have a supportive organizational climate?
15. How competitive are you with your job market?
16. Are you experiencing high turnover in any particular positions?
17. Are you having any recruitment problems?

Including part-timers increases the complexity of the plan and may cause the skewing of pay and ultimately the resentment of full-timers if the part-time employee's pay reaches that of a full-time employee working more hours. However, part-time employees contribute to the organization's goals, and in today's environment, they may constitute a large percentage of an institution's workforce.

Circuit Breakers

Circuit breakers are minimum achievements that must be met before any incentives are paid off. There needs to be a set of checks or circuit breakers in order to prevent large amounts of money being paid out where certain basic goals are not achieved, even though they may not be part of the stated goals in the official plan. One example might be that individuals in a department may achieve all their goals, yet the department fails the Joint Commission on Accreditation of Hospitals' survey. Examples of such circuit breakers include:

- Maintenance of accreditation
- Minimum profit level
- Employee must have passed probation for eligibility
- Employee must not be on disciplinary probation
- A person must be employed at the time awards are distributed in order to qualify to receive them.

By using the circuit breakers on the needs of the culture of the organization, the overall system will be more equitable to both employees and the organization itself.

Legal Concerns

For the not-for-profit health care organizations, there are a number of considerations regarding performance-based pay plans that should be reviewed with legal counsel. One important such concern involves the criteria determined by the IRS in order for the organization to maintain its tax-exempt status (Hranchak, 1985). The criteria include responsibilities, whether productivity is achieved, external review by the board of trustees, and whether there is a cap on the maximum pay-out.

Performance-based pay systems are becoming the future for health services organizations. It is important to keep in mind, however, that the details of each system are as varied as each organization that adopts one. Therefore, it is essential that the plan be designed and implemented in such a way as to focus on the particular organization's goals, culture, and history. (See Exhibits 6.3 and 6.4.)

REFERENCES

Browdy, J. D. (1985, July). Tips for tailoring an incentive compensation plan to your employee's needs. *Trustee*.

——— (1986). Incentive compensation in the health care sector. *Incentive Systems That Work: Rewarding High Performance*. Teleconference, Chicago, American Hospital Association.

Carner, D. C. (1984, September-October). Carner's Codes: Chapt. 15—Incentive compensation. *Hospital Forum* 27 (5): 59–61.
Cole, B. S. (1986, November 7). More facilities use incentives to reward executives. *Modern Healthcare*.
Doud. E., and Kazemek, E. A. (1986, February). Building an effective incentive pay plan. *Healthcare Financial Management* 40 (2).
Gupta, N. G. et al. (1986). *Explanatory Investigations of Pay-for-Knowledge Systems*. Washington, D.C.: U.S. Department of Labor.
Hranchak, W. H. (1985, Fall). Incentive compensation and benefits of profit-sharing plans. *Topics in Health Care Financing* 12 (1): 33–37.
Jones, K. (1986). Speech given at ASHRRA conference. *Employee Relations Weekly* 4 (30).
Lawler, E. (1981). *Pay and Organizational Development*. Reading, Mass.: Addison-Wesley.
Milkovich, G., and Newman, J. M. (1984). *Compensation*. Plano, Tex.: Business Publications.
O'Dell, C. (1986). *People, Performance and Pay: America Responds to the Competitive Challenge*. Scottsdale, Ariz.: American Compensation Association.
Sellentin, J. L. (1985). Survey says hospitals are currently more interested in incentive-pay-for-performance plans. *Incentive Systems That Work: Rewarding High Performance*. Teleconference, Chicago, American Hospital Association.
Shyavitz, L., Rosenbloom, D., Conover, L. (1985, November). Financial incentives for middle managers. *Health Care Management Review*.
Wallace, M. J., Jr. (1987). *Innovative Rewards: The Art of Strategy*. Designing Strategic Reward Systems Conference. Scottsdale, Ariz.: American Compensation Association.

7
Designing a Compensation System in the Strategic Human Resource Management Model

Lois Friss

Organizations compensate individuals for performing work necessary to make a product or perform the services that enable the organization to survive and prosper—to achieve strategic objectives. Individuals work for other reasons than pay, but most health care workers, like other workers, expect to be paid fairly considering education, experience, skills, responsibility, and working conditions.

Total payroll is a function of many elements: staffing mix and level, hourly rate, fringe benefits, and management's ability to control scheduling, absenteeism, and turnover. This chapter discusses only the basic system for direct pay. Trends of special concern to health care managers, such as recurring nursing shortages, supply of unskilled workers, corporate office relations, and government control of wage rates, are also examined. Now that organizations are being held accountable for both quality of care and cost-effectiveness, health care managers need a sound pay system as the base for paying differentials related to performance.

TRENDS

The major external forces affecting health care compensation strategies include the probability of nursing shortages, reliance on unskilled labor, tensions between local and corporate offices in multihospital systems, and government control of wage rates. Because hospitals dominate the pay systems of health workers, much of the literature and many of the examples are from these organizations. The trends and principles apply equally to other health care organizations, however, and can be adapted with little modification.

Recurrent Shortages of Professional Workers

Nurses and other allied health professionals are subject to recurring shortages. Nurses are the largest single group of health care employees. Because their pay effectively establishes the pay of many other groups—laboratory technicians and therapists, for example—and because much of the research has been conducted in nursing, this discussion is limited to nurses. The underlying dynamics can often be applied to other health professions. Considerable evidence suggests that when nurses' incomes rise relative to those of other workers, more nurses are available for hospital employment, and vacancy rates decline (Aiken, and Mullinix, 1987). A 1 percent increase in nursing wages relative to other professional, technical, and kindred occupations leads to a 1.5 percent increase in entrants to nursing schools within two years (nine dollars per month in the late 1970s) (U.S. DHHS, 1981).

The recurring shortage of nurses is thus attributed in part to the sluggish response of local markets to raise nursing pay, which eventually necessitates an above-average pay increase to attract enough nurses. This ratchet pay adjustment system has worked because female high school graduates had low career aspirations and few alternatives and benefited from the low unemployment rate and flexible hours. At the same time, the federal government subsidized basic nursing education ($1.6 billion since 1964), keeping the pipeline full.

Now that women have many career alternatives and higher aspirations for full-time careers, nursing and allied health schools are accepting less qualified students (as measured by SAT scores). Enrollments are dropping, especially in baccalaureate prgrams, which form the pool for teachers and administrators. The federal government no longer supports entry-level education since no national shortage of licensed nurses exists and nurses can obtain loans like other students.

To keep enough full-time competent nurses, hospitals need to lengthen the career ladder for bedside nurses. Current career ladders only partially compensate for the few grades and steps. Employers will need to offer a differential of 100 percent between entry level and retirement rather than the modest career plans they now provide (Ginzberg et al., 1982; Beyers et al., 1983). In addition, if the quality of the workforce is to be maintained, it will be necessary to have pay differentials for education, experience, and tenure. These differentials did not exist in 1980 (Institute of Medicine, 1983).

Placing nurses on salary may also be a method of improving job satisfaction, especially if they are also given authority to establish staffing schedules, expand nursing activities, and provide for peer review of performance (Dear, Weisman, and O'Keefe, 1985). Since salaried nurses are not eligible for overtime, shift, and charge differentials, they earned 12.2 percent higher base pay. Even if

Designing a Compensation System

salaried costs were higher, management can save by hiring fewer contract or replacement workers.

More Unskilled Workers

So long as the pay differential between the highly skilled and educated and other workers is modest, health care organizations can afford to have a high proportion of professionals. When health care organizations have to pay more to retain highly qualified professionals, it will be necessary to rely on more auxiliary workers and manage them better.[1] In some areas, a shortage of low-wage entrants exists because the effect of declining birthrates during the 1960s has not been offset by a high immigration rate. Even when the supply of low wage workers is adequate, employers will be challenged to find innovative ways to reward compassionate and competent auxiliary workers.

Corporate and Regional Office Mandates

An important trend is the influence of the corporate office of multihospital systems. Although over 30 percent of all hospital beds are owned, leased, or managed by multihospital systems, there is little literature on how they influence pay decisions of local organizations. There are predictable phases in the development of the systems (Freund and Mitchell, 1985). At first the systems emphasize financing, diversification, and employee benefits (incentives). Later strategic planning becomes important. Beyond that, corporate systems vary considerably on the amount of decentralization and autonomy they allow individual units in establishing staffing standards and pay rates.

Emphasis on Quality Control

Purchasers of services, especially governments, are increasingly asking if patient outcomes justify the costs of care. The Joint Commission on the Accreditation of Hospitals will be using computer protocols to compare hospital mortality rates. It is only a matter of time before awareness that quality outcomes depend on group effort will modify the pay system. There may be changes in structural arrangements between risk management, quality assurance, continuing education, performance appraisal, and pay.

Government Control of Wage Rates

There are many forces exerting downward pressure on hospital wages—four direct and the others indirect.

1. The Health Care Financing Administration uses a wage index provided by the Bureau of Labor Statistics to calculate routine, special care, and ancillary operating cost reimbursement under Medicare (Prospective Payment Assessment

Commission, 1985; Fackelman, 1985a, 1985b; Greene, 1980; Watland et al., 1983). This not only places an upper limit on the amount of money available for hospital operations but also perpetuates the relative position of hospital workers.

2. Budget pressures make it unlikely that Congress will permit more than marginal increases in DRG payments for the next few years. The continuing possibility that the rates will be frozen dampens employer willingness to enter into multiyear contracts with wage increases. Reports that 57 percent of hospitals received more than it cost to treat patients under prospective rather than cost-based reimbursement makes it difficult to convince legislators and bureaucrats that hospitals lack funds to increase salaries.

3. The courts have consistently reaffirmed state laws regulating health care, including costs. When reduced state funding limited hospitals' ability to increase wages, the federal courts ruled that the resulting loss in bargaining power of the employees is not an impermissible attempt to interfere with collective bargaining (Burda, 1986).

4. State rate commissions interfere with hospital bargaining settlements, limiting increases by use of a formula or retrospective review of labor settlements (Schramm, 1978).

5. Internal Revenue Service rulings limit innovative approaches, such as cafeteria benefit plans.

6. The tax code penalizes two-income families (Leuthold, 1984). Since the majority of female professionals are married, their real pay is less than management believes.

7. The American Hospital Association has a Comparable Worth Task Force whose mission is to counteract comparable worth activity.

8. In metropolitan areas, it is common for hospitals, through their trade association, to share wage information and adopt similar wage practices. This involves community, government, and investor-owned hospitals (Friss, 1987). These practices supplant but perpetuate formal wage setting agreements used until the 1960s.

9. Antitrust laws have not been enforced or amended to ensure that employers cannot collude to depress wages. The statute states, "Any combination that tampers with the price structure or pricing mechanism is engaged in an unlawful activity, even absent an agreement on particular prices. The fact that the combination . . . may have the effect of reducing rather than raising prices will not save the combination or agreement from illegality" (Thompson, 1979). Antitrust powers, however, are limited in markets where there is conscious parallel behavior without explicit agreements, the usual case in hospital wage setting.

10. Multihospital systems can use profits from one hospital to subsidize hospitals in other areas (U.S. Government Accounting Office, 1983). When this occurs, it is likely that employees in all areas are led to believe that economic pressures preclude wage increases.

11. The federal government is a major employer of registered nurses in the

Designing a Compensation System

military, Veterans Administration, and civil service. Pay is based in part on comparability with the private sector. This is achieved by relating grade level and pay to the private sector. Thus, the federal government picks up low pay practices of private employers (Friss, 1981).

The many downward pressures on salaries are partially offset by upward pay pressures. The most direct one is that the Fair Labor Standards Amendments of 1985 were recently extended to government hospitals. As a result, hospitals must pay overtime or compensatory time off to employees who work over forty hours a week. The definition of regular work time is tightened. The time a nurse spends driving to required seminars must be paid, for example. Some salaried positions will need to be changed to hourly positions with shift differentials and overtime pay. This federal oversight will probably extend to private hospitals (Poulos, 1984).[2]

Managers fear that unions will increase their membership and raise wages. Actually, this fear is exaggerated. The best estimate is that unions raise nurses' wages by 5 percent per year (Adamache and Sloan, 1982). The average impact on cost per day and cost per case is in the range of 3 to 10 percent (Salkever, 1983). Although economists do not agree on whether the union effect on wages continues over time, they do agree that union growth has not been an important cause of hospital inflation. It is unlikely that there will be rapid growth of unions in community hospitals because three prerequisites do not exist: homogeneous workforce, lack of alternatives, and a single employer.

OBJECTIVES

Because labor costs are the single largest cost to health care organizations, it follows that the pay system should be well designed, implemented, and maintained. At a minimum, aggregate salary outlays should attract and retain a workforce that provides quality services and keeps the organization viable in the short run. Additionally the pay system needs to be simple enough so that employees believe that they are being paid fairly. For the long term, pay systems should be easy to maintain and contribute to long-term organizational and industry success.

The objectives of any pay system are to establish a base rate for every job and to design an orderly procedure for justly compensating employees for performance rendered. As a practical matter, the federal and state minimum wage laws govern base pay and overtime pay, and local area wage rates establish threshold levels. At the top end, more variation and flexibility should exist for high-performing managers and valuable professionals.

ALTERNATIVE METHODOLOGIES FOR JOB EVALUATION

Job evaluation plans in combination with wage surveys have been used for more than fifty years in both the public and private sectors to maintain internal and external equity. Job evaluation is an analytic process used to identify and categorize job content and rank jobs in a hierarchy as the basis for paying workers holding different jobs equitably. The basic goal of a job evaluation system is to compare responsibility, skill, and ability requirements for diverse positions so that they may be compared, ranked, and placed in a small number of pay categories.

The major alternative systems for evaluating jobs are whole-job ranking, grading or position classification, point rating, and factor comparison. The first two are called qualitative methods; the latter two are quantitative methods. The popular Hay Plan Compensable Factors is a hybrid approach (Exhibit 7.1).

Another approach gaining popularity is the job-component method, which emphasizes job relatedness and is especially attractive for pay based on performance. One hospital-oriented version is ROPEP (results-oriented performance evaluation program). Used in connection with productivity, ROPEP is defined as the measurement of the results of a person's work effort compared with previously agreed-upon standards of performance. Thus, performance rather than the job is the focal point. Specific behaviors are written in measurable terms, frequently using anchor or identification statements (Ganong and Ganong, 1984).

In small firms, whole jobs are ranked from top to bottom by their worth or importance with little, if any, discussion of decision criteria. Implicit criteria are frequently organizational level of the position, perceived importance of the position to the organization's mission, and personal status of the incumbent. Paired comparisons can be used to refine this method. Once all jobs have been ranked, the ranked jobs are placed in categories and salary levels are assigned. This ranking method is highly subjective and not highly regarded by job evaluation experts.

The classification system, which is used by many governments, differentiates all positions by kind of work and level of work (Siegel and Myrtle, 1985: 103). Kind of work refers to the nature of work performed; level of work includes the elements (factors), such as the level of complexity, supervision, and technical knowledge required. The positions in each class are sufficiently alike in kind of work and level of difficulty that they can be clustered under the same broad qualification requirements, the same tests of fitness, and the same scale of pay. In contrast with the other methods, classification requires a decision beforehand on the number of pay grades.

First, brief descriptions of a number of levels and grades, or classes, are written. Then, based on job descriptions, jobs are assigned to classes. The range of classes, from least to most difficult within a specialized kind of work, is referred to as a series of classes. In the traditional federal positions classification plan, classes are, in turn, clustered into grades of difficulty and responsibility. A separate set of standards or allocation rules governs each zone, and together the zones form the basis for federal pay standardization. It is possible for a position in a class to be allocated to one of several grades depending on distinctions between the grade standards. Thus, a technician who is responsible for

Exhibit 7.1
Hay Plan Compensable Factors

Mental Activity (problem solving)	Know-How	Accountability
The amount of original, self-starting thought required by the job for analysis, evaluation, creation, reasoning, and arriving at conclusions. Mental Activity has two dimensions: ■ The degree of freedom with which the thinking process is used to achieve job objectives without the guidance of standards, precedents, or direction from others ■ The type of mental activity involved; the complexity, abstractness, or originality of thought required Mental activity is expressed as a percentage of Know-How for the obvious reason that people think with what they know. The percentage judged to be correct for a job is applied to the Know-How point value; the result is the point value given to Mental Activity.	The sum total of all knowledge and skills, however acquired, needed for satisfactory job performance (evaluates the job, not the person). Know-How has three dimensions: ■ The amount of practical, specialized, or technical knowledge required ■ Breadth of management, or the ability to make many activities and functions work well together; the job of company president, for example, has greater breadth than that of a department supervisor ■ Requirement for skill in motivating people Using a chart, a number can be assigned to the level of Know-How needed in a job. This number—or point value—indicates the relative importance of Know-How in the job being evaluated.	The measured effect of the job on company goals. Accountability has three dimensions: ■ Freedom to act, or relative presence of personal or procedural control and guidance; determined by answering the question, "How much freedom has the job holder to act independently?"; for example, a plant manager has more freedom than a supervisor under his or her control ■ Dollar magnitude, a measure of the sales, budget, dollar value of purchases, value added, or any other significant annual dollar figure related to the job ■ Impact of the job on dollar magnitude, a determination of whether the job has a primary effect on end results or has instead a sharing, contributory, or remote effect Accountability is given a point value independent of the other two factors.

The total evaluation of any job is arrived at by adding the points for Mental Activity, Know-How, and Accountability.

Source: Reprinted by permission from *Effective Personnel Management*, 2nd ed. by R. Schuler and S. Youngblood. Copyright © 1986 by West Publishing Company. All rights reserved.

the maintenance and calibration of exotic rather than mundane instruments could be placed in a higher pay grade without the need to create a new class. While a classification scheme arranges positions in classes on the basis of their similarities, the pay plan will establish ranges of pay for each class of positions. Consequently, if a position is improperly classified, the corresponding salary will not be in accord with the principle of fair play.

Two key limitations to this method have been identified. Well-trained and experienced classification experts are required. When jobs are high on one criterion and low on another, the analyst is forced to make an arbitrary decision. For example, some jobs may have educational requirements suitable for the class but not the requisite supervisory responsibility.

Critics of position classification note that decisions are influenced by market pay rates, tradition, and political consideratrions. Shafritz (1973) states that it is possible for classification decisions to be more intuitive than rational. Classes often have minimum education and experience requirements that reflect false credentialism rather than job-related requirements. Further, over time a tendency exists to reallocate positions upward, the so-called grade creep. This compensates for inadequate pay adjustments or solves personnel problems, which are difficult to resolve directly.

Point rating, the most widely used model in the United States,[3] is based on an identified set of compensable factors. Common factors for hourly rated jobs are skill, effort, responsibility, and working conditions. Common factors for salaried jobs (clerical, supervisory, and technical) include education, experience, complexity of duties, monetary responsibility, contacts, type of supervision, extent of supervision, and working conditions (Spector and Beer, 1985). The average number of factors used is about ten, but as few as three and as many as twenty-five are possible; studies suggest that a large number of factors is not necessary to determine the relative worth of jobs.

For each factor there is an ascending scale of points; the range of possible points is constant across all jobs. To increase reliability and validity of the ratings, anchor points have minidescriptions. Once points have been assigned based on the rating for each factor, the points are totaled to yield a job worth score. Worth is thus determined by the features of the jobs that are identified and measured. Total points are the basis for determining job level. The problem lies with the rigidity stemming from the fixed number of points throughout the organization.

Factor comparison is growing in popularity. A small (four to seven) set of compensable factors is chosen representing universally applicable factors. Common factors are mental requirements, physical requirements, skill requirements, responsibility, and working conditions. The result is a single overall job evaluation plan for the organization. In the usual case, analysis proceeds after analyzing key (benchmark) positions where consensus exists regarding their relative worth and importance of the chosen factors.[4] Then the benchmark jobs are ranked according to total worth. Finally, a judgment is made for each job regarding the contribution of each factor to the total worth of the job. Once the weight of each

Designing a Compensation System

of the factors and total scores for benchmark jobs have been ascertained, evaluators look for discrepancies and make necessary adjustments. Remaining jobs are compared to an appropriate benchmark factor by factor. Thus, every job receives a total score based on the sum of factor scores. The factor comparison method is becoming popular although it takes more time and cost to install; once it is established, it can be applied by trained staff with less classification experience. Once understood, the system is accepted by employees, especially lower-paid ones (Moore, 1985).

Several disadvantages have been identified for point factor plans:

1. They are difficult for employees, line managers, and legal experts to understand
2. Updating is expensive
3. Updating is necessary since the key positions on which scaling depends may change over time
4. It may be difficult to find universal factors that an organization wants to compensate

In spite of these disadvantages, many experts believe that the factor comparison method surfaces decision criteria and provides better checks and balances than the other systems. Successful hospitals have adopted the system (and have been able to expand it to a performance-based pay system). (Exhibit 7.2 summarizes these systems.)

The Hay Guide Chart Profile Method, a modification and simplification of the factor comparison method, was developed and used by the Hay and Associates consulting firm for over thirty years. Organizations have used this popular system primarily for higher managerial and professional jobs. There is little distinction among lower-level jobs; no weight is given to working conditions; subjective judgments are emphasized more than usual. The system compares jobs using three factors: know-how, problem solving, and accountability. Each factor has subfactors with points that are tailored for each client and portrayed on a chart. There are five implementation steps:

1. Updating job descriptions for benchmark jobs.
2. Profiling the benchmark jobs by using guide charts to determine the proportion of total job content attributable to the three factors. The purposes are to align the jobs relative to one another and establish a baseline for comparing point evaluation, which occurs later.
3. Comparing jobs by establishing steps scored on geometric scale. There is roughly a 15 percent difference between steps, which is compatible with the observations that salary differences between job levels typically approximate 15 percent. (Studies done in the 1940s suggest that it is possible to have a 15 percent error in measurement among trained raters. Therefore, if through some grouping of criteria, one job is no more than 15 percent different from another, most people will consider the two jobs to be equivalent and worthy of similar pay [Henderson and Clarke, 1981].)

Exhibit 7.2
Job Evaluation Systems

Characteristics	Whole Job Ranking	Methods: Classification	Factor Method	Point Ranking
Measures jobs:	Against other jobs in organization, based on importance to organization relative to chief's position	Against a standardized scale with skill levels determined qualitatively	Against other jobs by ranking them on multiple factors	Quantitatively on predetermined scale of factors with qualitative levels
Weights jobs:	No points given	No points given; pay level assigned by amount of skill required	Points given to factors; jobs ranked on each factor	Factors divided into levels and assigned points
Introduces bias:	When comparisons made about which jobs most valuable to organization	When standards developed	When factors, rankings, and weights determined	When factors and sublevels chosen and weighted

Source: E.O. Youngkin, "Comparable Worth: Alternatives to Litigation and Legislation," *Nursing Economics* 3 (1985): 40. Reprinted with permission.

Designing a Compensation System

4. "Sore-thumbing" or resolving discrepancies between the initial profile and the distribution of points.
5. Converting Hay points to salary rates. To do this, existing salary rates are plotted against Hay points for benchmark jobs, and the line of best fit is determined. Experience leads Hay to believe that point distribution has a linear relationship to salary and nonlinearities identify problems in the pay structure.

Lawler (1986), a compensation expert in the private sector, raises some fundamental objections to job evaluation. He believes that managers pay a high price for relying on job descriptions, which foster bureaucratic rigid management controls resulting in overstaffing, lost time, and poor coordination among specialists as workers "go by the book" and do not perform additional duties. In addition, productivity changes are difficult in competitive times. This happens because the point system emphasizes duties and supervisory responsibility rather than growth, development, and performance. Further, as the system matures, employees learn how to write creative job descriptions, often involving extra equipment and more subordinates, which reward those who increase rather than decrease expenses and salaries. The point system with its bias toward upward mobility may be particularly unsuited for health organizations where there are few promotional opportunities for clinicians. A fundamental but unanswered question is whether it makes sense to use a method that encourages static or declining pay for core workers in an industry where the majority of workers are developing steady-state professional careers and where promotional opportunities are limited.

SCOPE

Management needs a well-thought-out compensation philosophy that is publicly stated, including its use of salary surveys. Pay policies are influenced to some extent by the organization's maturity and strategic plan. Growing businesses should stimulate an enterprising entrepreneurial style of management; high cash payments and above-average rewards are appropriate. Mature firms need to protect markets; the matching pay policy is a blend of average cash payments, moderate incentives, and standard benefits. When cost control is paramount, benefits should be standard, salaries should be below average, and modest incentives should be tied directly to controlling costs.

Another key decision is whether to have a common job hierarchy or separate systems for various occupational groupings. Public jurisdictions have traditionally integrated most positions in one hierarchy of jobs. The federal government has done this using the Factor Evaluation System, a point system based on nine factors: knowledge required, supervisor controls, guidelines, complexity, scope and effect, personal contacts, purpose of contacts, physical demands, and work environment. The new Federal Executive Service is an example of an attempt to modify the uniform system to reward particularly productive career managers.

Organizations commonly maintain separate pay plans for hourly workers, professionals, and managers. Some analysts believe that organizations should have only one pay plan if workers at all levels are to be paid equitably, but this is a controversial recommendation. A National Academy of Science committee studying job evaluation was divided on this point (Treiman and Hartmann, 1981).

Before initiating a company-wide job evaluation program, management needs to draw boundaries around the project and establish guidelines. Time and money are wasted when a company or jurisdiction-wide job evaluation program is authorized unnecessarily. Perhaps the existing classification system needs redoing first. Or an analysis of the pay structure of jobs held by protected classes, union members, or difficult-to-fill jobs can identify target jobs and classes needing immediate attention. Remedies might be appropriately confined to updating job descriptions or the pay survey. Other alternatives are reclassifying target jobs, identifying new benchmark jobs, or creating bridge classes to provide career mobility.

PROCESS

Since the point factor method offers the most potential for developing a bias-free system and incorporates all phases—job description, classification, salary surveys—the process for this method will be described in detail. Internal equity depends on job analysis, internal job evaluation (including the establishment of rational and numerical class families and groupings), and establishing the pay structure. External equity (competitiveness) depends on matching the pay structure to data from salary surveys. Ultimately the organization assigns an individual to a specific pay category. A healthy system requires explicit resolution of inconsistencies and a high investment in maintenance. The process outlined below clearly separates market information from the internal analysis in the early stages, as recommended by consultants familiar with court cases.

Internal Equity

Job Analysis

The foundation for all job evaluation plans is an accurate job description developed by some combination of observing work activities, interviews, questionnaires to job incumbents, and interviews with supervisors. A written summary of worker requirements (job specification) together with the task-focused job descriptions comprise a job analysis. The process can be done by skilled job analysts employed by the organization, employees with special training, outside consultants, or some combination of the three. The job description process should allow incumbents to inspect and alter their job descriptions if actual position changes have occurred.

Internal Job Evaluation Analysis

Many of the evaluation systems in use today were developed by using a firm's existing pay structure to determine statistically which attributes of jobs best predict their pay rates. This policy-capturing approach uses multiple regression to predict current wages from job evaluation data. The factors and their weights thus obtained are then used to adjust rates of existing jobs that are overpaid or underpaid relative to the predictions of the formula (Treiman and Hartmann, 1981). To do this properly, points should be assigned to factors for nonprotected classes and be benchmarked to white male salaries (Thomsen, 1978). This process might include ranking each benchmark factor by factor or using whole job rankings with paired comparisons to determine clusters of benchmarks to approximate grades.

Statistical analysis of the point-factor scores obtained in the job evaluation can suggest classes that should be compensated at the same level, compensation relationships among classes within a series, and assignment for classes to salary grades. At the same time, analysts use their judgment to integrate job analysis information with the point-factor job evaluation system to create, abolish or combine classes; determine the number of levels within a class series; and allocate positions to the appropriate class.

The a priori method, in contrast to measuring what exists, requires that the employer define a set of factors and factor weights as legitimate bases of pay differentials before examining pay differences.

Establishing the Pay Structure

Once the job evaluation has been completed, pay grades are constructed. A pay grade is a grouping of jobs of approximately equal difficulty or importance as determined by the job evaluation. In the factor-comparison plan, a pay grade consists of a range of evaluated rates. (In ranking, a number of ranks are used; in the point method, each grade includes a range of points; in the classification method, pay grades are determined in advance.) This process is complex, but generally:

1. Jobs of the same general value should be clustered in the same pay grade
2. Jobs that clearly differ in value should be in different pay grades
3. There should be a smooth progression of point groupings
4. Any new system should realistically fit the existing pay system
5. The pay grades should conform reasonably well to pay patterns in relevant labor markets (Cascio, 1986)

A number of dilemmas can arise during this stage. Do factor scores match the pay grade assignment? Should all the incumbents performing jobs within a pay grade be paid the same? How many grades are appropriate? What should the relationship be between adjacent pay grades? Should seniority and performance be recognized in the pay grade? How can internal equity problems be addressed? This last step should be considered before as well as after "going to the market." There are no right answers to these questions. An objective analysis of existing practices will reveal implicit policies. Ultimately such questions are answered in response to the external environment, management priorities, and the power of competing advocates.

Sometimes pay grade boundaries, rate range limits, and the wage line are done simultaneously. First, a midpoint or average line is fitted. Next, trend lines are drawn for both the minimum and maximum rate of pay for each point total. Then pay grades, or ranges, characterized by a point spread from minimum to maximum for each grade are established. Within grades, management and staff determine the number of steps and criteria for advancement. At other times, the price is established through collective bargaining. Usually both present wage rates and external rates are used.

External Equity

External equity or competitive wages depends on a survey of what other employers are paying. Management jobs depend on comparisons within the industry (except for marketing), and nonmanagement jobs relate to competitive wages. These data are obtained in several ways. Consulting firms and health care journals conduct and publish industry executive surveys regularly (Cole, 1987). Locally the human resources staff may conduct its own telephone or mail surveys. Merchant and manufacturing associations conduct annual surveys of general positions and selected industry-specific jobs. Hospital councils survey their members; hospitals describe this common practice as the fifth most valuable service the councils provide (Strasser et al., 1983). The Bureau of Labor Statistics conducts salary surveys of hospital workers every three years, community wage surveys, and a national survey of professional, administrative, technical, and clerical pay.

Hospitals may be vulnerable to antitrust lawsuits because they are considered to be an employer-dominated industry and because female workers are becoming more assertive. Although there are no court interpretations about the legality of salary surveys, a consent degree agreed to by the Boston Survey Group suggests that employers should follow these guidelines:

1. Do not permit discussion of individual incumbent salaries with other firms or participate in surveys reporting such data
2. Use surveys that report results in aggregated, weighted averages for each job and that do not identify the data of each participant
3. Avoid participation in surveys that report on an industry-by-industry basis or that include job categories reporting fewer than ten incumbents
4. Decide under what circumstances company employees should be allowed to see the aggregated survey results for their own jobs

Designing a Compensation System

5. Do not exchange future intentions regarding wage and salary rates
6. Encourage the participation of other industries in salary surveys
7. Use disinterested, third-party surveys as much as possible
8. Eliminate company code exchanges for surveys reporting blind results
9. Avoid or cut short any discussions with companies suggesting that an agreement be made to pay certain rates for certain jobs (Fisher, 1985)

The final steps in designing the salary structure are to determine the midpoint differences between successive grades and the width of the salary range for each grade (Greene, 1982). Various experts recommend that the spread between midpoints be either 5 percent or 10 to 25 percent. One practical option is to use 5 or 7.5 percent for the nonexempt structure and 10 to 13 percent for the exempt structure.

Once the midpoint progression has been selected, the salary width needs to be resolved. In examining large survey samples, it appears that the first and third quartiles will generally range from 10 to 13 percent below and above the average, respectively. The basic decision that needs to be made is whether to use the same spread throughout the structure or have it fan out for upper management.

There is no standard number of pay grades or dollar spread of pay grades. In hourly jobs, the maximum may be 10 to 20 percent above the minimum; for salaried employees, the maximum may vary from 15 to 75 percent. Hospitals traditionally have had compacted salary ranges and few grades for professional employees.

Hospitals compete for employees in many labor markets. No single salary can be the necessary or right salary for a job. The "going rate" is difficult to obtain. First, job titles and descriptions may be misleading. Second, employers need to consider not only the mean or median but also the full range, the dollar spread of the frequently used middle range, and the number of employees at each salary level. Further, salary distributions are often skewed, bimodal, or flat rather than normal.

Paying Individuals

The compensation cycle is not completed until the salary has been assigned for each individual. The hiring process and employee handbook should concisely and accurately inform employees about pay policies and procedures. Realistic expectations minimize employee turnover among new workers. Employee morale depends on a perception that the performance appraisal and pay systems together are both fair and fairly administered. The best technical plan still needs the support of supervisors if it is to be accepted by the majority of workers.

Although most organizations claim to have a merit plan, pay rates for individuals within rate ranges also reflect an individual's pay history, position in the range, experience, time since last pay increase, amount of last increase, pay relationships within the department, pay relationships with other departments, labor market forces, and the organization's resources. A formal pay plan has several steps. Usually management provides supervisors with the necessary policy information and staff support to enable them to develop a pay adjustment forecast. The forecasts serve as the basis for approving budgets across the organization. After the budget is approved, supervisors then make individual pay decisions incorporating merit or pay-for-performance criteria, which are in effect.

Maintenance Program

A well-managed organization regularly re-evaluates its pay philosophy and supply and demand of labor in tandem with its strategic objectives to ensure that the pay system is legal, fair, and effective. Although this sounds like common sense, a well-maintained program is the exception rather than the rule. One analyst recommends that annually 10 percent of all positions should be randomly selected, audited, and evaluated according to factors. If few changes are required, the system may be considered to be functioning effectively. If extensive changes are required, a detailed analysis is necessary (Suskin, 1977). Inflation adjustment is also an essential component (Reynard, 1976).

CRITERIA FOR ASSESSING EFFECTIVENESS

Carey (1985) has identified fourteen symptoms of salary problems and recommends action when three or more are present:

1. Many employees leave for better pay
2. Complaints about pay are common
3. Employees often request salary increases
4. Employees often get increases when they ask
5. Morale is poor, as shown by high turnover, excessive tardiness and absenteeism, frequent requests for transfer, union militancy, low output, and poor-quality work
6. Attitude surveys show negative views about pay practices
7. Applicants are asked what salary they want
8. Recruiting competent people is hampered by pay offered
9. Departments classify and pay jobs differently
10. Supervisors cannot get routine salary actions approved (or rejected) promptly
11. Good employees leave in a year or two
12. Company labor costs are higher than those of competitors
13. Executives spend too much time on routine salary matters
14. Top executives lack confidence in salary administration controls

The system should also pass legal tests. Since subjectivity exists at each step of any individually tailored system—selecting factors and benchmark jobs, ranking benchmark jobs, assigning weights to factors based on market prices, matching jobs to benchmarks, and selecting market comparisons—pay outcomes should be analyzed for discriminatory impact on protected classes.

SPECIAL ISSUES

Physicians

A full discussion of physician compensation is beyond the scope of the chapter.[5] Health care managers are becoming increasingly involved in physician compensation issues. More organizations have full-time physicians, and managers also want to reward physicians for reducing unnecessary utilization (Weissburg and Stern, 1985).

Incentive compensation for physicians is possible because sophisticated computer programs can compare past performance, severity of illness indicators, and costs incurred with standards. In the prospective payment environment, health care organizations want to encourage low-cost producers and discourage high-cost producers. Incentive compensation poses legal risks since Medicare and Medicaid fraud and abuse statutes prohibit payment to anyone inducing a person to refer a patient or a "healthier" patient. Some states also have laws prohibiting kickbacks and referrals or the corporate practice of medicine.

Hospital-based physicians are paid on salary or fee-for-service basis (FFS). (Recent regulations have all but eliminated the percentage-of-patient-revenue approach.) Physicians paid on an FFS basis tend to bill separately from the hospital. Five factors increase the probability that a hospital will have salaried doctors: teaching hospital status, availability of foreign medical school graduates, high physician to population ratios, higher proportion of Medicaid patients, and lower proportion of Medicare patients (Steinwald, 1983).

Executive Compensation

In the compensation plan of a traditional hospital, 70 percent of the total package is the base salary, 25 percent is benefits, and 5 percent is special benefits, such as extra life insurance and extensions on coverages. (In industry, salary represents only 40 percent of the total.) Industry-wide salary comparisons rather than general wage levels are the most important for determining management salary levels. These surveys, conducted by consulting firms and published regularly (Redling and Daze, 1985; Egan, 1986), suggest that senior management salaries in the health care industry are considerably lower than in manufacturing companies with comparable dollar volume. Controllers, accountants, business office managers, and data processing managers are comparable, however. State hospital associations and individual health care organizations also conduct surveys of key positions.

A recent analysis suggests that hospital executive compensation is following the trends of other industries, with increased use of incentive pay based on criteria of unit performance and performance against predetermined objectives (Egan, 1986). The top administrator in a multiple hospital system has a higher base salary and receives higher bonuses. Because the roles of president and marketing manager are relatively new, pay ranges are not well established in relation to the top administrator. Other jobs (chief financial officer, associate administrator, directors of nursing services and directors of human resources) have a relatively stable relationship to the top administrator position over time. Executive pay in multiaffiliate corporations is more complex than in independent hospitals. The key to a successful program is linking position titles and salary structures to responsibility, whether it occurs at the corporate or affiliate level (Browdy, 1986).

Employee Involvement and Acceptance

Managers face common problems related to fairness as perceived by employees. Among these are the perceptions that the supervisor's personal preferences prejudice the evaluation, that insiders cannot be promoted, that quiet competence is overlooked, and that important decisions are made in secret. Although it is neither advisable nor possible to have all employees involved in all the technical decisions and tough compromises, insisting on management prerogative over all facets of the pay system may be costly in the long run. Enough experiments have been performed with employee involvement in setting pay to suggest that enlightenment is productive and does not lead to anarchy (Henderson, 1982). Involvement usually involves advisory committee representation, but the size and composition vary widely. A study of Chicago hospitals noted that size varied from small to large. Representation ranged from managerial only to managerial plus supervisory personnel to committees with nonsupervisory employees as well (Maxey, Kennedy, and Carlson, 1979).

Secrecy

When there is a wage contract, hourly workers are informed of the details of the wage and salary programs, but nonunion and salaried workers are more likely to have information about ranges rather than specific salaries. Full disclosure of pay policy and procedures, which is generally recommended, however, does not imply that individual salary information should be released.

Pay Satisfaction: Level and Administration

Unfortunately, different models of work have been used to understand work behaviors of men and women. For men, research is designed using the job model, which treats work as the primary variable explaining behavior on and off the job. The gender model used to study women's paid employment em-

Designing a Compensation System

phasizes personal characteristics and relationship to family. When studies are analyzed, additional distortions occur; data that do not fit the model are overlooked or ignored; significance of data violating assumptions is discounted or ignored; and when alternative interpretations are possible, the one most consistent with job or gender is favored without discussion (Feldberg and Glenn, 1982; Richardson and Kaufman, 1983).

The two basic theories managers use to understand motivation (and thus satisfaction) are the hierarchy of need and intrinsic-extrinsic motivation theories. Although they are easy to understand and have much intuitive appeal, their validity has been questioned (King, 1970; Dawis, 1984). Indeed, preference differences probably relate to goals and expectations workers bring to their jobs rather than job attitudes and opportunities. Since workers, both male and female, are now fashioning careers other than the traditional up-the-ladder or professional ones understood by researchers two and three decades ago, old paradigms are inadequate.

Motivations depend on the preferred balance between life interests and paid work. Alternative career styles (entrepreneurial, spiral) are possible as the industry has diversified and women, especially, have broader opportunities. Generalizations concerning worker satisfaction and pay should be made cautiously because of poor research design and also the diversity of workers, employment settings, influence of rapid cultural changes, and economic swings occurring in the industry generally.

Two generalizations are worth noting. Pay satisfaction is influenced by other factors than absolute income. Employees with higher pay, although not necessarily the highest, are usually more satisfied with their pay. Whether this is a function of the pay itself rather than the fact that high-paying jobs tend to be interesting and prestigious is hard to prove. Sex differences in pay satisfaction have been found (Sauser and York, 1978). The increased pay satisfaction among female employees in lower-level jobs has been explained as a function of their low expectations for pay and the lack of reference groups where pay is any higher. This may not hold for upper-level women, who were found to be less satisfied with pay and promotions than were upper-level men (Varca, Shaffer, and McCauley, 1983).

Among nurses, one-third of young graduates took the job that was best paying, while half gave job security as the primary reason (Munro, 1983). Both proportions are high enough that managers probably should not underestimate the importance of either one. Ivancevich and his colleagues (1980) found that among nurses and technologists, pay satisfaction was associated with demonstration that management was task oriented. This bodes well for results-oriented performance appraisals.

Pay Equity and Comparable Worth

Analysts agree that women generally earn much less than men.[6] Statistics show that the larger is the proportion of women in an occupation, the lower is the hourly wage. Statistics also show that the pay differential is not fully explained by measurable characteristics of men or women or jobs. Education and years in the labor force are common comparison characteristics. Statistics, however, cannot rule out that the remaining differential is caused by factors other than discrimination. However, just as it is reasonable to assume that cigarette smoking causes cancer even though it cannot be proved statistically, it is reasonable to accept that women have suffered discrimination in the workplace and that it has not been completely eradicated (Aaron and Lougy, 1986).

Sex is a better predictor of salary than the points assigned as a result of the job evaluation system (Exhibits 7.3 and 7.4). In the state of Washington, women were paid from 22.2 to 27.2 percent less than men. Similar patterns have been documented in Illinois, Connecticut, Iowa, San Jose, Los Angeles, and Denver.[7] Some advocates for pay equity argue, based on these data, that job evaluation systems have not been objective measures of internal equity but an elaborate method of perpetuating historical discrimination. The proposed remedy, paying for jobs of comparable value, is called comparable worth.

Comparable worth activity occurs in three major arenas: federal law enforcement and litigation, state and local activity, and organized labor. Several lawsuits have been filed during the past ten years. In one involving health workers (nurses), *Lemons* v. *City and County of Denver* (CA 10, 1980, 22 FEP Cases 959), the nurses lost on the ground that jobs had to be substantially equal. This restriction was subsequently lifted in the case of *County of Washington, Oregon* v. *Gunther* (25 FEP Cases 1521). In a second case, public health nurses failed to prove that the market rate defense was a "pretext" for "intentional" sex discrimination in favor of sanitarians (*Briggs* v. *City of Madison*, 536 F. Supp. 435; (W.D. Wis 1982; Moskowitz, 1983). The Equal Employment Opportunity Commission ruled against the American Nurses Association in Illinois, and public health nurses lost their case in Alaska. Employers are advised to design their human resource systems so that any wage differences between men and women can be explained on the basis of seniority, merit, quantity or quality of work, or any factor other than sex (Cooper and Barrett, 1984).

Comparable worth is only one approach to achieving pay equity. Even if it were pursued aggressively and widely applied, economists believe that most of the gap between men's and women's wages would remain (Aaron and Lougy, 1986). Achieving equity will require enforcement of executive order 11375 and the Civil Rights Act of 1964 by President Johnson, which brought women into the federal EEO program in 1967. In health occupations, where so many workers are employed in sex-segregated occupations in employer-dominated markets, at least one analyst has suggested that antitrust activity may be more appropriate than comparable worth (Killingsworth, 1986).

To avoid lawsuits and, more important, to remain competitive for competent workers of both sexes, private and public employers are advised to (Sape, 1985):

1. Work to eliminate job segregation. This is difficult in health care where many professions are over 70 percent female. However, careful examination of classes may reveal

Exhibit 7.3
Comparison of Salaries and Points for Selected Sex-Segregated Positions, State of Washington

Benchmark Title	Evaluation Points	Monthly Prevailing* Rates	Prevailing Rate as % of Predicted**	% Female Incumbents
AUTOMOTIVE MECHANIC	175	1646	120.4	0.0
CIVIL ENGINEER	287	1885	116.0	0.0
MAINTENANCE CARPENTER	197	1707	118.9	2.3
HIGHWAY ENGINEER 3	345	1980	110.4	3.0
CORRECTIONAL OFFICER	173	1436	105.0	9.3
HIGHWAY ENGINEERING TECH	133	1401	110.4	11.6
TRUCK DRIVER	97	1493	126.6	13.6
PHYSICIAN	861	3857	128.0	13.6
WAREHOUSE WORKER	97	1286	109.1	15.4
SENIOR ARCHITECT	362	2240	121.8	16.7
SR. COMPUTER SYSTEM ANALYST	384	2080	113.1	17.8
CHEMIST	277	1885	116.0	20.0
PERSONNEL REPRESENTATIVE	410	1956	101.2	45.6
LAUNDRY WORKER	105	884	73.2	80.3
LIBRARIAN 3	353	1625	90.6	84.6
LICENSED PRACTICAL NURSE	173	1030	75.3	89.5
REGISTERED NURSE	348	1368	76.3	92.2
ADMINISTRATIVE ASSISTANT	226	1334	90.6	95.1
TELEPHONE OPERATOR	118	887	71.6	95.7
DATA ENTRY OPERATOR	125	1017	82.1	96.5
INTERMEDIATE CLERK TYPIST	129	968	76.3	96.7
WORK PROCESS EQUIP. OPERATOR	138	1082	83.2	98.3
SECRETARY	197	1122	78.1	98.5
RETAIL SALES CLERK	121	921	74.3	100.0

* Prevailing rates as of July 1, 1980. Adopted State rates for midpoint of ranges, October 1981.
** Predicted salary from line of best fit = ($2.43)(points) + $936.19, r=0.8.

Source: Adapted from *Public Personnel Management Journal* 10 (4) (Winter 1981): 378. Reprinted with permission.

Exhibit 7.4
Selected Results of Point-Factor Job Evaluation Pilot Study for the Illinois Commission on the Status of Women

Job Title	Sex	Total Score Job Evaluation	Present average Monthly Salary
Nurse IV	F	1017	$2104
Nurse III	F	893	1794
Accountant V	M	889	2470
Public aid caseworker	F	760	1622
LPN	F	649	1298
Electrician	M	548	2826
Office manager I	M	543	2010
Secretary II	F	533	1486
Mental Health Tech II	F	494	1135
Secretary I	F	442	1283
Accountant	F	432	1426
Correctional officer	M	430	1438
Automotive mechanic	M	420	1681

Source: From the *American Journal of Nursing*, February 1984, pp. 256–57. Used with permission.

areas where progress can be made by aggressive recruiting, promotion, and cross-training strategies.

2. Audit the impact of pay practices on men's and women's salaries on a regular basis. When discrepancies are found, management should verify and document that factors other than sex account for the disparity.

3. Review key job evaluation determinants for bias. For example, unpleasant working conditions exist for male- and female-dominated jobs, but men's jobs get points for noise and dirt, while women's jobs do not get points for odors or steady machine noises. Variety, intricacy, and simultaneous processing of complex inputs characterize both secretarial positions and nursing but are commonly undervalued. Men may be compensated for lifting objects while women are not compensated for lifting patients.

4. Examine each element of the compensation system for controls on possible discrimination. Such safeguards include training on compensation for wage and salary administrators and periodic review by managers of salary decisions that affect male and female workers.

5. Take corrective action once a problem area has been identified. Phased-in and good-faith efforts are appropriate. Costs of correction are often overstated.

GUIDELINES FOR ADMINISTRATORS

Prerequisites

Although many pay systems are technically flawed, the problems in troubled health care organizations usually transcend technical correction, as important and necessary as these are. The basic problem often is a philosophy of pay that

Designing a Compensation System

is out of touch with both the real world of work and the opportunities available for workers of both sexes with intelligence, compassion, dedication, and skills. Progressive health care managers do not equate the bottom line with competitive entry-level salaries at the expense of a pay structure needed to ensure a balance of full-time workers and the development of experienced clinicians, administrators, and teachers. Labor-intensive businesses, including health care, depend on commitment and performance of workers who fit the culture, whose work is organized productively, and who accept the employer's mission. This precludes a use-and-dispose pay philosophy. When the cycle of shortages recurs, will the organization be positioned with enough career employees to manage and provide threshold level of services?

Establishing a pay philosophy also goes beyond whether to lead or follow the market. Are salary differentials enough to make a career difference? (Employees' inability to articulate either a career plan or a target salary does not mean that salary does not affect decisions.) Are we looking at pay from the employees' perspective? (The take-home pay of a secondary earner may not yield enough after-tax income to offset the disadvantages of full-time work.) Does our job and pay structure fit the demographics of our working population? More bluntly, why do we have few workers between ages 35 and 55, the prime career years, in some departments?

A trap to avoid is the chicken and egg argument over the relative importance of pay and psychic rewards. When an organization is gridlocked over this debate, both pay and working conditions deteriorate since a management reluctant to pay for performance and foster careers is unlikely to allow for worker autonomy and involvement.

Individual organizations also prosper or decline in response to external forces. Today's external forces are so complex that market surveys alone are not enough. Indeed, industry lobbying and salary surveys leading to low salary ceilings may be the underlying force driving potential health professionals to other careers even as the short-term economies enable more hospitals to survive with low occupancy. If shortages occur in key occupations, can't we expect policy analysts to argue that it would be less expensive to relocate workers and pay some workers more with the money saved from closing underutilized facilities?

Financial survival in the next decade will likely depend on being able to attract and retain professional workers necessary to provide revenue-generating services. Competition for new workers with an interest in science, who like people, and who possess good problem-solving skills from other businesses will be intense in the new service-oriented economy. Competition for already educated health workers will come not only from other segments of the health industry, such as alternative delivery systems, but also new alternatives, such as private practice, employee-owned hospitals, and group contracting.

Increasingly managers will need to examine the incentives needed to retain mature workers (tax reduction strategies), to encourage upward movement from unlicensed to licensed positions (pay for education), to foster specialization (meangful clinical ladders), and to balance specialization with flexibility (pay for competence across departments and shifts). In short, pay policies should be determined not from a historical or parochial perspective but a contemporary and dynamic perspective. Managers with a long-term perspective have an ethical responsibility to extend this new vision to the industry at large. Those with a long-term view realize that competition differs in health care organizations from production industries where jobs can be exported. Therefore leaders have a responsibility for ensuring that the basic pay structure for health care–based occupations remains competitive with other professional service opportunities. If not, the industry is doomed to have a higher total payroll as it overpays entry-level workers of less ability, relies on more part-time workers than it desires, and pays more supervisors to coordinate the work of these less productive workers.

Designing a Pay System

Employers are advised to make it clear by words and actions what attributes of jobs are deserving of compensation for all its employees and how they relate to the organization's mission. Further, the design, implementation, and evaluation should have integrity as evidenced by representative employee involvement, documentation, audits, appeals process, staff training, and employee understanding. There should be an explicit and open policy about what attributes of jobs deserve compensation. The development, installation, and operation of the system should include representatives of employees from all sectors of the organization and all races and both sexes.

The employer should ensure that choice of measured factors accounts for all compensable features of the job. These identified factors and the relationship of the factors to one another should not be biased against any particular race or gender. If the system results in jobs held mainly by women or minorities scoring lower on average than white males, then it is the obligation of the employer to justify the choice of factors. That is, they are valid measures and no other factors are available that would be equally valid but less discriminatory. Job titles should be periodically audited so that jobs with similar tasks are not titled differently based on the sex of the incumbents. For example, it is not appropriate to use *secretaries* for women and *assistants* for men.

In point-factor systems, the range of scores for each factor should represent the full range of variability of the feature being measured, and the division of the full range of levels should be accurately specified. The factor weights must also be chosen in a bias-free way. The use of existing wages to assign weights is unacceptable unless the employer can show that such weights are unbiased with respect to sex—that is, justified by business necessity. Factor-level descriptions should be written as concretely as possible with careful specification of equivalences for different types of jobs.

Implementation

The system should be well documented, and the documentation should be available to employees or their representatives. The personnel should be well trained and have enough practice to be up to date. There should be regular and documented audit procedures to review and update job descriptions. The system should have an appeals mechanism that is explained, along with other key features, during the orientation process.

Beyond these technical measures of program adequacy, managers need to look at general outcomes. Health care organizations are increasingly being held accountable for delivering quality care within an established price. Is the time, effort, and cost of maintaining the pay system contributing to achieving the larger outcomes? There is a great need for creativity and innovation in using data from quality assurance activities, management information systems, and monies budgeted for education and fringe benefits to redesign pay systems and integrate them with nonpay rewards for good performers.

SUMMARY

Compensation is a core activity of the health care organizations. Fair pay rests on a well-designed and well-maintained system for writing job descriptions, conducting job evaluations, relating jobs to one another, and matching pay rates with pay grades. Technical expertise and computer analysis provide the tools for maintaining both external and internal equity. Explicit policies and clear communications undergird employee acceptance.

In health care more than in other private businesses, government policies for reimbursement constrain management options. Simultaneously, cultural forces are demanding a different definition of fair pay if health care organizations are to attract and retain professionals and lower-paid workers. An enlightened pay philosophy is paramount. Clearly the compensation system must be integrated with all other organizational activities, especially quality control, job design and description, performance appraisal, and fringe benefits.

NOTES

1. There are two alternatives: assume that government outlays will increase enough to pay all workers more or close hospitals with low occupancy, thus consolidating valued workers in high-occupancy hospitals. Neither of these seems politically feasible.

2. This same act exempts companies from paying overtime beyond forty hours per week if a union management agreement provides that no employee will be required to work more than 1,040 hours during any twenty-six consecutive weeks (or 2,240 hours per fifty-two weeks). The employee must be guaranteed no fewer than 1,080 hours of employment per year. However, overtime must be paid beyond twelve hours in one day and fifty-six in one workweek. Executives, administrators, and professionals are exempt.

Hospitals use a flexible hour concept, especially for nurses, but a guaranteed annual wage does not accompany this practice.

3. Variations on the point method are the position analysis questionnaire (PAQ), the federal factor evaluation system, and the time span of discretion. There is considerable interest in the federal government in installing the time span of discretion method developed by Jaques (1964). Since it is not used in health care currently, it is not discussed here. However, its emphasis on broad bands of responsibility may make it attractive in health service organizations in the future.

4. The advantages of benchmarks, which are used in all individually tailored systems, are that employers can relate many disparate jobs using clusters tied by benchmarks to recreate the whole; newly created jobs can be fitted in without re-examining the whole system; market surveys are needed for only a few jobs.

5. For a theoretical discussion, see E. England, "Socioeconomic Explanation of Job Segregation," in Helen Remick, ed., *Comparable Worth and Wage Discrimination: Technical Possibilities and Political Realities* (Philadelphia: Temple University Press, 1985), pp. 28–46; D. Treiman and P. Roose, "Sex and Earnings in Industrial Society: A Nine-Nation Comparison," *American Journal of Sociology* 89(3) (1985): 612–50.

6. For a good overview see U. Reinhardt, "The Compensation of Physicians," *Quality Review Bulletin* (1985): 366–77.

7. Most of the comparable worth cases and decisions involve public agencies, primarily because they have well-developed job evaluation systems, many classes, and accessible data.

REFERENCES

Aaron, H., and Lougy, C. (1986). *The Comparable Worth Controversy*. Washington, D.C.: Brookings Institution.

Adamache, K., and Sloan, F. (1982). Unions and hospitals. *Journal of Health Economics* 1: 81–108.

Aiken, L., and Mullinix, C. (1987). The nurse shortage: Myth or reality? *New England Journal of Medicine* 317: 641–46.

Beyers, M., Mullner, R., Byre, C., and Whitehead, S. (1983). Results of the nursing personnel survey, part 3: RN salary and fringe benefits. *Journal of Nursing Administration* 13 (6): 16–20.

Browdy, J. D. (1986). Executive compensation in the multiaffiliate corporation. *Health Progress* 67 (5): 31–35.

Burda, D. (1986). Labor law may create trap for unwary hospitals. *Hospitals* 60 (4): 38.

Carey, J. (1985). *Salary Administration*. Atlanta: Association for Media-Based Continuing Education for Engineers.

Cascio, W. (1986). *Managing Human Resources*. New York: McGraw-Hill.

Chayes, A. (1974). Make your equal opportunity program court-proof. *Harvard Business Review* 52 (5): 81–89.

Cole, B. (1987). Average base salary increase slips a notch to 6–7% in 1986. *Modern Healthcare* 16 (23): 65–118.

Cooper, E., and Barrett, G. (1984). Equal pay and gender: Implications of court cases for personnel practices. *Academy of Management Review* 9: 84–94.

Dawis, R. (1984). Job satisfaction: Worker aspirations, attitudes, and behavior. In N. Gysber (Ed.), *Designing Careers,* 275–301. San Francisco: Jossey-Bass.

Dear, M., Weisman, C., and O'Keefe, S. (1985). Evaluation of a contract model for professional nursing practice. *Heathcare Management Review* 10 (2): 65–76.
Egan, P. (1986, September 5). Executive paychecks to jump 4.9% in '86. *Hospitals*.
England, E. (1985). Socioeconomic explanation of job segregation. In Helen Remick (Ed.), *Comparable Worth and Wage Discrimination,* 28–46. Philadelphia: Temple University.
Fackelman, K. (1985a). Fears about revised wage index draw protests from hospital groups. *Modern Healthcare* 15 (8): 60–61.
——— (1985b). Revised wage index won't create expected Midwest windfalls-study. *Modern Healthcare* 15 (18): 32–34.
Feldberg, R., and Glenn, E. (1982). Male and female: Job versus gender models in the sociology of work. In R. Kahn-Hut, A. Kaplan-Daniels, and R. Colvard (Eds.), *Women and Work: Problems and Perspective,* 65–80. New York: Oxford.
Fisher, G. (1985). Salary surveys: An antitrust perspective. *Personnel Administrator* 30 (4): 87–154.
Freund, C., and Mitchell, J. (1985). Multi-institutional systems: The new arrangement. *Nursing Economics* 3: 24–31.
Friss, L. (1981). Work force policy perspectives: Registered nurses. *Journal of Health Politics, Policy and Law* 5: 696–719.
——— (1983). Hospital nurse staffing: An urgent need for management reappraisal. *Health Care Management Review* 7 (1): 21–28.
——— (1988). Why don't nurses demand more pay? In Rita Kelly and Jane Bayes (Eds.), *Comparable Worth, Pay Equity, and Public Policy,* 63–76. Westport, Conn.: Greenwood Press.
Ganong, J., and Ganong, W. (1984). *Performance Appraisal for Productivity*. Rockville, Md.: Aspen.
Ginzberg, E., Patray, J., Ostow, M., and Brann, E. (1982). Nurse discontent: The search for realistic solutions. *Journal of Nursing Administration* 9: 7–11.
Greene, R. (1980). Geographic wage indexing for CETA and Medicare. *Monthly Labor Review* 103 (9): 15–19.
——— (1982). Issues in salary structure design. *Compensation Review* 14 (2): 28–33.
Henderson, R. (1982). *Compensation Management: Rewarding Performance*. 3d ed. Reston, Va.: Reston.
Henderson, R., and Clarke, K. (1981). *Job Pay for Job Worth*. Atlanta: Georgia State University.
Institute of Medicine, National Academy of Science (1983). *Nursing and Nursing Education: Public Policies and Private Actions*. Washington, D.C.: National Academy Press.
Ivancevich, J., Matteson, M., and McMahon, J. (1980). Understanding professional attitudes. *Hospital and Health Services Administration* 25: 53–68.
Jaques, E. (1964). *Time Span Handbook*. London: Heinemann.
Killingsworth, M. (1986). The economics of comparable worth: Analytical, empirical and policy questions. In Heidi Hartmann (Ed.), *Comparable Worth: New Directions for Research,* 86–115. Washington, D.C.: National Academy Press.
King, N. (1970). Clarification and evaluation of the two factor theory of job satisfaction. *Psychological Bulletin* 74: 18–31.
Laliberty, R., and Christopher, W. (1984). *Enhancing Productivity in Health Care Facilities*. Owings Mills, Md.: National Health Publishing.

Lawler, E. (1986). What's wrong with the point-factor job evaluation. *Management Review* 75 (11): 44–48.

Leuthold, J. (1984). Income splitting and women's labor-force participation. *Industrial and Labor Relations Review* 38: 98–105.

Levit, K., Lazenby, H., Waldo, D., and Davidoff, M. (1985). National health expenditures, 1984. *Health Care Financing Review* 7: 13.

Maxey, C., Kennedy, R., and Carlson, K. (1979). Approaches to wage and salary determination. *Journal of the American Dietetic Association* 74: 345–52.

Moore, P. (1985). *Public Personnel Management*. Lexington, Mass.: D. C. Heath.

Moskowitz, S. (1983). Pay equity and American nurses: A legal analysis. *St. Louis University Law Journal* 27 (4): 801–55.

Munro, B. (1983). Young graduates: Who are they and what do they want? *Journal of Nursing Administration* 13 (6): 21–26.

Poulos, M. 1984. Hospital cutbacks' effects on employee wages. *Health Matrix* 2: 95–96.

Prospective Payment Assessment Commission (1985). *Technical Appendixes to the Report and Recommendations to the Secretary, U.S. Department of Health and Human Services April 1, 1985*. Washington, D.C.: Government Printing Office.

Redling, E., and Daze, H. (1985). Healthcare senior management salaries lag behind general industry. *Healthcare Financial Management* 39 (8): 38–42.

Reynard, E. (1976). Updating salary information for scientific and technical positions: A statistical approach. *Compensation Review* 8: 36–43.

Richardson, R., and Kaufman, D. (1983): Social science inquiries into female achievement: Recurrent methodological problems. In Barbara Ricardson and Jeana Wirtenberg (Eds.), *Sex Role Research*, 33–48. New York: Oxford.

Salkever, D. (1983). Cost implications of hospital unionization. In Richard M. Scheffler and L. T. Rossiter (Eds.), *Advances in Health Economics and Health Services Research*, 4: 225–55. Greenwich, Conn.: JAI Press.

Sape, G. (1985). Coping with comparable worth. *Harvard Business Review* 85 (3): 145–52.

Sauser, W., and York, C. (1978). Sex differences in job satisfaction: A re-examination. *Personnel Psychology* 31: 537–47.

Schramm, C. (1978). Regulating hospital labor costs: A case study in the politics of state rate commissions. *Journal of Health Politics, Policy and Law* 3: 364–74.

Schuler, R., and Youngblood, S. (1986). *Effective Personnel Management*. 2d ed. St. Paul, Minn.: West.

Shafritz, J. M. (1973). *Position Classification: A Behavioral Analysis for the Public Service*. New York: Praeger.

Siegel, G., and Myrtle, R. (1985). *Public Personnel Administration: Concepts and Practices*. Boston: Houghton Mifflin.

Spector, B., and Beer, M. (1985). Note on job evaluation. In Michael Beer, Bert Spector, Paul R. Lawrence, C. Quinn Mills, and Richard E. Walton (Eds.), *Human Resource Management*, 494–97. New York: Free Press.

Steinwald, B. (1983). Compensation of hospital-based physicians. *Health Services Research* 18 (1): 17–47.

Strasser, S., Steinberg, J., Cummins, G., and Persels, J. (1983). Why some evaluation studies are useful and others are not: Facilitators and obstacles to the use of

evaluation research in hospital settings. *Health and Human Services Administration* 28: 69–95.
Suskin, H. (Ed.) (1977). *Job Evaluation and Pay Administration in the Public Sector*, 160–61. Chicago: International Personnel Management Association.
Thompson, M. (1979). *Antitrust and the Health Care Provider*. Germantown, Md.: Aspen.
Thomsen, D. (1978). Eliminating pay discrimination caused by job evaluation. *Personnel* 55 (5): 11–22.
——— (1980). Consideration for non-biased systems. In Joy Grune (Ed.), *Manual on Pay Equity*, 110–11. Washington, D.C.: Conference on Alternative State and Local Policies.
Treiman, D., and Hartmann, H. (Eds.) (1981). *Women, Work, and Wages*, 73, 79. Washington, D.C.: National Academy Press.
Treiman, D., and Roos, P. (1983). Sex and earnings in industrial society: A nine-nation comparison. *American Journal of Sociology* 89: 612–50.
U.S. Department of Health and Human Services (1981). *The Recurrent Shortages of Registered Nurses*. Washington, D.C.: Human Resources Administration.
U.S. General Accounting Office (1983). *Hospital Links with Related Firms Can Conceal Unreasonable Costs and Increase Administrative Burden, Thus Inflating Health Program Expenditures*. Washington, D.C.: Government Printing Office.
Varca, P., Shaffer, G., and McCauley, C. (1983). Sex differences in job satisfaction revisited. *Academy of Management Journal* 26: 348–53.
Watland, A., Morgan, B., Diviney, J., and Bodenhausen, A. 1983. Study shows adverse effect on hospital reimbursement. *Hospital Financial Management* 13 (8): 32–35.
Weissburg, C., and Stern, K. (1985). Can hospitals reward physicians for reducing unnecessary utilization? *FAH Review* 18 (5): 45–46.
Youngkin, Ellis O. (1985). Comparable worth: Alternatives to litigation and legislation. *Nursing Economics* 3:40.

8
The Role of Quality of Worklife in the Strategic Human Resource Management Model

*Paula L. Stamps
and Thomas E. Duston*

The purpose of this chapter is to present and describe methods for improving the quality of worklife in the health field. We begin by discussing the nature of the quality of worklife (QWL) movement and the relationship of this to the critical issue of productivity. A model for an integrated QWL program is presented with some final cautions about the implementation of these programs and their links to productivity.

This chapter does not draw on any examples in home care, nor has it many specifics on job redesign; Chapters 3 and 9 address those two topics. We will instead initially present some necessary theoretical constructs for both QWL and productivity and then follow up with specific and practical guidelines for health administrators. We feel strongly that we must return to some of these concepts. This may seem a waste of time to busy health care managers, but in fact this is exactly the problem; in our rush to apply new concepts, they often are applied erroneously, with the results being even more dissatisfied and demoralized employees.

Our own bias should be recognized regarding the roles of management and labor in QWL programs. Although we appreciate that even the most progressive managers have organizational constraints on their behavior, we also believe that better management with more open communication is clearly possible in almost every health organization. This communication is a necessary condition for increasing workplace democracy, the ultimate goal of QWL programs.

QUALITY OF WORKLIFE

The QWL movement is an example of a rediscovered concept. Its roots are in two works that all managers will recognize: McGregor's 1960 book that defined Theory X and Y and Herzberg's theory of job satisfaction that separates our satisfaction factors and "dissatisfaction" factors. (He is known as the "originator" of the job enrichment concept, another newly "rediscovered" term.)[1]

Theory X and Y became the focus of management of human resources—often called personnel supervision—with Theory X being the more traditional centralized management pattern that emphasizes the control necessary for good management. This Theory X model of management is particularly ineffective in organizations with many professionals, including most health care organizations. Theory Y is an alternative that emphasizes working with people and stresses their positive characteristics. Recently Theory Z has arisen from the Japanese model of management.[2] This recognizes that employees possess characteristics of both Theories X and Y and pose a challenge to managers to create the best working environment based on the needs of the individual workers. Of the five specific attributes of Theory Z, two have become particularly well known: lifetime employment relationships and participative decision making. The latter has led to participation in quality circles.

The quality circle receives a great deal of attention today. This concept is really an offshoot of the Theory Z participative management scheme. Quality circles depend on the joint interest of labor and management; small groups at various levels in the organization are involved in frequent and regular discussions. In industry these have been used as part of the quality control management responsibility. Quality circles have been used to decrease rank and age differences between supervisors and workers. The use of quality circles seems quite appropriate in an industry such as the health field where many professionals are involved but within which distinct hierarchical arrangements often exist.

An interesting—an ironic—aspect of this very brief history is that these QWL and job enrichment concepts have been around since the 1960s. Many industries have tried some model of them, and yet we still have reports of tremendous amounts of occupational dissatisfaction. Also left out in this brief history is the union movement. In fact, if participative management worked, including more control over wage determination, there would probably be no need for unions, although this level of participation by labor is probably inconsistent with capitalism. Union leaders have been generally cool to job enrichment, viewing it as a way of intensifying any given job ("a speedup"). Labor leaders who supported QWL did so not because QWL programs lead to increased productivity but because the purposes of this movement were democracy and dignity. If productivity also improved, that was fine.[3]

WORK ALIENATION

Where do these brief comments about QWL in the health field lead us? To answer this fully, we must add an additional concept that recurs in the QWL

The Role of Quality of Worklife

literature: work alienation. Work alienation is a difficult notion for many people to accept since it sounds much more extreme than work dissatisfaction. The latter is almost always preferred since it implies concerns related specifically to work within the organization and not to the nature of the organization itself. Work alienation involves wider social structure factors since it is not viewed as an individual maladjustment but rather as a characteristic of how the work process is organized.

There are three specific theories of work alienation. The first arises in the critique of capitalism and depends on Karl Marx's observation that workers have no part in deciding how tasks are to be achieved. Alienation occurs because the worker has no control over the methods of production; class conflict between workers and supervisors increases under a centralized management scheme. A second theory of alienation concerns the technology and structure common to large organizations. As size increases, so does the division of jobs and hierarchy. Alienation results from a feeling of powerlessness and increased separation from other workers and from the product itself. A third theory of work alienation arises from modern writings in political economy and focuses on the hierarchical nature of organizations. Work is increasingly divided into thinking (the manager) and production (the worker). This division of labor keeps workers and managers separated from one another and has as a primary function not productivity or efficiency enhancement but maximizing control over workers.[4]

We have listed some of the conflicts often viewed as being at the root of worker alienation.[5] Although they are phrased in general terms using the word *employees,* substitution of *nurses* for *employees* and *administrator* for *organization* underscores the relevance to the health field:

- Employees want change and personal growth; the organization wants work to be organized simply and according to specialty.
- Employees want to be included in participative management; organizations are hierarchical and dependent on status differentials.
- Employee commitment is influenced highly by the intrinsic nature of the work. The organization's reward system emphasizes material rewards and job security.
- Employees are likely to have a shorter time line for their own personal achievement than organizations.
- Employees value interpersonal aspects of organizational life; organizations strive to remove as much human variability as possible.
- Employees are less motivated by competition; organizations continue to arrange the reward system competitively.

Health care organizations, especially hospitals, continue to operate on a classic managerial style; this tends to centralize power and decision making, removing autonomy from a variety of professionals who have a lower rank within the organization. This loss of autonomy is one of the primary motivating factors in an increase in alienation. Additionally, the continued trend toward specialization and use of highly sophisticated technological innovations has taken away much of the human orientation of the health industry. This trend leads to increased isolation of direct care providers and to increased distance from the product—the health status of the patient.

The conclusion from this brief introduction to QWL is this: the language of the QWL movement is full of terms that do not seem exactly appropriate to the health field: *workers, alienation, supervisors,* and *means of production,* among others. However, the principles that are referred to in these concepts are most appropriate to the health field. The health industry has become more and more businesslike, but instead of adopting new methods of participative management, the management of most health care organizations, especially hospitals, has increasingly become centralized.

AN EXTENDED CAVEAT ON PRODUCTIVITY

Most management people assume that QWL programs are aimed at increasing productivity, although the theory behind QWL programs is related more to altruistic motives and concerns related to improving the work environment. However, behind that link is the assumption that happy workers are more productive. Even management books have become more explicit; *Management for Productivity* is a recent title.[6]

Productivity is generally defined as an increase in output relative to inputs used. This increase takes place through redesign of the job, improvements in work process and methods, changes in scheduling, increased efficiency of the people themselves, or just getting the people to work harder. Cost containment is another way of talking about productivity improvement; if output per hour of labor input is increased and wage costs are kept under control, the cost per unit of output will be reduced (or at least kept within acceptable bounds). Although the most common measure of productivity is output per unit of labor, productivity may also be measured by output per dollar spent on inputs.

A big problem with productivity in hospitals is that the outcome measure (treated patients, revenue generated, or something else) is a function of the whole array of inputs that go toward treating patients; a fair amount of trade-off is usually possible among the inputs, and experimenting with the substitution of inputs is done in both research and management. Examples of input substitution are abundant in the health field. In ambulatory care, substitution of a nurse practitioner for a physician for many primary care activities acts to increase the number of patients seen per dollar spent on direct care providers since nurse practitioners are paid less than physicians. The substitution of volunteer workers, aides, and licensed practical nurses for some of the nursing functions in hospitals has accomplished the same goal: the same output for fewer dollars spent on the input.

Deciding on the appropriate output measure has always been problematic in the health field. Increasingly, the output measure used for productivity purposes is being defined as total revenue generated by a particular service or department in a hospital. This use of productivity often leads to a decrease in services that generate less revenue per dollar spent on inputs and increasing services that generate more revenue per dollar spent on inputs. Output can also be defined in physical numeric terms, such as length of stay, number of laboratory tests performed, or number of prescriptions processed.

In for-profit industrial settings, both quality control and consumer acceptance are built into the output measure. The output measure commonly includes a product that has an acceptable quality, meaning that a certain proportion of products have been examined or inspected. The implication of most industrial quality control processes is that consumers will accept a certain low percentage of failures or of unacceptably low-quality products.

The health field has developed numerous output measures that are pseudomeasures for quality. Although there are many efforts to measure quality directly, they are obviously difficult and subject to much controversy. Consumer acceptance is also an issue in the health field, but this is more complicated than in private industry since the patient's perception of quality may be quite different from that of the clinician. In fact, it may be impossible to have highly satisfied patients and providers as outcomes of the health care system, even if we were to relax the present constraints on costs.

Demonstrating improvements in productivity in the health field is difficult. In many cases, even discussing productivity is difficult because of the many disagreements over measurements. However, attention to productivity improvement will not go away, nor should it. This attention should lead to increased efforts to define carefully the inputs, including both labor and capital. We should also be prepared to expand the definition of outputs to include not only services rendered or dollars generated but also acceptable patient and staff satisfaction levels. One example of a proxy output measure that is particularly appropriate but practically never used is turnover rate. Of course, as part of the emphasis on developing measures of output, we must continue to pursue measurements of quality, since that is really the output of most interest and most value to us. Using more appropriate measures will improve our ability to see productivity improvements.

Productivity improvements should be designed through managerial intervention, such as an ongoing organizational development program or what is now often called a quality of worklife program. Productivity improvements may also take place through collective bargaining activity.[7]

The ambiguity of measuring productivity should not be allowed to get in the way of trying to come to better measures. Many people in the health field are uncomfortable with the view of productivity that is being increasingly used in the health field: revenue per dollar spent on inputs. One way of dealing with this is to use the philosophy of quality circles and apply it to the productivity problem. A quality circle in a hospital setting could include clinicians, accounting staff, and representatives of patient and employee satisfaction interests. Incorporating financial concerns, clinical concerns, and concerns about turnover and patient satisfaction meets the philosophy of quality circles better than any other current experiment in participative management.

As a final caution, it must be noted that even with appropriate measures of productivity, a QWL program will not necessarily produce demonstrable results without a firm commitment to the philosophy of participative management. QWL programs, including participation in quality circles, are nothing more than new ways of organizing a critical resource (or input) in the health field—people. The health industry is a labor-intensive one, with wages and benefits constituting 60 to 65 percent of the costs of services. Despite this, we spend far more time analyzing the capital expenditures of the industry than on developing meaningful ways of organizing the human resources.

An additional caution concerns the results to be expected from a QWL program. QWL programs are not meant to improve productivity. They are meant to improve the working atmosphere and staff morale. It is the continuing assumption that these inputs are related to the outputs that causes us to link QWL programs with improved productivity.

If management is serious about improving the work situation of employees in the health field, what specific actions can be taken? The remainder of this chapter will focus on what seem to us to be the most relevant and honest efforts to improve the quality of worklife. Not all will be appropriate in every organization and not all are totally within the control of management, but these are suggestions that can be adapted to the health field.

QUALITY OF WORKLIFE PROGRAMS FOR THE HEALTH FIELD

QWL programs generally have four common goals: (1) creating a more democratic organization where everyone can participate; (2) sharing financial incentives; (3) creating greater job security; and (4) enhancing individual development by creating conditions that contribute to this development. There are a great variety of organizational interventions that are labeled QWL, but in most cases they are something less. In fact, a QWL program is just that—an ongoing, systematic *program,* not one experiment in job redesign. Any organizational intervention that meets any or all of the four goals noted here meets the requirements for a QWL program. We would like to discuss the ones that are most applicable to the health field. The following should all be viewed as part of a QWL program:

- Recruitment, selection, and retention
- Job satisfaction
- Career development
- Job redesign
- Alternative patterns of work
- Participative management

Not all of these innovations will be appropriate for all job situations within the health field, and in some cases there may be organizational or professional constraints. In many cases, however, the hesitation is simply a result of the old "we've never done it this way before" idea. The health industry is far behind other industries in terms of organization of human resources. Many of these programs do not require either money or drastic organizational change, but they do require a very different management style.

Recruitment, Selection, and Retention

To many people, recruitment and selection of potential employees is not a QWL program. This attitude is part of the problem. In a labor-intensive industry such as the health field, turnover is expensive, with estimates of replacing one hospital nurse varying from $800 to $5,000, depending on training and other indirect costs.[8] If the major motivation of a QWL program is the hope of improving productivity, having a high nursing turnover, which requires almost constant retraining of nurses, is a major barrier to the most efficient use of available personnel. If the motivation for a QWL program is employee satisfaction and workplace democracy, high levels of turnover disrupt the ability of the group to work closely together.

Recruitment and selection refer to the two phases of obtaining new employees; retention activities are directed at preventing these—and other—employees from leaving.

Recruitment is the first step and usually involves some sort of marketing activity through which the organization tries to make itself competitive with other possible organizations for what is often a limited pool of applicants. Developing a formal recruitment plan is the most appropriate mechanism; far too many organizations wait for the turnover to occur. A plan or a projection based on previous turnover figures will allow replacement or addition of employees in a timely, planned fashion.

After the organization has identified the type and number of people that it is likely to need to recruit, the next decision is where to recruit. Three factors are important here. The first is that the organization wants to recruit where the chance of success is the greatest. The second is to arrange the recruiting process so that no potential applicants are systematically screened out. For example, advertising in newspapers with a large circulation is far more likely to attract a wider diversity of applicants than advertising in small-circulation local newspapers. It is important that the spirit of affirmative action be met in advertising for new positions. The third factor in recruiting is honesty. The goal of the organization is to recruit the best applicants for any available position who will stay in the job or at least stay with the organization. This retention factor is often overlooked by managers who are too busy to see beyond the immediate turnover problem. Recruiting many highly qualified applicants who leave within a year is an indication of a poor recruiting strategy. Retention must be a primary goal in a recruitment strategy. The organization may conduct in-depth personal interviews, tours of the facility, or meetings with current employees. If the last is not viewed positively, within the organization, that fact itself is a sign of major problems with respect to retention. Research has shown that when new recruits are given realistic information about a job, no decrease will occur in the number of people who apply for the job, and a significant reduction is realized in turnover.[9]

There are, of course, alternatives to recruitment—overtime, temporary help, and subcontracting, among others. Although each may be appropriate in specific and limited situations, in general creating a stable, full-time team of people working together and viewing themselves as a group is a necessary condition for achieving the principles behind participative management.

Selection from among the screened pool of applicants is the next step. The selection process ranges from an almost random process to an extremely rigid interpretation of certain skills. Since the goal is to select an employee who will stay, it is worth the manager's time to collect as much information as possible. The more important and/or complicated the job is, the more information is needed. An additional principle is to remember that past behavior is one of the best predictors of future behavior, so references become an important part of the selection process. Personal interviews are an appropriate way of determining any past behavior that the applicant may feel is not indicative of future behavior.

The selection process is another place for the organization to demonstrate reality to the applicant. A very realistic view of the job and interviews with managers and supervisors as well as employees with whom they will work is appropriate and will do much to decrease turnover rate. Even if this results in a high rate of applicants withdrawing from the selection process, this is much better than those applicants coping with their unrealistic expectations by leaving the job.

If participatory management is a key part of the QWL program, as it should be, applicants should be made aware of this, and their willingness to participate in this system should be part of the screening process.

Retention is the final step in the recruitment and selection process. In fact, retention is a very appropriate goal of a QWL program in and of itself, and most of the rest of this chapter has retention as the goal of many of the programs. The first step in retaining employees is appropriate selection. After that, conducting a thoughtful orientation program for new employees will help in creating an appropriate atmosphere. A carefully designed orientation program will reduce employee turnover, reduce anxiety, create positive work values, reduce start-up costs, and will save time on the part of both supervisors and coworkers.[10]

It is important to know what not to do as part of an orientation program; new employees should not be flooded with factual information. Since most health professionals value professional autonomy and personal interaction with coworkers very highly, these are the two facets of an orientation program that

The Role of Quality of Worklife

should be emphasized. In designing an orientation program, the following questions should also be considered:

1. What information is needed to make the new employee comfortable in the immediate environmnent?
2. What impression and impact does the organization want to make within the first week?
3. What key policies and procedures must employees understand on the first day to prevent early mistakes?
4. What can be done to acquaint new employees and fellow employees with each other so that they might begin to work together?
5. What special facilities, such as desk or work area, are needed to make the new employee feel comfortable?
6. What job-related tasks can be done on the first day?
7. What positive experience can the new employee take home from the first day?[11]

Most often orientation is viewed as a one-day program. When the goal of an orientation program is to be an integral part of a QWL program whose larger goal is retention, this process becomes both more important and longer. The nature of the job partially determines the appropriate orientation period. It is important to interview a new employee after a short time (about a month) to document any problems and the level of satisfaction with the new job. This interview should take place after the person is comfortable with the job but may have some concerns or need some minor additional information. Additional personal interviews should be held periodically during the first year. These interviews should be clearly separated from the performance review of the employee.

Retention of both new and older employees is a process that leads to a discussion of job satisfaction, since it is assumed that dissatisfaction is one factor that leads to a variety of negative coping mechanisms, including high absenteeism, high turnover, and low morale.

Job Satisfaction

Concern with the level of job satisfaction of employees has been of interest for many years. The major motivation for this interest has been to discover the link between satisfaction and job performance and ultimately to be able to document the link between satisfaction and productivity. Investigations to this end have provided varied and often conflicting results; work dissatisfaction has been directly related to high rates of turnover, accidents, tardiness and absenteeism.[12] However, these results are not consistent, and other studies show no relationship to other measures of job performances, including productivity measures. Inability to document the relationships between satisfaction and a variety of job-related factors has not led to a diminution of interest in work satisfaction. In fact, interest has increased in recent years.

In addition to the intuitive relationship between productivity and work satisfaction, a second major focus is more humanistic. This focus examines the role of work in individuals' lives in relation to their overall quality of life and focuses on the personal and professional development of individuals as they work. This humanitarian focus has strong and partially altruistic roots in a portion of American society and draws heavily on the work of people who talk about alienation. Even this humanistic focus always notes the possible link between satisfaction and productivity, however.

The health field has room for both motivations; in fact, both are appropriate. The financial concern is obvious since labor costs are a high percentage of the budget of any direct care organization. As cost containment has increased in scope and power, it has become increasingly necessary to demonstrate efficiencies. Increasing attention has been paid to satisfaction as a way to achieve efficiencies and cost improvements. However, the health field is composed of many different health professionals who, although working in an hierarchical arrangement, have specific and important roles to play.

At a practical level, most managers will admit to being concerned about job satisfaction but will note the impossibility of measurement, which has been a significant problem. Most of the measurements have been developed by academics, including occupational sociologists and industrial psychologists, who have concentrated most of their measurement efforts on employees in nonprofessional lower-level jobs. This has had the effect of defining both the type and the content of investigation and of people's perceptions about their jobs. Since the motivations for developing these measurements have varied, the results of the studies have also varied. As a result there are few consistent trends and practically no measures that managers are willing to use.

Even the more recent measures that have been developed for professionals are not widely used, nor are the results consistent. Of these more recent tools, the Job Description Index (JDI) is the most common, although it has not been recently updated. Other scales that have been used include one that does not involve reading but depends on ranking expressions on faces and one that uses a semantic differential type scale.[13]

The health field has also developed specific measures of job satisfaction, with most of the research concentrating on nurses, specifically hospital nurses. Although these studies provide much insight into the nursing profession in particular, and into health care professionals in general, the studies use different measurements and study slightly different variables. As a result, most health care managers feel like other managers: job satisfaction is one of those aspects over which they have no control.

In fact, a major part of the problem has been the lack of a validated measurement instrument. Without one, it is impossible to try to relate the variables that are being evaluated. The first need is development of a validated measurement instrument for health personnel, and the second need is to develop this in such a way that it can be used as part of a management information system used to develop the critical human resources in the health field.

After over ten years of scale development, a validated measurement instrument exists. This has been specifically developed using nurses but has also been applied to many other groups of health professionals.[14] The instrument itself is composed of two parts: a ranking to obtain information on expectations and a forty-four-item Likert scale that gathers information about current level of satisfaction with a particular job. It is possible to utilize either or both of these parts and also to create a weighted index using the rankings from expectations to create weights for current level of satisfaction. The measurement scale demonstrates high levels of reliability and validity and has been utilized in many settings with a variety of health professionals. The results are generally consistent.

This scale has been developed for a specific purpose; it is meant to be included in a management information system. The results are meant to be used to increase communication within the hierarchical health care system and to provide information necessary for job redesign. Satisfaction measures are meant to be included along with other systematic inputs, including performance evaluations, information from exit interviews, and data on absenteeism and turnover rates. It is ironic that although the health field is very labor intensive, health care managers have paid very little attention to the need to develop systematic ways of organizing human resources.

Many administrators and researchers argue that work satisfaction is not directly manipulable and thus has little practical significance for making recommendations for any organization or behavioral change. A major rationale for this position—the lack of a valid measurement instrument—has now been eliminated. Use of the Stamps-Piedmonte Index as a management tool provides information about general expectations, as well as current satisfaction, and also provides guidance for possible job redesign measures. This scale is meant to be part of an ongoing process that is an integral part of a management information system; it is a mechanism to organize data and to point out areas amenable to organizational change. Another intent of this measurement instrument is to be sensitive to changes in level of satisfaction that may result from managerial decisions. Unlike other scales used to measure work satisfaction, this one is designed to go beyond the data collection and data analysis phases to the actual implementation of organizational change. This does not mean that work satisfaction is itself always directly manipulable, but it does imply that levels of work satisfaction can be—and are—affected by managerial decisions.

This measurement is meant to be used to increase communication and to start the process of job redesign. As such, measures of job satisfaction are critical to any QWL program. As with all other techniques, however, the success of this approach rests mainly with the managers using it.

In a QWL program, a measure of job satisfaction can—and should—be used as an outcome measure. Satisfaction is one of the variables the QWL program wants to affect. Levels of satisfaction are an important interest in and of themselves. Once we have enough data using validated and standardized measurement instruments, we will then address the next research question: the relationship between satisfaction and other characteristics of a job, including job performance and productivity, turnover rates, and health outcomes of patients.

Career Development

Most industries recognize that a very important part of managing human resources is to view the new employee as a person with a career within the current organization. This implies the goal of retention and provides for many moves within one organization for an individual. The health care industry is lacking in this understanding and typically hires a registered nurse to fill one particular slot without any thought for the future role of that individual within the organization. This shortsighted attitude by health and hospital administrators is reinforced by the health care industry in general since vertical mobility is very limited. This does not mean that a manager should ignore what can be done within an organization, however. In fact, a commitment to the principles behind QWL obviously leads to a manager's pushing for the best possible careers for employees.

Occupational sociologists identify four career stages that most people go through: exploration, establishment, maintenance, and decline.[15] In the early exploration stage, the person is involved in a personal self-identification and self-assessment process that often leads to the need to try a variety of occupational situations. Once this stage is accomplished, they usually work to establish themselves within a certain occupational niche. The importance of their job within their life becomes large, and their job changes are more focused on gaining necessary skills. The maintenance phase occurs in mid- to late career; it usually incorporates increasing responsibility and generally carries high expectations for productivity. Individuals in the decline phase must make preparations for formal retirement and often begin to phase out part of their job responsibilities.

Study after study on job satisfaction has demonstrated a relationship between age and satisfaction, with satisfaction increasing with age. This has been treated as a demographic variable but is far more likely reflective of the career stages of an individual. Obviously individuals in these stages need different management styles and different types of services from the organization. Although most hospital administrators view this as outside their scope of responsibility, the turnover rate, which is within their responsibility, would probably be much lower if career development were included as part of their managerial style. In most cases, activities and/or programs can be offered without great expense to the organization. As with so many other management areas, the most important variable is the attitude of the manager.

Perhaps the most basic aspect of career development in the health field is training programs. Training programs can be constructed so as to be part of on-the-job training or arranged to take place outside the job. Staff nurses, as well as all other health care professionals, are acutely aware of their needs for ongoing training and education. It is crucial that opportunities be made known to them and that their schedule be manipulated so that they have access to these programs. Many hospital nurses complain that their supervisors are not supportive of their need to go to educational sessions and are not willing to assist in the necessary schedule changes. This administrative shortsightedness is a big mistake; this complaint may lead to a qualified nurse or other health professional leaving the organization. An important extension of this commitment to education is to arrange for special sessions of particular interest to a group of health clinicians.

Although an explicit career pathing program may not be appropriate in a particular health agency, elements of it can be translated from industry. Once again, the major requirement is the willingness of the administrators. Most industries offer formal career counseling and career pathing, which refers to the identification of a sequential series of jobs through which individuals can gain skills and advance vertically in the organization. In some organizations, five-year plans are developed for employees and are reviewed periodically.

Within a hospital environment, a modification of career pathing can be developed. For example, all nursing staff should be informed of vertical positions that become available. Any nurse looking for another position outside the hospital should be interviewed and a position within the hospital sought that meets higher career needs. Supervisory positions that are available should be posted openly so that current nursing staff can apply. There should be a well-planned and well-known method for posting jobs, one that all employees are aware of. Opportunities for training to change careers within the hospital should also be available—for example, from nursing to administration, finance, or marketing.

Opportunities for horizontal mobility are as important to health professionals as opportunities for vertical mobility. Programs for horizontal mobility should be developed to allow clinical personnel maximum opportunity to develop their skills. This may be independent of those who want to develop their leadership skills and take increasingly administrative positions. This mobility plan should have a clearly stated and strictly observed transfer policy. This policy should be fair to each employee and should allow for mobility within the institution for professional growth and development.[16]

Two factors will be important to the success of a career development program being developed as part of a QWL program. The first is the attitude of the manager, administrator, supervisor. Without recognition of the importance of this type of program, it will no doubt fail. The second factor is communication. Of all the managerial skills, this is the one that is critical in the health field, not only for this type of program but for others as well. Ongoing communication with all levels is the backbone of any retention program. It can be achieved in a variety of ways: regular meetings, newsletters, unit meetings, and staff-level meetings, among others. The key to the participative management system crucial to all QWL programs is frequent and systematic communication. Also, the intent of communication is in fact to carry on a dialogue—to listen and respond. This provides a framework for both staff and supervisors to understand the parameters of individual and organizational situations.

Job redesign refers to major interventions in terms of the nature of the task requirements. Since Chapter 3 fully discusses job analysis and job design, we will mention this important component only briefly. Job redesign depends on an appropriate job analysis. As a result of that analysis, the nature of the task requirement is changed in some way so as to create more satisfaction. In some cases this is done by simplifying or specializing a task. In most cases, especially in the health field, this is done by job enrichment—that is, by making the job more complex and comprehensive and thus increasing the person's level of responsibility. Appropriate use of job enrichment strategies can make work less alienating and provide more satisfying elements for people. This must be done with great care since it must not be simply a way of pushing people to do more work for the same money.

In the health field one of the most likely candidates for enrichment strategies concerns redesign of work into teams. These may be interdisciplinary teams, as in care of severe head trauma patients, for example, that involve nurses, physical therapists, neurosurgeons, and rehabilitation therapists. It may be reconfiguring nurse staffing patterns to allow for team nursing. Primary care nursing fits into this model of job enrichment also. An extension of this is the autonomous work group, a small group of people who are totally responsible for achieving a certain outcome (total care of a given patient, for example). The group is directed by its own informal leadership rather than traditional supervisors. Although this concept has been used more commonly in private industry, it could be adapted to the health field easily since health professionals are used to working autonomously and this professional autonomy is viewed very highly by team members. These teams can then form the basis for quality circles.

Alternative Patterns of Work

An easily adaptable QWL program is to decentralize the staffing and scheduling function, allowing teams of health professionals to select the patterns of work time that are most appropriate. The hospital nursing world is full of personal anecdotes relating to the inability of any group of nurses to have any control over their work schedule. One of the most common examples concerns the inability to control division of holidays between Jewish and Christian nurses. This is clearly an example of a rigid set of expectations.

The first principle is to decentralize this function and allow the team to decide on its schedule. Within that, all options could be made available, including flextime, which allows a considerable amount of variation in beginning and ending hours of work. Permanent part-time work schedules are often used by hospitals, with job sharing as one way to encourage permanent part-time work.

Another possibility is the compressed workweek, which allows people to work longer hours in fewer days.

Participative Management

This is a generic attitude that is perhaps almost synonymous with quality of worklife, since the philosophy behind participative management is really workplace democracy. Quality circles are associated with participative management. In these groups managers and workers make joint decisions about the production process and also are jointly involved in the quality control process. Through this, quality assurance activities are built into the work schedule throughout the production process.

This concept, as with alternative work patterns, should be remarkably easy to incorporate into the fabric of the health industry. There are often no clear distinctions betwen workers and managers, as in industry. There are, however, hierarchical arrangements of the many health professionals involved in direct care. When an organization attempts a real experiment in teamwork, participative management and quality circles usually follow. In fact, working in teams is a necessary precondition for health professionals to become involved in quality circles. This is adaptable to a variety of settings, including ambulatory care, hospital care, and long-term care. The care of most patients demands multiple health professionals, and nearly all research on health professionals points to autonomy as the most highly valued component. Participative management can contribute significantly to better health outcomes and increased autonomy for direct care professionals.

CONCLUSION

Several additional issues arise as a result of reflection about QWL programs. The first is the relationship of all these programs to productivity. The first point to be underscored here is that we do not know if there is a relationship with increased productivity, although we assume that there is. However, QWL programs should be instituted as a means of improving the work environment, not primarily as a means of improving productivity. In fact, we should have several equally weighted outcome measures, including employee satisfaction and participation in decision making. These should be viewed as independent possible outcomes, not as primarily serving the function of increasing productivity or cutting costs.

Who is responsible for change within organizations? is a frequent question. In reality, most organizational change occurs when some level of management decides that some level of employee will behave differently. The motivation in industry is usually productivity and is expressed in terms of profit. The motive in the health field is also productivity but is expressed in terms of cost containment. Occasionally a change will take place because of pressure from employees—often a union.

Organizational development is a management responsibility, but the motivation for change is an important determinant in the type of change that occurs. The change process itself is very much like a decision-making process, with two basic criteria for evaluating effectiveness: the logic or soundness of the proposed change and the acceptance of the change and the commitment to its implementation by those who must carry it out.[17]

Appropriately diagnosing the problem is the necessary precursor to the first criterion, since the solution must be related to the problem. This is an important management skill that depends on communication from those who will be affected by the change. The job satisfaction scale is an example of a technique that is useful to the ability of a manager to diagnose the problem and also provides direction to creating a logical intervention.

Without this communication, moving to the implementation phase is very difficult. The implementation phase must draw on an understanding of behavioral science, especially when considering the problem of motivation. A helpful framework for implementation is the one developed by Kurt Lewin and expanded by Schein, which has three stages.[18] The first stage is "unfreezing," which creates the motivation for change. This unfreezing is the time during which the status quo is analyzed and it is demonstrated why the change is necessary. This impetus for diagnosing the problem and creating a logical intervention may come from external constraints, such as a funding cutoff, management concerns, such as too high a turnover rate of nurses, or an organized employee group's threatening to strike. Use of the suggested job satisfaction scale can create an unfrozen organizational climate by providing a data collection and feedback mechanism that can be used before the problems become critical.

Stage 2, the change phase, encompasses the acceptance of change and the implementation. This is the behavioral modification part of the change process. Personal motivation is important here; equally important is the communication of the image of the better way or better model of an organization. This communication can be from management to employees or from employees to management. The change must be seen as being achievable—that is, as being within the scope of the organization.

The third stage, refreezing, stabilizes the changed behavior and integrates the changes into the system. Many organizational changes fail at this point because the changes are not consistently supported by the organization. Perhaps the reward must be appropriately modified, training may be necessary, or a slightly different management or accounting system may be necessary. For example, if RNs are trained to have a slightly different role, physicians and aides will also have to be retrained or the newly trained nurse behaviors will not be adequately supported by the organization and will most likely result in resorting back to the previous situation.

Management must bear the primary responsibility for developing the skills to

The Role of Quality of Worklife

deal with organizational change and creating a climate that encourages participation in decision making. QWL programs often fail, and when they do, employees are usually blamed. More commonly, the lack of either adequate organizational supports to refreeze the change or the necessary motivation and attitudes of the managers leads to the failure.

Unions, the Legal System, and QWL

There is another answer to the question about who should be responsible for development of QWL programs, this one focusing on the unions and the legal system. The law involved in QWL programs is the federal labor law under the National Labor Relations Act (NLRA, or Wagner Act), as amended and expanded by the Labor Management Relations Act (LMRA, or Taft-Hartley) and the Labor-Management Reporting and Disclosure Act (LMRDA, or Landrum-Griffin Act).[19] Many health employees are not covered by these acts, but as union participation increases in the health field, it is important at least to recognize their clear legal standing. Most QWL programs do not deal with the mandatory subjects of collective bargaining—aspects that are grievable, including wages, hours, working conditions, work schedules, work assignments, work rules, and workloads. Permissive subjects, which are addressed by QWL programs, include all of those areas considered to be management prerogatives, including job design, product design, and quality control.[20]

Although there has not been a legal challenge to QWL programs yet, there surely will be soon. Organized labor often protests QWL programs on the grounds that job enrichment is an example of altering the nature of work and job responsibility. In fact, many union organizers feel that some organizations institute QWL programs and participative management in order to avoid having a strong union. Some critics claim that QWL programs are designed to provide even more control to management while making employees feel as if they are involved in the process.

Instituting QWL programs in a health organization that has active unions is more complicated than in an organization without an active union. However, this does not mean that QWL programs and unions are mutually exclusive. It merely means that the motives of management will probably be given stricter attention since there is an organized labor group. Instituting QWL programs in order to prevent a union is not what QWL programs are about. In fact, that is a prime example of an invitation to failure. A considerable literature exists on attitudes toward quality circles of various segments of the labor movement, and this literature shows significant differences in these attitudes.[21]

A Final Caution

The management work is full of tricks and clever techniques; the labor world is full of suspicions and antagonisms. There is nothing inherent in QWL programs that can rise above either of these two circumstances. There have been many years of experience with organizational changes in private industry, including many of what might be termed QWL programs. There have been many failures and some successes. When all these situations are reviewed, several factors emerge, and we offer them as a conclusion.

First is the importance of the attitude of the manager and his or her perceptions about those who work under his or her direction. This is perhaps the most important factor in predicting success or failure of QWL programs.

Second is the theoretical framework of the manager. If the manager has an understanding of the larger issues of work alienation and the role of the organization (as well as society), he or she will be far more sensitive to the possibilities of change. This is the major reason for the inclusion of the theoretical framework that began this chapter.

These two predicate the third, which is the nature of communication within the organization. Without adequate communication, which is a *dialogue,* these organizational changes cannot occur.

The fourth is related to the skills of the manager. Are managers trained so that they can correctly diagnose the problem, design a solution, motivate the employees, and structure changes in the organization to provide support for the organizational interventions?

The fifth conclusion is the understanding that QWL programs should not be used as a substitute for improvements in salaries for health care professionals. Job satisfaction and income are clearly related, although in the health field and other service sectors, the relationship may not be as direct. With the exception of physician incomes, however, wages and salaries in the health care sector tend to be quite low. Improving these salaries may not be within the direct control of the manager, but QWL programs should not be used as replacement of efforts to improve salaries.

Finally, the structure of the QWL program itself is an important issue. In our opinion, it is far better to create a whole program than to create one or two changes, for several reasons. One is practical: these programs result in outcomes that are very difficult to measure, much like medical care itself. Changes may be subtle and are always hard to measure. There are many variables interacting with one another, and if a specific QWL program affects only one, it may not be the one that is perceived by the workers as being the most important. Also, and most important, QWL programs are supposed to improve the quality of worklife, and that is a complicated procedure that requirese a comprehensive program, not one specific change.

An ideal QWL program would begin with recruitment and selection of employees. It would continue with an attitude that all employees make valuable contributions and that it is better for both the employee and the organization to retain them than it is to replace them. A program to collect data routinely (such as the job satisfaction scale described here) should be developed, and strategies for change should result from collection of the data. Finally, strategies for change should be given organizational support. This implies that the goal is a long-term one, related not to specific quick changes but to a long-term goal of organizational development.

QWL programs are not quick fixes. They arise from a theoretical base that posits a change in management style from the traditional to one where power and decision-making authority are shared. Participative management is not common in the health field, despite the preponderance of autonomous health professionals. Unlike private industry, health professionals understand the problem of not having clear-cut outcome measures by which to evaluate the process. After all, our discussions of quality of medical care usually rely far more on process measures. This should lead us to a clearer understanding of the importance of a program whose goal is to improve the quality of worklife.

NOTES

1. Douglas McGregor, *The Human Side of Enterprise* (New York: McGraw-Hill, 1960); F. Herzberg, B. Mausner, and P. Snyderman, *The Motivation to Work,* 2d ed. (New York: Wiley, 1959).

2. W. G. Ouchi, *Theory Z: How American Business Can Meet the Japanese Challenge* (Reading, Mass.: Addison-Wesley, 1981).

3. Mike Parker, *Inside the Circle: A Union Guide to QWL* (Boston: South End Press, 1985).

4. G. Ramirez-Sosa, "An Analysis of the Framework and Implications of Work Satisfaction Research and Practice" (Ph.D. diss., University of Massachusetts, 1980).

5. R. E. Walton, "Alienation and Innovation in the Workplace," in *Work and the Quality of Life: Resource Papers for Work in America,* 227–45, ed. James O'Toole (Boston: MIT Press, 1974).

6. J. R. Schermerhorn, *Management for Productivity* (New York: John Wiley, 1984).

7. M. D. Fottler, and W. P. Maloney, "Guidelines to Productivity Bargaining in the Health Care Industry," in Norman Metzger (Ed.), *Handbook of Health Care Human Resources Management,* 697–707 (Rockville, Md.: Aspen, 1981).

8. T. Filoromo, and D. Ziff, "Some Thoughts on Job Satisfaction and Retention," in Norman Metzger (Ed.), *Handbook of Health Care Human Resources Management,* 363–73 (Rockville, Md.: Aspen, 1981); G. A. Wolf, "Nursing Turnover: Some Causes and Solutions," *Nursing Outlook* 29 (4) (1981): 233–36.

9. D. J. Cherrington, *Personnel Management: The Management of Human Resources* (Dubuque, Iowa: Wm. C. Brown, 1983).

10. Ibid.

11. Ibid.

12. K. Azumi, and J. Huge, *Organizational Systems* (Lexington, Mass.: D. C. Heath, 1972).

13. P. C. Smith, L. M. Kendall, and C. L. Hulin, *The Measurement of Satisfaction in Work and Retirement* (New York: Rand McNally, 1969); T. Kunin, "The Construction of a New Type of Attitude Measure," *Personnel Psychology* 8 (1955): 65–68; W. E. Scott, and K. M. Rowland, "The Generality and the Significance of Semantic Differential

Scales as Measures of 'Morale,' " *Organizational Behavior and Human Performance* 5 (1970): 576–91.

14. P. L. Stamps, and F. R. Piedmonte, *Nurses and Work Satisfaction: An Index for Measurement* (Ann Arbor, Mich.: Health Administration Press, 1986).

15. J. von Maanen, and E. Schein, "Career Development," in *Improving Life at Work*, ed. J. Richard Hackman and J. Lloyd Suttle (Santa Monica, Calif.: Goodyear Publishing Company, 1977); G. W. Dalton, P. H. Thompson, and R. L. Price, "The Four Stages of Professional Careers," *Organizational Dynamics* 7 (Summer 1977): 19–42.

16. Filomoro and Ziff, "Some Thoughts."

17. I. M. Rubin, R. E. Fry, and M. S. Plovnick, *Managing Human Resources in Health Care Organizations: An Applied Approach* (Reston, Va.: Reston Publishing Company, 1978).

18. E. Schein, "Mechanisms of Change," in *Planning of Change,* ed. Richard Bennis et al. (New York: Holt, Rinehart and Winston, 1969).

19. Ramirez-Sosa, "Analysis of the Framework."

20. Ibid.

21. Ibid.

9
Strategic Management of Quality of Worklife in the Home Care Industry

Penny Hollander Feldman and Alice M. Sapienza

This chapter focuses on the jobs of more than 300,000 homemaker–home health aides in the United States who provide such services as maintenance of prescribed routines (e.g., exercises and medication), observation of physical and psychological changes in the client and/or the family, provision of an adequate diet, personal care activities such as bathing, assistance with activities of daily living (e.g., shopping and cooking), and psychosocial support (Trager, 1980). The homemaker–home health aide (whom we call for the sake of brevity home aide) is the least skilled worker in the hierarchy of home health service providers that includes physicians, nurses, social workers, physical and other therapists. Quality of worklife (QWL) is an important issue for home aides; the job can be advertised, as one recent newspaper article pointed out, as offering "low pay; poor benefits; sometimes quirky clients" (*Hackensack Record*, 1987).

This chapter has three objectives. The first is to put the home aide job in the context of two major trends affecting nearly every country in the world: (1) the shift in demographics resulting in aging of the population, and, partially related to this, (2) the increase in national resources allocated to health care expenditures. In addition, the job is part of a labor market characterized by part-time, service sector employment. The second objective is to familiarize readers with the U.S. home care industry. What types of organizations provide home care services?

The research and writing of this paper were supported in part by the Ford Foundation, Grant 850-0361.

Who pays for them? As far as QWL is concerned, what effects do industry structure and financing have on the job of the home aide and on the options open to managers to improve this job? Finally, the third objective is to illustrate what managers are doing to improve quality of worklife. We describe a range of activities and research across the United States and what influences the adoption, implementation, and outcome of these activities. This section concludes with a brief discussion of the implications for managers.

A GLOBAL PERSPECTIVE ON HOME CARE

Demographics and the Rising Cost of Health Care

The job of the home aide is influenced by the shift in demographics resulting in the aging of the population and the increase in national resources allocated to health care expenditures. Exhibit 9.1 illustrates how life expectancies increased from 1950 through 1980 for twenty-four Organization for Economic Cooperation and Development (OECD) countries. In the United States alone, life expectancy increased by about one month for every year between 1970 and 1980. Life expectancy in the United States has been increasing for well over a century as a result of public health measures (e.g., sanitation), medical technology (e.g., anti-infective drugs), and life-style changes (e.g., changes in eating, drinking, smoking, and exercise habits). But over the next few decades, Americans and those in other industrialized nations will witness a tremendous growth in the proportion of the population over 65 years of age.

Today individuals over 65 years old account for about 12 percent of the total population in the United States. By the year 2030, people in this age group could account for more than 21 percent; that is, one person out of every five will be over 65. This, coupled with the lower birthrate, results in a phenomenon called the squaring of the pyramid. Exhibit 9.2 illustrates the squaring of the population pyramid in Japan. In short, we are growing older as a world.

The second trend is the ominous rise in the cost of health care. In the United States and three nations with socialized health care, the cost of hospitalization and ambulatory care more than doubled between 1975 and 1983 (Exhibit 9.3). This trend is so serious that a recent OECD report states:

Over the last fifteen years the growth of expenditures on health care has been a major concern to all OECD countries.... Both current and future cost pressures challenge the capacity of [these] societies to enhance the quality of life of their citizens through general economic growth while at the same time providing essential health and other social services. Without mastery of the cost problem, the economic and social trade-offs will be onerous and unacceptable. (OECD, 1985: 7)

The squaring of the population pyramid is not readily amenable to public policy intervention; however, we can change how much is spent on health care. Because

Exhibit 9.1
Life Expectancies in OECD Nations

	At birth								At age 60							
	Females				Males				Females				Males			
	1950	1960	1970	1980	1950	1960	1970	1980	1950	1960	1970	1980	1950	1960	1970	1980
Australia	71.7	74.0	74.2	78.0	66.5	67.9	67.4	70.9	18.5	19.5	19.5	22.0	15.3	15.6	15.0	17.2
Austria	67.3	72.0	73.4	76.1	62.2	65.4	66.4	69.0	17.6	18.7	18.8	20.4	15.3	15.1	14.8	16.4
Belgium	69.0	72.7	74.2	75.5	63.8	66.7	67.8	69.8	17.8	18.5	19.2	20.0	15.6	15.4	15.3	16.5
Canada	70.5	73.9	76.2	79.0	66.3	68.2	69.3	71.0	18.6	19.7	21.3	23.0	16.5	16.6	16.9	18.0
Denmark	71.7	74.1	76.1	77.6	69.2	72.3	71.0	71.4	18.0	19.1	20.7	21.7	17.2	17.2	17.3	17.2
Finland	68.1	72.4	74.5	77.6	61.4	65.4	66.2	69.2	17.0	17.7	18.7	20.7	14.2	14.5	14.5	15.6
France	69.7	74.1	76.7	78.3	63.9	67.5	69.1	70.1	18.5	19.7	21.4	22.3	15.4	15.7	16.6	17.2
Germany	68.3	71.9	73.6	76.5	64.4	66.5	67.3	69.7	17.5	18.1	19.0	21.7	16.3	15.3	15.2	16.4
Greece	71.0	73.5	76.0	77.8	69.0	70.3	71.6	73.2	20.0	20.3	21.1	21.7	18.5	18.6	18.7	19.0
Iceland	73.6	74.8	77.4	80.5	68.7	72.5	70.7	73.6	20.4	20.2	20.9	23.5	17.7	19.5	18.1	19.5
Ireland	66.8	71.8	73.2	75.0	64.5	68.5	68.5	69.5	17.1	18.3	18.5	18.8	15.7	16.3	15.4	15.5
Italy	67.9	71.8	74.6	77.4	64.3	66.8	68.6	70.7	18.5	19.0	20.1	21.3	16.9	16.4	16.4	17.1
Japan	60.8	70.4	74.9	79.2	57.5	65.5	69.5	73.7	16.5	18.0	19.5	22.4	14.1	15.0	16.1	18.7
Luxembourg	65.7	71.9	73.9	75.1	61.7	66.1	67.0	68.0	16.9	18.3	19.0	19.8	15.0	15.9	14.7	15.1
Netherlands	72.8	75.5	76.6	79.2	70.5	71.6	70.9	72.5	18.5	19.0	20.7	22.7	17.8	17.8	16.9	17.5
New Zealand	71.1	73.9	74.4	76.4	67.4	68.7	68.1	69.7	18.4	19.5	19.7	21.2	16.0	16.3	15.6	16.6
Norway	73.4	75.9	77.5	79.0	70.0	71.4	71.0	72.2	19.3	20.1	21.1	22.1	18.1	18.0	17.3	17.7
Portugal	61.3	67.2	70.3	75.0	56.1	61.7	64.1	67.0	18.1	18.6	18.8	20.0	15.5	15.9	15.7	16.0
Spain	64.3	72.2	75.4	78.0	59.8	67.6	70.0	71.5	17.1	19.0	20.3	21.0	14.9	16.5	17.2	18.0
Sweden	72.4	75.0	77.4	78.9	69.9	71.3	72.3	72.6	18.1	19.4	21.2	22.3	17.1	17.3	18.0	17.9
Switzerland	71.3	74.2	76.3	79.1	66.9	68.7	70.1	72.4	18.3	19.1	20.5	22.6	16.1	16.2	16.8	18.0
Turkey			60.9	62.3			55.2	58.1								
United Kingdom	71.3	74.2	75.2	75.9	66.5	68.3	68.8	70.2	18.2	19.3	19.9	20.5	15.1	15.3	15.2	15.9
United States	71.2	73.3	74.7	76.7	65.6	66.7	67.2	69.6	18.6	19.6	20.7	22.4	15.8	15.9	16.1	17.2

Source: "Measuring Health Care, 1960–1983," *OECD Publications* (Paris: OECD, 1985).

Exhibit 9.2
The Squaring of the Pyramid: Japan

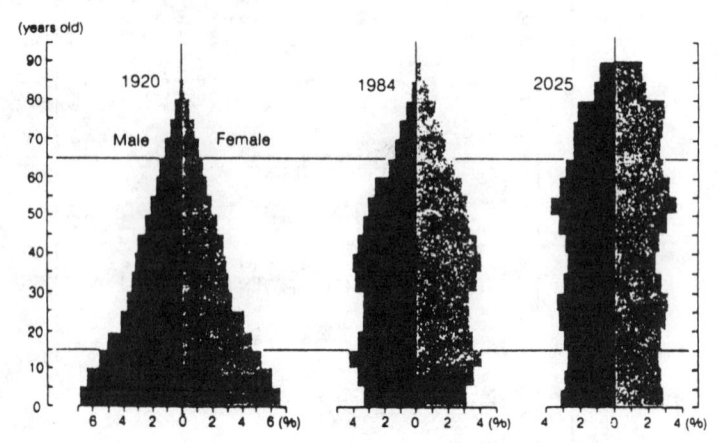

Source: Japan 1986: An International Comparison (Toyko: Keisai Koho Center).

Exhibit 9.3
Cost of Hospitalization and Health Care

	1975	1983
Hospital Care Price Indices		
US	100	206.4
UK	100	253.8
Canada	100	210.3 (1982)
Denmark	100	199.5
Ambulatory Care Price Indices		
US	100	197.3
UK	100	NA
Canada	100	203.8
Denmark	100	207.1

hospital costs account for the largest single bite out of the U.S. health care budget—nearly 40 percent of the total—incentives have been introduced to decrease the amount of time a person spends in the hospital for a given illness.

In 1970 the average length of stay (ALOS) for diseases of the circulatory system—such as atherosclerosis, a disease affecting many of those over 65 years—was 12 days. In 1981 ALOS for this category had dropped to 9.6 days, and in 1982 it had dropped to 9.4 days. This decline continues. However, at the same time as length of stay is being reduced, the average expenditure on health care for persons over the age of 65 is still more than four times the average expenditure for persons under 65, primarily because their hospitalization rate is nearly four times higher.

What are the implications of these trends and issues for home care and home care workers? With the continued aging of the population, demand for services can be expected to grow almost indefinitely. Home aides are seemingly assured of a job for what has been described as "an *enormous* dependent group in the population" (Pifer and Broute, 1986: 5). One recent study conservatively estimated that by the year 2040, 9 million noninstitutionalized elderly would require 240 million hours of care per week, both paid and informal (Manton, 1987). At the same time, efforts to reduce the time people spend in hospitals mean that people over 65 years are discharged in a frailer condition. Thus, the home aide also faces a needier client. In management parlance, service intensity has increased, with important implications for quality of worklife in terms of training, supervision, and scheduling of home aides.

The job of the home care worker must also be understood within the context of the relevant labor market. The next subsection addresses the inescapable fact that QWL, especially for the home care worker, is a gender issue. (By "gender" we mean "all the social and psychological attributes linked to the social roles of men and women" [Rossi, 1986: 113].)

Women in the Workforce

There have been two major structural changes in the labor markets of all OECD countries over the last several decades. The first is the growth of the services sector. If we divide civilian employment into three component sectors—agriculture, manufacturing, and services—then services account for at least 50 percent of the total in the large industrialized nations. In the United States in 1985, 3 percent of workers engaged in agriculture, 28 percent in manufacturing, 69 percent in services.

Growth of the services sector is expected to continue for two reasons. First, productivity increases more rapidly in manufacturing (Paukert, 1984). Thus, labor shifts from manufacturing to services naturally. Second, "as a country gets richer, it can be expected to spend more on services, particularly services such as health and education, and demand for these services increases" (Paukert, 1984: 47). In the United States, for example, the proportion of gross national product (GNP) spent on health increased from 5.3 percent in 1960 to 10.7 percent in 1985—or $26.9 billion in 1960 and $425 billion in 1985 (nominal dollars, not adjusted for inflation).

The second major structural shift in labor markets is the growth of part-time employment, which is concentrated in the services sector (OECD, 1985). In the United States, about 14 percent of the civilian labor force works part time, but 80 percent of this part-time employment is in the services sector.

Why is part-time employment so pronounced in services? In manufacturing, productivity increases faster primarily because of the substitution of machinery for labor (e.g., the use of robots in automobile factories). But in most services, no such substitution can take place. Services tend to be labor intensive and characterized by a high fixed-cost structure: the cost of nonsubstitutable labor. In manufacturing, a decline in demand for a product can be matched by a decline in production. Factories are run at less than full capacity. Within certain limits, an increase in demand can be matched simply by running factories at higher and higher percentages of full capacity.

In a service business, there is very little machinery to slow down or speed up, so when changes in demand occur, the matching of labor to demand can be difficult. Most hospitals employ the same number of nurses in December as they do in June, despite the fact that admissions in December are always much lower than in June.

One alternative to keeping this high fixed-cost structure in services is to employ part-time staff, thus shifting some of the fixed (full-time staff) cost to variable (part-time staff) cost. Fast food restaurants handle the peak hours of mealtimes by employing part-time workers. Rather than hire, for example, five full-time workers who will be frantically busy for twenty hours and have little to do for the remainder, they will hire seven twenty-hour workers for mealtimes and two twenty-hour workers for the remainder. The difference in worked hours will be twenty hours, but the savings in wages is even greater because part-time workers earn less and are usually not entitled to such benefits as paid holidays, sick time, vacations, and health care insurance. It has been noted that the "greater flexibility and low cost of part-time work have been ... factors of interest to employers, particularly in times of fluctuating business" (Paukert, 1984: 50).

These labor market changes affect women in general and home care workers in particular. There has been a large increase in the number and proportion of women working since World War II in all industrialized nations. More recently, in the United States the proportion of men working stayed at 85 percent between 1975 and 1983, while the proportion of women working rose from 53 percent to 62 percent. In 1980 more than 80 percent of working women worked in the services sector. Women, not surprisingly, also account for the lioness's share of part-time workers. In the United States in 1981, 25 percent of all women worked part-time, accounting for 70 percent of all part-time employment (Paukert, 1984).

Part-time employment may be advantageous to women because it allows them to continue bearing the larger share of household responsibilities. On the other hand:

Part-time workers may experience a depreciation of any skills they do have, since on-the-job training is rarely offered to them. Advancement opportunities are often minimal; furthermore, the exclusion of part-time workers from pension schemes ... means that there will be no retirement income on the basis of employment-related pension schemes. Part-time workers frequently have less job security since they are often the first to be laid off. (OECD, 1985: 17)

Labor markets are clearly segmented by race, gender, and occupation, and "the labor market segments in which women are concentrated tend to be disadvantaged in terms of skill, status, security, and earning" (OECD, 1985: 38). These disadvantages are characteristic of what labor economists term secondary labor markets—those providing marginal jobs with low pay, poor working conditions, and little chance of advancement (Piore, 1975).

Where does home care fit in this picture? It is a services sector occupation. Almost all home aides are women, and many are also minority women. Most are the financial head of the household. The average wage of home care workers is between four and five dollars per hour. The average number of hours they work is fewer than forty per week. A survey of about 1,200 home care workers across the United States showed that 95 percent are women, 50 percent are minority, and 60 percent are head of household. The average wage is $4.41 per hour, with twenty-nine hours being the average number worked per week. The average age is 45 years (Feldman and Sapienza, 1987).

OVERVIEW OF THE U.S. HOME CARE INDUSTRY

Home care is a high-growth industry in the United States. Combined Medicare and Medicaid home care expenditures rose from $994 million in 1980 to $2.8 billion in 1985 (HCFA, 1987), an average annual growth rate of 37 percent. With the aging of the population, private out-of-pocket payments for home care have also grown. Liu, Manton, and Liu (1985) estimate that in 1982, 608,000 disabled elderly paid an average of $164 per month out of pocket for personal assistance at home, or $1 billion in total. Even assuming modest population growth and price inflation, we estimate that out-of-pocket expenditures reached $1.44 billion in 1985, an average annual increase of 15 percent.[1] Yet despite the enormous growth in demand for home care, the typical home aide is poorly paid, rarely salaried, lacks important benefits such as health insurance or paid sick leave, receives minimal training and organizational support, and enjoys few opportunities for advancement.

The home aide's job does provide opportunities for personal fulfillment. However, the objective conditions of employment, typical of the secondary labor market, are relatively poor. The industry structure and financing have significant effects on QWL for home aides.

Quality of Worklife Issues

Wage Levels

The average wage of a home aide is between four and five dollars per hour (Feldman and Sapienza, 1987). Even if she worked full time year round, the average aide would earn less than $10,000 per year. As head of household with one or two dependents, her income would be barely above poverty level, defined as $8,738 for a family of three in 1986 (U.S. Bureau of the Census, 1987).

Wage Parity

In addition to low wages, there is a disparity in pay between home- and institution-based workers. Although home aides do essentially the same work as nurse's aides in hospitals, often under more difficult working conditions, they receive at best three-quarters of their hospital counterparts' pay (Commonwealth of Massachusetts, 1986).

Job Stability

Most home care agencies prefer flexible part-time workers whose schedules can be readily adapted to changing client caseloads. Many agencies act as temporary help agencies, contracting with individual aides from a roster of those available. Aides are rarely guaranteed a minimum number of hours per week and rarely salaried. As a result, they often cannot be sure of full-time, year-round work. A recent survey in five metropolitan areas—Boston, Milwaukee, New York City, Syracuse, and San Diego—found that the average home aide worked twenty-nine hours per week for her primary employer and would have liked to work five or six hours more (Feldman and Sapienza, 1987). About one-fifth worked at an additional job as well.

Benefits

As part-time workers, aides are generally ineligible for benefits such as health insurance, paid vacation, or sick leave. Home care agencies rarely offer health insurance coverage to their aides. On average, Feldman and Sapienza (1987) found, only 16 percent of workers had health insurance coverage through the home care agency. About 8 percent had to rely on Medicaid, and about 20 percent had no health insurance at all.

Training and Support

Training requirements for home aides vary across states and by funding source. Relatively few agencies adhere to the sixty-hour training requirement put forward by the National HomeCaring Council, a voluntary accrediting body, as the minimum industry standard. The lack of adequate training has become an issue because many of the most difficult chronic cases with developmental disabilities, mental health and geriatric problems, and even terminal care are referred to home aides for personal care and emotional support (Mootz, 1986). The inadequacy of training is compounded by the lack of organizational support systems to help workers cope with difficult clients, feelings of isolation, or personal problems affecting their job performance and satisfaction. The typical home aide spends minimal time at the agency, has limited contact with coworkers, nurses, service coordinators, and schedulers, and receives little organizational recognition of her contributions to her clients' welfare (Canalis, 1987).

Opportunities for Advancement

Job titles, like training requirements, vary across states and by funding source as well. Home health aides, homemakers, personal care workers, and home attendants, to name just a few, perform similar work but receive different pay depending on their funding source. These largely artificial distinctions create the illusion of career ladders, which in fact do not exist (Surpin and Grumm, 1987). The industry as a whole does not provide systematic rewards to home aides for experience, good performance, acquiring increased skills, or serving more difficult cases.

Industry Structure and Financing

Four key features of the industry affect the QWL issues and the options available to managers to address them:

1. Industry fragmentation, impeding efforts to standardize employment conditions, regulate employers, and organize workers to effect reform
2. Increasing competition and for-profitization of the industry, accentuating the temporary help aspects of home aide employment
3. Narrow margins and declining profits for basic home services, encouraging agencies to pursue growth and diversification strategies that divert resources from potential QWL improvements
4. The increasing importance of high-technology home care, with its uncertain impact on career prospects for lower-tier workers

Industry Fragmentation

Because the home care industry is so fragmented, it is difficult to describe employers and employees, much less coordinate or control them. A variety of organizations provide primary home care services: visiting nurse associations (VNAs), other community-based private nonprofit agencies, government agencies, hospital and nursing home–based home health agencies, regional and national for-profit home health chains, and large temporary help companies.

Nearly 6,000 of these organizations are certified; they are eligible for direct Medicare and Medicaid reimbursement because they meet certain conditions specified by the federal and state governments. In addition to the certified agencies, approximately 2,000 uncertified or unlicensed agencies provide home care services under contract to certified agencies, to state and local governments, to health maintenance organizations (HMOs) and other institutions, to private insurers, or directly to clients who pay for services out of pocket.

With the exception of VNAs and government agencies, the number of home care organizations—both certified and uncertified—has increased since the enactment of Medicare and Medicaid made third-party financing available. Proprietary agencies grew fastest—from 2 percent of total certified agencies in 1972 to 30 percent in 1986—followed by hospital and nursing home–based agencies, which grew from 11 percent in 1972 to 25 percent of total certified agencies in 1986.[2]

Variations in payment source and organizational type are important to QWL for several reasons. First, evidence suggests that such variations correspond to differences in employment conditions. For example, a 1983 survey of twenty-seven nonprofit and proprietary agencies in eleven states found that wage ranges were somewhat higher among the nonprofit agencies surveyed ($3.20 to $7.00 per hour) than among proprietary agencies ($3.50 to $5.00 per hour) (Cohen et al., 1984). That survey also found that ten out of eighteen nonprofit agencies provided some benefits to their home aides, compared to only two out of nine proprietary agencies. Second, the multiplicity and variety of payers and providers make it virtually impossible for any single authority to standardize or regulate job requirements, compensation, benefits, or other aspects of employment in the industry. While agencies that seek Medicare certification are subject to uniform regulation by the U.S. Health Care Finance Administration (HCFA), others are subject only to the discretion of the states and their localities, which have been slow to monitor or regulate them. Third, fragmentation impedes the diffusion of successful quality of work life innovations from one organization to another.

Increasing Competition and For-Profitization

With increased demand, home care has become a highly competitive industry. Barriers to entry are minimal: "capital requirements and start-up costs are low, and regulatory and licensure requirements are not excessively burdensome" (Dyckman et al., 1985). According to Dyckman and his colleagues (1985: 5–9), the service network "has changed in many localities from that of a single or small number of charitable, community supported, non-profit agencies providing services in a relatively non-competitive environment, to a highly competitive market, characterized by extensive marketing and aggressive agency behavior to solicit new business." Heightened competition, in turn, has led to the "for-profitization" of the industry, inasmuch as proprietary agencies have proliferated and nonprofits have begun to emulate their business practices.

VNAs, for example, long considered model service providers and employers, have been profoundly affected by for-profitization. In some areas, once-dominant VNAs have undertaken aggressive marketing and joint ventures with hospitals in order to retain their market shares (Dyckman et al., 1985). Other VNAs have spun off for-profit home care subsidiaries to lower their overhead and tap the market for uncertified services (Kane and Herzlinger, 1986). This movement into the for-profit business represents, for the home aide, a shift away from full-time, occasionally salaried work with accompanying benefits to temporary, part-time work without benefits.

Narrow Margins and Declining Profits in the Primary Services Sector

Four factors contribute to narrow operating margins and apparently falling profits in the primary services segment of the home care industry. First, between

20 and 30 percent of home care expenditures are paid out of pocket by individual consumers (Kane, 1987). Most of this demand comes from people over age 75, and these frail, elderly, usually widowed clients cannot afford to pay high prices. Second, federal Medicare reimbursement policies, which affect the second major source of home care revenues, are increasingly stringent, exerting tighter pressure on profit margins and reducing the financial flexibility of providers (Perspectives, 1986). A third factor contributing to narrow operating margins is the attitude of other public payers. States and localities, facing a trade-off between cost of service and volume, generally allocate additional dollars to meet increased demand rather than to improve wages, benefits, training, or quality of service significantly. Fourth, because direct labor costs are the largest cost component in the primary services segment, there is little productivity gain to be achieved.

Even the home care chains providing $30 million or more of home care services per year have exhibited very low to negative profit performance in recent years. Kane's (1987) financial analysis of the twelve largest publicly owned companies indicated that "of all reporting any information, only three indicated consistently positive profitability over a multi-year period; in one of those two, profit margins were dropping precipitously; in another, profits were improving as the company shifted from primary to high technology services; and in a third, the company was recently indicted for Medicaid fraud and forced to sell all of its operations" (p. 11).

Increasing Importance of High-Tech Home Care

It is still too early in the development of high-technology home care to determine whether the industry's pursuit of higher profits in this area will undermine the tenuous status and marginal working conditions of the home aide or will provide opportunities for upward mobility through specialized training and service to technology-dependent clients.

The increasing industry emphasis on specialized medical services could reinforce the distinctions and mobility barriers between lower-tier home aides and upper-tier workers who administer increasingly sophisticated therapies to a sicker and more debilitated client population. Elderly patients (and others) "frequently return home with an intravenous line, receiving a variety of antibiotics, narcotics, chemotherapy, or intravenous nutrition—typically at about 1/3 the cost of the same type service given in a hospital setting" (Hankwitz, 1987: 7). Nurses generally set up the necessary equipment in the home and train patients and their families in its use.

Theoretically there is no reason that a home aide could not be trained in the same fashion as a family member to administer one of these therapies to a dependent client. Practically, however, several obstacles stand in the way. State regulations prohibiting aides from performing medically related services, medical risk and liability issues, as well as concerns about aides' cognitive and literacy skills all deter managers from assigning aides increased responsibility for technical care.

Home health agencies report that they have increased the number of specialists on staff and have retrained existing staff in the use of highly technical services and their possible complications (Seifer, 1987). To what extent home aides have benefited from such retraining efforts is unknown.

Improvements in QWL require the investment of resources in higher compensation, adequate benefits, better training and supervision, redesign of jobs to increase satisfaction, development of opportunities for advancement, and the like. Industries and firms with poor working conditions and low profits or operating deficits are not likely to make such an investment. The evidence is clear on poor working conditions for home aides, low profits in the primary service sector, competitive pressures to keep prices low, regulatory pressures to cut costs, and legal pressures to prevent aides from carrying out tasks deemed medical in nature. Such evidence provides little basis for optimism that the growth of high-technology home care will create new opportunities for home aides. Indeed, it is possible that the move to high-tech care will detract from the QWL for home aides by increasing their burdens and responsibilities without increasing their status or their pay. The latter scenario is entirely consistent with what is known about QWL in other industries. The editors of a major volume on the subject observe:

Organizations that have gone farthest in changing their structures, job content, and relationships are by various social and economic indicators the better ones. As they continue these developments, the quality of working life in the best organizations becomes even better and that in poor organizations becomes relatively worse. (Davis and Cherns, 1975: 8)

QUALITY OF WORKLIFE EFFORTS

Why are managers of home care agencies concerned about QWL for home aides, and what are they doing to improve it? In this section, we describe the management concerns that motivate QWL efforts, the range of activities that have been undertaken, and the factors that influence their adoption and implementation.

Management Concerns

Managers cite five concerns that lead them to address QWL issues: worker recruitment, worker turnover, productivity, quality of service, and, in some circumstances, union pressures.

Worker Recruitment

In recent years, increasing demand for home care and decreasing unemployment rates have created home aide shortages in many surburban areas and in high employment states. Recruitment is most difficult in states with the lowest unemployment rates, such as Massachusctts and New Jersey, where low-wage employers face the greatest competition from employers offering more attractive employment opportunities (*Boston Globe*, 1987; *Hackensack Record,* 1987). In Massachusetts, the state Rate Setting Commission estimated a 20 percent gap between hours of service authorized for the home-bound elderly and hours actually provided by the state's home care corporations in 1986 (*Boston Globe,* 1987). A statewide provider task force concluded in March 1987 that "worker availability has become *the* critical resource issue for the years ahead—and for the present" and recommended a variety of actions to make the home aide's job more attractive through improved compensation, better supervision and support, changes in job scheduling, and enhanced job status (Task Force, 1987: 5). The key to the success of these recommendations, it noted, is a "regulatory environment that will allow and encourage innovative wage, benefit and recruitment policies" (Task Force, 1987: 5).

Worker Turnover

Human service agencies experience particularly high turnover rates (Montgomery, 1981). Reliable data on turnover rates among home aides are difficult to find because there have been few systematic studies and because agencies tend to compute turnover in different ways. The industry-wide rate for home aides is thought to be about 60 percent (Beck, 1987). Feldman (1986) found a six-month turnover rate of 53 percent among a cohort of new workers hired by a California for-profit agency in 1986. Twenty-two nonprofit home care agencies in Massachusetts reported an average turnover rate of 29 percent in 1985, with a range of 5 percent to 67 percent (Massachusetts Council for Homemaker/Home Health Aide Services, 1985). Montgomery's (1981) study of turnover among direct service providers employed by forty-two health and human service organizations in a midsized metropolitan area found a one-year turnover rate of 33.3 percent among in-home service workers compared to 19.4 percent for hospital workers. The study sample included nurses as well as aides.

Because home aides receive little formal training from their employers and because many home care employers function essentially as temporary help agencies, high turnover is not necessarily as disruptive to the home care industry as it would be to an industry heavily reliant on permanent full-time labor. Nevertheless, even for agencies accustomed to relying on temporary part-time workers, turnover can cause burdensome recruitment and orientation costs, decreased productivity, and decreased client satisfaction.

Productivity

Increased productivity has not traditionally been a major concern of home care managers. However, as third-party payers tighten their payments for home visits, agencies face the challenge of providing quality care at a lower cost per visit (Bonstein and Mueller, 1985). One response is to require aides who work as full-time staff to increase their number of visits—that is, increase their productivity. A second response is to place increased reliance on part-time nonbenefited workers. Even these workers are being asked to increase their productivity by accomplishing their tasks in a shorter time and visiting more clients per day (Liebman, 1986). Worker stress associated with efforts to improve productivity is increasingly perceived by home care managers as a QWL issue, promoting interest in improved scheduling practices, travel pay, and support services to reduce its disruptive effects.

Quality of Service

Studies of the quality of care delivered by health organizations have rarely considered the possible impact of care givers' satisfaction on clients or the potential for management to influence quality by providing working conditions conducive to staff satisfaction (Weisman and Nathanson, 1985). Yet home care managers generally believe that well-trained, satisfied home aides will provide better care than minimally trained aides dissatisfied with their working conditions. Worker reliability, a critical dimension of quality to dependent clients with chronic needs, is perceived to be especially sensitive to QWL life issues and job satisfaction. A recent article in the industry magazine *Caring* advised managers to "listen to the needs" of home aides and "improv[e] their work situation" to promote quality and excellence in care (Canalis, 1987: 89).

Home care managers are also paying increased attention to home aides' skills in providing social support, counseling, problem identification, and crisis intervention—dimensions of quality that home care training programs by and large ignored in the past (Kaye, 1986). In particular, heightened public and professional awareness of the mental and emotional problems of elderly patients suffering from Alzheimer's and other debilitating conditions has sparked agency interest in efforts to improve the interpersonal and coping skills of aides who serve these difficult clients.

Union Pressures

Scattered across multiple worksites, home care workers are far more difficult to unionize than health care workers in institutional settings. The vast majority of home aides do not belong to unions, and the prospects for large-scale unionization of the industry appear dim. Nevertheless, in some large cities, unions have successfully organized aides who work for agencies that contract with state and local governments to provide publicly financed services. Freedom of information laws affecting government contracts, plus centralized program funding and administration, apparently facilitate unionization of workers in contract agencies. Unions in Boston, New York City, San Diego, and San Francisco have successfully gained paid holidays, vacation leave, sick time, and, in some cases, modest health insurance benefits for home aides employed by contract agencies serving publicly funded clients. In areas where government funds can be garnered to finance increased program costs, managers have found it advantageous to join unions in lobbying public officials for funds to support QWL improvements.

RANGE OF QWL ACTIVITIES

The circumstances described have provided the impetus for a number of activities to improve the working conditions of home aides. Most of the QWL activities undertaken by the industry have been ad hoc, limited to a single agency, and heavily oriented toward training and support provided at relatively low cost (Joseloff, 1986; Stockton, 1986; Canalis, 1987; Shulman, Steinberg, and Kahn, 1987). Other efforts include guarantees of full-time employment, measures to enhance worker status, enriched compensation and benefit packages, an experiment in worker ownership, and a statewide regulatory initiative. Here we describe four QWL efforts that are notable for their scope, design, and intent: the High-Tech Training Module of the National HomeCaring Council; the Ford Foundation Home Care Project; Cooperative Home Care Associates, a worker cooperative sponsored by the Community Service Society of New York; and the Homemaker/Home Health Aide Service regulations of the Massachusetts Rate Setting Commission. Each addresses more than one aspect of QWL, and each aims to have an impact beynd the workers immediately affected.

The High-Tech Training Module

With support from the federal government and in conjunction with the Visiting Nurse Association of Metropolitan Atlanta, the National HomeCaring Council has developed a training module, Homemaker–Home Health Aide Services in Support of High-Tech Patients and Their Families (National Home Caring Council, 1987). The model curriculum and teaching guide outline twenty-four hours of supplemental aide training in the functioning of high-technology equipment and the provision of specialized personal care to the technology dependent.

The purpose of the training is to help aides cope with the needs of technology-dependent patients and to provide an opportunity for aides to achieve higher status and compensation. The designers of the training program anticipate that it will lead to a new step on a career ladder from homemaker–home health aide to high-tech aide, a position that will command greater respect and better pay than home aide (Copeman and Weigel, 1987). They clearly state, however, that high-tech aides will not be trained to provide "skilled care" or perform "skilled tasks"—duties that remain the province of nurses and other professionals.

Because the high-tech program has been developed by a national body well known for its standard-setting and voluntry accreditation functions, it will likely receive wide industry exposure. Neither the widespread use of the curriculum nor its role in creating a new career ladder for home aides is assured, however. Advancement for home aides within the home care industry is far more dependent on state licensing regulations and on federal and state payment policies, which rarely recognize gradations in home aide skills, than on the availability of suitable curriculum materials or skilled trainers.

Ford Foundation Home Care Project

In spring 1985, the Ford Foundation funded a three-year research and demonstration project focusing on the employment conditions of home aides. The project combined data gathering on the home aide workforce and its working conditions with implementation and evaluation of several "modest interventions" (Grinker, Walker & Associates, 1985) intended to demonstrate the potential for improving QWL, increasing worker satisfaction, reducing turnover, and improving quality of service.

Home care managers representing both for-profit and nonprofit agencies in four demonstration cities—San Diego, New York City, Milwaukee, and Syracuse—designed QWL interventions with the assent of relevant unions and in conjunction with the research team. Each agency implemented a somewhat different set of interventions, depending on the economic and regulatory climate and the perceived needs of managers, workers, and clients. The interventions were as follows:

- Basic training and guaranteed full-time employment: In San Diego, a large for-profit agency providing in-home supportive services under contract to the county developed a QWL program with four main components: specially designed supplementary basic and refresher training; a professionally guided employee support and development group, focusing on work-related and personal needs, professional identity, and self-esteem; measures to enhance worker status, including a special title and special uniforms and identity badges; and guaranteed full-time employment (thirty-five hours per week) for participating aides.
- Career development through skills training: In New York City, two nonprofit agencies providing home attendant services under contract to the city Medicaid program developed a QWL program with four main components: advanced training for aides who would serve behaviorally difficult, mentally ill, or mentally impaired clients; ongoing professional support for these aides; measures to enhance worker status, including special titles, badges, and program publicity; and a thirty cent per hour wage increment for program graduates.
- Career development as an award for worker loyalty and accessibility: In Milwaukee and Syracuse, two branches of a national for-profit chain selected a group of aides for demonstrated dependability and high performance. From this group, the research team randomly chose twenty to become "staff aides." The main components of the associated QWL program were enhanced status as a staff aide; guaranteed full-time work (forty hours per week); enriched benefits, identical to those of office staff and including employer contributions to a health insurance plan; and a fifty cent per hour wage increment as a reward for past performance and for a commitment to serve clients on short notice, at odd and weekend hours, in difficult circumstances, and for shorter terms than ordinary home aides.

Analysis of the implementation and wind-down phases of the programs yielded two important preliminary findings. First, implementation of the full-time work guarantee encountered major obstacles: fewer workers agreed to participate than expected, and a number who participated subsequently declined to accept a full-time caseload. Agency supervisory staff found it difficult to schedule workers full time given the logistical constraints of matching clients and aides; and in San Diego, government funding constraints led to cutbacks in authorized hours of service that impeded vigorous implementation of the full-time work component. Second, the costs of employer-subsidized health insurance benefits were so burdensome that when foundation funding expired, the Syracuse and Milwaukee agencies opted to continue their staff aide programs but without the health insurance benefit.

Cooperative Home Care Associates, a Worker Cooperative

Perhaps the most ambitious QWL effort is a newly formed worker cooperative, Cooperative Home Care Associates (CHCA), sponsored by the Community Service Society of New York. Founded in 1985 with one service contract and twelve home health aides, CHCA had four major contracts and 130 aides by early 1987.

As a low-income worker cooperative enterprise, CHCA sees itself going against the grain of the existing home care industry:

The mainstream industry fosters low-paying, part-time employment with no opportunities for advancement; CHCA seeks to establish a permanent workforce with adequate pay and benefits, full-time employment, and opportunities for career mobility, participation in governance and profit sharing. (Surpin, 1987)

The initial starting wage for CHCA aides in 1986 was $4.75 per hour, the highest in New York City. After a year of full-time employment, aides receive a twenty-five cent per hour increment, and there is a twenty-five cent per hour increment for weekend work. Approximately two-thirds of CHCA aides are employed full time, a high proportion achieved with considerable administrative effort. All CHCA aides receive limited benefits: life insurance, five paid personal or vacation days, and a uniform allowance. The company's long-term plans call for a more extensive benefit package, including health insurance; a career development program for training aides in allied health professions; implementation of a profit-sharing plan; and predominantly worker ownership.

The benefits of worker ownership include the right to elect and be elected to the company's board of directors and to receive a share of company profits, if and when they occur, in proportion to hours worked. To become owners or members, workers must satisfactorily complete a three-month performance probation period, participate in team meetings, and purchase a share of the company at $1,000. (Purchasing a share can be done by an initial payment of $50 plus a $3.50 weekly payroll deduction over about five years.)

Ordinarily a company comparable in size and structure to CHCA would require a worker-owner investment of $3,000 to $5,000 each; however, because home aides do not have the financial resources to make this kind of payment, CHCA relied on grant funds for start-up and development costs. Even with the reduced worker investment requirement, significant worker ownership is a difficult goal to achieve given the structure of the industry and the company's inability to provide full-time employment to all workers on an ongoing basis. After two years of operation, approximately 25 percent of workers were participating in the ownership plan, and CHCA hoped to reach 50 percent within the near future.

Homemaker–Home Health Aide Service Regulations of the Massachusetts Rate Setting Commission

The Massachusetts Rate Setting Commission has responsibility for setting reimbursement rates for all homemaker–home health aide services paid for by state funds. Each year, the commission establishes through regulation a uniform wage rate for all covered providers. That rate was $6.21 per direct service hour in fiscal year 1987. The total reimbursement rate in fiscal 1987—including the wage rate, overhead, and travel add-on—ranged from $8.47 per direct service hour to $9.78, depending on the provider's volume. (There is also a fifty-cent per hour differential for weekend, evening, and holiday hours.)

Wages for homemakers have increased dramatically in Massachusetts over the past five years. The wage component of the reimbursement rate increased from $4.42 in fiscal 1982 to $6.21 in fiscal 1987. Home aides reported an average take-home pay of $5.55 per hour in 1987 (Massachusetts Rate Setting Commission, 1987). While rate regulation is the proximate cause of the increase, the underlying factors are, to some extent, growing unionization and, to a large extent, the strength of the Massachusetts economy.

Despite the increase in wages, home care agencies in Massachusetts continue to struggle with recruitment problems stemming from the tight labor market in the state. To address recruitment issues, the Rate Setting Commission in 1987 created an "optional incentive add-on to encourage the retention and recruitment of direct care workers" (Shark, 1987). Under the incentive add-on mechanism, agencies wishing to offer workers optional incentives such as health insurance, paid vacation or sick leave, guaranteed hours, or wage increments for tenure or performance can be reimbursed for these after applying to the commission and receiving approval. The maximum reimbursement for such add-ons is eighty-four cents per hour in fiscal 1988, plus overhead. At this writing, the regulation had just been adopted, and providers were planning to develop and document various job enhancement proposals intended to qualify for the optional reimbursement. Thus a single regulatory initiative will likely reinforce some of the QWL activities already underway in the state and spawn a number of others.

Factors Affecting Adoption and Implementation

Our overview of the home care industry and our discussion of ongoing QWL efforts have already suggested a number of factors affecting the successful adoption and implementation of job enhancement measures. Here we briefly summarize those critical factors: market conditions, regulatory and reimbursement conditions, agency capacity, and workforce characteristics.

Market Conditions

In our industry overview we pointed to the entry of for-profit organizations into the home care industry, increased competition among nonprofit and for-profit agencies, and pressure on the nonprofits to cut their costs by adopting some of the temporary help features of the for-profit chains. These conditions generally imply retrenchment in QWL for aides who are employed by nonprofit agencies, traditionally known for providing higher wages and more benefits than their for-profit counterparts.

The prospects for QWL improvements under conditions of heightened competition and for-profitization are not entirely bleak, however. Providers' quests for profits from high-technology home care may lead to higher skills and better pay for aides who complete high-tech training, such as that developed by the National HomeCaring Council. Tight labor markets, competition with other agencies to attract home aides, and the desire to increase agency volume can provide incentives for managers to experiment with QWL improvements, as developments in Massachusetts and among participants in the Ford Home Care Project have demonstrated.

Although market conditions may provide home care managers with an incentive for job enhancement, they also establish limits on the magnitude of associated costs that managers will bear. However ambitious the job enhancement goals of CHCA, for example, the board of directors could not justify the provision of subsidized worker health insurance as a financially feasible policy. In a similar vein, the managers of the Milwaukee and Syracuse staff aide programs could not financially justify continued provision of subsidized health insurance benefits after foundation funds in support of the staff aide program expired.

Regulatory and Reimbursement Conditions

As with market conditions, regulatory and reimbursement conditions impose clear constraints on QWL improvements. Downward pressure on payment rates from Medicare and other third-party payers leads home care managers to seek increased productivity, which, in turn, can provide incentives for improving worker support and compensation. The problem is that managers can less easily afford the costs of such improvements when payers are tightening reimbursement.

Sympathetic public officials and relatively generous reimbursement conditions in New York City facilitated development of career advancement opportunities and associated wage increments for home attendants trained to serve difficult clients. Similarly the Massachusetts Rate Setting Commission's program of optional incentive add-ons demonstrates how a supportive regulatory climate can work to foster QWL improvements advocated by providers. These examples, however, are the exception rather than the rule. For the most part, third-party payers are more concerned about constraining expenditures than improving the quality of work or of service.

Agency Capacity

No matter how conducive market or reimbursement conditions may be to QWL improvements, successful implementation depends to a large extent on managerial capacity. The large home care chains have substantial management capacity at the corporate level, but at the agency level—whether in chain-affiliated or independent agencies—resources for carrying out innovative QWL programs are thin. Thus successful implementation of such activities may depend on an agency's willingness and ability either to divert management resources from routine operations or to pay for outside help in the implementation process.

Agencies participating in the Ford Foundation Home Care Project adopted both strategies. All the training and support activities implemented as part of the Ford Project's QWL experiments relied on outside institutions and consultants for development and operation. Furthermore, their continuation beyond the demonstration period depended on the extension of consultative agreements arranged as part of the demonstration. On the other hand, all the guarantees of full-time work depended on in-house resources, which were considerably strained by the commitment.

Cooperative Home Care Associates, too, noted that the commitment to provide full-time work to a substantial portion of their workforce almost exceeded the capacity of their scheduling staff to make appropriate assignments. Because the scheduling of full-time workers is a complex task that imposes a heavy burden on the routine scheduling operations of an agency, QWL efforts designed to increase the proportion of full-time workers in an agency may succeed only to the degree that they affect small numbers of workers or that an agency, such as CHCA, makes them the highest priority.

Workforce Characteristics

Finally, successful implementation of QWL activities depends on the workers themselves. Poor pay, part-time hours, and low status have undoubtedly dampened the work expectations of some home aides. Others have adapted by finding outside jobs or pursuing schooling to prepare them to leave the home care field. Many are coping with personal and family problems such as chronic illness, children's schooling difficulties, and inadequate housing. All of these situations conspire against the success of QWL improvements by placing obstacles in the way of workers' active participation.

Problems in implementing the guaranteed full-time work component of the Ford Foundation Home Care Project are a prime example. Workers overwhelmingly expressed the desire to work more hours than were usually available and to work full time if asked by their company. However, of all the home aides in the three agencies that offered the work guarantee, only 15 to 25 percent expressed initial interest in participating in such a program, and a smaller proportion finally decided to participate. Furthermore, although all program participants had agreed to work thirty-five or forty hours per week on a regular basis, a number subsequently declined to accept client assignments. Reasons for declining included inconvenient hours or client location, personal problems, family commitments, and conflicts with outside jobs or schooling. Failure to keep the full-time commitment occurred at all three sites, regardless of whether the aide received an hourly wage increment as well. As a good-faith gesture, one site paid aides for forty hours even when they declined assignment, but the practice became too costly and was discontinued after several months. These findings suggest that the success of major changes in the structure of work will require significant changes in the life circumstances of the home care workforce.

GUIDELINES FOR MANAGERS

The manager concerned about the quality of worklife for the home aide is acutely aware of the structural constraints that hamper improvement: gender and race issues regarding women—many minority—who provide home and personal services on a part-time basis to the elderly. One of the implicit reasons for the low reimbursement of home services is the traditional undervaluing of "women's work." This, in conjunction with racial prejudice and a perspective of the disabled elderly as burdensome members of society, results in a pay and status gap that will be hard to overcome.

Other structural constraints derive from the financing and organization of the industry. Perhaps the most obvious constraint is the squeeze on margins in the primary services sector—manifested in the wage and benefits package that agencies can offer to home aides.

What, then, are options for the manager? What are the implications of the previous discussion?

First, as has been accomplished in New York and Massachusetts, managers should unite to lobby state and local governments for better compensation for publicly financed home care services. Furthermore, in their quest for more generous reimbursement, they should ally themselves with unions and consumer groups, who stand to benefit from improvements in worker satisfaction and quality of service.

Second, managers should allocate training resources to help the home aide deal with the increased frailty of the client population, help her cope with difficult and mentally impaired clients, and prepare her to handle more of the high-tech equipment that will be found in clients' homes.

Third, managers should use wage differentials, expanded benefits, and visible status symbols—such as uniforms, badges, and employee awards—to reward home aides for tenure, accessibility, performance, and the acquisition of advanced skills.

Fourth, managers should look upon full-time, year-round employment as a goal to be achieved for a target group of aides willing to make the necessary commitment of time, energy and responsibility.

Fifth, managers should ensure that there is an organizational support system to assist the aide in dealing with problems on and off the job, as well as with endemic isolation. In the interest of both career development and quality assurance, managers might explore the feasibility of training and promoting a select group of aides to serve as field support staff fulfilling this function.

Finally, managers should be prepared to commit significant managerial resources and, in some cases, to rely on outside experts, to implement innovative QWL improvements.

NOTES

1. This estimate assumes a 2.5 percent per year increase in the number of elderly disabled (Manton, 1987: 208). Annual price inflation is assumed to equal the annual rise in the consumer price index—3.8 percent in 1983, 4.1 percent in 1984, and 3.6 percent in 1985—although medical prices rose more steeply.

2. Figures for 1986 are unpublished data from the Health Care Financing Administration, Bureau of Health Care Standards and Quality, telephone communication (May 1987). Precise information on the numbers and kinds of uncertified agencies is lacking because few states license or regulate them.

REFERENCES

Beck, B. (1987, June 20). Better home health care by worker-owners. *New York Times*.
Bonstein, R., and Mueller, J. (1985). Improving agency productivity. *Caring* 4 (11): 4–9.
Boston Globe (1987, April 9). A home care pay travesty.
Canalis, D. (1987). Homemaker/home health aide attrition: Methods of prevention. *Caring* 6 (4): 85–89.
Cohen, D., Patrizi, P., Wagner, C., and Brunelle, M. (1984). A planning study of alternative home health ventures that improve employment opportunities for the homemaker/home health aide. Final report submitted to the Ford Foundation. Philadelphia: Wharton School, University of Pennsylvania.
Commonwealth of Massachusetts. Division of Employment Security (1986). *Employment Trends in the Health Care Industry*. Boston: Division of Employment Security.
Copeman, E., and Weigel, L. (1987). Training homemaker/home health aides for high tech home care. *Caring* 6 (5): 34–37.
Davis, L., and Cherns, A. (1975). *The Quality of Working Life*, Vol. 1: *Problems, Prospects and the State of the Art*. New York: Free Press.
Dietz, J. (1986, June 26). State home care workers get 11 percent pay raise. *Boston Globe*.
Dyckman, Z., Hurwitz, N., Bishop, C., and Cohen, M. (1985). Market study for home health care services. Prepared for Health Care Financing Administration, HCFA Contract No. 500–84–0033. Columbia, Md.: Center for Health Policy Studies.
Feldman, P. (1986). Preliminary turnover analysis, California. Unpublished report. Boston: Harvard University School of Public Health.

Feldman, P., and Sapienza, A. (1987). Comparison of questionnaire results across sites: Homemaker/home health aide survey, January 27, 1987. Unpublished report. Boston: Harvard University School of Public Health.

Grinker, Walker & Associates, Feldman, P., Kane, N., and Sapienza, A. (1985). A proposal for improving employment conditions of entry level service workers: Lessons from the home care industry. Proposal submitted to the Ford Foundation, February 1985. Boston: Harvard University School of Public Health.

Hackensack (N.J.) *Record* (1987, February 26). A dearth of care.

Hackmann, J. R., and Lawler, E. E. III, (1979). Job characteristics and motivation: A conceptual framework. In L. E. Davis and J. C. Taylor (Eds.), *Design of Jobs*, 75–84. Santa Monica, Calif.: Goodyear Publishing Co.

Hankwitz, P. (1987). A welcome to our readers. *Journal for Physicians in Home Care* 1 (1): 6–7.

Health Care Financing Administration (HCFA) (1987). *Trends in the Utilization of Medicare Home Health Agency Services: Persons Served, Visits, Charges, and Reimbursements for Selected Years: 1974–1985*. Baltimore: Department of Health and Human Services.

Health Industry Today (1985, February). The market for home healthcare products and services. *Health Industry Today*, 47–51.

Janson, D. (1985, December 21). Low paying jobs go begging at suburban shopping malls. *New York Times*.

Joseloff, A. (1986). The home health aide: A member of the hospice team. *Caring* 5 (10): 37–38.

Kane, N., (198). Day care crisis of the 'Nineties—taking care of Mom. Unpublished manuscript. Boston: Harvard University School of Public Health.

Kane, N. and Herzlinger, R. (1986). "The Visiting Nurse Service of New York." Unpublished, Harvard Business School Case No. 2–186–251.

Kaye, L. (1986). Worker views of the intensity of affective expression during the delivery of home care services for the elderly. *Home Health Care Services Quarterly* 7 (2): 41–54.

Liebman, J. (1986). Rate setting for homecare services in Massachusetts. Unpublished report. Boston: Harvard University School of Public Health.

Liu, K., Manton, K., and Liu, B. (1985). Home care expenses for the elderly. *Health Care Financing Review* 7 (2): 51–58.

Manton, K. G. (1987). The interaction of population aging and health transitions at later ages. In C. J. Schramm (Ed.), *Health Care and Its Costs*, 185–221. New York: W. W. Norton.

Massachusetts Council for Homemaker–Home Health Aide Services (1985, Summer). Survey of member agencies on personnel practices. Boston.

Massachusetts Rate Setting Commission (1987). *The Homebound Elderly: Who Cares?* Boston: The Commission.

Montgomery, D. (1981, May). Working in aging services: Job satisfaction, regulation and turnover. *JHHRA*, pp. 477–93.

Mootz, A. (1986). Do we support standards in the homemaker–home health aide field? *Caring* 5 (4): 32–33.

Mundinger, M. (1983). *Home Care Controversy: Too Little, Too Late, Too Costly.* Rockville, Md.: Aspen Systems Corporation.

National HomeCaring Council (1987). *Homemaker-Home Health Aide Services in Support of High-Tech Patients and Their Families: A Trainer's Manual.* Washington, D.C.: National HomeCaring Council.

Organization for Economic Cooperation and Development (1985). *The Integration of Women into the Economy.* Paris: OECD.

Parks, C. (1986). A study of home care workers in the Boston area. Unpublished report. Boston: Harvard University School of Public Health.

Paukert, L. (1984). *The Employment and Unemployment of Women in OECD Countries.* Paris: OECD.

Perspectives (1986, August 18). Hard times for home health. *Medicine and Health* 40: supplement.

Pifer, A., and Broute, L. (1986). Squaring the pyramid. In A. Pifer and L. Broute (Eds.), *Our Aging Society,* 3–13. New York: W. W. Norton.

Piore, M. (1975). Notes for a theory of labor market stratification. In R. Edwards, M. Reich, and D. Gordon (Eds.), *Labor Market Segmentation,* 125–50. Lexington, Mass.: D. C. Heath.

Rossi, A. (1986). Sex and gender in the aging society. In A. Pifer and L. Broute (Eds.), *Our Aging Society,* 111–39. New York: W. W. Norton.

Seifer, S. (1987). The impact of PPS on home health care: A survey of thirty-five home health agencies. *Caring* 6 (4): 10–12.

Shark, M. (1987, April 15). Overview of proposed regulation. Letter to Homemaker Task Force. Boston: Massachusetts Rate Setting Commission.

Shulman, E., Steinberg, G., and Kahn, R. (1987). Senile dementia: The new market in home health care. *Caring* 6 (5): 58–62.

Stockton, M. (1986). Who's taking care of you? Hospice worker burnout: Its diagnosis, prevention and cure. *Caring* 6 (4): 60–63.

Surpin, R. (1987). *Cooperative Home Care Associates: A Status Report.* New York: Community Service Society.

Surpin, R., and Grumm, F. (1987). Ending workers' hidden subsidy for home care services. Unpublished report. New York: Community Service Society, Worker Cooperative Development Project.

Task Force (1987, March). *Problems on the Supply Side: The Homemaker Shortage in Massachusetts.* March 1987 Task Force Report. Boston: Massachusetts Council for Homemaker–Home Health Aide Services.

Trager, B. (1980). Service definition. *Home Health Care Services Quarterly* 1 (2): 7–25.

U.S. Bureau of the Census (1987). Poverty level for a family of three. Telephone communication. Boston: U.S. Department of Commerce.

Weisman, C., and Nathanson, C. (1985). Professional satisfaction and client outcomes: A comparative organizational analysis. *Medica Care* 23 (10): 1179–92.

10
The Role of Organizational Development in the Strategic Human Resource Management Model

Ruth B. Welborn

The health care sector is facing changes more extensive, more far-reaching in implication, and fundamental in transforming quality than ever before. Faced with the accelerated growth of expensive technologies, numerous ethical and policy dilemmas, the reallocation of financial resources, and the shift from a patient-centered way of thinking to a bottom-line perspective by both health care administrators and health care professionals, an unstable and frustrating health care service environment has been generated for all who are concerned with and involved in health care.

Health care organizations must learn to operate in a wholly new mode. The total scope of what needs to be done is, of course, highly variable, in large part because it depends on the unstable nature of the health care industry. What is clear, however, is the need for innovation and creativity, with particular emphases on the way that organizations operate, in their view of themselves, and in the mechanisms that can be developed to maximize services to health care recipients. Most important, organizations need to shift from the present tendency to deal with their tasks in a relatively single-minded, top-directed way and to a capacity to respond innovatively and promptly to a wide variety of organizational changes. To be successful, health care organizations must be, above all, flexible and to an extent become risk oriented. They must be organizations with more contact with the environments both near and far that affect all aspects of health care and incorporate an array of sensing mechanisms for recognizing emerging changes and their implications. In such an organization, more people with greater skills than ever before will link the organization to the health delivery environments. Structured flexibility, which increases the capacity for effective reaction, needs major attention. The health care sector has emerged from a heterogeneous environment of thousands of individual ambulatory, acute, and long-term care units to a collective of institutions. Large multihospital systems have appeared in both the for-profit and not-for-profit sectors. Mergers and acquisitions are continuing to proceed, moving these multi-institutional health care systems to a more centralized structure.

As never before, the health care sector needs creative organizational systems that provide new paths, new methods, and new approaches. In this respect organizational development has the potential to assist.

THEORETICAL PERSPECTIVES ON ORGANIZATIONAL DEVELOPMENT

A term that became popular in the 1950s, *organizational development* has moved over the years from the techniques developed from social psychology, organizational theory, systems theory, and mangement practices to a diffuse but recognizable body of work focusing on a person that facilitates changes needed to maintain organizational viability. In 1972, Margulies and Raia contended that organizational development was "essentially a systems approach to the total set of functional and interpersonal role relationships in organizations" (p. 2). Miles (1975) wrote that in practice, *organizational development* is a term used to describe the activities that people are doing with the title. Lippitt (1982) described organizational development as "any planned, organization-wide effort to increase the effectiveness and health of an organization through various 'interventions' in the organizational processes using behavioral and management sciences technologies" (p. xiv).

In 1982, Margulies and Adams cited Beckhard and Burke and Hornstein's definitions of organizational development. Beckhard defined organizational development (OD) as "an effort (1) planned, (2) organization-wide, and (3) managed from the top, to (4) increase organization effectivenes and health through (5) planned interventions in the organization's 'processes', using behavioral science knowledge" (Beckhard, 1969: 9). Burke and Hornstein defined it as "a process of planned change—change of an organization's culture from one which avoids an examination of social processes to one which legitimizes this examination, and from one which resists change to one which promotes the planning and use of procedures for adapting to changes on a day-to-day basis" (Burke and Hornstein, 1972). Specifically they see OD as consisting of two major phases: diagnosis and intervention.

Harvey, as described by Margulies and Adams (1982), said a successful OD program must "(1) respond directly to important organizational problems, (2) be based on a comprehensive theory which has utility for solving problems, (3) be an extension of the CEO, (4) be based on the authentic use of power by all managers in the organization, and (5) be supported by an OD staff competent to provide 'Socratic Consultation' assistance'' (Adams, 1974: 184). Harvey goes on to caution against focusing too much attention on the consultant's responsibilities and suggests that the line manager should assume more responsibility.

Although there are many definitions of OD and a lack of total agreement on the term, some basic characteristics can be identified. Bennis (1969) noted:

1. An educational strategy adopted to bring about organizational change
2. A means to address problems of mission, of human satisfaction and development, and of organizational effectiveness
3. Educational strategies that emphasize experienced behavior (i.e., data-based strategies)
4. A collaborative relationship between consultant and members of the client system. When consultants are utilized they are generally not members of that specific organization but they share the social philosophy of the client system (cited by Margulies and Adams, 1982: 13)

Margulies and Adams have identified a set of values that support the involvement of individuals with organizations as they contribute to the functioning of the organization as a whole:

1. The value of providing opportunities for people to act as human beings rather than as resources in the productive processes
2. The value of providing opportunities for each organization member, as well as the organization, to develop to full potential
3. The value of striving to increase the effectiveness of the organization in terms of all its goals
4. The value of striving to create a work environment in which it is possible to find exciting and challenging work
5. The value of providing an opportunity for people in the organization to influence the way in which they engage in work and relate to the organization and the environment
6. The value of treating each human being as a person with a complex set of needs, all of which are important (Margulies and Adams, 1982: 13)

The nature of the individual appears to assume a main role in OD. The individual in some organizational settings is viewed as having vast amounts of untapped potential and the capability to grow, to participate, and to be creative within an organizational environment. On the other hand, the individual may be viewed as follows:

1. All of us are self-centered, suckers for a bit of praise, and generally like to think of ourselves as winners. But the fact of the matter is that our talents are distributed normally—none of us is really as good as he or she would like to think, but rubbing our noses daily in that reality doesn't do us a bit of good.

2. Our imaginative, symbolic right brain is at least as important as our rational, deductive left. We reason by stories as least as often as with good data. "Does it feel right?" counts for more than "Does it add up?" or "Can I prove it?"

3. As information processors, we are simultaneously flawed and wonderful. On the one hand, we can hold little explicitly in mind, at most a half dozen or so facts at one time. Hence there should be an enormous pressure on managements—of complex organizations especially—to keep things very simple indeed. On the other hand, our unconscious mind is powerful, accumulating a vast storehouse of patterns, if we let it. Experience is an excellent teacher; yet most businessmen seem to undervalue it in the special sense we will describe.

4. We are creatures of our environment, very sensitive and responsive to external rewards and punishment. We are also strongly driven from within, self-motivated.

5. We act as if express beliefs are important, yet action speaks louder than words. One cannot, it turns out, fool any of the people any of the time. They watch for patterns in our most minute actions, and are wise enough to distrust words that in any way mismatch our deeds.

6. We desperately need meaning in our lives and will sacrifice a great deal to institutions that will provide meaning for us. We simultaneously need independence, to feel as though we are in charge of our destinies, and to have the ability to stick out. (Peters and Waterman, 1982: 55)

The value of the individual in terms of establishing a relationship with an organization needs to be understood in terms of the individual's role, expectations, and contributions to the total organizational picture.

Generally organizations imply structure. Kast and Rosenzweig (1970) suggest that organizations are goal oriented, a place where people work with a purpose, psychosocial systems where people work in groups, a technological system where people are using knowledge and techniques, and an integration of structured activities where people are working together. Organizations may be functional or dysfunctional, depending on whether the structure supports effective and/or efficient organizational performance. Toffler (1980) suggested that organizations are emerging to specifying multiple goals, weighing them, interrelating these goals, and finding synergic policies and systems that accomplish more than a single goal at a time. The new organization requires policies that optimize not for one but for several variables at the same time, making a major shift from the single bottom line to multiple bottom lines—environmental, ethical, informational, political, and social. The organization today has moved to one of new complexity.

Lippitt, Langseth, and Mossop (1985: 2) suggest that OD has a value-based focus that gives attention to the following concerns:

- increased organization complexity
- increased world interdependence and relationships

- mission and goal coordination
- increased interface between special interest groups, government, education, business, and the community
- maintaining financial perspectives
- new organization structures
- interunit competition
- managing change and conflict
- changing worker values
- clarifying roles and accountability
- effective resource utilization
- increased interface between machines and people
- finding ways and means to increase productivity

Naisbitt (1982) identifies trends that necessitate the attention of organizations: from an industrial society to an information society; from forced technology to high tech, high touch (face-to-face contact and communication between people); from a national economy to a world economy; from short-term to long-term concerns for the future; from centralization to decentralization; from institutional help to self-help; from representative democracy to participative democracy; from hierarchies to networking (people sharing ideas, information, and resources, thus creating linkages between people); from North (decline of northern industry) to South (really West, Southwest, and Florida); and from either-or (narrow choices) to multiple options.

Inherent in change is modification. Tichy (1983) views change from a spectrum of causes in which a shift in any one can set off a compelled adjustment; he refers to this phenomenon as the rope theory. The rope is made of strands of politics, culture, and technology that appear as one but are interdependent; separation and unraveling will weaken the organization. Therefore, when change occurs, the organization and the individual associated must modify their environment, technology, goals, motivations, and perceived values.

Once a need for an OD activity has been established Margulies and Adams (1982: 10) identify general OD practices that need to be taken by a client system. These include:

- inviting OD consultant(s) to review the situation
- consultant(s) meet with key management people to review the problem situation in general terms
- a contract is negotiated to clarify goals, methods and specifics
- data are collected
- feedback is given to the client system
- agreement is reached on the course of action

- course of action is implemented
- implemented actions are monitored
- all efforts are evaluated at each step

PROCESS AND TECHNIQUES OF ORGANIZATIONAL DEVELOPMENT

The basic OD process features three major activities: organizational assessment or data collection, diagnosis, and action. The OD process follows that of planned change first described by Lewin (1947). Also known as the action-research model, the process features a number of techniques to carry out the major phases of the process.

In the assessment phase, the major activity is the collection of data, with consideration being given to the techniques and methods used to access and generate data. All environments that touch the organization should be included in the various collections of data. A technique of identifying the strengths, weaknesses, opportunities, and threats (SWOT analysis) is a worthwhile technique to use during this assessment phase.

The second phase of the process is analytical; it uses data gathered during the first phase of the process to make a diagnosis. Techniques may be used to identify concerns and issues, establish priorities, and settle on goals. Alternative strategies and plans for implementation are included in this phase. Testing of suggested approaches to resolve problems is also one technique.

In the implementation phase, action, the techniques are varied but include typically training and development. The action that is taken is based on the data collected and the diagnosis made, taking into consideration the organization's unique problem or situation. Follow-up techniques are incorporated in this phase.

Lippitt (1982) identifies sixteen OD processes, which he groups into four major categories: organizational characteristics approaches, environmental approaches, quality of worklife and climate approaches, and managerial policies and practices approaches. Each category features the basic OD process of assessment and/or data collection, diagnosis and action within the context of the structure of the organization. Attention needs to be given to the various environments that affect and bring pressure to the organization: the work climate inclusive of the nature of work and work output, and the management policies and practices, which affect operational, financial, and human resource accounting. When all of the supportive processes are given attention, a comprehensive OD process is in operation.

A multidisciplinary approach to OD adds to the success of the OD process. Attention must be given to behavioral changes, a system view of the organization, and top management support and involvement, with the expectation of moving the organization to success.

OD IN THE HEALTH SECTOR

In part because of the many changes occurring in the health care industry, the OD process is being examined as a means to assist the health care sector to manage the unique and complex organizations. Tichy and Beckhard (1982) contend that OD can help health care organizations respond to the following tasks.

1. Health care organizations are becoming more aware of the need to learn how to manage both internal and external demands.
2. Health care organization managers increasingly are concerned with systematically planning and controlling their organizations.
3. The trend in health care education is toward more emphasis on the quality of practitioner-patient relationships and toward patient-oriented prevention treatment.
4. Of those interns who graduate with an area of specialization, 90% are in general practice within five years. This has implications for medical school curricula.
5. There is a growing inconsistency between what health care practitioners of all types are taught in school and what they end up doing on the job.
6. Recently medical students have shown deeper social concern and interest in social intervention and in humanizing medical care.
7. Nearly all of the professional associations of the various health care practitioners have sponsored programs for raising their members' competencies in managing organizations and change. (18)

Attention should also be given to the areas of patient and community education, training techniques in health care settings, and attitudes associated with shifting the focus of health care services from treatment to prevention. The nature of the health care organization's mission, which has a life-and-death aspect, the complexity of numerous professional and nonprofessional groups, and environmental pressures that must be balanced and managed emphasize the complexity.

There are some limitations to OD. First, health care organizations are increasingly being charged with not managing themselves for performance and efficiency. This has led to numerous mandates, of which the latest is reimbursement of health services under the diagnostic related groups (DRGs). Second, their management structures are often inadequate for task performance. Health care organizations still rely on a hierarchical structure that depends on simple functional organizational forms for coordination. More complex organizational techniques—task forces, multidisciplinary teams, and matrix structures—are not being used. Information and control systems are primarily designed to meet the needs of external financial and accrediting groups rather than the needs of internal management. Third, health care organizations use to a lesser degree than business professionally prepared managers and available management techniques. Management expertise is still acquired all too frequently by "on the job training" (Nadler and Tichy, 1982: 366).

Nadler and Tichy contend that given these three limitations, traditional OD problems addressed by business should be placed aside while attention is given to core problems of the health care sector. They suggest that lack of professional management coupled with an uncertain environment will place pressure on health care administrators to interact with the environment, but prior to the interaction, the issues of the managerial competence of administrators needs to be confronted. They suggest three types of assessments for health care organizations:

1. Assessment of the management competence of individuals.
2. Assessment of the organization's capacity to carry out effective strategic planning.
3. Assessment of fit, or congruence, between strategy and overall organizational design. (367)

After these assessments are made, the following actions should be followed in the order given:

1. Competent managers need to be put into key positions. This may be possible via training and skill development. In many cases, however, it may require personnel changes. Until competent players are on the management team, none of the other interventions can be successfully implemented.
2. Highest priority should be given to environmental relations and environmental strategy. This issue is vital to the survival of the organization.
3. Once a strategy has been decided upon, systems of organization must be developed to achieve the coordination and control necessary to implement it.
4. Working relationships, team functioning, intergroup conflict, and other human relations issues should be dealt with. (368)

Other considerations the health organization must attend to are the political problems of determining organizational goals and the allocation of rewards. The major power hierarchies in health care organizations are the medical and the administrative. Tension usually exists between the two, resulting in a great deal of political bargaining between them over control of the health care resources and the determination of the organization's mission and goals. Physicians give commitment to quality of patient care, scientific medical practice, and research; administrators are committed to quality of care and cost efficiencies. To complicate the problem associated with a bihierachical system, the boundaries of authority are not clearly defined. Weisbord (1979) sees that lack of attention to the political activities among physicians and administrators creates a difficult climate for OD.

Health care organizations are more explicitly and intensely political than many others, not only because of the administrators' and physicians' conflict of interest issues but the existence of numerous professional and paraprofessional groups, each with its own language, credentials, problems, and defined turf. The competition for resources has also contributed to the intensity of conflict and political action. In addition the external environments of health care organizations are highly political.

Nadler and Tichy (1982) recommend that because of the unique and complex nature of health care organizations, a shift in the focus of OD intervention activities should encompass the following points:

1. Take an open systems perspective. Health care organizations display the characteristics of open systems. The nature of their mission combined with the political context in which they exist today mandate that they conduct numerous intense and continuous transactions with the environment. During the diagnostic phase of the OD process, OD practitioners should collect data about the environment and about the organization's interactions with the environment.
2. Aim interventions at the critical systems issues. An open systems perspective allows the OD practitioner to ask, What issues are most critical to the survival and continued health of a particular organization?
3. Emphasize strategic and structural concerns. Although each organizational situation is different, it is safe to assume that in most cases strategic and/or structural concerns should be addressed.
4. Plan for political dynamics. Health care organizations are highly political. OD practitioners must take the political system into account and must deal with key power groups, different professional orientations, and conflicts. (375)

Health care organizations should focus their OD efforts on the external environments, which provide input to the organization, the resources that are available to the organization to accomplish its tasks, and the inputs of previous patterns of decisions and behaviors along with the history of the organization as to the strategies utilized to make decisions about mission, goals, and plans.

Useful techniques for health care organizational OD are team building, continuing education, and quality circles. Team building is a technique in which groups of individuals work together to accomplish a task. The numerous teams used in the health care setting make this OD technique familiar. Continuing education, training, and development keep individuals well informed on the latest skills, techniques, and developments associated with the various health care professions, with a focus on the organization and on the individual. Quality circles feature small-group problem-solving meetings in which individuals give attention to changes needed in their areas of operation and with the organization in general.

THE ROLE OF TRAINING

The term *training* suggests a process whereby the trainee gradually learns to do exactly what the trainer wants the individual to do. The training of organizational participants is a very different kind of process, and its final outcome generally represents a compromise between the plans of the trainer and the preferences of the trainee, further modified by the accidents of the training period.

Fombrun, Tichy, and DeVanna (1984) describe training as a means of enhancing an individual's present and future effectiveness. The areas of training focus on performance, attitudes, identity, and adaption. Performance and attitude typically focus on the short term, giving attention to the attainment of present work goals and present feelings about the career, such as involvement, commitment, and conflict. Adaptability is the extent to which the individual is preparing to meet future career demands. Identity is a measure of congruence of integration of the person's self-perceptions over time.

Good selection and position management are not enough to bring high technical competence to an organization. Continuing training and development are essential even if experienced competent people are selected and job assignments take full advantage of their strengths.

Before deciding on training as a way to resolve a knowledge or skill deficiency, it is worthwhile to look at whether a training need really exists or whether other problems stand in the way of a particular achievement. Training time should be devoted to those matters that deserve highest priority.

Four elements involved in getting individuals and organizations to improve performance are identified by McLean (1982): the systematic study of job principles and guidelines, the use of available knowledge, analysis of one's own performance, and the willingness to make innovations on the job a regular practice.

A number of activities can enhance the individual's performance, attitudes, identity, and adaptation: coaching, increased effort and self-improvement to increase job performance, socialization, job experiences, counseling, peer interaction, job assignments, education, self-examination, self-assessment, and feedback. All too frequently organizations define training as attending a task procedural–oriented lecture.

The design of training programs should examine the assessment of need for the program, selection of goals and objectives, employment of appropriate learning principles, utilization of supportive learning strategies that take into consideration the organizational climate, adult learning principles and organizational resources, and the evaluation of the training encounter. Administrative support should also be considered in the design of the training program.

In health care organizations, the training effort can be organized into staff or line training, or both. Staff training is usually found in large health care organizations where a group of educators is responsible for in-service and training needs. Line training approaches are department specific and are typically performed by department heads. In addition to training, management development is usually made available in health care organizations. The need for a strong management development program often results from the fact that managers are frequently selected from the health professionals educated in a specific clinical specialty. These individual have been promoted because of their superior technical expertise. Essentially management development is the means to increase the capabilities of managers. Most often such development focuses on attributes such as communications, delegation, and problem solving.

In the vast majority of organizations, the importance of training is underestimated, and training procedures are less than adequate, with the result that many promising individuals leave the organization. Training in the sense that individuals in organizations try to improve the performance of other people through some type of learning experience is probably a basic process in any system, particularly at the informal level. Because many organizations do not use training as a major change activity, managers should evaluate their programs carefully and take measures to determine if the training produces the desired results.

GUIDELINES FOR ADMINISTRATORS AND PROFESSIONALS

OD has the potential to assist health care administrators and professionals in participating in the various aspects of change that affect the health care sector. It is reasonable to say that no skill leading to effective management in the future will be more important than those that contribute to managing change. All changes occur through a process that unfolds in stages: recognition, identification, implementation, and adaption. Rakich, Longest, and Darr (1985) suggest that change proceeds in a series of steps:

1. Recognition of the need to change;
2. Diagnosis of the problems;
3. Identification of alternative methods and strategies;
4. Selection of the method and strategy;
5. Implementation of the change, and
6. Evaluation of the change. (500)

Lippitt, Longseth, and Mossop (1985) identify a checklist that administrators can use to take action toward implementing change within their organization:

1. Appoint a credible manager and give him or her the authority, time, and resources to bring about the desired change
2. Ensure that the project manager has clout and the required skills, has change facilitators at all levels and in all parts of the organization, has interpersonal and organization development skills to help, train, and coach those affected, understands and can facilitate the phases of the change project, selects and trains the best people to carry out the action plan, motivates throughout the process people trying to change themselves, and makes available time and resources to those responsible for implementing the desired change

3. Give the project manager external and internal consulting help in managing the change process, help to differentiate and integrate all change activities, give those responsible for action access to internal and external facilitators who collect data on change effect and who can recommend assistance needed by specialists
4. Provide an impartial evaluation to evaluate the effect of actions taken against the purpose of the change
5. Maintain and demonstrate top management's full support for the projected change and for the actions taken to achieve it (105)

The optimum design for an organization cannot be completely specified, but there are well-established principles for managing an organization in a creative manner:

1. Identify the creative individuals on whom the success of the organization depends, on the basis of their demonstrated performance
2. Make sure that you and they share a common view of the organization's goals, whether broadly or narrowly defined
3. Provide them with all the support the organization can muster
4. Protect them from bureaucratic interference
5. Reward them as lavishly as possible (Caplow, 1983: 180)

If an OD program is to be successful, top management must do more than make funds available. A successful OD program will quickly generate requests for changes in policies and practices that demand top-level approval; and failure to respond thoughtfully and quickly can doom the effort. Top management should be directly involved in the OD process from the beginning. The OD effort does not proceed in lockstep down the system but flows down into the system and then up again, with top management members learning not only from their own internal processes but also from being confronted with the impact of their behaviors on those below them.

Deal and Kennedy (1982: 176) give this advice on successful change: (1) position a hero in charge of the process, (2) recognize a real threat from outside, (3) make transition rituals the pivotal elements of change, (4) provide transition training in new values and behavioral patterns, (5) bring in an outside consultant, (6) build tangible symbols of the new direction, and (7) insist on the importance of security in transition.

Beckhard (1969: 96) identifies a number of conditions that appear to contribute to the failure of OD efforts:

1. The existence of a credibility gap between top management statements of values and styles and their actual behavior
2. The use of pieces of an OD program or ad hoc activities that are not based on systematic goals for change

3. A short time perspective or an unrealistic expectation of short-term results
4. Overdependence on and improper use of external and internal consultants
5. A lack of communication and lack of integration of OD efforts between the various levels within the organization
6. Perceiving good relationships as an end goal of OD rather than as a condition of organizational effectiveness
7. Searching for quick solutions or cookbook prescriptions for organizational health
8. Applying an intervention inappropriately or without proper data gathering and diagnosis

Contrary to opinions generally held in the past, the best available information suggests that OD has been used and is now being used in a variety of health care settings; the failure of OD health care projects is more attributable to the lack of knowledge and skill on the part of the OD practitioner than to the uniqueness of the health care setting; and the application of OD concepts and techniques can result in a wide variety of benefits for the organization and its administrators and health care professionals.

REFERENCES

Adams, J. (Ed.) (1977). *New Technologies in Organization Development*. San Diego: University Associates.
Beckhard, R. (1969). *Organization Development: Strategies and Models*. Reading, Mass.: Addison-Wesley.
Bennis, W. G. (1969). *Organization Development: Its Nature, Origins, and Prospects*. Reading, Mass.: Addison-Wesley.
Burke, W., and Hornstein, H. (1972). *The Social Technology of Organization Development*. Fairfax, Va.: NTL Learning Resources Corp.
Caplow, T. (1983). *Managing an Organization*. 2d ed. New York: Holt, Rinehart and Winston.
Deal, T. E., and Kennedy, A. A. (1982). *Corporate Cultures: The Rites and Rituals of Corporate Life*. Reading, Mass.: Addison-Wesley.
Demone, H. W., and Schulberg, H. C. (1985, Spring). Human services and health administration education: Management development issues. *Journal of Health Administration Education*, 185–212.
Flory, J. (1986, September-October). Leadership: Doing does it: An interview with Warren Bennis. *Healthcare Executive*, 28–29.
Fombrun, C. J., Tichy N. M., and Devanna, M. A. (Eds.) (1984). *Strategic Human Resource Management*. New York: John Wiley.
Kast, F. E., and Rosenzweig, J. E. (1970). *Organization and Management*. New York: McGraw-Hill.
Lewin, K. (1947). *Research Center for Group Dynamics*. New York: Beacon House.
Lippitt, G. (1982). *Organizational Renewal*. 2d ed. Englewood Cliffs, N.J.: Prentice-Hall.
Lippitt, G. L., Langseth, P., and Mossop, J. (1985). *Implementing Organizational Change*. San Francisco: Jossey-Bass.

McClure, L. (1985, July-August). Organization development in the healthcare setting. In *Hospital and Health Services Administration*, 55–64.

McLaren, R. I. (1982). *Organizational Dilemmas*. New York: John Wiley.

McLean, H. A. (1982). *There Is a Better Way to Manage*. New York: American Management Association.

Margulies, N., and Adams, J. (1982). Introduction to organization development. In N. Margulies and J. Adams (Eds.), *Organizational Development in Health Care Organization*. Reading, Mass.: Addison-Wesley.

——— (Eds.) (1982). *Organizational Development in Health Care Organizations*. Reading, Mass.: Addison-Wesley.

Margulies, N., and Raia, A. P. (Eds.) (1972). *Organization Development Values, Process, and Technology*. New York: McGraw-Hill.

Margulies, N., and Wallace, J. (1973). *Organizational Change Techniques and Applications*. Glenview, Ill.: Scott, Foresman.

Miles, R. E. (1975). *Theories of Management: Implications for Organizational Behavior and Development*. New York: McGraw-Hill.

Nadler, D. A., and Tichy, N. M. (1982). The limitations of traditional interventional techniques in health care organizations. In N. Margulies and J. Adams (Eds.), *Organizational Development in Health Care Organizations*. Reading, Mass.: Addison-Wesley.

Naisbitt, J. (1982). *Megatrends*. New York: Warner Books, Inc.

Peters, T. J., and Waterman, R. H., Jr. (1982). *In Search of Excellence*. New York: Harper & Row.

Rakich, J. S., Longest, B. B., and Darr, K. (1985). *Managing Health Services Organizations*. Philadelphia: W. B. Saunders.

Ridderheim, D. S. (1986, May-June). The anatomy of change. *Hospital and Health Services Administration*, 7–21.

Shortell, S. M., and Kaluzny, A. D. (Eds.) (1983). *Health Care Management: A Text in Organization Theory and Behavior*. New York: John Wiley.

Tichy, N. M. (1983). *Managing Strategic Change: Technical, Political and Cultural Dynamics*. New York: John Wiley.

Tichy, N. M., and Beckhard, R. (1982). Applied behavioral sciences for health care organizations. In N. Margulies and J. Adams (Eds.), *Organizational Development in Health Care Organizations*. Reading, Mass.: Addison-Wesley.

Toffler, A. (1980). *The Third Wave*. New York: William Morrow.

Weisbord, M. R. (1976). Why organization development hasn't worked (so far) in medical centers. *Health Care Management Review*, 17–28.

11
Occupational Safety and Health Strategies

James Hill

The modern health organization is an incredibly complex ecosystem. The delivery of safe patient care is dependent on the coordinated efforts of a myriad of clinicians and technicians, each of whom routinely works with sophisticated technology and potentially hazardous materials. In the absence of a comprehensive occupational safety and health program, both the patient and the health care worker are at grave risk, for a hospital can be an exceedingly hazardous place.

The vast array of chemicals, diagnostic imaging hazards, and anesthetic and sterilization gases, to name but a few, are commonplace in both the small community-based hospital and the enormous tertiary-care facility. The presence of these hazards—although indispensable for the delivery of patient care—raises a host of safety and health concerns. Moreover, the beneficiary of this care, the patient, may be inflicted with a communicable disease, complicating the safety mission of the organization to the extent that the patients themselves may represent additional safety and health risks to the hospital worker.

OVERVIEW OF EMERGING ISSUES

The typical hospital safety or safety surveillance function has long been accountable for routine safety matters such as fire and electrical safety and the administration of safety precautions governing the operation of biomedical equipment, the training of personnel in proper moving and lifting techniques, and the like. However, in recent years, increasingly sophisticated technology and medical evidence suggesting causal links between exposure to substances commonly used in the delivery of patient care and adverse health effects have imposed new and difficult burdens on the coordination of the hospital safety effort.

The emerging safety issues in health care may be categorized in the following groups:

- Workplace exposures
- Hazards identification
- Communicable diseases in the workplace
- Hazardous waste storage and disposal
- Employee concerns

Workplace Exposures and Hazards Identification

Despite the significant efforts of the various federal, state, local, and private bodies charged with the development and enforcement of safety standards in health care, little is currently known about the safe exposure levels of numerous chemicals and medical gases. Compounding this problem is the possibility that an existing standard provides employees with a false sense of security; that is, where a standard does exist, it may be meaningless to the extent that it does not adequately control safe exposure levels.

Workplace exposures are a particularly acute issue as to reproductive hazards. The National Institute for Occupational Safety and Health (NIOSH), the research arm of OSHA, ranks reproductive hazards sixth in the top ten occupational diseases, yet OSHA has issued only three standards based on reproductive effects.[1] Health care unions cite a higher rate of spontaneous abortions among nurses who are exposed to antineoplastic or anticancer drugs as further evidence of the reproductive hazards in health care.[2]

One other significant workplace exposure concerns the presence of asbestos, originally used as an insulation and building material, in older hospital facilities across the nation. The link between prolonged exposure to asbestos and a greater risk of developing certain cancers is now well known. In response, safety personnel at older facilities have moved ahead with plans to remove the asbestos and replace it with other building materials.

Communicable Diseases in the Workplace

The acquired immune deficiency syndrome (AIDS) and the hepatitis-B (HBV) viruses present serious concerns to workers in the health care industry. Workers subject to blood, body fluid, or needle stick exposures face the greatest risk of contracting either virus. In a typical hospital these workers include nurses, physicians, dentists and dental hygienists, podiatrists, laboratory and blood bank technicians, phlebotomists, dialysis personnel, morgue workers, housekeepers, laundry workers, and others whose duties include contact with blood or other body fluids or with corpses.

Infection with the AIDS virus in the workplace represents a minor but real health hazard. Fortunately, only a few such cases have been reported to date. According to the Center for Disease Control (CDC), HBV infections occur in 8,000 to 12,000 health care workers per year and ultimately result in over 200 deaths per year due to acute and/or chronic effects.[3]

In October 1987, OSHA, in conjunction with the Department of Health and Human Services, issued guidelines to protect health care workers against occupational exposure to AIDS and HBV.[4] Recommendations to the health care employer included the development of standard operating procedures and practices for the safe handling of blood and other body fluids, as well as items soiled with blood and other body fluids. Where the hospital assigns responsibility to a safety committee to implement protective practices and procedures, the federal agencies recommend that the committee include both management and worker representatives.

Hazardous Waste Storage and Disposal

This issue has received renewed attention from personnel charged with hospital safety to the extent that right-to-know laws require the employer to make available information governing the safe storage and disposal of hazardous materials. Additionally, there is an increased awareness on the part of hospital safety personnel that certain hazardous waste materials must not be combined with other such materials for risk of potentially lethal chemical reactions.

Improper venting of the by-products of various laboratory tests, for example, may contaminate the work environment. These by-products must be allowed to exhaust either from the hospital roof for safe dispersion into the air or, if permissible, allowed to dissipate safely in the work area itself after employees have sealed off the area.

Finally, as with other industries, the Environmental Protection Administration (EPA) monitors the health care industry to ensure that hazardous waste is not illegally released into the environment.

Employee Concerns

Paralleling the new technologies in health care is an increasingly astute and concerned workforce. As a result of the federal government's imposition of cost controls on the health care industry in the mid–1980s in the form of fixed payments for treatments rendered under Medicare and Medicaid diagnostic related groups (DRGs), hospitals were forced to reduce the cost of patient care. Almost immediately, hospitals in precarious financial positions closed beds, reduced employee merit compensation pools, and moved ahead with reductions in force (RIF), the last a phenomenon almost unheard of in the industry.

Not surprisingly, health care workers, particularly unionized employees, began to shift their focus from monetary benefits to other employment issues, like job security and job safety. Thus, it is not uncommon in this new financial era of health care for health care unions to devote considerable effort to safety issues during collective bargaining. Some unions have demanded and won the right of access to employee chemical exposure records. Members of the American Nurses Association (ANA) at three Oregon public hospitals won the right in late 1985 to be transferred from assignments or equipment they consider dangerous while their complaint is investigated. Other nursing bargaining units have been successful in securing contractual language providing for additional staff to handle heavy or violent patients.

ORGANIZATIONAL SAFETY AND HEALTH STRATEGIES AND APPROACHES

In order to be effective, a hospital safety program is generally organized along interdisciplinary lines. That is, recognizing that the ultimate safety effort is contingent on the safe behaviors and practices of all employees, personnel from key functional areas should be represented in the safety program. Primary accountability for occupational safety and health is delegated to a safety or safety surveillance department. The department is, by its nature, a staff function and the chief safety officer in the hospital typically reports directly to administration.

Administrative Structure of the Safety Surveillance Department

The scope of responsibilities of this department is a function of the size of the institution. In large urban medical centers, the department may employ a number of safety specialists, each accountable for areas or departments that routinely use hazardous materials or operate potentially hazardous equipment. For example, a senior safety officer may be assigned responsibility for laboratory services, including microbiology, hematology, immunology, the blood bank, and the patient specimen acquisition unit. This employee would be charged with safe chemical and reagent disposal, as well as the development and enforcement of protocols for the proper labeling and storage of these chemicals. Special procedures may be necessary for the safe handling of blood samples and blood products. Chemicals and reagents routinely used in laboratory tests often emit noxious fumes or odors. Thus this employee would ensure that laboratory personnel are properly outfitted with protective respiratory devices and that the individual workstations adequately vent the adverse by-products of laboratory tests.

Hazardous waste technicians assume the responsibility for the safe disposal of waste generated by the hospital. Duties might include the disposal of patient isolation waste, blood products and pathological waste, and the destruction and disposal of expired pharmaceuticals. In large academic medical centers, animals are used for a variety of research purposes. Their carcasses are ordinarily disposed of by incineration.

Other technicians are delegated accountability for safety matters in the central supply and sterilization department. Duties would include the maintenance of passive monitors to control ethylene oxide (ETO) exposure, the gas used for the sterilization of surgical instruments. These employees are also ordinarily responsible for the passive monitoring devices in operating rooms to ensure safe exposure levels of anesthetic gases.

The Safety Surveillance Department as Organizational Liaison

In a typical hospital a number of other functional areas are routinely involved in both employee and patient safety beyond their representation on the hospital safety committee. These areas include risk management, employee health service, and an infection control body.

Risk Management

While it is not unusual for the safety department to be called a risk management department in some hospitals, in a larger facility the latter usually refers to the function allocated responsibility for assessing and correcting safety problems that may contribute to the filing of a malpractice action. For example, it is not uncommon for a typical hospital to be sued several times a year by patients who fall and injure themselves while in the hospital. Often an unsafe work condition or improper supervision of the patient by care givers may contribute to the injury. Another example of an unsafe work condition that may lead to a malpractice action could be a malfunctioning passive monitor in the hospital operating room. A resulting claim may allege that overexposure to an anesthetic gas gave rise to the malpractice.

Given the significant risk of extensive monetary damages associated with some malpractice claims, the safety surveillance department communicates regularly with risk management personnel in the development and enforcement of protocols to minimize these risks.

Employee Health Service

This function is responsible for providing on-site care to the employee population. The department ordinarily administers both the pre-employment physical to the newly hired and provides first aid to employees injured on the job.

The employee health service (EHS) is a key element in a comprehensive safety program. It may assist in establishing specific standards for physical fitness for some positions, and it may develop screening tests for applicants whose jobs pose physical demands or have special agility standards. EHS may also assist the employment department in carrying out its obligation to hire handicapped individuals by identifying these persons during the pre-employment process and suggesting appropriate workstation modifications or other accommodative measures.

Infection Control Committee

The Joint Commission on the Accreditation of Hospitals (JCAH) requires the establishment of an infection control committee to monitor biologic safety. The committee's span of control normally includes all patient care areas, the emergency room, the operating room, food and nutrition services, and the hospital laundry. The committee is typically authorized to mandate all measures necessary for the hospital to control the risk of infection, including the isolation of patients and the imposition of work restrictions on employees who may manifest a contagious condition like chicken pox or measles.

Emergency Responses

Rounding out the scope of responsibilities of the safety surveillance function is a series of established emergency response protocols. These include plans for evacuation of the facility in the event of a fire or bomb threat and emergency electrical capability in case of a power failure. The department may also coordinate logistical details associated with the hospital's disaster drill, another JCAH requirement.

In the event of the malfunction of a surgical instrument sterilizer, the safety personnel department may authorize a lockout procedure whereby the contaminated sterilization area is sealed off until released gases have dissipated to safe exposure levels.

LEGAL CONSIDERATIONS IN IMPLEMENTING AND ADMINISTERING AN OCCUPATIONAL SAFETY AND HEALTH PROGRAM

The legal considerations attendant to the implementation and administration of occupational safety and health standards in a health care organization are considerable. Given the omnipresent hazards in the typical hospital, what may the administration do to protect the safety and health of its employees without violating other statutes designed to protect employee rights? Stated another way, may the hospital administration, for example, implement an employment policy that excludes women of childbearing age from holding certain positions where the prolonged exposure to gases or toxins may cause genetic injury or reproductive harm? May the hospital legally hire only male anesthesiologists because medical evidence establishes a causal link between exposure to some anesthetic gases and a higher incidence of miscarriage? Or should employment laws favor the hospital that wishes to restrict employment opportunities in its central service department to males because the gas typically used in hospitals to sterilize surgical instruments, ETO, has also been associated with a higher rate of miscarriages than normal? May health care workers legally refuse to work with a coemployee who may suffer from a communicable disease like hepatitis-B or AIDS? Finally, may the health care employer legally restrict the employment opportunities of workers suffering from a communicable disease?

Fetal Protection Policies and Title VII

The development and implementation of fetal protection policies in health care and other industries represent an important occupational safety goal. These policies are generally designed in one of two fashions. The first such policy excludes only pregnant women from work activity that may have detrimental effects on the unborn. The other, a much broader policy, attempts to exclude all women capable of bearing children from specific job assignments. While both of these policies may be commendable to the extent that each protects the developing fetus, their enforcement seriously compromises the employment opportunities of women and, as such, may be violative of Title VII of the Civil Rights Act of 1964.[5]

In a recent case, a certified radiology technician was discharged after her employer learned she was pregnant.[6] Her discharge was based on recommendations of the medical director of the radiology department and the radiation safety director, both of whom believed that the protection of the unborn fetus required the employee's removal from exposure to X-rays. The discharged employee brought suit, charging that the hospital's fetal protection policy discriminated against women. The court agreed that the policy operated to exclude pregnant women from employment opportunities in the radiology department and was therefore discriminatory on its face.

In addition to evidence establishing that the employee's actual exposure to radiation was less than the prescribed hazardous level, the court found that the hospital had failed to consider other, less restrictive alternatives, to protect the fetus. For example, the hospital chose not to pursue the possibility that the employee could perform other duties, both within the department and the hospital as a whole, that would reduce her exposure to radiation.

In a similar matter from outside the health care industry, a court upheld a fetal protection policy that excluded all women of childbearing age from positions involving regular exposure to known or suspected reproductive hazards.[7] The employer had adopted its broadly restrictive policy only after the completion of a comprehensive study, which included extensive medical evidence. In short, the court concluded there was no other acceptable alternative to protect the unborn fetus other than altogether barring women of childbearing age from jobs where they would be exposed to the toxins. As such, the court held that the employer could, as a matter of business necessity, impose restrictions on the employment opportunities of women that were reasonably necessary to protect the unborn fetus.

Considered together, these decisions indicate that the health care organization may legally restrict the employment opportunities of women in the interest of guarding against exposing women to reproductive hazards. However, the health care employer is well advised to support such a decision with detailed medical evidence before implementing a policy that excludes a class of female workers.

Refusals to Work with an AIDS Victim

A related question is whether a health care employee may legally refuse to work with a coemployee afflicted with the AIDS virus on the theory that to do so would present an unsafe work condition in violation of the Occupational Safety and Health Act. Given the existing body of medical knowledge about the AIDS virus—that it cannot be transmitted by casual contact—it is doubtful that such conduct would be protected by the act since the Supreme Court has determined that OSHA regulations require such a refusal be made with a reasonable belief that no alternative is available.[8]

Similarly, there is the issue of whether unionized health care employees are afforded protection under the National Labor Relations Act to refuse to work with an AIDS victim. Again, this must be answered in the negative because of current medical knowledge about AIDS.

Generally, concerted activity is protected under the National Labor Relations Act so long as that activity is engaged in with other employees and not on behalf of the employee alone.[9] However, a well-established Supreme Court decision provides for the protection of concerted activity, in the context of work refusals, only if there exists a good-faith belief that employees may be subjected to unsafe working conditions.[10]

Status of Communicable Diseases as an Employment Handicap

The Rehabilitation Act of 1973 forbids an employer from discriminating against an "otherwise qualified handicapped individual" on the basis of a handicap.[11] While the definition of *handicap* in the statute does not expressly mention diseases, the Supreme Court has interpreted the act as covering diseases, including those that are communicable.[12]

In *Arline*, the employee was discharged by her employer elementary school after she was stricken with tuberculosis three times in less than two years. The employer justified its action on the basis of the perceived risk to others and on public opinion, arguing that the act does not protect against discrimination based on the person's perceived ability to communicate the disease to others. Since in this case the fear of contagion of tuberculosis may not have had a rational basis, the Court rejected this argument and held that there was not sufficient cause to justify excluding the employee from employment opportunities within the school system.

A few lower courts have held that AIDS is covered as a handicap under the Rehabilitation Act.[13] Although an AIDS case has not yet been decided by the Supreme Court in this context, the reasoning in *Arline* seems to support this view. Many state employment statutes expressly apply to diseases,[14] while others mirror the definition of the federal Rehabilitation Act and therefore should be interpreted to the same effect. In any event, the clear trend among the states is to find that AIDS is a covered handicap.[15]

With respect to AIDS and some other diseases, an individual may be diagnosed as having been exposed to the disease while not being disabled by it. However, the definition of *handicap* in the federal statute and in many state statutes applies to individuals who are "regarded" or "perceived" as handicapped. As such, these persons are likely protected against discrimination on these grounds.[16]

Right-to-Know Laws

In late 1983, OSHA issued its Hazard Communication Standard.[17] This standard requires employers to disclose information related to the hazardous nature of workplace chemicals and other potentially toxic materials. Shortly after, a number of states enacted legislation providing employees with the protective right to know about hazardous materials with which they may work.[18] The policy reasons for these laws are quite simple; if workers understand and better appreciate the risks involved in using hazardous materials, they will adjust their work practices accordingly.

As a result of these laws, a manufacturer of a material identified as hazardous is required to supply the buyer and user of that material with material safety data sheets (MSDS). This information essentially specifies methods of safe use, hazardous exposure levels, and required remedial action in the event of an accident. The user of the hazardous materials must maintain these data sheets on record. Moreover, the information about a given substance—from a cleaning agent to a medical gas—must be made available to an inquiring employee upon demand. The employer must also post information in conspicuous places (most commonly in laboratories and central supply areas) advising employees of their statutory right to request and receive information about hazardous materials.

Protection of Employee(s) Who File Safety Complaints

Under the general duty clause of the Occupational Safety and Health Act, an employer must provide "employment and a place of employment which are free from recognized hazards."[19] Workers whose employers refuse or neglect to correct hazardous situations may file a complaint with OSHA and/or with the comparable state occupational safety and health agency.

In order to protect the complaining worker from the possibility of employer retaliation in the form of discharge, discipline, or other unfavorable treatment, complainants' identities are not revealed to the employer. OSHA also investigates employee complaints of discriminatory treatment by employers against employees who have exercised their statutory safety and health rights.

GUIDELINES FOR ADMINISTRATORS AND PROFESSIONALS

The development and implementation of an effective workplace safety program, one that discharges its statutory obligation under the Occupational Safety and Health Act to provide a safe work environment, while also providing safe patient care, requires a formidable effort. The intricacies of record keeping and compliance reporting alone can be an overwhelming task. Moreover, a tangle of legal issues confronts the health care professional as safety plans are developed and implemented. Following is an itemization of some basic strategies to keep in mind.

Job Descriptions and Pre-employment Physicals

Often injuries occur in the workplace because employees are not physically capable of performing the duties for which they were hired. In order to ensure that an applicant may be suitable for the physical demands of a given position, hospital personnel involved in the hiring decision ought to refer to a job description that clearly reflects these demands. During the course of the employment interview, any special physical demand should be clearly communicated to the applicant.

Under both Title VII and many individual state antidiscrimination laws, it is illegal for the employer to base an employment decision on an applicant's handicap or disability. However, before the selection of an applicant, it may be advisable to conduct a pre-employment physical to verify an applicant's ability to perform safely specific duties of the job. The physical may be administered by a physician or nurse assigned to the hospital's employee health service. To avoid charges of discrimination, however, the pre-employment physical should be given to all final applicants prior to the selection.

Positive Discipline

Once on the job, an employee may suffer injuries that are entirely preventable. Usually they are the result of an employee's neglecting to use proper lifting techniques or to seek assistance when confronted with a particularly physically demanding task. The negative management outcomes of preventable injuries include staffing disruptions and increased workers' compensation exposure.

If management is objectively satisfied it has met its burden of training the employee in safe workplace conduct and that it has accurately communicated and demonstrated to that employee the techniques and precautions necessary to perform the job safely, management should not be reticent to authorize progressive discipline for repeated safety violations. However, under no circumstances should the supervisor authorize discipline or discharge an employee because that employee filed a workers' compensation claim as the result of an on-the-job injury.[20]

Training

The proper training of employees is a critical element in the reduction of on-the-job injuries. Teaching safe workplace methods aids the employee in developing both a knowledge base and a desire to maintain good work safety habits. Training must be vivid, recent, and important in order to have a clear impact upon employees. Regular safety in-service instruction can be an excellent motivator; it reaffirms to employees the need to be aware of safety as they perform their jobs.

Interdisciplinary Safety Committee

Consistent with the premise that a truly effective occupational safety and health program integrates and coordinates safety issues across the house, the hospital should employ a committee model, comprised of representatives from key functional areas, to manage the overall safety effort. Since occupational safety and health standards are mandatory subjects of bargaining, it is likely that the language in the collective bargaining agreement of the unionized hospital provides for union representation on the safety committee. As such, one or more union stewards should be designated to serve on the committee.

The committee should meet regularly—at least once a month—to review injury reports from the preceding month and to implement corrective action. Safe exposure levels should be reviewed and revised as needed, and information as to the proper handling, storage, and disposal of hazardous materials should be communicated to the appropriate personnel. The committee should also regularly review and update, as needed, standard operating and emergency procedures.

In terms of organizational authority, the committee, through the chief safety officer, should be empowered to mandate compliance with its programs and procedures, subject to review perhaps only at the highest levels of management. In other words, the recommendations of the committee must not be merely advisory if its objectives are to succeed.

Senior Management Support

Senior management must endorse and actively support the safety mission if it is to enjoy credibility and eventually succeed. As with other segments of the employee population, top management is similarly responsible for providing a safe workplace.

Awareness of Legal Issues

Before developing and implementing occupational safety and health plans that may restrict the employment opportunities of classes of employees (e.g., women of childbearing age, pregnant women, and the handicapped), proposals should be reviewed by a member of the hospital's employee–labor relations staff. Goals may be laudable, but a legal obstacle may force some modifications or revisions of plans.

NOTES

1. *BNA Employee Relations Weekly*, July 20, 1987, p. 922. The article goes on to quote a report authored by the Congressional Office of Technology Assessment: "What is known about reproductive hazards is far outweighed by what is unknown."

2. Ibid., p. 924.

3. *Protection against Occupational Exposure to Hepatitis B Virus (HBV) and Human Immunodeficiency Virus (HIV)* (Washington, D.C.: Joint Advisory Notice of the Department of Labor and the Department of Health and Human Services, October 19, 1987), p. 1.

4. Ibid.

5. 42 U.S.C. sec. 2000e.

6. Hayes v. Shelby Memorial Hospital, 726 F.2d 1543 (11th Cir. 1984).

7. Wright v. Olin Corp., 697 F.2d 1172 (4th Cir. 1982).

8. Whirlpool Corp. v. Marshall, 445 U.S. 1 (1980).

9. Meyers Industries, Inc., 268 NLRB 493 (1984).

10. NLRB v. Washington Aluminum Co., 370 U.S. 9 (1962).

11. 29 U.S.C. Sec. 701 et seq.

12. School Board of Nassau County v. Arline, 107 S. Ct. 1123 (1987). See also New York Association for Retarded Children v. Carey, 612 F.2d 644 (1979) (court held that retarded children infected with hepatitis-B virus could not be segregated unless a significant risk of infection was present).

13. See, e.g., Thomas v. Atascadero Unified School District, 1986 DLR 123: A–1 (C.D. Calif., November 17, 1986).

14. See, e.g., the Illinois Human Rights Act, Ill. Rev. Stat. ch. 68, par 2–101 *et seq*.

15. See, e.g., Cronan v. New England Telephone Co., 1986 DLR 179: D–1 (Mass. S. Ct., Suffolk County, August 15, 1986); Shuttlesworth v. Broward County, 639 F. Supp. 654 (S.D. Fla. 1986).

16. See, e.g., Cronan v. New England Telephone Co.

17. 29 C.F.R. sec. 1910.1200.

18. For example, among large industrial states, California, New York, New Jersey, and Illinois have such disclosure laws.

19. 29 U.S.C. sec. 651 et seq.

20. To do so may constitute an illegal retaliatory discharge. See, e.g., Kelsay v. Motorola, Inc., 74 Ill. 2d 172, 384 N.E. 2d 353 (1978) (discharge for filing a workers' compensation claim against employer) and Wolcowicz v. Intercraft Industries, Inc., 133 Ill. App. 3d 157, 478 N.E. 2d 1039 (1st Dist. 1985) (retaliatory discharge where employee was preemptively fired in order to deter him from filing a workers' compensation claim).

12
Employee Rights Strategies

John Bernat

Put yourself in their shoes...

You are a newly graduated female nurse, and it's your fourth day on the job. After an exhausting two hours of continuous and stressful work, you take a brief break. An older male attending physician puts a friendly arm around your shoulders and tells you how attractive you are. When you politely tell him to remove his arm, he informs you that he can make or break careers in the hospital based on his influence, and you should be more cooperative...

You are a laboratory technologist. You learn that certain control agents with which you are working are in fact toxic and should be handled according to certain well-established guidelines for sterility and safety. When you tell your supervisor that you will not continue to work with the substance until these precautions are observed, she tells you that if you refuse to continue working, you may as well go home on a disciplinary suspension.

You are a transporter of patients. A patient files a complaint against you, which is completely unfounded, stating that you used profane language in his presence. Based on this information alone, the hospital discharges you. When you ask about a published nonunion employee grievance procedure, an administrator responds, "Well, since we put that into the employee handbook, we

---

The author would like to acknowledge and extend thanks for the support and ideas of Lynne Wolfe, director of human resources, Ravenswood Health Care Corporation, Chicago, Illinois, and Suzanne Klinetop, employment manager, Rush-Presbyterian-St. Luke's Medical Center.

have the right to change it at any time. Because of all these employee lawsuits, we changed that policy. There is no grievance procedure any more.''

In employee relations work, the question most often asked by employees is, ''Can they do that?'' This chapter examines legal rights that nonunionized employees have gained very recently and sound management strategies to address these rights and still maintain an effective and efficient workplace.

HISTORICAL EMERGENCE OF EMPLOYEE RIGHTS IN HEALTH CARE

In the past, employees in the United States generally had very few rights. As laws changed and more rights began to apply to employees, health care employees were frequently not included. Now, virtually any employee right applicable to a non–health care worker applies to health care workers as well. This creates a legal environment of potential jeopardy for the health care administrator. To understand why we have such a tangled legal environment, we must explore the antecedents of the balance of rights between employers and employees.

The Original Employment-at-Will Doctrine

Most U.S. law descended from English law, the major departure being the creation of sovereignty by Constitution and elected officials as opposed to the rule of a monarch. In the early days of the United States, the doctrine that applied to the relationship between employer and employee was called ''master-servant'' law (appropriately named), borrowed from Great Britain. Under this body of common law (''judge-made law''), virtually all rights in this relationship were reserved to the employer, who could hire or fire employees at his will. The employment-at-will doctrine, then, is just that: an employer can end the relationship at any time and at his or her total discretion for a good cause, bad cause, or no cause at all.[1] The employee had no legal power to affect that decision whatsoever. In a similar fashion, the employee had no power whatever to affect rate of pay or hours of work; a dissatisfied employee had the free prerogative to take his or her services elsewhere for higher compensation.

In the early history of the United States, the seemingly satisfactory nature of this legal framework largely was grounded in several salient characteristics:

1. The entrepreneurial nature of the American economy of the time was a major factor. The mainstay of the economy was farming and various skilled occupations. Mass production of goods by larger groups of semiskilled or unskilled employees did not exist.
2. Large concentrations of capital, while not nonexistent, were rare.
3. The early existence of a slavery-based economy profoundly affected the socioeconomic outlook of paid employees in the South.

4. The continuing westward expansion of the nation largely meant that dissatisfied employees with marketable general skills could move on to other areas.

Emergence of Collective Bargaining: First Incursions into Employment at Will

The first restrictions on employers' rights respecting their workers came from the unions and the rights they achieved for their members. Employers could typically not fire a union worker, for example, except for just cause (as opposed to unjust cause or, for that matter, no cause at all). These rights are typically enforced by a private grievance procedure ending in a voluntary third-party judgment process called arbitration. The right of a union to demand just cause of an employer was legally secured by the passage of the Labor-Management Relations Act of 1935 but had effectively been asserted by many unions through their economic power long before then. Unions in hospitals, however, were quite rare.

Child Labor, Minimum Wages, and Overtime

As the nation became increasingly industrialized, abuses of economic power disturbed the social conscience of the nation. In more and more cases, industries employed young children to work in hazardous and physically taxing jobs, such as mining, textiles, and heavy manufacturing. Additionally, large concentrations of capital in fewer hands operated increasingly mechanized factories that could employ great numbers of people. This concentration of economic power meant that unskilled or semiskilled factory workers with little bargaining power could be paid extremely low wages.

After the turn of the century, some states regulated or outlawed child labor, but the Fair Employment Standards Act of 1938[2] effectively outlawed child labor for the entire country. Additionally, it established that there would be a minimum hourly wage paid for most occupations and mandated overtime pay for hours worked in excess of forty per week. In addition, certain occupations are considered to be especially hazardous for minors and are set aside in the law.

Equal Pay for Equal Work

In the early 1960s but before the passage of the 1964 Civil Rights Act, an increased number of women in the workforce pressed for the passage of the 1963 Equal Pay Act, which is a comprehensive amendment to the Fair Labor Standards Act. This act provided that for jobs involving equal levels of skill, effort, responsibility, and working conditions, equal pay would have to be provided, irrespective of favorable job market conditions (more women seeking employment then men) allowing the recruitment of women for lower wages.

Civil Rights Movement

The 1964 Civil Rights Act was a landmark federal law outlawing discrimination on the basis of race, color, religion, sex, or national origin.[3] Title VII of the law outlaws such discrimination in employment. Another law was passed in 1967 to outlaw discrimination against persons over the age of forty, and Title VII was later amended to bar discrimination against pregnant employees.

The reach of Title VII is extremely broad; it asserts jurisdiction over virtually every employer in the United States.[4] Additionally, many states have enacted their own antidiscrimination laws, which may go beyond the federal law—covering, for example, sexual preference (homosexuality), marital status, military discharge status, ancestry, and physical handicap.

Relief is provided for victims of employment discrimination through governmental agencies (the U.S. Equal Employment Opportunity Commission [EEOC] and various state fair employment practices agencies) and directly through the court system as well. An individual need not retain a lawyer to take his or her complaint to the EEOC. And entire classes of individuals (for example, "all black candidates for employment") can join in lawsuits with awards in hundreds of thousands of dollars.

Affirmative Action

If a hospital receives federal funds,[5] it is covered by a series of executive orders[6] mandating affirmative action in recruitment, training, and promoting targeted minority groups. The theory of affirmative action is that minority groups, most notably blacks, have been victims of discrimination for decades, and affirmative action exists as a means to remedy past discrimination.

Age Discrimination in Employment Act

The Age Discrimination in Employment Act (ADEA) was enacted in 1967 to protect individuals over the age of 40, through the age of 70, from discrimination in employment on the basis of age. In 1986 it was amended to remove the upper limit of 70; it now covers anyone over the age of 40, and "mandatory retirement" for all but executives is now unlawful. While similar in form to Title VII, there is a different administrative structure for the ADEA, and the remedies provided can actually be greater in some circumstances than in Title VII cases.

Vocational Rehabilitation Act

In 1973, Congress passed the Vocational Rehabilitation Act (the Rehab Act), which requires employers with government contracts to make reasonable accommodations to the physical or mental limitations of applicants and employees. Employers that do more than $50,000 per year of government contracting must prepare plans to hire the handicapped affirmatively. Before or after the Rehab Act, many states adopted legislation prohibiting discrimination on the basis of handicap unrelated to ability to perform the work in question.

Health Care Amendments to the National Labor Relations Act

It was not until 1974 that the 1935 Labor-Management Relations Act (sometimes called Taft-Hartley) was amended to include not-for-profit hospital and health care workers. By this time, though, many unions had become active in hospitals. With certain exceptions, health care workers now have the same rights to unionize as other workers.

Pregnancy Discrimination Act

In 1978, Congress passed an amendment to Title VII of the Civil Rights Act—the Pregnancy Discrimination Act—in response to a U.S. Supreme Court decision that declined to characterize discrimination based on pregnancy as a form of sex discrimination.[7] An employer must treat pregnancy exactly as the employer would treat any other form of medical disability, including the payment of medical benefits and paid or unpaid sick leave. This law does not mandate any special set of pregnancy benefits; it simply provides that the employer do for the pregnant employee precisely what it would do for any other medically disabled employee. Many individual states have extended the reach of pregnancy discrimination into certain mandated benefits, such as a guarantee of return to work after pregnancy and paid time off.

CURRENT LEGAL FRAMEWORK OF EMPLOYEE RIGHTS

Employment-at-Will Doctrine

In the majority of states, the long-standing employment-at-will doctrine has been eroded. This means that hospitals are still vulnerable to lawsuits even when the individual employee is not represented by a union, is not a member of a class of people protected by Title VII or the ADEA (i.e., the employee is a white male under the age of forty) and cannot allege violation of any employment-related statute. Under the law of court decisions (the common law), judges in state courts have increasingly been sympathetic to making broad exceptions to the employment-at-will doctrine, much to the advantage of the individual employee. Bear in mind that these legal avenues vary greatly (or do not exist at all).

Contract Theories

The Express Contract

Most people think of a contract as a piece of paper outlining rights and obligations between parties. Courts will certainly take signed, written contracts of employment (called express contracts) very seriously. The general rule followed by the courts is to construe such contracts strictly against the party having greater power—and that party is presumed to be the employer. Therefore written contracts of employment should address all possible legal issues that might arise out of the employment relationship, including termination of employment, the length of employment, the impact of separation, establishment of compensation, and a myriad of other employment-related issues.

Breach of Employment Contract Implied in Fact

A gathering trend is to consider other written documents or patterns of conduct as contracts (previously no such implication existed). For example, only ten years ago very few courts would have taken an employee handbook as a contract; now such an assertion is commonplace. The previous logic was that the employment contract consisted of money exchanged for services; if a handbook was issued, there was no "new consideration" (beyond the exchange of services for wages) given by the employee to support management assuming a new set of legal obligations.

Courts have increasingly accepted the handbook as a contract on the theory that when an employee accepts employment, he or she is persuaded to accept by relying on the existence of the handbook. This reliance on the handbook to the employee's detriment replaces "new consideration" with something called "promissory estoppel." The result is that more and more states are requiring employers to live up to what is promised in employee handbooks, personnel policy and procedure manuals, and statements made in employment applications.[8]

In addition, even in the absence of written materials, many courts have concluded that statements made by managers before employment can also be considered contractual obgligations. If, for example, a candidate for employment says during the interview, "I am interested in the position, but since you're asking me to relocate from Ohio to Iowa, how is the job security?" and the manager responds, "Don't worry, you'll have a job here as long as you do it well," the manager may have just waived management's right to lay that employee off for lack of work.[9] In other words, the candidate relied to his potential detriment on a promise by management that there would be a job for him—and that created a binding contractual obligation on management. Such obligations can be created by managers who are not authorized to make such contracts so long as the manager had "apparent authority" to make the contract.

Breach of Employment Contract Implied in Law

Additionally, courts have forced contractual interpretations onto situations where no contract could even be discerned from the facts. The contract implied in law is really not a contract but a court-imposed determination that to remedy an apparent injustice, contractual theories of relief must be applied.

Summary of the Contract Theories

Generally when a contract theory is utilized, it gives the court access to remedies such as specific performance and injunctive relief, in addition to compensatory damages. That means that a court finding of breach of contract gives the court authority to direct the reinstatement of the employee, with retroactive compensation. Contract theories generally do not, however, permit the awarding of punitive damages. Therefore the contract theories typically do not involve damage awards of extensive magnitude but can result in management's being forced to rehire a terminated employee with back pay.

Retaliation and Public Policy

The pursuit of legal rights under the law is a protected public policy in the United States. Various state and federal laws dealing with unionization, workplace safety, and workers' compensation may contain internal provisions prohibiting management from retaliating against the employee for filing complaints or charges against the employer. This protection is intended to prevent management from intimidating other employees interested in pusuing their rights under the law. Therefore, management must take extra care to support factually any actions taken against employees who have filed discrimination complaints, unfair labor practice charges, workers' compensation claims, and so on.[10]

Discharges against public policy also extend into areas such as discharges motivated only by an employer's desire to avoid responsibilities to its employees established by law. For example, a federal law (ERISA) regulates an employer's obligations regarding pensions.[11] In a case where there was no technical ERISA violation, a court still found legal liability when an employer discharged an employee for no other apparent reason than that the employee was about to become eligible to receive a pension.[12] Certainly a discharge for refusing to perform illegal acts will be held to be against public policy.[13]

Finally, in an area sometimes headed whistle-blowing, the law has some interest in protecting employees performing activities in the general public interest even though those activities might be contrary to the employer's best interests. An employee who goes public with a complaint about the unsafe manner in which a hospital cares for patients, for example, might have protection under a state whistle-blower statute or might find a judge who regards discharge of the employee as against public policy.[14]

Torts

A tort is a wrongful act that can be the basis for a lawsuit. No contractual relationship need exist between the parties, but the sued party must typically have some duty of care to the wronged individual. A simple example of a tort is negligence resulting in personal injury: if I hit you with my car, you can sue me for damages. While we did not have a contract between us, the law imposes a duty of care to operate my car safely (and not hit you), and I breached that duty by hitting you. This tort is under the heading of negligence. Other torts can be intentional, meaning that the wrongdoer acted for the purpose of doing wrong. In either case, both compensatory and punitive damages are awardable in tort; therefore, the price tag of tort actions can be exceedingly high, although a pure tort suit cannot result in an order reinstating the employee to work. Punitive damages are awarded where the employer acted in malice toward the employee, "malice" defined as consciously disregarding the rights and safety of others.

Intentional Torts in Employee Rights

The first such tort we examine is intentional infliction of emotional distress. Courts have found that where a high level of animosity existed between employee and manager, it could be said that the manager intentionally performed such flagrant acts of vindictiveness, or willfully ignored the rights or safety of employees, that he or she should be liable for the emotional distress suffered by the employee. This was once rare, but is becoming more common.[15] Punitive damages can be extensive.

Defamation, the second intentional tort, is the communication of a false statement of material fact that results in damage to the victim of defamation. When defamation is written, it is libel; when oral, it is slander. Most commonly, defamation actions arise from the giving of employment references, which the former employee believes to be false and injurious to his or her reputation. The traditional employee defense to a defamation action is called qualified privilege. In the former law of defamation, employers were universally granted the ability to provide references without fear of defamation actions, the theory being that employers have a legitimate business interest in learning as much as possible about new employees. Without such a privilege, undesirable or even dangerous employees could be hired to the general injury of business. The qualified privilege is so called because it can be lost through abuse, such as overpublication (communicating the references to disinterested parties) or a reckless disregard for the truth or falsity of the reference information (whether I personally know the reference to be true or not, I repeat it anyway).

The law in this area has changed dramatically. Consider the facts of a recent Minnesota case where damages were awarded to a former employee: the employee was discharged for grounds that ultimately could have been false (insubordination).[16] The former employer did not disclose these grounds to any party other than the employee. The court upheld the defamation action on the grounds

Employee Rights Strategies

that the employee himself would have to "publish" (communicate) the "slander" whenever the employee applied for another job and was asked about why he had left his former employer. In other words, if a new employer asked the employee about circumstances surrounding his last job, the employee would have to give truthfully the reason he was given by his former boss. Therefore, even if the former employer does not tell anyone else about the circumstances of discharge, the manager can be held liable because his former employee will have to republish the manager's slander. This case, highly controversial in its findings, is an example of how far courts will stretch the law to favor discharged employees.

Defamation is a personal tort. This means that a corporation cannot be sued for defamation, only an individual. Successful defamation actions must therefore be paid personally by the manager.

Many state courts have pursued a new tort action under a general heading of wrongful discharge. While it is hard to generalize about this, courts have analyzed an overall pattern of conduct by management, which it then declares to be wrongful.[17] Such cases could also fit under "infliction of emotional distress" in terms of their legal analysis (and the awarding of punitive damages).

Negligence Theories

A few courts have gone so far as to impose a duty of care on employers to their employees, which can be breached and therefore create tort liability. The process of evaluating an employee, for example, was held in one case to impose on management a duty of care that could be breached.[18] As with intentional torts, punitive damages can be awarded for negligence.

Fair Labor Standards Act

The Minimum Wage

The 1938 law placed the minimum wage at twenty-five cents per hour. Nongovernmental[19] hospitals and health care organizations were not covered by the minimum wage until 1966 and at that time pegged a lower hourly minimum wage than the national standard.[20] Currently health care workers covered by this law receive the same minimum wage as workers in all other segments: $3.35 per hour. This level has not been changed since 1981, although Congress has recently discussed raising it.

Overtime and Hours of Work

Employees in positions that are not exempt from the provisions of the wage and hour law must be paid overtime at a rate of at least one and a half times their hourly rate for all hours in excess of forty in a week. A special alternate rule for hospitals provides that the period of time triggering overtime can be altered from forty hours per week to eighty hours in a two-week payroll period and over eight hours in a given day.

Recently some hospitals have moved to place more health professionals into the exempt category. Managers and executives are overtime exempt, but the law further provides for a professional exemption. Since the dollar salary criteria placing employees as either exempt or nonexempt ($150 or $250 per week) have not been changed in many years, some hospitals have placed their nurses on salary, arguing that their work is "professional" in the standards of the law.[21]

Child Labor

The federal law prohibits employment of children under the age of fourteen. Between fourteen and sixteen, employment in hospitals can be authorized via a work permit from the child's school. Between sixteen and eighteen, employment in "hazardous" occupations is prohibited but it is not otherwise restricted. "Hazardous" occupations may be defined by individual states and can cover jobs in health care.[22]

Equal Pay Act and Comparable Worth

Equal pay for substantially equal work is still the rule.[23] While the 1963 Equal Pay Act was heralded as an advance for women, it quickly became obvious that certain female-dominated occupations, notably secretarial work and nursing, still suffered depressed wage levels, while paying all incumbents (regardless of gender) the same rate. This led to the comparable worth controversy of the early 1980s, the theory of which has been that jobs not equal but comparable in value should pay equally. For example, if a male nurse makes more than a female nurse, clearly that would violate the Equal Pay Act. However, if a female nurse makes less than a male garbage collector, that would not violate the Equal Pay Act; the work is not literally equal in skill, effort, responsibility, and working conditions. Advocates of comparable worth say that the latter situation should warrant relief if an objective finding can be made that the work of the garbage collector, while perhaps requiring more physical effort and having worse working conditions, certainly does not require the level of skill and responsibility nursing does. Thus far, comparable worth has succeeded in the courts only on very narrow grounds. If a company performs a wage study, and it reveals that the company should pay nurses more than garbage collectors, and then the company ignores the study and pays the garbage collector more, then and only then is the company liable under a comparable worth theory as being guilty of intentional sex discrimination. Otherwise, though, pure comparable worth has not found sympathy in American courts generally.[24]

Title VII of the 1964 Civil Rights Act

It is a bad idea to discriminate on any grounds other than individual performance in hiring, promoting, compensating, or discharging employees. The employer is well advised to be race blind, gender blind, age blind, and so forth in all employment practices.

Race and National Origin Discrimination

Discriminatory Effect versus Intent

An early test of the meaning of discrimination was *Griggs* v. *Duke Power and Light* (1971).[25] In this case, preemployment tests administered were race neutral on their face but in result excluded a higher proportion of blacks than whites. It is clear that an employer who states that he or she wants to hire no blacks is guilty of intentional discrimination. *Duke Power* established that even where an employment practice gives no evidence of intent to discriminate, it is still actionable if its ultimate result or effect is to have a discriminatory impact on a minority group. Thus, if a preemployment test is administered, it must be directly related to the performance of the work in question so that it does not unfairly exclude members of a minority group in its effect.[26] If any employment practice is shown to have a discriminatory impact on minorities, a case of discrimination is made out, which must then be rebutted by the employer to show some business justification for the practice. In hospitals, requiring the ability to speak English has a discriminatory impact on minorities but has been regarded as justified by business necessity.[27]

Intentional race or national origin discrimination cannot be permitted even where a business's clientele demands such a practice. While Title VII created an exception permitting discrimination based on BFOQs (bona-fide occupational qualifications), race-based BFOQs virtually do not exist. An American company doing business in South Africa, for example, cannot limit its sales representatives to whites only, even though its South African customers will refuse to do business with blacks.[28] This is of potential relevance when patients might demand care givers of a particular race or national origin; patients have no legal right to make such a demand.

In the area of national origin discrimination, certain difficulties have emerged with the passage of the 1986 Immigration Reform and Control Act (IRCA), which requires employers to verify the work eligibility of all new employees hired after November 1986. This law mandates that employers discriminate against (by refusing to hire) aliens who are not lawfully eligible to work based on their immigration status—either as illegal aliens or aliens admitted for nonwork purposes (such as students). This puts the employer in a difficult position; it forces the hospital to discriminate against ineligible aliens, and that can have the effect of discriminating against people on the basis of their national origin. The U.S. Justice Department issued new rules, effective November 7, 1987, stating that an employer cannot set up rules or hiring procedures that systematically exclude persons from one particular country of origin, irrespective of a given individual's right to work in the United States. For example, a hospital cannot refuse to hire any applicants of Mexican origin under an assumption that most Mexican applicants are illegal immigrants. However, neutral conduct by employers with an unintended disparate impact is not an unfair immigration-related employment practice. To continue the example, say an employer requires that all applicants present a state driver's license to confirm identity for IRCA purposes. Mexican applicants could not allege that since, statistically, fewer Mexican than others possess driver's licenses, discriminatory effect exists, which gives grounds for a charge or lawsuit. In essence, the employer is expected to exclude ineligible aliens, but if one nationality group is intentially treated differently, a charge of national origin discrimination can be pursued.[29]

Title VII has also been interpreted to impose an obligation on employers to control national origin harassment in the workplace. This means that the administrator cannot condone or permit name calling or other ethnic references in the workplace such that it creates a hostile, offensive work environment for the members of minority groups.

Sex Discrimination

Intentional sex discrimination can be practiced only if strong business justification can be shown—and instances of such business justification are rare indeed. For example, locker room attendant positions or athletic coaches may be limited to members of the gender in question, and some health delivery positions—notably OB/GYN—can be gender defined to suit the sensibilities of the patients.[30]

Requirements limiting the employment of married women are violations of Title VII unless the employer similarly restricts employment of married men.[31]

In 1980, the definition of sex discrimination under Title VII of the 1964 Civil Rights Act was expanded to include sexual harassment in the workplace. The legal theory used to expand Title VII was roughly that if you were not female (or male), the unwelcome sexual harassment would not have happened; therefore, it is a form of sex discrimination. Sexual harassment was then defined as receiving unwelcome sexual advances, being told that granting sexual favors was a condition of employment, or the creation of a hostile, offensive working environment through sexual jokes and other references. Unwelcome sexual advances is distinguished from involuntary sexual conduct in a legal sense. One can "volunteer" to have sex without "welcoming" it, and unwelcome sex is chargeable.

Management is responsible not only for controlling its own sexual conduct but also protecting employees from sexual harassment from coworkers and even customers (patients) to the extent management could control such conduct and to the extent management "knew of or should have known of" sexual harassment. A recent Supreme Court case set forth certain clarifications:

- Sexual harassment is a form of sex discrimination, as a matter of law.
- A hostile working environment caused by sexual harassment is actionable. This means that sexual jokes, gestures, and references could, if pervasive, be adequate cause for a charge, and management will have to control this environment.

Employee Rights Strategies 259

- No refusal or loss of employment, or loss of promotion or other job-related benefits need have been actually suffered by a complainant to give basis for a lawsuit.[32]

Other courts have stated that even where management did not know of the harassment, legal liability exists,[33] that additional lawsuits for intentional infliction of emotional distress can be filed for punitive damages[34] where the employer knew of the harassment and did nothing to stop it quickly and that the employee need not complain formally of the offensive work environment created by sexual harassment.[35]

Religious Discrimination

Not-for-profit religious-owned businesses are free to hire only members of their own faith[36] due to a special provision of Title VII. Beyond that, discrimination on the basis of religious belief is strictly prohibited and, in fact, reasonable accommodation of religious practices is expected of employers.

"Reasonable accommodation" poses some situations of exquisite delicacy. If a nurse refuses to perform abortions on religious grounds, for example, at least one court has imposed a duty on the hospital to make reasonable efforts to accommodate the nurse[37] and not assign her to abortion cases.

Scheduling work is the more typical problem. If an employee must take every Sunday off as a matter of religious faith, the employer must accommodate that request within reason. This, of course, poses special problems for hospitals, which must operate around the clock, seven days a week. What is reasonable? The employee must notify in advance of his or her intent to take religious holidays and the reasons for the holidays. If the hospital makes no effort to accommodate, liability will be found. The best strategy is to ask coworkers whether such an accommodation is possible.[38]

Affirmative Action: Executive Order 11246

The practical effect of affirmative action is difficult to reconcile with the goal of race-blind hiring. In effect, the employer must actively seek out targeted minority applicants, monitor race representation in the workplace, and give some preference to underrepresented minorities. Underrepresentation is tyically established by an analysis of the racial composition of the relevant labor market in the employer's geographic area. Quotas in the strictest sense are not required or lawful,[39] but goals for racial representation in the workforce are expected. When faced with two qualified candidates for hire or promotion, the plan means hiring a lesser-qualified minority in futherance of the affirmative action goal[40] but cannot state that "this job must next be filled by a minority candidate."

An affirmative action plan should contain detailed specifications for strategies for minority recruitment, requirements for training and internal upward mobility, and regular assessments of success in attaining preestablished goals.

Recent cases have reinforced the legal status of affirmative action. Once an employer undertakes an affirmative action plan, it will be held strictly to its own plan and cannot subsequently claim it should have been exempted because it received no federal funding.[41] No affirmative action plan can call for more severe discipline for nonminorities than minorities to further affirmative action goals.[42] The same discipline should be given out to all for the same infractions, without regard to race.

Age Discrimination in Employment Act

The ADEA bars discrimination based on age against candidates for employment or employees over the age of 40. Only executives can be compelled to retire; mandatory retirement no longer exists for all other employees. While the law provides for BFOQs based on age, it is not likely that any health care occupation would qualify for such treatment. In most respects, age discrimination law operates the same as other areas of discrimination law.

Pregnancy Discrimination Act

In addition to state-mandated benefits for pregnant employees, actions under the federal Pregnancy Discrimination Act are still prevalent. Failure to hire a pregnant applicant because she is pregnant is a violation unless the employer can show objective scientific evidence that the decision was motivated by prevention of hazards to the fetus.[43] Unwed motherhood is also a prohibited ground for discrimination; hospitals would have to prove that being a married mother is somehow a BFOQ.[44]

The entire thrust of the Pregancy Discrimination Act is to treat pregnancy the same as any other disability. If a pregnant employee is advised that her job will be filled while on pregnancy leave, for example, such action is permissible only if the employer has similarly filled jobs of employees on sick leaves; internal consistency is the key.[45] Finally, any benefits given to employees on medical disabilities must be given to pregnant employees—and this covers the spouses of employees where spousal health insurance is available.[46]

Handicaps

Most hospitals already have redesigned their facilities for access by handicapped individuals; this is most often a basic business decision. The Rehab Act can require affirmative action for the handicapped, in addition to reasonable accommodation for handicaps in the workplace. The reasonable accommodation obligation exists for virtually any health care institution touching the federal government in any way.[47] Almost all federal courts agree that accepting Medicare and Medicaid payments brings a hospital under the act.[48] Employers can ask applicants about their ability to perform the work in question but can pose no direct questions about physical or mental handicaps that are not linked to the job itself. Many hospitals have mistakenly assumed that the Rehab Act means that anyone who is handicapped must be hired. Nothing in the law prohibits an employer from maintaining a qualified workforce for the best possible patient care; the spirit of the law is to overcome stereotypes about handicaps and instead analyze their actual impact on job performance.

Reasonable accommodation of a handicap means any sort of strategy that does not impose an undue hardship on the employer, such as modified work schedules, job restructuring, physical modifications to the workplace, and even the relocation of particular offices or jobs. However, the Supreme Court in 1979[49] defined "qualified" to mean someone "who is able to meet *all* of a program's requirements in spite of his handicap [emphasis added]."[50] Thus, it appears that "qualifications for the job" will outweigh extensive accommodations to the handicapped job applicant.

The Right to Privacy

The Federal Privacy Act of 1974 provided a skeleton for employee privacy laws subsequently enacted by various states. In 1987, the Supreme Court ruled that public employees have some reasonable expectation of privacy in the workplace, the first Supreme Court ruling of its kind.[51] In addition to guarantees of privacy in the workplace, state laws fall into general categories.

Employee Records

The legitimate distribution of employee files is controlled by a variety of state laws. Additionally, many of these same laws provide employees right of inspection of their own personnel records.[52]

Personal Employee Finances

Employers are in a position to learn a great deal about the personal finances of employees. In fact, many companies until only recently had a strict rule regarding wage garnishment; one such garnishment was cause for immediate discharge. The Consumer Credit Protection Act[53] forbids an employer to discharge an employee for receiving a garnishment for any one indebtedness.

Employee Drug and Alcohol Testing and the Polygraph

In a nutshell, federal law does not prohibit pre-employment drug testing. There is some controversy concerning the methods by which samples for testing are obtained; it is a good idea to advise applicants for employment that they are being asked to provide test samples and give them the opportunity to decline. Such declinations can be valid grounds for refusing employment.

I doubt the reliability of broadly based pre-employment drug and alcohol screens, however, and do not recommend their use for that reason. Congress recently considered a bill that would ban the use of polygraph either pre-employment or during employment.[54] Generally mechanical methods of screening employees of any kind (drug screens, personality testing, "honesty" tests, or the polygraph) are at best poor substitutes for managerial judgment and may result in poor personnel decisions. Further, these approaches are vulnerable to challenge on disparate impact grounds; the polygraph has been so challenged.[55]

While pre-employment drug screens are lawful, far less clear are the standards relating to continuing employees. Most labor arbitrators will not allow discharges based solely on a refusal to provide a necessary sample for testing. Some independent cause must first be shown before soliciting the sample, such as outward observable symptoms of intoxication. If the employee appears intoxicated and then refuses to provide a sample for testing, many arbitrators will "imply consent" for the test and allow the discharge to stand, based on the weight of the evidence for intoxication. If no independent basis for suspecting intoxication exists, however, refusal to provide a sample will probably not suffice as grounds for termination.

EMPLOYEE RIGHTS ISSUES PECULIAR TO HEALTH CARE

Relationships among Health Care Professionals

In health care organizations, almost stereotypical role conflict exists in abundance, making the enforcement of laws a very real challenge. We have higher-paid predominantly male physicians directing the activities of predominantly female nurses. The sexual interplay between physicians and nurses has become part of the popular culture. Additionally, in urban hospitals, there are vast numbers of minority group members occupying relatively menial job categories (housekeeping, orderlies, porters) but still relatively few minority administrators and physicians.

To coordinate the activities of such groups, let alone ensure the protection of their employee rights, is a highly complex task. Schuler and Youngblood[56] set forth two valuable concepts for health care human resources management: cooperative acceptance and cooperative systems.

Cooperative acceptance is defined as "the right of employees to be treated fairly and with respect regardless of race, sex, national origin, physical disability, age or religion while *on the job* (as well as in obtaining a job and maintaining job security)." To foster such acceptance, top management must endorse this simple concept (one that really is basic to human dignity) and back it with effective communications systems, including grievance procedures, responsive systems to punish individuals responsible for undermining cooperative acceptance, and general organizational awareness of management's investment in everyone's right to cooperative acceptance.

The concept of cooperative systems is most often applied to union-management relations to describe situations where the union and management work jointly rather than against one another to solve problems. Awareness of employee needs can give rise to cooperative systems, such as expanding grievance procedures into joint employee-employer meetings for the purpose of solving problems of entire work groups.

The key to both is the willingness and ability of top management to meet the needs of its employees on all levels for basic dignity in the workplace.

Predominance of Women in Health Occupations

Most hospitals are from two-thirds to three-fourths female. Therefore, issues of sex and pregnancy discrimination become critically important. In the past, a great deal of comparable worth pressure was being exerted by nursing groups particularly, but two successive worldwide nursing shortages, not to mention the relatively successful incursions of unionism into nursing, have caused nursing compensation levels to rise of their own accord. Another significant issue concerning gender-defined classification has since largely resolved itself as well: differences in pay levels for "male" versus "female" housekeeping employees. In some litigated cases, however, additional physical strength requirements alone were upheld so long as the hospital did not restrict the entry of women into the higher-paying male-dominated classification.[57]

RESPONSIBILITY FOR EMPLOYEE RIGHTS

A classic view of this topic is that a health care organization creates a department (called employee relations, personnel, human resources, or some other convenient label) vested with responsibility for maintaining employee rights. A highly placed health care official once told me that a primary responsibility of human resources was to clean up messes made by management. Of course, this view is shortsighted. Every managerial employee in the organization has an employee rights responsibility to the extent that the manager is responsible for subordinates. And the business justification is clear: the "messes made by management" carry dear price tags in court these days.

The vehicle for placing this responsibility and seeing to its exercise is managerial and supervisory awareness of the legal scene and inculcation of the managerial advantages to recognizing and making cooperative acceptance happen. People who believe that they are being treated fairly tend to work more productively.

FUTURE TRENDS IN EMPLOYEE RIGHTS

We have just completed eight years of a conservative Republican administration in Washington. The expectation of a resulting promanagement (or antiemployee) legal environment has not been entirely realized, however. Unions organizing in health care have indeed encountered a more hostile legal environment. However, the 1980s have instead seen a vast expansion in legal actions available to individual employees through largely unchecked discrimination litigation and a panoply of private causes of action considered unthinkable only a decade ago. Therefore, the health organization must make the preservation of employee rights a high priority, if for no other reason than as an article of economic survival in an intensely competitive economic climate.

Individual Litigation

Plaintiffs tend to use theories that afford the maximum recovery. Therefore, while contract-based individual causes of action will still be used (and more and more courts will find them valid), the high-recovery tort-based cases will rise in popularity. The practical reality is that the individual litigant is represented by an attorney compensated on a contingency fee[58] basis (although the ethical status of such fee arrangements is questionable). Since the lawyer controls the litigation strategy, the press for tort-based claims will increase.

Affirmative Action

Affirmative action was also thought to be moribund under the Reagan administration but has been, to paraphrase Mark Twain, prematurely reported dead. Affirmative action is by its nature self-extinguishing and not a permanent fixture, being a remedy for past discrimination—once past discrimination has been remedied, affirmative action is supposed to disappear. Despite that, authority as high and recently as the U.S. Supreme Court in 1987[59] has endorsed it in the employment setting and affirmed the employer's obligation to carry forward already-developed plans.

This area may see further legal action, although controversy has surrounded less-than-energetic enforcement of affirmative action by the Office of Federal Contract Compliance Programs (the federal agency charged with its maintenance). While federal affirmative action does not give rise to private lawsuits without OFCCP involvement,[60] various state-based programs may do so. To sum up: if a hospital has an affirmative action plan, it is a good idea to enforce it at least until its expiration. If a case ever presents itself to clarify whether a given funding pattern in health care (Medicare or Medicaid receipt alone) constitutes federal contracting status for affirmative action we will better know the legal ramifications of dropping it altogether.

Employment Discrimination

There are some signs that enforcement agencies and the courts have taken a more conservative (or certainly less expensive) posture toward equal employment opportunity (EEO) litigation. Despite that, none of the major prior expansions of EEO (sex discrimination, sexual harassment, national origin harassment) has

Employee Rights Strategies

seen serious effects of judicial contraction. It is highly unlikely, though, that EEO law will expand into new areas at the federal level, such as protecting sexual preference or marital status. The various individual states have been far more aggressive in this area.

Summary

The judicial direction of all these areas is very much up in the air. The primary determinant of employee rights law in the United States is the predisposition of the Supreme Court. Owing to the uncertain nature of its ideological leanings, predicting the future course of employee rights is problematic. It is clear, though, that the various states are increasingly sympathetic to creating and enforcing employee rights on an individual basis, and that trend shows no sign of slowing.

As the general composition of the urban workforce shifts more heavily into new immigrant groups (Hispanic, Middle Eastern, and Far Eastern), there will be new legal activity among these groups, where existing legal structures provide class-based relief for employment discrimination.

GUIDELINES FOR ADMINISTRATORS AND PROFESSIONALS

Despite the legal intricacies, the two most important principles to bear in mind concerning employee rights are good common sense in judging employees and something like the Golden Rule. Would you yourself want to be treated as you are now treating an employee? Empathy and responsiveness to employee concerns go a long way in resolving even the most difficult employee rights issues.

From a strictly legal standpoint, having explicit written policies and procedures, clearly communicated in writing to employees, is still the method of choice for good employee relations. Yes, courts are now telling us that we will be legally held to these rules, and care should thus be exercised in promulgating them, but isn't that just common sense? Grouped around critical events in the employment relationship, there are key points to be observed.

HIRING

1. Set forth job requirements that are realistic and related directly to the work to be performed.

    - Unrealistically high job requirements violate EEO principles.
    - While hospitals can require English language facility without violating EEO requirements,[61] flexibility in hiring is still a good practice.
    - Be prepared reasonably to accommodate handicapped individuals.

2. Avoid use of mechanical preemployment screening criteria.

- Polygraph examinations are of still-dubious scientific validity and may not withstand a legal challenge on the basis of discriminatory impact. They also could be attacked on the basis of invasion of privacy; many states have outlawed their use in the employment process.
- Preemployment drug screening, while popular, suffers from potential attack on the basis of privacy invasion, discriminatory impact on minorities, and discrimination on the basis of handicap (addiction) unrelated to the ability to perform the work in question.

3. Exercise care in interviewing applicants.

- Do not make promises you cannot keep; you could be making a contract with the applicant. Here are examples of unwise statements: "You'll have a position here as long as you do your job." "We'll start you at $35,000" (when you actually do not know whether you can deliver that rate without speaking to a superior). "You'll never have to type your own letters" (or perform some other duty the interviewee would view as undesirable—never say *never*!).
- Certain questions are regarded as leading toward intentional discrimination on the basis of race, gender, pregnancy, or national origin. Do not ask:

  For candidates of a specific race, national origin, or gender.

  About arrangements for child care.[62]

  Whether an applicant has ever been arrested. You can ask about whether an applicant has ever been convicted of a crime, if the crime was materially connected with the performance of the work in question.[63]

  About ethnic origin, even indirectly (examples: "What sort of name is Brennan: German or Irish?" or "What neighborhood were you raised in?").

4. Be very careful with references. The greater legal risk of a defamation action lies with the giver of the reference, not the receiver; do not repeat it to others. Nevertheless, if you receive an unfavorable reference, how do you know it is true? You could be "republishing" slander or libel and thus assume legal liability. Do not share the reference with the candidate either, for the same reason. It is best either to say nothing or to cite other independent grounds for the refusal to hire.

Everyday Employee Relations

1. Schedule work equally and equitably. Rotate holidays, weekends, and other time off as evenly as possible. Using seniority as a tiebreaker in scheduling desirable holidays is a widespread and legally safe practice. The only exception is reasonably to accommodate the religious practices of subordinates. The practical rule is that if you ask the staff whether they would be willing to bend their schedules around the religious practice, and they agree, the accommodation must be made. It is a violation not to ask; you cannot presume that staff would not agree to it. The religious practitioner cannot "pick and choose" among alternative accommodations, however.[64] Once an accommodation is reached, it does not have to be subject to further negotiation.
2. Maintain a workplace free from sexual references or references to national origin (joking or not).

Employee Rights Strategies

3. Avoid sexual relationships with subordinates. The law regards supervisors as "inherently coercive" with respect to their employees.

4. Give pregnant employees the same treatment as though they were medically disabled, unless your state provides more pregnancy benefits as a matter of law.

Performance Appraisal and Administering Wages

1. Establish and enforce, wherever possible, pay for performance, not pay based on other considerations. Do not, for example, give raises based on family size, "head of household" status, and so on; this invites charges of illegal discrimination. Documentation of the appraisal has been an essential turning point in many cases of alleged discrimination; courts will defer heavily to your managerial judgment in administering wages if you have objective and documented reasons to show support for your decisions.

2. Comparable worth is not as big a topic as it once was, but if you conduct a salary study showing that a female-oriented job or job group ought to be paid more, the law will require you to heed that study and pay more or risk a charge of sex discrimination.

Employee Discipline

Consistency is the key to effective employee discipline, not only in the legal sense (avoiding allegations of discrimination) but also from a managerial standpoint. If an employee feels that you are treating him or her differently from others, he or she is far less likely to respond positively to the discipline than if convinced everyone was treated the same way for the same infraction.

Confidentiality is equally important. Legally, it reduces the likelihood of defamation actions and respects employee rights to privacy. Managerially, there is nothing to be accomplished by public humiliation. It does not influence the desired behavioral change, which is the objective of effective discipline.

Documentation is again critical, from a legal defense standpoint. Objectivity is crucial. Focus on the facts, not opinions, stereotypes, or suppositions. Listen carefully to the employee's side of the story and impartially assess its credibility.

Do not perform drug or alcohol testing unless you have some objective reason to conclude that an employee may be intoxicated (via physical symptoms).

Finally, acknowledgment by the employee (via signature showing receipt) and filing are important. Many states have statutes controlling employee files and providing for employee inspection of same. "Secret discipline" can often be invalidated by such statutes.

Do not discipline employees for engaging in union activity, protesting safety hazards or reporting OSHA violations, filing discrimination charges, whistleblowing, filing worker's compensation claims, or otherwise cooperating with the government. Each of these areas is protected.

Discharge from Employment

Use of the "just cause" standard for discharge is mandatory now, even in nonunion settings. "Just cause" means:

1. The employee was warned previously of possibility of discharge, except in cases of extreme first-time offenses (such as unprovoked physical assault or stealing). Prior warnings are appropriate in cases of incompetence, poor attendance, or violations of minor work rules.
2. The penalty fits the offense (or repeated series of offenses).
3. Other similarly situated employees were also discharged for the same offense (consistency).
4. Adequate factual proof exists to support the discharge, not just suppositions.

For all these reasons, it is wise to double check the decision to discharge with another person, either an employee relations expert or a superior within the organization, before acting. A good vehicle for this is to suspend pending investigation for termination of employment to afford you the time needed to investigate thoroughly and get opinions before acting.

Finally, exercise extreme caution in giving employment references on discharged employees—or any other employees, for that matter. Remember that the greater legal risk of a defamation action lies with the provider of a reference. Even giving an erroneous reason for dismissal to the employee can give grounds for a defamation action.

Grievance Procedures

An express, written grievance procedure is invaluable in meeting employee rights issues:

- It allows the employer to gather and analyze evidence that might become vital in a subsequent trial. The employee who "changes his story" can be impeached at trial.
- It shows a court or other reviewing body that the employer tried in good faith to give the employee a fair shake.
- Management can reverse erroneous decisions before lengthy and costly legal proceedings.
- An employee's refusal to use an established grievance procedure can, in some instances, be used as a legal defense (called "failure to exhaust internal remedies").

The grievance procedure has many managerial advantages as well. It is better for an employer to be viewed as willing to listen to employee concerns and complaints in an organized way. If individual concerns are addressed and remedied, it reduces the likelihood of discontent spreading beyond the affected individual to others. And many view the grievance procedure itself as therapeutic.

It is better to get complaints and concerns on the table rather than have them fester and grow into much more serious discontent.

A typical grievance procedure consists of a policy statement of what constitutes a formal grievance, and a series of steps of appeal. To be effective, a grievance procedure should be straightforward, contain a minimum of exceptions (with all exceptions clearly delineated in the procedure itself), and contemplate the expeditious and timely processing of grievances, since justice delayed is justice denied.

It goes without saying that if a formal procedure is adopted, the courts will now ensure that the hospital follow it closely.[65] Considering the important managerial credibility this brings about, it is not a bad idea to adhere to your word.

NOTES

1. "All may dismiss their employee at will, be they many or few, for good cause, for no cause, or even for cause morally wrong without thereby being guilty of legal wrong" (Payne v. Western & A. R. R. Co., 1884).

2. 29 U.S.C. Sec. 201.

3. 42 U.S.C. Sec. 200e.

4. Any employer of fifteen or more workers is covered by Title VII.

5. The exact meaning of "receipt of federal funds" has been much debated. There is a yet-untested line of argument that Medicare money, for example, is paid not directly to the hospital but instead to the individual Medicare patient. Some hospitals have therefore adopted the posture that, absent receiving other federal aid (such as block research grants), they are not obliged to adopt or enforce affirmative action (AA) plans just because they receive Medicare payments. Although this line of argument has not yet been tested in court, it is clear that once a hospital does adopt an AA plan, it must conform to it. It cannot argue retroactively that it was never obliged to make one.

6. Executive Order 11246 of September 24, 1965, was the first and most frequently cited. An executive order is not an act of Congress; in essence, the president is issuing additional conditions for parties contracting with the federal government. EO 11246 was amended in 1967 by EO 11375 (changing contracting thresholds) and in 1978 by EO 12086 (consolidating enforcement of EO 11246, the Rehab Act, and certain other federal contracting programs in the Office of Federal Contract Compliance Programs).

7. Gilbert v. General Elec., 429 U.S. 125 (1976). The EEOC had taken a position that pregnancy discrimination was a form of sex discrimination, and the Supreme Court disagreed, indicating that pregnancy is a physiological condition not relating directly to sex as defined by Title VII. The Court's conclusion stirred Congress into passage of the Pregnancy Discrimination Act.

8. See John D. Coombe, "Employee Handbooks, Asset or Liability?" *Employee Relations Law Journal* 12 (1) (1986): 4–17. Also Hoffman-LaRoche Inc. v. Campbell, Ala. Sup. Ct. 1987, 2 IER Cases 739, and Duldulao v. St. Mary Nazareth Hospital, Ill. Sup. Ct. 1987.

9. Toussaint v. Blue Cross and Blue Shield, Michigan, 1980.

10. Monge v. Beebe Rubber Co. 1974; Kelsay v. Motorola Corp., Ill. Sup. Ct. (1982); Beauvoir v. Rush-Presbyterian-St. Luke's Medical Center, Ill. Sup. Ct. (1985).

11. The Employee Retirement Income Security Act of 1974.

12. Savodnik v. Korvettes, Inc., 482 F. Supp. 822 (E.D.N.Y., 1980). Savodnik had to work less than another month to vest in a pension and was discharged.

13. Tameny v. Atlantic Richfield Co., 27 Cal. 3d 167, 610 P.2d 1330 (Cal. Sup. Ct., 1980).

14. An employee who complained that a coworker did not have a certification required by city ordinance to work as an EMT was discharged for that reason; the discharge was held to be against public policy. Gould v. Campbell's Ambulance Service, 474 N.E.2d 740 (Ill. Sup. Ct., 1980).

15. Ford v. Revlon, Inc. (Ariz., 1987); intentional infliction of emotional distress found where the employer permitted a sexually harassing supervisor to go unpunished for a year and employee attempted suicide.

16. Lewis v. Equitable Life Assurance Society of U.S., 361 N.W.2d 875 (Minn. App., 1985).

17. Agis v. Howard Johnson Co., 371 Mass. 140 (Mass. Sup. Ct., 1976).

18. Chamberlain v. Bissell, Inc., 549 F. Supp. 1067 (W.D. Mich., 1982).

19. Hospitals operated by units of government are not covered by wage and hour law. National League of Cities v. Usury, 426 U.S. 833 (1976).

20. $1.00 per hour for health care workers versus $1.25 per hour for all other workers.

21. Those standards are: work requiring knowledge of an advanced type in a field of science or learning customarily acquired by a prolonged course in specialized intellectual instruction and study, work that is original and creative in character in a recognized field of artistic endeavor, or teaching, tutoring, instructing, or lecturing in the activity of imparting knowledge. (29 C.F.R. Sec. 541.3(a)(1)–(3)). Hospitals argue that nurses fall into the first category and typically earn more than $250 weekly.

22. Such as working with caustic chemicals or animals. These regulations vary greating from state to state.

23. EEOC v. Madison School District, 818 F.2d 577, 28 Wage & Hour Cas. 105 (7th Cir. 1987). Female athletic coaches were paid less than male athletic coaches; while the jobs were not "identical," they did involve "substantially equal work."

24. Gunther v. County of Washington, 452 U.S. 161 (1980). Subsequent cases have shown no inclination to expand the *Gunther* guidelines.

25. 401 U.S. 424, 3 FEP Cases 175 (1971).

26. The EEOC has developed guidelines approved by the Supreme Court to determine whether preemployment tests are job related; these guidelines relate to the "validity" of the tests as to the job in question. Albemarle Paper Co. v. Moody, 422 U.S. 405 (1975).

27. Garcia v. Rush-Presbyterian-St. Luke's Medical Center, 660 F.2d 1217 (7th Cir., 1981). In this case, a requirement that nearly all employees speak and read English "in some fashion" constitutes a BFOQ for hospital employment.

28. Note that this is not necessarily true for gender as a BFOQ. Two major cases have upheld health care employers' rights to honor patient preference for care givers of their own gender: Fesel v. Masonic Home of Del., 447 F. Supp. 1346 (D. Del., 1978), and Backus v. Baptist Medical Center Hosp., 510 F. Supp. 1191 (E.D. Ark., 1981).

29. *B.N.A. Employment Guide*, October 19, 1987.

30. Backus v. Baptist Medical Center Hospital.

31. This does not invalidate the use of a no-spouse rule, however. "No-spouse rules" are employer policies prohibiting the hiring of relatives or spouses of current employees. Such rules must, however, be gender neutral. A rule that wives of employees cannot be hired is illegal. Yukas v. L.O.F., 562 F.2d 496 (7th Cir., 1977).

32. Meritor Savings Bank v. Vinson, 106 S. Ct. 2399 (1986).

33. College Town v. Rizzi, 508 N.E.2d 587 (Mass., 1987). Bear in mind that the Massachusetts state supreme court was interpreting and applying a state sexual harassment provision—not the federal law—which was more restrictive on this point.

34. Ford v. Revlon, Inc., 734 P.2d 580 (Ariz., 1987). The employer waited nine months to receive and act on a valid complaint of sexual harassment; the harassing supervisor was discharged only after the employee attempted suicide a year after the initial complaint.

35. Meritor Savings Bank.

36. Corporation of the Presiding Bishop of the Church of Jesus Christ of Latter-Day Saints v. Amos, 107 S. Ct. 2862, 44 FEP Cases 20 (1987). There is still some question as to whether for-profit corporations owned by religious organizations would be treated the same way.

37. Kenny v. Ambulatory Center of Miami, Fla., Inc., 26 FEP Cases 322 (Fla. Dist. Ct. App., 1981).

38. Four factors have been discerned in cases where no discrimination has been found: (1) it was impossible for the employer to train a suitable replacement; (2) the replacement was not available in the current workforce; (3) the employer would suffer severe economic hardship if it accommodated the religious belief; and (4) the employee was required by the nature of the job to be available on the Sabbath. Murphy v. Edge Memorial Hosp., 550 F. Supp. 1195 (D. Ala., 1982).

39. Bakke v. Regents of the University of California, 438 U.S. 265 (1978); Kaiser Aluminum v. Weber, 443 U.S. 193 (1979). These two Supreme Court cases barred a strict quota approach to affirmative action but endorsed it as a legitimate means of rectifying the wrongs done by past discrimination.

40. Johnson v. Transportation Agency, Santa Clara County, 107 S. Ct. 1442, 43 FEP Cases 411 (1987).

41. Fang-Hai-Liao v. Dean, 658 F. Supp. 1554, 43 FEP Cases 1199 (N.D. Ala. 1987), and Johnson v. Transportation Agency, Santa Clara County, 107 S. Ct. 1442, 43 FEP Cases 411 (1987). Both cases also reinforce the viability of an affirmative action plan to remedy the effects of past sex discrimination.

42. McDonald v. Santa Fe Trail Trans. Co., 427 U.S. 273 (1976).

43. Hayes v. Shelby Memorial Hospital, 726 F.2d 444 (11th Cir., 1984).

44. Doe v. Osteopathic Hospital, 3 FEP Cases 1128 (D. Kan., 1971).

45. For example, in Gammon v. Precision Engineering (D. Minn., August 27, 1987), a pregnant employee was awarded over $18,000 in back pay and damages for mental pain and suffering when her employer advised her that her job would be filled while she was on leave. The evidence showed that the company had held open jobs for other employees who had been on sick leave.

46. Newport News Shipbuilding Co. v. EEOC, 462 U.S. 669 (1983).

47. In Conrail v. Darrone, 34 FEP Cases 79 (1984), the U.S. Supreme Court clearly stated that the receipt of any federal funds for any program, employment related or not, places the "reasonable accommodation" obligation on the employer. The obligation only runs, however, to the program receiving financial assistance, and not throughout the organization.

48. Of course, this differs sharply from the position taken by many hospitals concerning affirmative action for racial minorities—but it is well accepted in six federal circuit courts.

49. Southeastern Community College v. Davis, 442 U.S. 397 (S. Ct., 1979).

50. Ibid. While this case concerned the application of the Rehab Act to an educational program, its analogy to employment is regarded as quite strong.

51. O'Connor v. Ortega, 107 S. Ct. 1492 (1987). A psychiatrist's desk was searched without permission during an investigation; the Court remanded the case for further proceedings to determine what reasonable expectation of privacy the psychiatrist had.

52. Twenty-six states give employees the right of access to their personnel files. *BNA Employment Guide*, November 2, 1987, p. 10:202.

53. 15 U.S.C. Sec. 1674(a).

54. HR 1212, 1987. Such legislation was passed by the House in 1986 but died in the Senate. At present, twenty-eight states either regulate or bar the use of the polygraph. *BNA Employment Guide, November 2, 1987.*

55. A theory of disparate impact on Latinos was advanced and caused settlement of a class action case involving Latino applicants for employment in a Chicago firm. Nevertheless, this theory was rejected in New York City Transit Authority v. Beazer, 440 U.S. 568 (1979). Transit Authority policy prohibited employment of persons in methadone maintenance programs and was sued by black and Hispanic groups who offered statistics that over 60 percent of all methadone users were minority. The Court indicated that there was no discriminatory intent and that the disparate impact the policy might produce was warranted by the business justification of public safety and efficiency. This is probably not true of general application of polygraph exams, however.

56. Randall S. Schuler and Stuart A. Youngblood, *Effective Personnel Management*, 2d ed. (St. Paul: West Publishing Co., 1986), pp. 522, 526, 575.

57. Marshall v. Building Maintenance Corp., 587 F.2d 567 (2d Cir., 1978); EEOC v. Mercy Hospital, 26 Wage & Hour Cas. 539 (7th Cir., 1983). These cases were almost entirely distinguished on the "effort" factor alone, since almost all other duties performed were identical in character.

58. Contingency fee arrangements are those where the attorney takes little or no retainer and is paid a flat percentage fee, typically 33 percent, out of any awards secured for the client. If the plaintiff loses, the attorney is paid little or nothing. If the plaintiff wins, the bigger the award (preferably a case involving punitive damages; ideally a class-action suit involving truly large damage awards), the handsomer the fee to the lawyer. The most-often-registered argument in favor of contingency fee arrangements is that this provides the indigent plaintiff with access to justice he or she would otherwise not have. The most-often-registered argument against such fee arrangements is that it presses the plaintiff's bar to secure damage awards all out of proportion to actual damage sustained by the client.

In certain types of litigation (personal injury, worker's compensation, employment discrimination), the contingency fee arrangement is the rule and not remotely considered unethical. In other areas (attorneys representing unions in labor matters, for example), contingency arrangements are considered unethical. The ethical issue in the newly minted individual plaintiff's bar of "employment at will" litigation is not yet settled due in part to its nature. If the lawsuit is tort based, the contingency fee is part of a long-established tradition of contingency charges for personal injury litigation. Most local bar associations have accepted this practice as ethical, so most attorneys do use contingency fee arrangements in the representation of individual litigants in employment-at-will matters.

59. Johnson v. Transportation Agency.

60. Manuel v. International Harvester Co., 23 FEP Cases 1477 (N.D. Ill, 1980).

Employee Rights Strategies

61. Garcia v. Rush-Presbyterian-St. Luke's Medical Center, 660 F.2d 1217 (7th Cir. 1981).

62. This is regarded as a form of sex discrimination.

63. Use of arrest records is racially discriminatory in its adverse impact on minorities. Arrests are not the same as convictions. Recall that under the American system, we are innocent until proved guilty (and thus convicted). A federal appeals court reasoned that blacks had a significantly higher instance of arrests than whites and that there was no business justification for asking about arrests (versus convictions). Gregory v. Litton Systems, Inc., 472 F.2d 631 (9th Cir., 1972).

64. Ansonia Board of Education v. Philbrook, 106 S. Ct. 848 (1986), Pet. Granted, 107 S. Ct. 20 (1987).

65. Duldulao v. St. Mary Nazareth Hospital (Ill. Sup. Ct., 1987) (cause of action for breach of implied employment contract upheld on grounds that employee was denied access to a published grievance procedure).

13
Collective Bargaining and Legislation: Implications for Strategic Human Resource Management

Howard M. Leftwich

IMPLICATIONS OF COLLECTIVE BARGAINING FOR STRATEGIC HUMAN RESOURCE MANAGEMENT

Collective bargaining results in significant changes in the human resource management system and process. Prior to collective bargaining, management could unilaterally determine wages, hours, and other terms and conditions of employment, subject, of course, to certain contraints such as the labor market (registered nurses are not available at four dollars per hour) and government regulation (there shall be no discrimination on the basis of race, gender, religion, national origin, age, or handicap). But under collective bargaining, employment terms are determined by negotation between the management and the union and are codified in the collective bargaining agreement, a legally binding document. Management now has discretion in changing employment terms only to the extent that it is allowed by the agreement. (For example, the agreement may provide for a pay range of $6.00 to $6.50 per hour for a particular job classification, with employee progression within the range to be determined by management on the basis of performance evaluation.) But any changes in employment terms during the term of the agreement beyond those allowed by the agreement itself require that management requests that the union agree to reopen negotations on the particular issue(s), the union voluntarily agrees to do so, and management and union agree to the new terms.

In interpreting and applying the terms of the agreement, management is subject to challenge and possible reversal of its decisions. Most collective bargaining agreements provide that employees and the union may challenge such decisions through the grievance procedure. Grievance procedures usually require two or more steps of bilateral negotiations over the alleged violation of the agreement. If a mutually satisfactory resolution is not reached, the grievance may go to arbitration, in which a neutral third party makes a final decision binding on both the management and the union. Thus, managerial authority in establishing terms and conditions of employment and in administering them on a daily basis at the workplace is restricted significantly by the existence of a collective bargaining agreement.

THE DEVELOPMENT OF COLLECTIVE BARGAINING AND LEGISLATION: A BRIEF OVERVIEW

Collective bargaining came to the health care sector relatively late. Although there were a few examples before 1960, widespread collective bargaining in health has developed only since that date. In contrast, collective bargaining was common in building construction and railroad transportation before World War I and became widespread in manufacturing during the 1930s. Among the reasons for the absence of collective bargaining in health care before 1960 are the following: the relatively small size of many employer organizations, workforces fragmented into a large number of occupational specialties, high turnover rates in some job classficiations, the belief that collective bargaining and strikes were inappropriate in health care organizations (especially for professional employees), a large proportion of female employees, and lack of legislative protection for the right of employees to organize and bargain collectively. There was no legislative protection for federal employees and those of most states, and private sector nonprofit health care organizations had been removed from coverage under the National Labor Act by the Taft-Hartley Amendments of 1947.

Beginning in the early 1960s, a number of developments began to spur the growth of health care unionization. The civil rights movement and the women's movement promoted increased militance among many health care workers in some areas. Employer organizations became larger and more impersonal. The increasing flow of funds into health care from third-party payers created the possibility that larger economic rewards might be won through collective bargaining. Unions began to show increasing interest in organizing the rapidly growing numbers of health care workers. Finally, comprehensive legislative frameworks began to be developed for labor relations in health care. Labor relations for federal employees, including those in health care facilities, began to be regulated by presidential executive orders beginning in 1961 and are now subject to the Civil Service Reform Act of 1978. States began to pass labor relations legislation applicable to their employees and those of political subdivisions. In 1974 Congress brought private, nonprofit health care organizations under coverage of the National Labor Relations Act. Thus, although some states still lack legislation, most health care workers are now covered by statutes that protect the right to organize and otherwise regulate labor relations.

LABOR ORGANIZATIONS IN THE HEALTH CARE SECTOR

Unlike manufacturing, in which all employees in an industry are often represented by a single comprehensive union like the United Auto Workers, a number of labor organizations represent health care employees. Among the more prominent are the Service Employees International Union, the National Union of Hospital and Health Care Employees, and the state affiliates of the American Nurses Association. Public sector unions such as the American Federation of State, County, and Municipal Employees often represent health care workers in public sector facilities. In addition, a significant number of unions concentrated mainly in other sectors also represent some employees in health care organizations. Even within an organization, collective bargaining is often fragmented. Workforces tend to be divided into subgroups for collective bargaining purposes, often with a different union representing each subgroup.

THE LEGAL FRAMEWORK FOR COLLECTIVE BARGAINING IN HEALTH CARE ORGANIZATIONS

The most significant legal guidelines for collective bargaining in health care facilities are in the negotiating process, the subject matter of collective bargaining, and the use of economic pressures and counterpressures to gain more favorable contract terms. The discussion focuses mainly on private sector health care organizations subject to the National Labor Relations Act (NLRA). Where significant differences exist in the public sector legal frameworks, they will be noted.

The Negotiating Process

Under the NLRA, employers and lawfully established unions are mutually obligated to meet at reasonable times and bargain in good faith over wages, hours, and other terms and conditions of employment. The basic meaning of good faith bargaining is that both sides negotiate with a sincere desire to reach agreement if at all possible, as opposed to stalling purposely and avoiding an agreement. Employers are sometimes tempted to stall, especially in negotiations for a first contract, in the hope that disillusionment and turnover among employees will dissipate the union's support, with the end result that the employer will ultimately avoid collective bargaining. The parties are not legally obligated to reach an agreement, however; the only obligation is to try. Moreover, neither side is legally required to make concessions.

In good faith bargaining, the parties are obligated to meet and confer at reasonable times. This means that actions that may be interpreted as attempts to avoid or delay meetings can constitute evidence of bad faith bargaining. If the meeting time(s) proposed by the union are satisfactory to management, reasonable alternatives should promptly be offered. Pleading that management is too busy to schedule bargaining meetings is not acceptable.

The employer is usually obligated to negotiate with whomever the union designates as its bargaining representatives. A preference to negotiate with persons who are not on the union's bargaining team or the judgment that union bargainers have insufficient qualifications are not permissible grounds for refusing to negotiate. Only in rare circumstances where it may be proved that the presence of particular individuals is extremely disruptive to the bargaining process or that they in effect represent a union that is not officially a party to the negotiations may the employer legally refuse to negotiate with the union bargaining team. Expert legal counsel should always be sought before taking such a step.

Management is obligated to make proposals. They can be offered at the beginning of negotiations or can be counterproposals in response to the union's demands. But it is inconsistent with good faith bargaining to reject the union's demands and tell it to come back with a more acceptable set of proposals; management must make proposals of its own.

If management rejects union proposals on the basis that it cannot afford them, good faith bargaining requires that it open its books to the union and make full disclosure of all information relevant to evaluating this contention. If management wants to avoid disclosing confidential cost or financial data to the union, it should reject union proposals on grounds other than inability to pay. Some examples would be inconsistency with settlements or pay rates in other organizations, creating inequities in the organization's pay structure, or simply being "excessive" (with no statement regarding inability to pay).

Good faith bargaining requires that management maintain the status quo with respect to terms and conditions of employment prior to reaching agreement with the union. An exception to the status quo rule is allowed in situations of bargaining impasse. Management can unilaterally put into effect employment terms that were offered to the union but on which negotiations have reached an impasse. Because determining whether an impasse exists is not a simple matter, a labor attorney should be consulted before relying on the impasse rule to institute changes in employment terms unilaterally. Finally, the parties must put into writing and sign any agreement reached if either party requests it. Insisting on an oral agreement is considered to be evidence of bad faith bargaining.

The legal obligation to bargain in good faith also exists in most public sector jurisdictions that have comprehensive labor relations statutes. The concept of good faith bargaining developed under the NLRA has generally served as the model for the public sector. Therefore the good faith requirements for public sector negotiations are generally similar to those in the private sector.

Subject Matter of Bargaining

A critical question is to what types of managerial decisions the legal obligation to bargain is applicable. Arguably most managerial decisions can affect employees in some way, however indirect. Because of a desire to retain a broad range of decisions as managerial prerogatives, management would prefer that the obligation to bargain apply to a relatively narrow range of subjects.

Under the NLRA, the obligation to bargain in good faith ("mandatory issues") applies to wages, hours, and other terms and conditions of employment. Pay systems and pay rates, types and levels of benefits, and hours of work, including scheduling issues, time off, and premium rates for less desirable shifts or overtime work, clearly are mandatory issues of bargaining. (A variety of issues that comprise "other terms and conditions of employment" are also mandatory: workloads, procedures and criteria for layoffs and recalls, disciplinary procedures and practices, and procedures and criteria for making other kinds of choices among employees, such as promotion decisions, job assignments, shift preferences, and vacation preferences).

For management, a management rights clause stating that decisions regarding terms and conditions of employment are to be left to managerial discretion is also a mandatory issue of bargaining. Such clauses often reserve to management the right to make decisions on such mandatory issues as workloads and job assignments. Thus, management can meet its obligation to bargain in good faith on mandatory issues by negotiating over *how* decisions shall be made—at its discretion or according to guidelines specified in the collective bargaining agreement. The legal right to negotiate a management rights clause covering mandatory issues is of considerable significance to managers who want to limit union encroachment on their decision-making prerogatives.

Nonmandatory issues may be negotiated if both parties agree to do so, but there is no legal obligation to bargain over them. Moreover, if a nonmandatory issue is under negotiation and one party decides it wants to remove it from the bargaining table, the other party is legally obligated to agree. (As a practical matter, however, it is not always so easy to separate nonmandatory from mandatory issues; the party asked to drop the nonmandatory issue may do so but suggest that as a result it will be forced to take a tougher position on a mandatory issue.) Nonmandatory issues comprise such basic managerial decisions as the size and location of the enterprise, the outputs to be produced, and the means used to produce them. Thus, management is not obligated to bargain about such decisions as closing a location, eliminating some of the organization's activities, or introducing new equipment and technology. It is obligated, however, to bargain about the effects of such organizational changes on the employees. Therefore, although it can usually shut down a location or introduce new equipment unilaterally, it is legally obligated to negotiate with the union on transfer rights, advance notice, retraining and relocation assistance, severance pay, and other measures the union might propose to ease the burden on affected employees.

Finally, there are the prohibited issues—those that would result in illegal contract clauses. Examples include proposals for a closed shop clause, which would require a person to belong to the union before being hired, and proposals that would constitute discrimination against blacks, women, or other protected workforce categories.

The situation regarding scope of bargaining under public sector legal frameworks is summarized in the following passage:

The range of subjects negotiated between public employee unions and government managers varies considerably among jurisdictions. Frequently, there is a threefold division made between types determined by legislative bodies, those left exclusively to civil service regulations and public managers, and those within the scope of bargaining. At the federal level, negotiations are narrowly confined to personnel policies and practices, while wages, fringe benefits, and other major conditions of employment are excluded. At the state and local levels, the range of bargainable items is generally much broader, yet it is difficult to find much uniformity among jurisdictions. (Herman, Kuhn, and Seeber, 1986: 423)

Thus, some of the key issues in private sector collective bargaining cannot be negotiated in federal health care facilities, and unions are forced to rely more on political action and lobbying to gain their objectives. The scope of bargaining at facilities subject to state law is generally broader than at federal facilities, although there is some variation among states. (A state-by-state survey is beyond the scope of this chapter.)

Economic Pressures and Counterpressures

Unions have a legal right to strike to obtain better contract terms, subject to several limitations pertaining to timing, procedures to be followed before striking, and bargaining issues over which a strike can occur. First, there shall be no collective bargaining agreement in effect that contains a no-strike clause because such an agreement is legally binding. A strike in violation of its terms could be restricted through court action. If the existing contract contains a no-strike clause, it must expire before a strike can take place.

Second, a number of procedural requirements must be met. The crux of these requirements is that before a strike can begin in a health care facility covered by the NLRA, there must be (1) at least a ninety-day advance notice of the intent to change contract terms coupled with an offer to bargain, (2) at least a thirty-day period during which the Federal Mediation and Conciliation Service (FMCS) shall attempt to mediate an agreement, and (3) at least a ten-day strike notice to the employer to allow time for measures to protect the welfare of patients. In addition, if one director of the FMCS determines that a work stoppage will substantially interrupt the delivery of health care in the community, he or she may establish a neutral board of inquiry (BOI) to investigate the dispute and recommend settlement terms. Both mediation and the BOI may be helpful in resolving a dispute, but neither guarantees a settlement without a stoppage.

The procedural requirements pertaining to health care facilities are more stringent than those applicable to other kinds of organizations. The latter are subject to only a sixty-day notice-and-bargaining requirement and a thirty-day notice to the FMCS. The use of mediation is at the discretion of the parties rather than mandatory, and there are no provisions for boards of inquiry or ten-day strike notices. The more rigorous requirements for health care organizations are in recognition of the important public services they perform and are intended to increase the likelihood of a settlement without a strike.

Regarding issues, strikes may be over mandatory issues of bargaining only. Nonmandatory issues may be raised during negotiations, but the union may not condition the signing of an agreement on management's acceptance of its proposal on a nonmandatory issue. In other words, the union may not push a nonmandatory issue to impasse and strike over it. The rationale for this rule is that insistence on a nonmandatory issue is, in effect, refusal to bargain in good faith over mandatory issues. However, as a practical matter, it may be difficult to separate nonmandatory from mandatory issues completely.

Although the restriction on strikes over nonmandatory issues is derived from the duty to bargain in good faith, in general, strikes or other economic pressure are not inconsistent with good faith bargaining. On the contrary, they are viewed as an integral part of good faith collective bargaining in the private sector—an important incentive for the parties to negotiate effectively and reach agreement.

If the strike is lawful, the union may support it by picketing at the strike site. By picketing the union will attempt to ensure that members of the striking bargaining unit do not work. The picketing may also be intended to prevent nonunit employees from entering the site. Other purposes of picketing may be to keep out potential users of the facility and to prevent the employees of other employers, such as delivery or repair personnel, from entering the struck site. Picketing may be restricted, however, if it is conducted in an improper manner, such as physically blocking entrances and exits or if the picketers engage in violent acts.

Although the union has a right to strike, the facility management is free under the law to continue to operate and has broad discretion as to the means utilized. For example, it can encourage bargaining unit members to stay on the job or return to the job after the strike has begun. It can utilize nonbargaining unit personnel such as supervisors to fill positions left vacant by strikers. It can hire replacements for strikers or utilize temporary help agencies. It can also subcontract tasks and functions to other organizations.

Moreover, management is free to begin the work stoppage by means of a lockout if it so desires, subject to restrictions similar to those that are applicable to strikes. No collective bargaining agreement containing a no-lockout clause shall be in effect. The same procedural requirements applicable to strikes must be followed before the lockout occurs. As is true of strikes, lockouts cannot be used to force acceptance of proposals on nonmandatory issues of bargaining. Finally, the purpose of the lockout must be to obtain more desirable contract terms, not to destroy the union.

If the strike fails to achieve the desired results and the employer continues to operate, the union might wish to pressure organizations that do business with the employer, such as suppliers of goods and services, to cease dealing. Successfully disrupting the flow of necessary goods and services could eventually achieve results similar to a successful strike. Unions are prohibited by law from promoting job actions at the sites of secondary organizations to force them to cease dealing with the struck employer and cannot threaten or coerce secondary organizations for this purpose. An exception would be if the other organization performed functions or tasks that, except for the strike, would have been done at the employer's site ("struck work"). In this case the union could picket or use other means to force the cessation of "struck work." The restrictions on pressuring other organizations do not make it illegal to picket the struck employer's site even if the picketing deters the employees of other organizations from entering the premises. This is regarded as an incidental effect of lawful picketing in support of a lawful strike. Under certain circumstances unions can picket retail stores to discourage the purchase of a struck employer's products and can use publicity means other than picketing to encourage total boycotts of stores that sell such products. These kinds of activities are generally not relevant to collective bargaining in health care organizations.

The final legal aspect of economic pressure to be discussed is the reinstatement rights of strikers when the strike has ended. This is an especially important issue to both management and union when replacements have been hired. Reinstatement rights differ between economic strikes and unfair labor practice strikes. Economic strikes are for the purpose of obtaining better contract terms. Unfair labor practice strikes are caused at least in part by, or are prolonged by, an employer violation of the NLRA, such as refusal to bargain in good faith. The National Labor Relations Board must uphold the union's charge of an NLRB violation if a strike is to be classified as an unfair labor practice strike; simply filing a charge is not enough.

After an economic strike, the ex-strikers must be reinstated if their old jobs are available and vacant but not if they have been filled by replacements or eliminated. If only some of the jobs previously held by strikers are available, management cannot discriminate against persons who are union activists when deciding who shall be reinstated. Ex-strikers whose jobs have been filled must be placed on a preferential hiring list for two years, which gives them preference over persons from the external labor market for jobs that become available. Ex-strikers who have been found guilty of serious acts of violence or sabotage during the strike need not be reinstated even if their old jobs are vacant.

After an unfair labor practice strike, the ex-strikers must be reinstated if their former jobs exist, even if replacements occupy them. Only if their jobs have been eliminated, as in the case of a cutback in the employer's operations, or if they are guilty of serious misconduct during the strike may ex-strikers be denied reinstatement. Therefore, if replacements are hired, the union may scrutinize the employer's conduct very closely in order to find grounds for a viable unfair labor practice charge. The reinstatement rights of its members may depend on its ability to do so.

In the public sector, strikes and lockouts are prohibited in many jurisdictions. Where comprehensive legal frameworks exist, there are usually provisions for the use of other dispute resolution techniques, such as mediation, fact finding, and arbitration, as alternatives to work stoppages. Even in jurisdictions where stoppages are allowed, statutes usually provide for the use of other techniques first so as to reduce the probability of strikes or lockouts.

Thus, the legal frameworks for labor relations contain significant guidelines for a number of important aspects of the collective bargaining process.

PREPARATION FOR BARGAINING

Few negotiators would disagree that adequate preparation is a prerequisite for success in collective bargaining. But adequate preparation requires scarce resources that have alternative uses within the organization: personnel, time, money, attention, and effort. Where preparation is inadequate, the reason is usually the unavailability of adequate managerial resources or the reluctance to allocate enough resources to preparation for bargaining in the light of competing demands for them.

In this section we examine four areas of preparation for collective bargaining negotiations: gathering information and data, establishing objectives, planning the bargaining team, and planning for a possible strike.

Preparing Information and Data

It is an axiom of collective bargaining that preparation for the next contract negotiation began the day your present contract took effect. Carefully examining experience under the present contract can provide information useful in determining objectives in the next negotiation. Which clauses have caused problems for supervisors in carrying out their jobs? Which clauses have been a source of confusion, resulting in inconsistent practices among supervisors, disputes over interpretation between management and employees, and the filing of grievances? Which clauses have had unexpected and undesirable results? The primary source of information regarding these matters is the supervisors who administer the contract daily and are often the first managers to be aware of the problems that arise under it.

It is important that supervisors make a written record of contract problems as they occur. Because memories are imperfect, contract administration is only one concern of a busy supervisor, and contracts are often of multiyear duration, trying to recall experience prior to negotiations may yield poor results. To minimize record-keeping effort, each supervisor can be provided with a copy of the contract with a blank page after each printed page so that he or she can note occurrences that indicate problems with particular clauses. If conscientiously done, these notes provide an excellent basis for planning revisions in the next contract. During preparation for negotiations, supervisors should be asked to review their notes and specify which clauses they think need revision, why revision would be helpful, and how the clauses should be revised.

In addition to consulting supervisors, the labor relations staff of the health care organization should study the grievance file, paying special attention to cases that have gone to arbitration. Where arbitrators' decisions have contradicted management's interpretation of the relevant clauses, changes in language may be called for. Where the management interpretations were upheld, it still may be worth asking if contract language could be made clearer in order to reduce the potential for future misunderstandings and grievances.

Management should also review experience with human resource policies and practices on matters not covered in the present agreement. Objections by employees to particular policies and practices may suggest that an effort will be made by the union to limit managerial discretion in these areas during the next negotiation. While management cannot prevent the introduction of such limiting proposals, it is better to anticipate them and prepare a response rather than be taken by surprise.

In addition to reviewing experience under the existing contract, management should be knowledgeable about the union with which it negotiates. What is its organizational structure? At what level are collective bargaining decisions made? What is its power structure, both formal and informal, and its financial situation? Are there internal problems and conflicts? What pressures are likely to be applied to union negotiators by the membership or various elements of union leadership? What kinds of people are the union's negotiators? Do they have any special likes and dislikes? Knowledge of these matters can be useful in anticipating the positions and behaviors of union bargainers and their reactions to management proposals and actions.

Knowledge of other contracts can help management to anticipate union proposals and positions and to establish realistic objectives. Copies of contracts can be obtained from other health care organizations, particularly those dealing with the same union. While contracts negotiated in one's community would be most relevant, a general knowledge of bargaining results throughout the country may be useful in anticipating union proposals and positions. Contracts from major local employers outside the health care sector may be useful if these have established community patterns in the past. But following precedents established elsewhere should be done with caution. It is crucial that management analyze their implications for its own organization. Arrangements suitable for one kind of facility may be totally inappropriate in another facility operating under different circumstances.

Data on a number of economic variables are often relevant to the negotiations. Data on changes in consumer prices, as measured by the consumer price index (CPI), should be obtained. Statistics on employment and unemployment trends in the area labor market, particularly for occupations or skills utilized in the health care organization, can also be useful in negotiations. Management should obtain information on pay rates, including benefits, for nonunion health care employees in comparable area facilities. (A word of caution is necessary, however, regarding pay comparability: in some cases jobs with similar titles may have different content.)

Finally, management needs to prepare a comprehensive assessment of its current financial situation and as good a forecast as possible of its financial situation during the term of the new contract. This information may be the most relevant kind to many of the issues in negotiations. It is clearly relevant to economic issues, such as wages, salaries, and benefits, but it is also relevant to noneconomic issues such as staffing levels, workloads, work rules, and other matters relating to effective utilization of the workforce.

Establishing Objectives and Formulating Proposals

A critical step in preparing for bargaining is establishing management's objectives and formulating the proposals with which they will be achieved. Proposals may be modified during negotiations in the light of new information or other considerations. But the formulation of well-thought-out proposals as part of the preparation process gives negotiators a plan, which can be helpful in achieving management's objectives in bargaining.

The information and data discussed in the last section provide a basis for formulating objectives and proposals. The labor relations staff is usually responsible for gathering and analyzing information and drawing up a first draft of proposals. This draft may then be circulated to all departments and managers affected by the contract and to the top management of the facility for review and comment. It is important that all managers who will be affected by the new contract be able to give input regarding proposals.

Several important considerations are involved in formulating management's objectives and proposals. Two related considerations are the needs and expectations of the employees and their union and the difficulty (and possibly the cost) of gaining acceptance of management proposals. For example, if there is a high rate of inflation coupled with large pay increases at other facilities, it is likely that there will be a strong expectation among employees and their union leadership of a sizable pay increase in the next contract. Gaining acceptance of a pay freeze because the particular organization cannot afford an increase will be relatively difficult as compared with circumstances of price stability and modest settlements elsewhere. (It may also be costly if acceptance can be obtained only by outlasting the employees in a strike. In addition to the direct costs of the strike, lower morale and productivity and higher absenteeism and turnover after the strike may result.) The difficulties (and costs) of gaining acceptance of a pay freeze may be increased if there is a political struggle within the union and a militant rival faction is ready to criticize the present leadership for being soft on management.

Another major consideration in formulating management's bargaining objectives and proposals is what is needed for organizational effectiveness. What are the short-term and long-term objectives of the health care organization? What are the characteristics of a collective bargaining agreement that will contribute to these objectives? A minimum package of contract terms that management may wish to consider is one that will enable the recruitment and retention of an adequate workforce. Related considerations are maintaining adequate morale and keeping absenteeism and turnover to acceptable levels. Another important consideration is whether the contract provides adequate incentives for good performance, which may include cooperation with other employees and sharing knowledge of how to improve job performance as well as "working hard." In addition, what are management's objectives regarding flexibility in managing the workforce? Efficiency? The quantity and quality of output per unit of labor input? The cost-effectivenss of the organization? These matters need to be explored as part of the process of establishing objectives. Once objectives are established, contract proposals can be developed to further them.

Planning the Bargaining Team

Another important step in preparation for negotiations is determining the size, composition, structure, and authority of management's bargaining team. Although there is no precise formula for making these determinations, a number of general statements regarding considerations and practices can be made. As to the related matters of size and composition, often there are conflicting objectives that must be reconciled. On one hand, it would be desirable to have on the bargaining team representatives from all management areas and from all subunits of the organization that may be affected by bargaining outcomes. On the other hand, the larger the team is, the more unwieldy it may be, possibly impeding the negotiating process. Usually the practice is for bargaining teams to consist of no more than five or six persons. Where it is not possible to have someone from each management area on the team, there should be close and continuous two-way communication with each area so that the interests of all are considered in the final settlement.

Team members should be selected on the basis of their capabilities for effective bargaining, as well as their expertise in particular areas of management. Ideally, they should be knowledgeable about bargaining and have had bargaining experience in which they showed themselves to be effective negotiators. As a practical matter, however, it is not always possible to organize a team comprised totally of experienced bargainers. Where this is the case, it may be a worthwhile investment of organizational resources to send inexperienced negotiators to

Collective Bargaining and Legislation

courses or seminars on collective bargaining. At a minimum, they should be encouraged to read about the process. The attitudes and personality traits that are desirable for team members can vary with the nature of the collective bargaining relationship. Where the relationship is strongly adversarial and union behavior is likely to be militant or unfriendly, management may want a bargaining team that can respond in kind. On the other hand, if a more cooperative relationship exists or is desired, members who can be firm but less abrasive are preferable.

One person should be designated as the spokesperson or chief negotiator for management and make the major presentations to the union negotiators, assign roles and duties to other members of the team, and generally perform supervisory and leadership functions in bargaining. Other team members must clearly understand and accept that they are subordinate to the spokesperson. It is critical that spokespersons be experienced and effective negotiators, good at planning and directing the actions of the bargaining team, and capable of exercising effective leadership. Frequently the spokesperson is the top labor relations or human resource management official in the organization. If no one has the qualifications necessary to be a spokesperson (as in some small organizations or where there has been little or no previous bargaining), it may be worthwhile to employ a professional negotiator, such as a labor attorney or a labor relations consultant, to act as management's spokesperson. In some organizations it is best to consider this as a temporary measure, to be utilized only until the necessary in-house expertise has been developed. In general, a member of management is likely to have a better understanding of the needs of the organization and the implications of collective bargaining decisions than is someone from the outside. In a small organization, however, where there is limited specialization among managers, the time, effort, and expense necessary to develop a capable spokesperson may exceed the benefits of doing so. In this case it may be more cost-effective to hire professional negotiators as needed.

Another matter to be resolved is the authority of the bargaining team to make binding commitments. Practice varies. Some managements have largely delegated to their bargaining teams the authority to make an agreement with the union. Although approval by top management may be a formal requirement, it will normally be granted almost automatically. In other cases negotiators must clear each concession with higher management. In some cases the bargaining team is empowered to reach agreement on some issues but must get approval from top management on others. While restricting the authority of the bargaining team may help top management to retain control over bargaining outcomes, lack of adequate authority to make commitments and reach agreement can frustrate the bargaining process and reduce its effectiveness.

Planning for a Possible Strike

Although a strike may seem remote during preparation for bargaining, some early analysis and planning can be useful in helping to shape management proposals and positions during negotiations and protecting the welfare of patients. The strike is not something separate and distinct from the bargaining process. Rather, a strike, or the possibility of one, can have a major impact on the terms offered by the parties and the concessions and compromises they are willing to make.

A key decision for management is how unacceptable a strike would be. If it would be highly unacceptable, management will tend to be relatively accommodating and responsive to union proposals even at the expense of significant concessions. If a strike is less unacceptable, management may be less willing to make concessions in order to reach agreement with the union.

A key decision for management is whether to accept a shutdown in the event of a strike or to try to keep operating, totally or at least partially. In assessing the ability of management to maintain operations, some relevant considerations include how many bargaining unit employees may be expected to cross picket lines, the number and skills of striking employees, the extent to which nonunit employees or supervisors could be substituted for strikers, the availability of replacements from the external labor market, and the potential for violence resulting from the crossing of picket lines. Additional considerations are the anticipated duration of the strike and anticipated community reaction to alternative management responses if a strike occurs.

In assessing the potential impact of a strike on patients or clients, a major issue is the availability of alternative sources of services. Management may wish to make contingency arrangements for the transfer of patients to other facilities in case it decides to accept a shutdown if a strike is called or is unable to maintain services at prestrike levels. Inventory buildup, a major prestrike tactic of goods producers to reduce the burden of a strike to themselves and their customers, is not as readily available to health care organizations or other producers of services. The closest equivalent would be to accelerate the scheduling of procedures to serve as many patients as possible before a strike.

Strikes are a relatively rare outcome of the collective bargaining process. Nevertheless, prudence requires that during planning for negotiations, some thought be given to management attitudes toward a strike and its response in case one occurs.

THE BARGAINING PROCESS

We now turn our attention to the bargaining process: the stages of bargaining, the conduct of bargaining negotiations, and strikes and other pressures in the collective bargaining process.

Stages of Bargaining

The negotiating process can vary considerably in detail, and it is not possible to specify a single procedure that will be optimal for all organizations. There

Collective Bargaining and Legislation

may be differences according to the type of union-management relationship (e.g., adversarial or cooperative), the relative bargaining power of the parties, their attitudes toward bargaining and toward each other, the personalities of the negotiators, and other variables. Most negotiations, however, may be divided into five stages: (1) opening, (2) settling in, (3) consolidation, (4) finalization, and (5) wrapping up (Herman, Kuhn, and Seeber, 1986: 223–27; Richardson, 1977: 148–49).

The opening phase is usually characterized by the initial exchange of proposals and a general exploration of the issues. Although there are few if any commitments and compromises at this stage, an atmosphere may be established that will affect all subsequent stages of negotiations. The details of exchanging proposals can vary. In the past, the most common procedure was for the union to present its initial proposals together with a supporting rationale, after which there would be a recess of some days or even weeks for management to develop or complete its initial set of counterproposals. During recent years an increasing number of managements have taken more initiative in presenting their initial proposals, either presenting them first or simultaneously exchanging proposals with the union. This increased initiative is often more likely to lead to desirable outcomes than if management merely responds to union proposals. It also requires the planning of objectives and proposals before negotiations begin.

A question that frequently arises is to what extent management should offer trade-off proposals, that is, proposals in which it is not really interested but later may be dropped in return for union concessions on significant issues. Some negotiators make liberal use of such proposals. There may be problems, however, if they are used to excess. If the union negotiators perceive that trade-off demands are a significant element in management's bargaining strategy, they may infer that all management proposals are tradable. If this happens, it may be difficult to convince them that any particular proposal is truly important to management.

During the second stage of negotiations, settling in, there is a fuller discussion of all issues and each party attempts to find out the other side's true objectives and priorities. The parties will try to identify and resolve issues on which agreement can be easily reached. Sometimes fuller discussion of issues is sufficient to resolve them to the satisfaction of both parties. Such discussion can also serve to identify at least some of the trade-off proposals, which may result in removing them from the table.

The third stage of negotiations, consolidation, is marked by reiteration and elaboration of the arguments and positions presented during the settling-in stage and the beginning of concessions and trade-offs on items of relatively low priority. These tend to be mainly noneconomic issues. (It should not be inferred, however, that all noneconomic issues are relatively unimportant. During recent years many employers have given a high priority to contract changes that give them greater flexibility and discretion in managing the workforce.) Also during the consolidation stage, a beginning is often made toward reaching agreement on economic issues. By the end of the consolidation stage, most of the easily settled issues have been removed from the table either through mutual agreement or by the proposing party's withdrawing them. Each party has reached some conclusions about the true objectives and priorities of the other. Management and union are now ready to deal with the difficult issues.

At the beginning of the finalization stage, a relatively small number of items remain unresolved, but these are important, high-priority issues to both sides. Therefore differences are hard to resolve because each party views concessions and compromises as significant costs of reaching an agreement. It is at this stage that the union may threaten to strike, and management may respond that it is willing and able to withstand a strike successfully and would rather do so than make the concessions demanded by the union. Where the timing of a work stoppage is a significant determinant of its impact, management sometimes threatens a lockout if this could result in a stoppage at a relatively more favorable time. More thought is given to work stoppage because the high cost of reaching agreement without one (concessions on important issues) may make the cost of forcing terms on the other side through a stoppage relatively more attractive. Preparations by both sides for work stoppage may intensify and take on added significance. Bargaining is now characterized by longer, more frequent, and more intense bargaining sessions and a growing sense of urgency. It is at the finalization stage, too, that mediation or some other form of third-party intervention may be utilized to avoid a work stoppage. Although a sense of urgency and the threat of a work stoppage make life hectic for negotiators, they provide strong incentives for a maximum effort to reach agreement.

The last stage of negotiations, wrapping up, occurs after basic agreement on the total contract has been reached. It consists of drafting contract language that clearly expresses the intent of the parties on each item. Careful drafting can facilitate contract administration and help to avoid grievances that arise because of unclear language.

Conduct of Bargaining Negotiations

There is no precise formula for the conduct of collective bargaining negotiations. There are, however, a number of general guidelines that should be helpful to management in negotiating with the union.

It is generally preferable for management to adopt a positive approach to bargaining. Following the positive approach, management will work toward the kind of agreement it wants rather than simply taking a defensive position and working against the kind of agreement the union wants. Increasing the use of the positive approach is indicated by the trend toward management's presenting its proposals first, or at least simultaneously with the union's presentation, rather than just reacting to union proposals.

Management negotiators should be able to view bargaining from a union perspective as well as their own. This will give them a better idea of how easy or difficult it will be to achieve the various management objectives and which compromises and trade-offs are likely to be acceptable. It may also help management negotiators to develop arguments in support of their position that are acceptable to the union.

Expectations of the union members must be kept in mind. These expectations must be met to some reasonable degree if the agreement is to be acceptable to the union leadership, which must periodically stand for reelection. Acceptability to the membership is also necessary if they are to ratify the agreement, a post-negotiation step required in most unions before the agreement can become effective.

Expectations that are unrealistically high from management's perspective pose a difficult challenge. Meeting such expectations may require concessions that are unacceptable to management. The alternative is to reduce expectations to more realistic levels. This may be done through persuasion. It must be demonstrated to the union bargainers, through the use of information, data, and arguments acceptable to them, that member expectations are indeed excessive. Should this be accomplished, there remains the task of persuading the members. In many cases this has proved to be more difficult than persuading the union leaders, who often have a broader perspective regarding the needs of the organization than does the membership. Selling the membership on a realistic contract may not be something that can be done by management alone; it is likely to require the active cooperation of the union leadership. In cases where union expectations cannot be lowered by persuasion to levels that allow a realistic agreement, the costs of a strike may be necessary to accomplish the task.

Keep in mind the differences in perspective that union and management negotiators often bring to the bargaining table. What may seem apparent and logical to a management representative may seem less so to someone with an employee-union perspective. Bridging the perspective gap is a process of education and persuasion, which may require skill, understanding, and patience.

It is basic to effective negotiations that management's bargainers have credibility with their union counterparts. Building and maintaining credibility requires the avoidance of deception, misrepresentation, and trickery in negotiations. Once discovered, such acts will cause union negotiators to treat all management statements and actions with suspicion. Credibility in the eyes of the union also requires that care be exercised in making promises; those that are not certain to be kept should be avoided. A promise that cannot be fulfilled is likely to reduce management credibility even though it was made in good faith. To maintain credibility, negotiators must distinguish between "no" and "we don't like that" or "maybe." Those who say "no" must mean it. If you do not mean it, find another way to indicate a negative attitude without foreclosing the possibility of a future concession or compromise. For example, in reply to an objectionable proposal from the union, management's spokesperson might say, "We're not receptive to that," and then explain the rationale for management's response. A position has been taken, but the possibility of future compromise has not been foreclosed.

Practice good human relations during negotiations. Remember that bargaining can flounder because of poor human relations, as well as differing positions on the issues. Respect the sincerity, intelligence, and skills of the union negotiators. Even if they prove themselves deficient in any of these areas, it may be best not to attack them with direct criticism. Such attacks are likely to antagonize the union bargainers and make them less willing to be flexible and to compromise. The net result may be greater difficulty in reaching an agreement on terms consistent with management's goals.

Accept that union negotiators have reasons for taking the positions they do. Realize that to get them to accept a different position, you must offer them reasons acceptable to them for doing so.

Good negotiators should be able to control their emotions. Losing one's temper and directing an angry tirade at the other side may be emotionally satisfying, but the cost may be greater difficulty in reaching an acceptable agreement. (Occasionally, anger may be used as a tactic in bargaining, but such a planned use of anger is far different from the unplanned explosions of temper that sometimes disrupt bargaining and even cause the breaking off of negotiations.)

A good human relations rule for negotiations is to personalize praise and depersonalize criticism. Thus, if the union's spokesperson makes a proposal with which management agrees or could agree with minor modifications, its spokesperson might respond, "Bill, that's a good idea" or "Bill, that idea is very promising." If Bill makes a poor proposal, however, criticize it but do not link it with him. Say, for example, "That proposal is a poor one." An even gentler way to deal with Bill's proposal would be to avoid beginning management's reply with an adverse judgment. Instead the chief negotiator might say, "Let's see how that would work out in practice," and then demonstrate that it would be unfeasible. Separating the proposal from Bill makes it easier for him to accept its withdrawal or modification.

Bargainers should always remember the importance of face saving in negotiations. Union negotiators may be more flexible toward a proposal that is undesirable to them if the management negotiators offer them a way to save face while accepting it—perhaps by offering the union new information regarding the issue or offering in return concessions on other issues of less importance to management. Face saving is important in overcoming psychological barriers to the acceptance of management proposals. It can also be important in gaining membership acceptance of these proposals and therefore in gaining ratification of the contract.

Patience is an important attribute of a good negotiator. Do not rush your team or the union negotiators. Take adequate time to analyze and to evaluate before making decisions. If in doubt, interrupt negotiations for a caucus. Allow the union to do the same. Although patience should not be carried to the point of allowing negotiations to drag on without movement, it should be remembered that decisions made in haste are sometimes repented in leisure.

Negotiators should be good listeners. Bargaining involves two-way commu-

Collective Bargaining and Legislation

nication. Sometimes important feelers regarding possible compromises or signals of change in positions are communicated in subtle ways and may be overlooked by negotiators who are not listening carefully. Good listeners may learn a great deal from what is said by union negotiators, which can be of value in reaching a mutually acceptable agreement.

Last, management negotiators should remember that their organization must live with the results of collective bargaining for the duration of the agreement. What is negotiated, and how it is negotiated, can influence relationships with the union and the employees and can affect the performance and cost-effectiveness of the organization. This should be constantly kept in mind by management bargainers during negotiations.

Strikes and Other Pressures

The basic role of strikes and other kinds of economic pressures in the collective bargaining process is a critical one: to provide an incentive for the parties to make concessions, to compromise, and to reach an agreement. It is not necessary that a strike actually take place for this incentive to be present; the possibility of a strike is often sufficient.

To understand the incentive role of the strike, let us begin with the layperson's usual conception of strikes: a union weapon to force concessions from management. If the union's demands exceed what management is willing to give "voluntarily," further concessions to meet these demands can be considered as a cost to management. That is, management would be agreeing to higher pay and benefits or more generous work rules than it desires. If there are costs in making concessions but no cost in refusing concessions, management will stand pat. But if there are costs in standing pat as well as making concessions, the optimal decision for management may be to make the concessions necessary to reach an agreement. The strike is the cost of standing pat and failing to reach an agreement—the cost of disagreement.

With the possibility of a strike, management must compare the estimated costs of reaching agreement (further concessions and compromises) with the estimated costs of disagreement (undergoing a strike). If the estimated agreement costs exceed disagreement costs, management will accept a strike rather than agreeing to union demands. But if estimated agreement costs are less than disagreement costs, management will make concessions and reach agreement with the union. (It is stressed that costs of agreement and disagreement are estimated by the parties and are subject to revision during negotiations and during a strike.)

But a strike imposes costs on the strikers and their union as well as on management. Strikers lose pay, and the union may be obligated to give them strike benefits, to allocate staff resources to the conduct of the strike, and possibly to incur other kinds of costs, such as legal fees. Therefore the strike is a cost of disagreement to the union as well as to management and provides an incentive to the union as well as to management to make concessions and reach an agreement.

Each side may take steps to increase the cost of disagreement (strikes) to the other side while reducing the cost to itself. Management, for example, may keep the facility operating by encouraging bargaining unit employees to remain on the job, substituting management or other personnel for strikers, hiring replacements, subcontracting tasks and function, or by any combination of these measures. Keeping the facility operating can reduce the cost of the strike to management, thereby increasing its ability to hold out. Holding out longer, other things remaining equal, will increase the cost of disagreement to the union. This may make it more amenable to concessions and compromise. For its part, the union may try to increase the militance of its members to make them more willing to strike and to stay out for a long time, thereby (all other things remaining equal) increasing strike costs to management. It may also build up a strike benefit fund to replace part of the earnings lost by strikers, thereby reducing the cost of the strike to them.

A common but erroneous conception is that management's major counterweapon to the strike is the lockout, in which management closes down to pressure the union into concessions. In most cases there is little incentive for management to use the lockout. As long as the facility operates, there is no cost of disagreement, and management can continue to function under the existing employment terms. (It may even institute new and less costly employment terms, such as lower pay or benefits, without union consent if the old contract has expired and these terms have been offered to the union and have been negotiated to an impasse.) Furthermore, having a test of strength by a work stoppage begun by the union (a strike) rather than by the employer (a lockout) increases the likelihood that public opinion will hold the union more responsible than the employer for any loss of services resulting from the stoppage. Where the lockout is used, it is usually because either the timing of a work stoppage is an important consideration and management chooses an earlier time more favorable to itself, or the union engages in slowdown tactics that are disruptive and cannot be dealt with effectively through usual disciplinary procedures. Thus, in most cases, management's major counterweapon to the strike is not the lockout but the ability to withstand a strike successfully and to outlast the union—and to communicate this to the union in a credible manner.

Pressures other than work stoppages may be used where strikes and lockouts are prohibited by law or restricted by custom or where a stoppage fails to accomplish its objectives (as where the facility continues to operate with little disruption). A barrage of public criticism by the union against the facility would be an example. Publicity, including picketing, to discourage use of the facility or to disrupt deliveries of goods or the performance of services by outside vendors may be employed by the union. (Causing or threatening to cause job actions at vendors' locations to pressure them not to supply the target facility is now generally prohibited by law.) All of these pressures are designed to increase the cost of disagreement.

A basic question regarding facilities in which work stoppages are prohibited should now be apparent: are there any effective substitutes for strikes and lockouts in motivating the parties to make concessions and move toward agreement? There may still be intangible pressures resulting from actual or threatened public criticism of one party by the other. There may be behind-the-scenes efforts to enlist the support of influential persons and decision makers outside the facility, such as public officials, legislators, or officials of private third-party payers. (One approach, in which union and management might join forces, would be to convince legislators to increase funding, or third-party payers to raise reimbursement levels, to allow facilities to afford larger concessions to the union.)

Moreover, there may be a number of costs to the parties arising from the continuation of negotiations. Bargaining unit employees may become demoralized and embittered, with a resulting increase in turnover and absenteeism and a decline in effort and productivity. Management may continue to devote resources to negotiations, resources that could be employed in other tasks if an agreement were reached with the union. The union, too, may continue to allocate resources to negotiations and wish to redeploy them elsewhere. While these costs of disagreement are less dramatic and may be lower than those resulting from a strike, they remind us that even where strikes are prohibited, the cost of disagreement may be greater than zero.

In addition, there are the dispute resolution procedures that involve third-party interventions, such as mediation, fact finding, and arbitration. In public sector jurisdictions where strikes are banned but comprehensive labor relations legislation exists, legal requirements for utilizing these procedures tend to be more highly developed than in the private sector where there is a broader right to strike.

COLLECTIVE BARGAINING IN A CHANGING ECONOMIC ENVIRONMENT

Every collective bargaining negotiation takes place within a framework of economic constraints. These constraints limit the improvements in pay, benefits, and working conditions that can be granted without impairing the ability of the organization to function successfully.

A major change in the economic environment for collective bargaining in health care organizations during the 1980s has been the tightening economic constraints imposed by third-party payers, both government programs and private insurance carriers, and a more competitive market for health services. As compared with the 1960s and 1970s, it has become increasingly difficult to pass on increased costs. Furthermore, with the long-term increase in capacity in health care organizations, coupled with pressures to limit usage in order to control costs, the marketplace for health services has become increasingly competitive. Tightening economic constraints have resulted in growing pressure on management to be more cost-effective.

In collective bargaining, tightening economic contraints mean that management is less able to offer sizable pay and benefits increases or to make other kinds of concessions that might restrict employee productivity or otherwise raise the cost of providing services. In some cases, management is taking the initiative in demanding union concessions on pay and benefits or changes in work rules that might improve the organization's cost-effectiveness.

To what extent, if any, these developments will make it more difficult to reach agreement and increase the probability of conflict will depend on the willingness of employees and their union leadership to accept the need for restraint on pay and other employment terms. The degree of willingness may be influenced by management's general credibility with the employees and the union leadership, the kind of relationship that has been developed (cooperative or confrontational), and the ability of management to support its position with arguments and information acceptable to the other side.

The changing economic environment makes it especially important that management assess the total impact on the organization of each package of employment terms on the table during collective bargaining. This is not always easy because it is sometimes difficult to identify and estimate the indirect effects of a particular change in employment terms. But failure to make such an assessment can result in unanticipated and costly results from collective bargaining agreements. For example, after obtaining concessions from the union on pay, benefits, and work rules, management may think that the new agreement will significantly improve the organization's cost-effectiveness. If, however, worsened employment terms also lead to a demoralized workforce, a higher quit rate, greater difficulty in filling vacancies, more absenteeism, and less effort by employees, the contribution to cost-effectiveness of the new contract may be much less than anticipated or even nonexistent. This is not to argue that improved employment terms granted during collective bargaining always pay for themselves or that obtaining concessions from the union is always self-defeating. It is only to reinforce the basic point that management should continually assess the total impact on the organization of the process and outcomes of collective bargaining.

In the late–1980s environment of tightening economic constraints and an increasingly competitive marketplace for health services, the consequences of collective bargaining agreements that inadequately meet the needs of the organization can be drastic for both parties: decline and even extinction for the organization and the elimination of jobs for the employees. This sobering prospect is not likely to change much in the foreseeable future.

GUIDELINES FOR PRACTITIONERS

1. Understand and keep in mind the significance and implications of collective bargaining for management, particularly for human resource management.

Collective Bargaining and Legislation

This will help you to bargain more effectively in the light of the strategic objectives of your organization.

2. Know which legal framework applies to your organization: private sector, federal, or state.

Guidelines 3 through 10 are based on the assumption that a comprehensive legal framework for labor relations is applicable to the practitioner's organization. This is true of private sector and federal facilities and of facilities subject to state labor relations law in many states.

3. Know the procedures and practices that must be followed to comply with the good faith bargaining obligation.

4. Know the distinction among mandatory, nonmandatory, and prohibited issues of bargaining and understand the implications of each category for the bargaining process and the utilization of strikes and lockouts.

5. Understand the implications of the distinction between mandatory and nonmandatory issues for management's ability to retain control over decision making.

6. Know how a management rights clause can be used to retain control over decision making on both mandatory and nonmandatory issues of bargaining.

7. Understand the difference between decision bargaining and effects bargaining. Although management may not be legally obligated to negotiate over basic managerial decisions such as closing a facility, it may still be obligated to negotiate over the effects of such decisions on employees.

8. Know the legal guidelines applicable to economic pressures that may be utilized by the union, such as strikes.

9. Know the legal guidelines applicable to counterpressures that management might utilize, such as hiring replacements for striking workers.

10. Know the legal provisions regarding the use of third-party dispute resolution mechanisms, such as mediation, fact finding, and arbitration, as alternatives to economic pressures.

11. If in doubt regarding the legal status of any aspect of the collective bargaining process, consult a labor attorney or other person with the necessary expertise.

12. Review experience under the previous agreement to identify troublesome clauses for which changes in language may be desirable.

13. Review experience with human resource policies and practices not covered by the present agreement as an aid to anticipating union proposals in the upcoming negotiations.

14. Be knowledgeable about the union with which you will negotiate.

15. Be knowledgeable about other contracts that may be used as models in the upcoming negotiations. Analyze the implications of similar contract terms for your organization.

16. Prepare data on relevant external economic variables such as trends in consumer prices, conditions in the local labor market, pay rates at area health care facilities, and others.

17. Be knowledgeable about your organization's financial situation and cost structure and its anticipated financial situation during the term of the new collective bargaining agreement.

18. Establish objectives for the upcoming negotiations and prepare proposals in the light of these objectives. Among the relevant considerations in formulating objectives and proposals are the needs of the organization and the acceptability of your proposals to the employees and their unions.

19. Regarding the bargaining team, make a reasonable compromise between the objectives of giving all elements of management representation on the team and limiting the team to a reasonable size.

20. Select team members on the basis of their potential to be effective negotiators, as well as their knowledge of particular areas of management.

21. Plan team organization. Designate a spokesperson and assign roles and duties to each member of the team.

22. Clearly define the authority of the bargaining team to make binding commitments to the union.

23. Develop contingency plans for a possible strike.

24. Understand the importance of adequate preparation for achieving satisfactory outcomes in collective bargaining and of allocating sufficient resources to the preparation process.

25. Understand the development of the collective bargaining process through its various stages from the beginning of negotiations to the reaching of agreement.

26. Adopt a positive approach to bargaining; work toward the kind of agreement management wants rather than against the kind of agreement the union wants.

27. Be able to view negotiations from the union's perspective, as well as from a management perspective.

28. Build and maintain credibility with the union negotiators. Avoid trickery and deception, say what you mean, and mean what you say.

29. Practice good human relations with the union negotiators. Respect their sincerity and ability. Control your temper and have patience. Personalize praise and depersonalize criticism.

30. Remember the importance of face saving in negotiations. To the maximum extent possible, give proposal negotiators the opportunity to retreat gracefully.

31. Be a good listener.

32. Be familiar with the various kinds of economic pressures and counterpressures that may be applied in the collective bargaining process.

33. Understand the role of economic pressures in collective bargaining: to impose a cost or penalty on the parties for failing to reach agreement. Avoiding these costs is a significant incentive to compromise and reach agreement.

34. Understand tactics that management might use to reduce the cost of disagreement to itself and/or to increase this cost for the union.

35. Understand how to determine whether it is preferable to make the conces-

sions necessary to reach agreement with the union or to accept a strike. (In the light of all relevant considerations, which is the least-cost alternative?)

36. Understand the third-party dispute resolution procedures available for resolving differences between union and management without resorting to strikes or other kinds of economic pressures. (In some cases, use of one or more of these alternatives may be required by law.)

37. Constantly remember that your organization must live with the agreed-upon terms for the duration of the contract and what is negotiated and how it is negotiated can influence ongoing relationships with your employees and their union and can significantly affect the performance and cost-effectiveness of your organization.

REFERENCES

Herman, E. E., Kuhn, A., and Seever, R. L. (1986). *Collective Bargaining and Labor Relations*. 2d ed. Englewood Cliffs, N.J.: Prentice-Hall.

Richardson, R. C. (1977). *Collective Bargaining by Objectives*. Englewood Cliffs, N.J.: Prentice-Hall.

14
The Technostress Challenge: Implications for Strategic Human Resource Management

*Amarjit S. Sethi
and Denis H.J. Caro*

In this chapter,[1] we shall present the concept of technostress and examine its implications for strategic human resource management. Our philosophical view is that a health care organization has a responsibility to introduce, diffuse, and manage information technology (IT) in such a way that it is congruent with the principles of strategic human resource management. This chapter rests on the fundamental premise that within an enviroment where the introduction and diffusion of technology is viewed as supportive and builds and maintains the worker's personal worth, the organization can maintain a high level of patient care while delivering the maximum positive benefits from the new technology. Our hypothesis is that technostress management is a strategic choice that human resource specialists need to include in accordance with the strategic choice model presented in Chapter 1.

OPERATIONAL DEFINITIONS

The terms *information technology* and *technostress* need to be defined before we present our conceptual model of technostress management and its implications for strategic human resource management (SHRM).

Information technology (IT) refers to developments in microelectronics and current and advanced computers, including artificial intelligence and telecommunications. The emerging trends in artificial intelligence and associated devices include information-related technologies such as expert systems, computer vision, machine translation, picture processing, industrial robots and computer-assisted manufacturing, decision-making systems, electronic office machines, and intelligent information banks. The combined impact of IT represents a turning point for industrial societies and has significant implications for SHRM.

Technostress is defined as a perception of uncertainty and an adaptive response mediated by sociopsychological processes and influenced by the introduction or exposure to technology. Technostress is viewed as a process of adaptation to the introduction and experience of IT. The term *technostress* describes stress resulting from the introduction of new information technology in the work environment in health care organizations. Important determinants include technological innovation and policies for its implementation, as well as the rate at which new technology is diffused into the workplace.

Technology is essentially a stressor that affects the individual who is using the technology (the techno-user). The techno-user's experience of stress depends upon his or her personality characteristics, coping mechanisms, adaptive capabilities, and value system. To what extent technology is viewed as important for one's job is a significant variable in the perception of technostress. Technostress is thus a form of social stress but is presented as a distinct form of stress arising from pervasive evolution of technology in an emerging information society to which hospitals and health care systems need to adapt to function successfully and effectively. Technostress is thus affected by a number of factors:

1. The nature of intended informational technology and its ecology
2. The rate of technological change
3. The nature of work design components needed to introduce technology
4. The nature of social group change needed to use technology
5. The nature of organizational power and culture, particularly in relation to participation and worker involvement
6. Demographic factors, such as age, sex, and marital status
7. Cognitive factors, such as personality characteristics and tolerance for ambiguity
8. Cultural values regarding technology and change
9. Response to perceived technostress
10. Results of technostress and their impact on individual and organizational health

These multiple factors of technostress are schematically depicted in Exhibit 14.1.

THE CONCEPT OF TECHNOSTRESS

IT emcompasses the totality of dynamic and complex information strategies covering microelectronics, computers, and telecommunications, including the following components: hardware, software, ergonomic workstations, expert systems, knowledge-based systems, data base management systems, advanced tele-

Exhibit 14.1
Technostress: A Working Model

TECHNOLOGY AS STRESSOR

ecological environment
- light
- noise
- temperature
- humidity
- pollution

rate of change
- technological innovations
- technological policies/procedures
- rate of technological diffusion

work design
- role conflict
- role ambiguity
- workload
- lack of career mobility
- job management
- training

social group change
- peer group conflict
- lack of supportive relationships
- lack of good congruence
- conflict in values and norms
- group think

organizational culture
- lack of participation
- weak organizational structure
- occupational level
- lack of clear policies
- lack of procedures

TECHNOUSER MODERATORS

demographic moderators
- age
- sex
- marital status

cognitive moderators
- type A behavior pattern
- level of self-esteem
- tolerance for ambiguity

cultural values
- social values about technology
- cultural perceptions about technology

attitude to change
- adaptability
- orientation to change

STRESS MANIFESTATIONS

Positive Technostress

Negative Technostress

TECHNOUSER MANIFESTATIONS

synergistic relationship to technology
high degree of self-automatization

ORGANIZATIONAL MANIFESTATIONS

higher savings
higher quality of patient care and research
good place for innovation and entrepreneurship
drive toward the future

TECHNOUSER MANIFESTATIONS

higher psychosomatic disease and incidence
lower self-esteem

ORGANIZATIONS MANIFESTATIONS

higher absenteeism
lower productivity of patient care
higher turnover
greater interpersonal conflict
drive toward status quo

communications, computer integrated manufacturing systems, and robotics. Technostress has assumed particular importance because of the rapid technological changes facing organizations (Landes, 1969; Winner, 1977; Weizenbaum, 1976; Brod, 1984; ILO, 1984). In order to adapt to technological change, organizations can use SHRM in a proactive manner to increase personal efficiency of organizational members, as well as maintain organizational performance (Friedman and Rosenman, 1974; Kets de Vries, 1984; Tapscott, Henderson, and Greenberg, 1985).

In our definition of technostress, we have given importance to a perceived and dynamic state of uncertainty in the face of technological change that occurs at individual, organizational, and societal levels. Technostress thus refers to uncertainty experienced by the person in different contexts in adapting to the new technological environment (Caro and Sethi, 1985; Sethi, Caro, and Schuler, 1987).

The process of adaptation is moderated by technology, task, structure, and individual and organizational power and value systems. In this process of wanting and acting to achieve a desired state, the individual worker must face certain constraints, demands, uncertainties and opportunities that may result in negative outcomes (technodistress) or positive outcomes (technoeustress) (Caro and Sethi, 1985).

There are a number of factors that add complexity to technological uncertainty: the nature of the technological task and its associated change, the condition of inputs, the tools and training available to workers to perform the task, the worker's attitude toward new technology and his or her knowledge and skill, and the structural arrangements among workers that govern information flow (Turner, 1987).

Technostress is not an isolated category of merely response but a state of adaptation combining (1) sources (e.g., technology), (2) dimensions (how the source is transmitted and perceived), and (3) responses (reaction to uncertainty unique to each level of analysis). Technostress is a dynamic adaptive state, which has three key ingredients in the environment: the nature of the stressor, the reaction or response to this stressor, and the results from this reaction, leading again to a cycle of new reactions and formulations at various levels of analysis, including the individual, organization, and society. This definition is in accordance with a transactional approach and pays attention to perceptual variables. Stress is both a physiological and psychological state and is mediated by the environmental factors, which again are both psychophysical and sociological.

There are two components to technostress: technoeustress and technodistress (adapted from Selye, 1974). This is based on the assumption that technology can have differential effects on their users. Technoeustress is the stress that is beneficial or has a positive effect on the functioning of the individual and his or her contribution to the level of organizational productivity. Organizational effectiveness and quality of worklife are balanced. Technodistress is that stress that has a negative impact on the individual's functions, with consequent negative effect on the overall organizational productivity and quality of worklife. These stress levels will manifest themselves in an individual and in an organization in a variety of ways. The employee may display a high level of anxiety, an increased disposition to accidents, and an inability to make decisions and may have more psychological complaints and disorders, such as backaches, migraines, and increased depression. The organization may show a high rate of absenteeism, more labor relations problems, and reduced organizational commitment and loyalty. There may be an overall imbalance between organizational effectiveness and quality of worklife (Turner and Karasek, 1984).

Indicators of technodistress include a propensity toward psychosomatic diseases (e.g., cardiovascular disease) and could be reflected in higher absenteeism, lower productivity, higher turnover, and lower quality of worklife. Indicators of technoeustress would be characterized by a symbiotic and synergistic relationship with information technology, resulting in higher level of job performance as well as better quality of workife.

MODERATING VARIABLES

Any of several moderating variables may be expected to contribute singly or collectively to the degree of perceived uncertainty and/or to the responses to uncertainty. These variables refer to transactional elements that are either factual or value oriented and exert a moderating influence. As shown in Exhibit 14.2 these include relative power, time pressure, individual ability, importance of issue, task interdependence, tolerance for ambiguity, field dependence, availability of feedback, locus of control, and group cohesiveness.

The moderators are likely to influence response to uncertainty. For example, individuals with a low tolerance for ambiguity are more likely to invoke response quickly. Since moderating variables have the potential to exert significant impact on perceived uncertainty and responses to it, it is important that they be diagnosed along with the dimensions of uncertainty and the sources of uncertainty in any analysis of technostress and organizational culture.

IMPLICATIONS OF TECHNOSTRESS AS A STRATEGIC CHOICE

Strategic choice has been used in economics, organizational behavior, and industrial relations (Bain, 1968; Porter, 1980; Simon, 1957; Braybrooke and Lindblom, 1970; Cyert and March, 1963; Kochan, McKersie, and Capelli, 1984). The term has been defined either as "actions or rules for choosing actions in a conflict situation" or high-level or "long-term planning" with reference to "issues of mission" (Rumelt, 1979: 197). Kochan et al. have used it as a frame of reference to cover both process and content in decision making, where "parties have discretions over their decisions" (Kochan, McKersie, and Capelli, 1984: 21).

Exhibit 14.2
Dimensions of Technostress

Factual Factors[b]
• Number of elements • Nature and rate of technological change • Heterogeneity of elements • Clarity of elements • Relationship among elements • Predictability of change

Human or Value Factors[b]	
• Relative power	• Ambiguity of tolerance
• Time pressure	
• Importance of issue	• Field dependence
• Individual ability interdependence	• Availability of feedback
• Locus of control	• Task and group cohesiveness

[a] The dimensions of technostress are common to all levels of analysis including unit, group, departmental and organizational levels.

[b] The "factual" and "value" factors are inter-related and separated here for showing their importance in the experience of technostress.

Source: R.S. Schuler, S.E. Jackson, and A.S. Sethi, "Human Resource Strategies in Technostress Management," in A.S. Sethi, D. Caro, and R.S. Schuler (Eds.), *Strategic Management of Technostress in an Information Society*, © 1987 by C.J. Hogrefe Publishers, Inc., Toronto, p. 75. Reproduced with permission.

The concepts of uncertainty and decision choices have been dealt with in decision theory and analysis. Raiffa (1970) has examined the significance of a person's degree of belief—his or her subjective probability assignments in decision making—in addition to the role of rational thinking and analysis based on choice behavior and bargaining strategies (Von Neumann and Morgenstern, 1947; Schlaifer, 1967; Pratt, Raiffa, and Schlaifer, 1976). To us strategic choice is not an expression of only a logical, rational, or necessary degree of belief but also an expression of a subjective degree of belief incorporating values of the choice maker, as well as influenced by power in and around decisional contexts (Raiffa, 1970; Mintzberg, 1983).

IMPLICATIONS FOR STRATEGIC HUMAN RESOURCE MANAGEMENT

Strategic choice in an SHRM context implies internalization of the aim of human resource management effectively for both health care organizations and workers by identifying and assessing organizational and technological environments and choosing those strategies that reduce uncertainty and increase productivity and quality of worklife.

The effective coping of technostress may help the health care executive in increasing his or her power base over organizational choices and decision-making processes in general. Pfeffer, Salancik, and Leblebeci (1976) and Goh (1985) confirm that as uncertainty increases, power differences become more important in influencing decision-making outcomes. It can be argued that in technological situations where there is greater uncertainty, those who are able to cope with uncertainty faced by an organization have greater power (Pettigrew, 1973; Crozier, 1964; Hinings et al., 1974).

We believe that the concept of strategy, or strategic choice, adds a dynamic component to the transitional model and in so doing helps explain changing response patterns in technostress management at both macrolevels and microlevels of a health care system. The strategic choices are made at different levels, and the effect of these decisions may have an impact throughout the health care system and society. The major purpose of these strategic decisions, regardless of their specific target, is to manage the state of uncertainty. Management of uncertainty results in either the actual reduction of uncertainty or ways to mitigate its otherwise harmful effects. The key components of the model (shown in Exhibit 14.3) are:

- The environment and its dimensions, including microlevels and macrolevels of IT, the number of elements in IT, rate of change, heterogeneity of IT elements, relationship among elements, and predictability of change
- Actor's perception and creativity in interpreting the environment based on his or her values, experience, and coping ability
- Moderators of the experience and reactions to uncertainty generated by new technology
- Strategic choices and decisions made at individual, organizational, and societal levels
- Outcomes measured in terms of organizational effectiveness and quality of worklife

Miles and Snow (1978) argue that neither natural selection (a more or less chance process by which organizations cope with change) nor rational selection (a completely conscious process of coping) is at work. Rather, the strategic choice model of technostress management argues that organizational adaptation is partly determined by environmental conditions beyond the control of managers and partly by top-level decision makers who have knowledge and power and make choices about structure and process to realize desired outcomes (Child, 1972; Anderson and Paine, 1975; Beer, 1980). In addition, they manipulate the environment itself to bring it into alignment with the organization.

Strategic choices can be reactive or defensive, proactive or analytical, or interactional or transactional. For successful technostress management, we hypothesize that proactive and transactional strategic choices should prove to be more effective, although research is needed to refine the relationship between different types of strategy and technological change (Lazarus, 1978a).

Exhibit 14.3
A Strategic Choice Model of Technostress Management

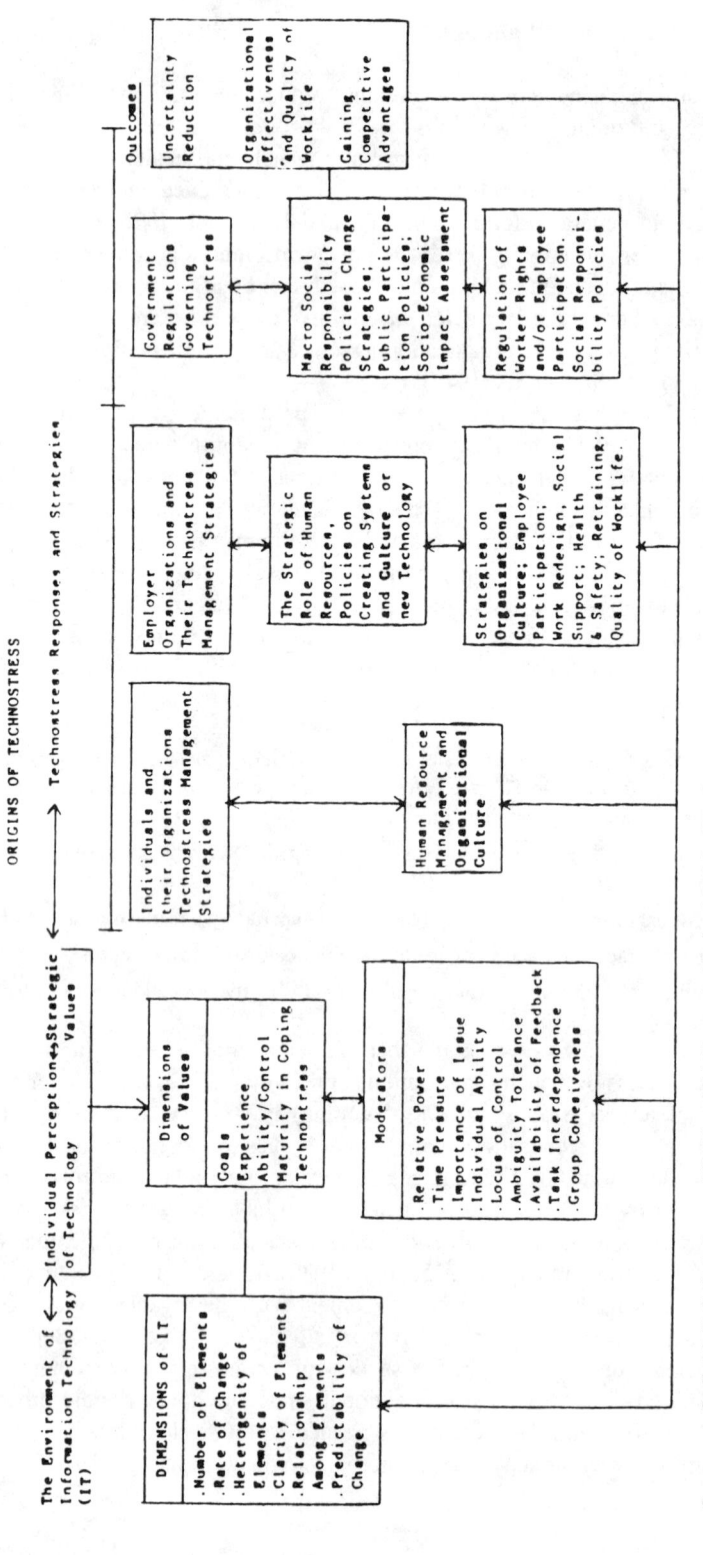

The Environment of ⟷ Individual Perceptions ⟷ Strategic Values
Information Technology   of Technology
(IT)

ORIGINS OF TECHNOSTRESS

⟶ Technostress Responses and Strategies

DIMENSIONS of IT
- Number of Elements
- Rate of Change
- Heterogeneity of Elements
- Clarity of Elements
- Relationship Among Elements
- Predictability of Change

Dimensions of Values
- Goals
- Experience
- Ability/Control
- Maturity in Coping Technostress

Moderators
- Relative Power
- Time Pressure
- Importance of Issue
- Individual Ability
- Locus of Control
- Ambiguity Tolerance
- Availability of Feedback
- Task Interdependence
- Group Cohesiveness

Individuals and their Organizations Technostress Management Strategies

Human Resource Management and Organizational Culture

Employer Organizations and Their Technostress Management Strategies

The Strategic Role of Human Resources, Policies on Creating Systems and Culture or new Technology

Strategies on Organizational Culture; Employee Participation; Work Redesign; Social Support; Health & Safety; Retraining; Quality of Worklife.

Government Regulations Governing Technostress

Macro Social Responsibility Policies; Change Strategies; Public Participation Policies; Socio-Economic Impact Assessment

Regulation of Worker Rights and/or Employee Participation. Social Responsibility Policies

Outcomes
Uncertainty Reduction

Organizational Effectiveness and Quality of Worklife

Gaining Competitive Advantage

Source: A.S. Sethi, R.S. Schuler, and D. Caro, "A Strategic Choice Model of Technostress Management," in A.S. Sethi, D. Caro, and R.S. Schuler (Eds.), *Strategic Management of Technostress in an Information Society*, © 1987 by C.J. Hogrefe Publishers, Inc., Toronto, p. 21. Reproduced with permission.

In examining the role of strategy in technostress management in health care, we have adopted the strategic choice concept with three specific characteristics of the concept. First, we believe that strategic choices are not only made by top decision makers but also by individuals in the organization as well as outsiders (societal representatives, government, consumers) who may affect the adaptational resources of the organization. Second, we have hypothesized that these choices are not merely interactional; they tend to be organic. The organizations and their environments function in multilinear fashion; influences can cause changes in both organizations and environments. Finally, we have given special emphasis to the role of values in the determination of strategic choices for managing technostress in health care (Kluckhohn et al., 1951; Mumford, 1981).

ASSUMPTIONS OF THE STRATEGIC CHOICE MODEL

The first assumption is that managing IT effects in health care requires prospective planning or the capacity to meet multiple demands and the managerial competence and skills to formulate and make strategic decisions. To quote Schönpflug (1983: 355):

Prospective planning, clear priority of decisions, and wise renunciation of goals of low priority may help to prevent multi-demand situations.... Lack of prospective planning inability in setting priorities and blind fixation to various incentives may in contrast, serve as the *via regia* to the creation of an entangling stress situation, finally also leading to fatigue. This, at least, is one of the lessons taught by the theory of action and its good companion, the theory of behavior economics.

The second assumption of the model is that technology may have both negative and/or positive impacts. The definition put forward by Brod (1982) that technostress has a negative impact on human performance is not supported by research. Negative impact is only one side of the coin of uncertainty of stress; the other side is the opportunity the new technology creates and therefore may be beneficial to workers, patients, and the organization.

The third assumption of the model is that technostress in health care can be positive if preventive strategies (such as strategic planning and organization culture) are adopted. Alcalay and Pasick (1983: 1082) explain:

Where innovations are simply adopted by virtue of their proclaimed benefits and intended functions and where work environment is structured around such innovations, technology may indeed be in control. However, where planning takes into account benefits, functions, and possible technologies, is structured around the health and well-being of workers, then technology is certainly the object of human choice.

Mann and Williams (1960), in one of the first empirical studies on the impact of computers on work, suggested that changes on jobs were stressful for some and a game for others. Recent studies indicate that outcomes cannot be determined as a foregone conclusion and that although IT does bring about broad changes in content of work, the level of employment, and the quality of worklife, specific changes should be understood based on impact assessment of each situation in a growing industry. This assessment may focus on factors such as the nature of the task, the way in which the new technology is introduced, conditions of inputs, the tools available to the worker for performing the task, the worker's perceptions and values, the health care system, and organizational values and structural arrangements of a given situation (Turner, 1987).

EMPIRICAL SUPPORT FOR THE STRATEGIC CHOICE MODEL

The literature on stress research reveals a wealth of perspectives and findings on both the nature of stress and its impact on individual and organizational effectiveness (Selye, 1976; Lazarus, 1978b; Howard, Rechnitzer, and Cunningham, 1978; Brown, 1984; McLean, 1979; Gibson, Ivancevich, and Donnelly, 1985; Dunham, 1984; Beehr and Newman, 1978; Friedman and Rosenman, 1974; Winner, 1977; Brief, Schuler, and Van Sell, 1980). Although a few studies, such as those by Johansson, Aronsson, and Lundström (1979), Frankenhaeuser (1979), Frankenhaeuser and Johansson (1981), OECD (1983), ILO (1984), Blumberg and Gerwin (1984), and Johansson and Aronsson (1984), have looked at the impact of technology on stress, more research is needed. Attewell and Rule (1984) have provided a comprehensive review of the literature on the effects of computing in organizations and point out that these effects are complex and require rigorous and broad-based contextual studies.

In a review of recent research on positive and negative impacts of technology in relation to whether technology controls workers or workers control technology, Alcalay and Pasick (1983: 1080–81) come to the following tentative conclusions:

1. The use of new technologies can increase job strain, job overload, and underload and can decrease the level of workers' control over work

2. Technologically intensive work can have an impact on the individual's social support networks

3. Workers who benefit the most from new techologies are usually high-level management and/or professionals

4. Workers who suffer the most from technology-centered task are in lower-status blue-collar or clerical positions

Based on a review of several successful companies in the United States that implemented IT, Benjamin et al. (1984: 3–10) support the proposition that IT impacts can be utilized by senior management to gain competitive advantage through generating awareness of the potential advantages of IT, and by creating a cultural environment in which "information technology is considered an important strategic weapon."

Recent ILO-initiated research shows that the impact of microcomputers on an organization can lead to perceived stress where there are poor supportive relationships (group stressors), a lack of supportive management (organizational stressor), unclear job definition (individual stressor) and a high-noise-level environment (physical environmental stressor) (ILO, 1984; Fraser, 1983; Levi, 1984; Wereneke, 1983; Rada, 1980). A recent empirical study supports the proposition that technological innovation produces a lack of fit between demands made by the technology and the needs, skills, procedures, structures, and equipment embodied in the social and technical structure of companies. The result is that new technology raises both cognitive and motivational problems with which managers, staff specialists, and workers have great difficulty in coping (Blumberg and Gerwin, 1984).

TECHNOSTRESS MANAGEMENT: RECOMMENDED STRATEGIES

Organizations can employ both preventive and curative strategies to manage technostress (Albrecht, 1979; Dunham, 1984; Sethi, Caros, and Schuler, 1987). These strategies relate to stressors, stress reaction, and personality characteristics of the individual. Effective technostress management in health care organizations may include human resource management strategies at individual and organizational levels. The key to effective technostress management is the introduction of preventive surveillance and adaptive strategies.

ORGANIZATIONAL STRATEGIES: TECHNOLOGY STRATEGY

Health care organizations can employ both preventive and curative strategies to manage technostress (McLean, 1979; Albrecht, 1979; Sethi, 1982, 1983; Dunham, 1984; Toffler, 1985; Ivancevich and Matteson, 1980). The key to effective technostress management at the organizational level is the introduction of preventive and adaptive strategies. Technology strategy is recommended as a preventive strategy; to be successful, it should be flexible and adapted to an individual health care organization's work environment. The nature of a technology strategy will vary with the size and structure of the organization, leadership style, rate of technological change, intensity of technostress experienced, commitment to technology, and available resources (Tapscott, Henderson, and Greenberg, 1985).

Technostress has assumed particular importance because of the rapid technological changes facing organizations today (Landes, 1969; Winner, 1977; Brod, 1984; ILO, 1984). On order to manage this change, technology strategy can be used in a proactive manner to increase personal efficiency of organizational members as well as maintain organizational performance (Friedman and Rosenman, 1974; Kets de Vries, 1979, 1984; Tapscott, Henderson, and Greenberg, 1985).

In the multiple-level health care system in Canada, there is a need for a clear understanding of the role of technological diffusion and the successful adaptation to technology. The technological revolution, with its increase in speed, reliability, improved efficiency, and portability, requires fundamental changes in human thought and action. There is a recognition in policy statements of both governments that IT will pose significant management and policy challenges. Francis Fox, the former minister of communications in Canada, emphasized the pervasive effects of new information-based strategies, which include integrated office systems, robotics, and office automated systems, when he stated:

These technologies will open new sources of wealth and affect the productivity of established industries. These changes will, quite obviously, exert *great stress* on the Canadian federation. There will be horizontal stresses between regions that are quick to adapt to the transformed environment and those which are not so quick. And there will be vertical stresss between individuals and groups who are able to take advantage of new opportunities and those who are not. (Canada Tomorrow Conference, 1984).

COMPONENTS OF TECHNOLOGY STRATEGY

A technology strategy has four main components: strategic technological planning, technostress monitoring systems, strategic implementation stage, and technostress research. These components can be productively employed in combination with other strategies discussed in this chapter, such as organizational culture programs and employee self-development programs.

Strategic Technological Planning

In order to minimize the dysfunctional impacts of IT, it is desirable for a health care organization to prepare a strategic plan for its introduction and effective implementation. The need for top management's support is critical, and the establishment of an operational technological advisory committee is helpful. The planning phase may consist of three fundamental stages: the desirability stage, the feasibility stage, and the strategic implementation stage.

During the desirability stage, the fundamental question posed is whether the technology to be introduced is desirable a priori. The potential employees should ideally participate in this decision-making process. With participation and feedback from the employees, the technology may in fact become a major factor in promoting efficiency and productivity.

Once a decision has been made that the technology is desirable, the health care organization, through its strategic planning mechanisms, must move to the second initial stage: feasibility. Four fundamental questions (Exhibit 14.4) are posed during this phase as the essence of technological assessment:

Exhibit 14.4
Phases in Strategic Technological Planning

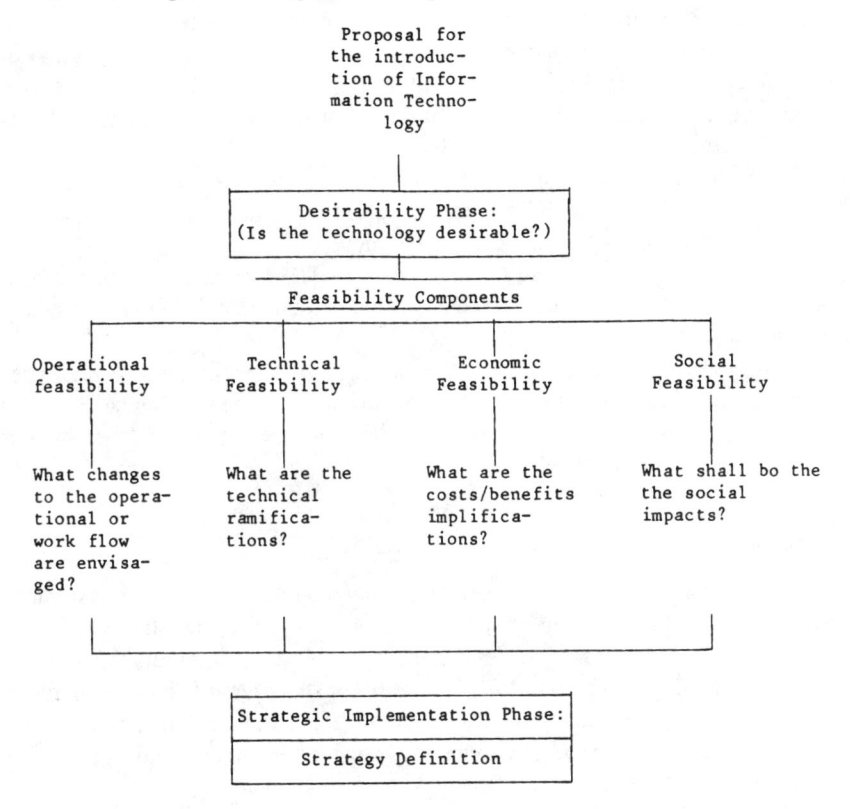

```
                    Proposal for
                    the introduc-
                    tion of Infor-
                    mation Techno-
                        logy
                          |
              ┌───────────────────────────┐
              │   Desirability Phase:     │
              │ (Is the technology desirable?) │
              └───────────────────────────┘
                          |
                 Feasibility Components
    ┌─────────────┬─────────────┬─────────────┬─────────────┐
 Operational    Technical     Economic       Social
 feasibility    Feasibility   Feasibility    Feasibility
    |             |             |             |
 What changes  What are the  What are the  What shall bo the
 to the opera- technical     costs/benefits the social
 tional or     ramifica-     implifica-    impacts?
 work flow     tions?        tions?
 are envisa-
 ged?
    └─────────────┴─────────────┴─────────────┘
                          |
              ┌───────────────────────────┐
              │ Strategic Implementation Phase: │
              ├───────────────────────────┤
              │    Strategy Definition    │
              └───────────────────────────┘
```

Source: D. Caro and A.S. Sethi, "Technology Strategy: The Role of Strategic Planning and Monitoring Systems," in A.S. Sethi, D. Caro, and R.S. Schuler (Eds.), *Strategic Management of Technostress in an Information Society*, © 1987 by C.J. Hogrefe Publishers, Inc., Toronto, p. 37. Reproduced with permission.

1. Is the technological proposal operationally feasible? What changes to the operations or work flow are envisaged?
2. Is the technology technically feasible? What are the technical ramifications of the technology?
3. Is this technology economically feasible? What are its cost-benefit implications?
4. Is this technology socially feasible? Will it have a beneficial impact on the social functioning of the organization?

Out of the four assessment questions, the social feasibility question, which deals with the social impact on the organization, is the most critical in any organizational strategy to manage technostress. This social impact assessment can lead to important preventive strategies for the mitigation of negative impacts of technology (Wolf, 1983).

The outcome of the feasibility study phase as it pertains to technostress would be: (1) a statement or projection of the potential impact of the introduction of technology on the levels of stress within the organization; and (2) a set of organizational strategies to prevent, mitigate, or minimze the potential effects of technostress.

Technologies should be assessed before introduction for contributions to efficiency and quality of life. Widespread adoption of IT should be delayed pending the results of rigorous technological assessment.

The policy implications are to identify major IT components, conduct technology assessment in a timely manner, and disseminate information to key decision makers.

Although evidence is incomplete, Feeney (1986) states that new technologies do contribute to increases in the cost of health care, and the widespread adoption of new technologies generally precedes the availability of hard evidence in their effectiveness and efficiency.

Technostress Monitoring Systems

Fundamental to the development of a technology strategy is the systematic surveillance and monitoring of the stress levels within the health care organization. The examination of various sources of stress for individuals within an organization is called a stress audit. The causes of stress identified in the literature can relate to organizational structure, interpersonal relationships, roles, organizational change, physical environment, career development, and intrinsic job qualities (Kets de Vries, 1984; Wereneke, 1983).

In the case of technostress, one can identify a number of conditions related to organizational structure as a source of stress. For example, the employee may experience high levels of technodistress when he or she does not participate in the decisions to introduce the technology, there is a general lack of social cohesion or an absence of supportive relationships within his or her working environment, there is poor communication, there are organizational restrictions on the technouser's behavioral patterns, there is a lack of opportunity for advancement, and there is an inequity in salary and performance evaluation (Schuler, 1984). In such cases, the employee may experience and exhibit a number of physiological, behavioral, and affective and cognitive psychological responses, which can be monitored systematically through the use of a technostress monitoring system as shown in Exhibit 14.5. Such a system documents the overall physiological, behavioral, and psychological factors that make up the employee's health profile. Routine health examinations can highlight health pattern changes, which, subjected to statistical analyses, could be significant and indicate appropriate individual or organizational corrective actions.

The health care organization could monitor the organizational manifestations

Exhibit 14.5
A Technostress Human Resource Monitoring System

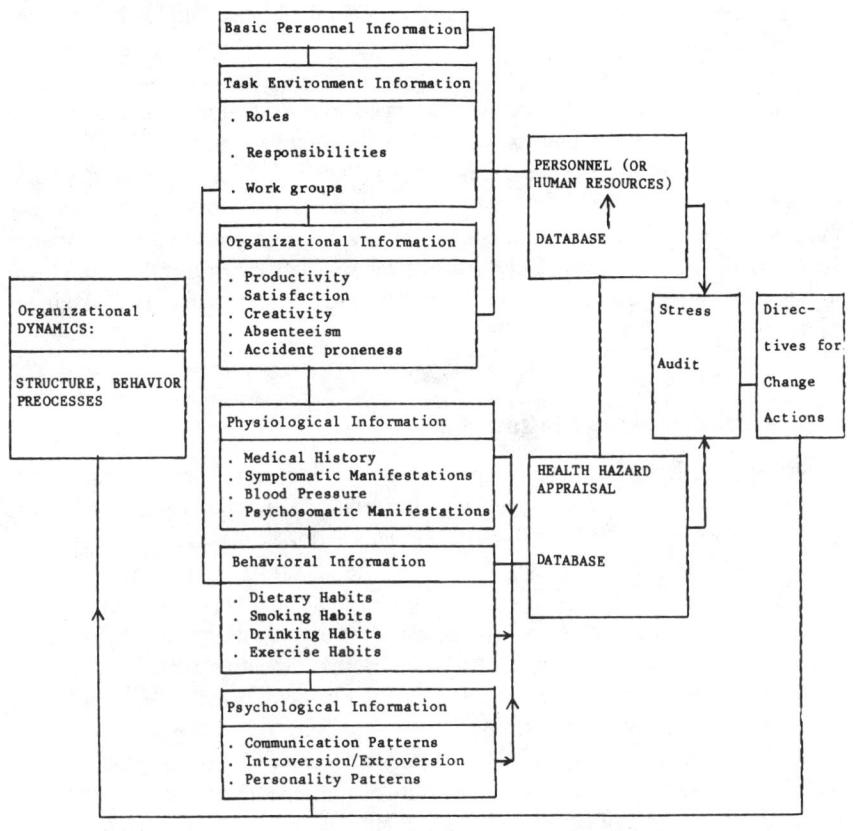

```
                    ┌─Basic Personnel Information─┐
                    ├─Task Environment Information┤
                    │  . Roles                    │
                    │  . Responsibilities         │────┐  ┌──────────────┐
                    │  . Work groups              │    │  │ PERSONNEL (OR│
                    ├─Organizational Information──┤    └──│ HUMAN        │
                    │  . Productivity             │       │ RESOURCES)   │
┌──────────────┐    │  . Satisfaction             │       │    ↑         │
│Organizational│    │  . Creativity               │       │ DATABASE     │  ┌────────┐ ┌────────┐
│ DYNAMICS:    │────│  . Absenteeism              │       └──────────────┘  │ Stress │ │Direc-  │
│              │    │  . Accident proneness       │                         │        │ │tives for│
│STRUCTURE,    │    ├─Physiological Information───┤                         │ Audit  │ │Change  │
│BEHAVIOR      │    │  . Medical History          │       ┌──────────────┐  │        │ │Actions │
│PROCESSES     │    │  . Symptomatic Manifestations│──────│HEALTH HAZARD │  └────────┘ └────────┘
└──────────────┘    │  . Blood Pressure           │       │APPRAISAL     │
                    │  . Psychosomatic Manifestations     │              │
                    ├─Behavioral Information──────┤       │ DATABASE     │
                    │  . Dietary Habits           │       └──────────────┘
                    │  . Smoking Habits           │
                    │  . Drinking Habits          │
                    │  . Exercise Habits          │
                    ├─Psychological Information───┤
                    │  . Communication Patterns   │
                    │  . Introversion/Extroversion│
                    │  . Personality Patterns     │
                    └─────────────────────────────┘
```

Source: D. Caro and A.S. Sethi, "Technology Strategy: The Role of Strategic Planning and Monitoring Systems," in A.S. Sethi, D. Caro, and R.S. Schuler (Eds.), *Strategic Management of Technostress in an Information Society*, © 1987 by C.J. Hogrefe Publishers, Inc., Toronto, p. 39. Reproduced with permission.

of technostress, including productivity levels, job involvement, responsibility or loyalty changes, creativity levels, job satisfaction, absenteeism, voluntary turnover, and accident proneness. These elements could be seen to constitute a human asset data base provided that this information is integrated with basic personnel and task environment information, as illustrated in Exhibit 14.5.

The data needed for the stress audit could be collected through questionnaires, clinical interviews, and physiological examinations (Kets de Vries, 1984). A typical questionnaire would include a stress symptom survey; an organizational survey, with questions about job demands, task characteristics, role demands, such as role conflict and ambiguity, organizational characteristics, career and performance variables, and factors related to the organizational environment, including a social readjustment rating scale (Holmes and Rahe, 1967); and personality profiles (Friedman and Rosenman, 1974).

Through parametric or multivariate statistical techniques, such as factor analysis, discriminant analysis, and multiple regression, technostress reaction patterns can be identified and relationships could be established of causal, mediating, and end result variables. Stress peaks could be identified and predicted, triggering individual and organizational preventive and corrective actions.

In summary, these three basic components—a health hazard appraisal system, a human asset data base, and stress audit reports—constitute a technostress monitoring system. A director of human resources within a hospital, for example, could routinely review these stress audit reports and recommend actions—individual or organizational—designed to prevent, mitigate, or correct dysfunctional levels of technostress.

Strategic Implementation Stage

Strategy implementation means providing a unified comprehensive framework that guides those choices that determine the strategic direction of the health care organization (Glueck and Snyder, 1982). This requires managerial skills of vision, integration, and reflection on the part of health care administrators; the design and implementation of a technology strategy involves an examination of the future impacts of technological change in an organization. Successful health care executives use reflection and feedback in implementing a relevant strategy for coping with technostress resulting from information technology. The hypothesis that orientation and control processes may be effective strategies in coping with stress and problems is supported by several studies (e.g., Newell and Simon, 1972; Meichenbaum, 1977). It is significant to design an appropriate strategy because an ineffective technostress coping strategy means that the person will either go back to the phase of strategy selection or engage in compensatory activity (Schönpflug, 1983; Lazarus, 1966, 1974).

According to the strategic choice perspective, ineffective coping may actually increase the degree of stress. Schönpflug (1983: 300–301) explains:

In the interest of coping the need for optimal selection of mediating processes arises. Competition may occur (a) within the orienting mode (e.g. whether to reduce concern for a problem rather than to search for new coping strategies), (b) within the control mode (e.g. which operation to apply), or (c) between orienting and control (e.g. a choice between the immediate application of a well-practised skill or a search for a new coping strategy).

Each process will have its costs and benefits, and the selection should be based on balancing the account to provide an optimal relation between losses and gains.... Balancing of psychological costs and benefits may be regarded as a central issue for the regulation of internal states of stress and external stressors. It is referred to ... as behavior economics.

Technostress Research

Developing research hypotheses may not only be desirable but a real necessity for adequate and further understanding of technostress management (Sethi and Schuler, 1984). Research on stress management strategies is fraught with difficulties (Burke and Weir, 1980) because coping is a complex and dynamic process with multiple decision points (Ray, Lindop, and Gibson, 1982). Nevertheless, such research efforts are underway in the attempt to capture this richness and complexity in the coping process (Folkman and Lazarus, 1980; Johansson, Aronsson, and Lundström, 1978; Johansson and Aronsson, 1984; Levi, 1984; OECD, 1983; Rada, 1980; Blumberg and Gerwin, 1984).

The area of organizational technostress represents a new and rich frontier for human resource research that could significantly affect organizational policies and procedures. Research on the social aspect of managing technological change is a major issue in an emerging health care system.

ORGANIZATIONAL CULTURE IN STRATEGIC HUMAN RESOURCE MANAGEMENT

The concept of culture is a broad one and has been used both as a metaphor and a variable in recent human resource management literature (Deal and Kennedy, 1982; Jelinek, Smircich, and Hirsch, 1983). The literature emphasizes one common point that there is some underlying structure of meaning that persists over time, constraining people's perceptions, interpretation, and behavior that we call culture. This persistent structure is simultaneously adapted and changed over time as a function of people's perception, interpretation, and behavior. The underlying structures emphasized differ: myths, unconscious organizational dynamics, or even economic transaction agreements. The process, however, is common (Jelinek, Smircich, and Hirsch, 1983).

The core element of culture rests with the dynamics of creating and sharing internal and external values. Wilkins and Ouchi (1983) recognize culture as a mode of control in the sense of a clan paradigm (such as stories, special language, and other cues) and emphasize a transaction cost perspective, but their emphasis on using culture to promote efficiency may tend to hide moral or ethical issues involved in introducing change. However, Wilkins and Ouchi (1983) and Jones (1983) provide a connection between economics and an organization's cultural processes. In their view, culture is an outcome and not a precondition. Wilkins and Ouchi do not seem to emphasize, as Jones does, that culture is the set of shared values about property rights, obligations, equity, and exchange rules. We concur with Jones that the role of shared social reality is crucial to understanding the economics of the exchange process.

According to Deal and Kennedy (1982), culture is "the integrated pattern of human behavior, that includes thought, speech, action and artifacts, and depends on man's capacity for learning and transmitting knowledge to succeeding generations." Several elements shape each organization's unique culture in coping with change:

1. The external economic, and technological environment, perhaps the most important influence in cultivating culture, since it determines what the institutions must do to be successful.
2. Values, which are the basic concepts and beliefs that an organization possesses. Values are the essence of a health care organization's philosophy for achieving successful change. They provide guidelines and a sense of direction, shared by employees and propagated by health administrators.
3. Heroes, who act to personify the values of the organization and represent its strength. These people are role models.
4. Rites and rituals, which are the "systematic and programmed" daily routines of the hospital. Rituals illustrate the expected kinds of employee behavior; rites or ceremonies provide pictures of what the hospital represents about technological change.
5. Cultural network, the most important means of communication within the hospital. Although not readily visible, this source of information exchange and its management are critical to the success of technological change. It is through this network that corporate values and myths are propagated (Deal and Kennedy, 1982).

Ulrich (1984) has argued that a culture of a given organization may be manifested through indicators such as symbols, rituals, ideologies, languages, stories, myths, relationships, and humor, although the emphasis may vary in each of these elements in different subcultures of an organization's culture. Managers can identify and reinforce desired values, which may then be manifested through cultural indicators such as stories and language. While cultural analysis can focus on ideology and values, it should also explain the nature of language and stories used to signify a given value system. For example, stories and languages may emphasize the values of conservatism or radicalism, equality or inequality, change or status quo, security or risk taking. In other words, an integrative cultural analysis of a hospital will be concerned with exploring assumptions about work and technological change of the various subcultures, and design strategies in coping with conflicts among these subcultures, in a given health care environment.

The assumption is that shared values are a cultural atlas and climate of a health care organization, and an understanding of these values will assist in introducing IT. Health administrators can use corporate culture as a positive strategy. Some of the methods that they can use may include delegation of decision making, making employees more accountable for their work, and rewarding the risk takers. In the private sector, culture is understood by large corporations such as Shell or Westinghouse as a set of the company's strategic and operating philosophy, employee attitudes and values, and work behavior. "Corporate culture," says C. W. Daniell, Shell Canada's president, "is dear to my heart these days. It has evolved from many of the changes that have occurred within the company over the past several years. We're tackling the final leg in the restructuring process, which is to change the way people think about their work" (Hubbard, 1984). One of the prime elements in this rethinking is a cultural analysis of employee values and corporate values, and as is done at Westinghouse, a combining of systems strategy with cultural analysis. "I reiterate my philosophy every day in meetings with managers," says Franz Tyaack, president of Westinghouse Canada. "You must be passionate to accomplish the goals of changing culture and entire management systems" (Hubbard, 1984).

CULTURAL ANALYSIS AND TECHNOSTRESS

Managing technostress involves strategic analysis of three components: a source (such as new computer system), a transmission (the way in which the information about the new computer is transmitted), and a user or a recipient (the characteristics, perceptions, and coping behaviors of the person or persons to whom the information is directed). The three components are interactive and help to develop a value system of an organization.

Cultural analysis can help different subcultures to become aware of various levels of technostress generated through information technology in three key ways (Ulrich, 1984; Sethi and Caro, 1987).

1. Recognition of differences among subcultures: The level of technostress will vary among different groups—top management, doctors, nurses, allied health manpower, general workers—due to different cultural perspectives
2. Modification of technostress coping practices: Since the various subgroups have different expectations, technostress management practices within the different groups should also be modified to be consistent with each subculture's values
3. Integration of subcultures: The positive mode of technostress impacts can be generated through problem-solving strategies by integrating various subcultures

The technological environment is the source of a number of stressors. The reactions to these stressors—physiological, psychological, and sociological—underlie the formation and development of the culture of a hospital. Transmission events such as control intervene between the technological stressor and the user and have further impacts on the evolution of culture within the organization (Baum, Singer, and Baum, 1981). The understanding of each of these components is helpful in developing sensitivity to the integrated management of culture in managing technostress in hospitals.

Cultural Matrix

A corporate cultural matrix can be used by health administrators and professionals to use culture as a strategy of managing technostress (Exhibit 14.6). The information system component may be subdivided into decision making, communicating, organizing, monitoring, and appraising-rewarding. "Relationships"

Exhibit 14.6
Cultural Matrix

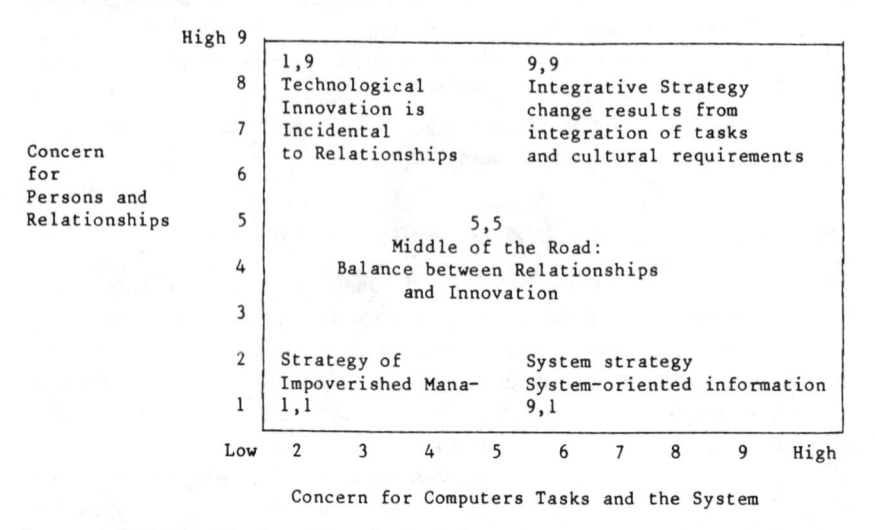

```
              High 9 ┌─────────────────────────────────────────────┐
                     │ 1,9                      9,9                │
                   8 │ Technological            Integrative Strategy│
                     │ Innovation is            change results from│
                   7 │ Incidental               integration of tasks│
  Concern            │ to Relationships         and cultural requirements│
  for                │                                             │
  Persons and      6 │                                             │
  Relationships    5 │              5,5                            │
                     │         Middle of the Road:                 │
                   4 │      Balance between Relationships          │
                     │              and Innovation                 │
                   3 │                                             │
                     │                                             │
                   2 │ Strategy of              System strategy    │
                     │ Impoverished Mana-       System-oriented information│
                   1 │ 1,1                      9,1                │
                     └─────────────────────────────────────────────┘
                Low   2    3    4    5    6    7    8    9   High

              Concern for Computers Tasks and the System
```

Source: A.S. Sethi and D. Caro, "Organizational Culture in Technostress Management," in A.S. Sethi, D. Caro, and R.S. Schuler (Eds.), *Strategic Management of Technostress in an Information Society*, © 1987 by C.J. Hogrefe, Inc., Toronto, p. 205. Reproduced with permission.

include categories such as company-wide, boss-subordinate, peer, and interdependent (Schwartz and Davis, 1981). Key values of each group are essential in assessing strategies. The completed matrix will assist in increasing cultural sensitivity to managing technostress in four key areas: adaptation to the new technology, overcoming workstation stress dealing with office automation and ergonomics, coping with workload stress involving on-the-job strain and burnout, and dealing with management stress covering the problems unique to information processing managers (McDonald, 1983).

It is essential that health administrators understand how their corporate cultures work and be able to fit them into the needs of the informational processing society in the outside world so that the organization is better able to adapt to the new demands. Cultural awareness can help to improve the introduction of change process, may improve productivity by allowing workers to feel better about their new role or job, and by providing them with guidelines for behavior congruent with the information technology. The manager can act to modify the culture by influencing desired values, creating a common vision, and providing appropriate leadership (Caro and Sethi, 1985).

CULTURAL FACTORS TO CONSIDER IN THE CHANGE PROCESS

Several cultural factors may be considered helpful in instituting IT change: putting a corporate hero in a position to implement change; creating employee dissatisfaction with existing workloads and processes, thus unfreezing them from current values; implementing transition rituals and providing transition training in new values and behavior patterns so as to give employees an idea of what is expected; using consultants to bridge the cultural gap; instituting structural changes that reveal the company's new focus in the light of new technology; and reinforcing the idea of stability despite the changing culture (Deal and Kennedy, 1982).

Some of the key questions to ask include the following:

What are the critical dynamics of our organization's environment? How do things really work?
- What trends are changing the nature of our technology? What represents the state of the art in the industry? Does it pose opportunities or threats?
- What are our competitors doing? Are they gaining competitive advantage at our expense? Are we seeking new ways to gain our own advantage?
- What do our patients really want? How do they value what we offer? Can we add greater value?
- Who are we as an organization? How do our people feel about who we are? How do they view our purpose?
- How is our organization distinctive and unique? What opportunities does our distinctiveness afford us?
- What are our most important and dominant capabilities, skills, and relationships? Can we further exploit them? Do we sufficiently understand them?
- What is our potential as an organization? Where can we be five, ten, twenty years from now?
- If I could rewrite the history of my own achievements or those of our industry, or organization, or our people, what would I change?

The most difficult part of handling technostress is altering culture. Managers who are sensitive and can manipulate the values, rituals, and heroes of the culture will have the best chance of coping with technostress. An open-systems approach to cultural analysis is recommended.

EMPLOYEE SELF-DEVELOPMENT STRATEGIES

The work of Howard, Rechnitzer, and Cunningham (1978), Lazarus (1978a), and Beehr (1984) suggests that when individuals are methodical in their analysis of stressful situations, they are more likely to produce a wide range of potentially effective coping strategies than if they are not.

It is the responsibility of human resource management to set up appropriate in-service programs to assist employees in becoming familiar with new technology. Their responsibility, however, does not stop there. They must initiate and offer alternative stress coping strategies that the person can adapt to unnecessary technodistress. Such strategies must be within an identifiable well-defined program, which we call the Employee Self-Development Program (ESP).

An ESP program consists of a number of behavioral self-management components that mitigate the effects of technodistress:

- Management practices, including time management, managerial styles, delegation, and communication behaviors (Schuler and Sethi, 1984)
- Nutritional programs
- Physical fitness programs
- Meditation programs (Sethi, 1982, 1983; Sethi and Schuler, 1984)
- Yoga programs
- Biofeedback programs (Brown, 1984)

These are examples of only a few components of employee self-development programs to increase the employee's adaptive capabilities. The provision of these options to employees becomes a key responsibility of human resources management within health care organizations. A brief overview of these strategies is given below.

Time Management

Time management practice raises several important questions for managers and organizations in new environments of technological change. If someone uses time management and actually gets more done in less time, should the individual be rewarded more? Are there enough duties to do to warrant time management programs, since they do take time, effort, and money to learn new skills required by technology? What are the gains and losses of everyone's really knowing his or her job? Do the managers really want to delegate, or will this be seen as a loss of power?

As Schuler and Sethi (1984) have pointed out, time management is a process in which an individual engages in order to accomplish or achieve the tasks or goal(s) he or she needs to and wants to that enable the individual to be effective in his or her job and career. With this process are several necessary phases, the essential theme being to identify those needs and wants in terms of importance and match them with time and resources available or potentially available.

A number of practices deal directly or indirectly with the stumbling blocks to time resources. A key practice is awareness: awareness of one's job duties, authority, and responsibility and their importance; awareness of one's own skills, needs and abilities; and awareness of how one adjusts to change generated by IT.

One technique is to review one's job description and its real meaning with one's supervisor and perhaps coworkers and subordinates. Occasionally individuals find it necessary to bring together all those individuals who have expectations, or ask favors, or make demands on them. These sessions can help clarify job authority, and responsibility expectations that these individuals have for the local individual and also help reduce expectations that these individuals have for the focal individual and also help reduce the conflict potential from these various "role" senders.

Frequently, time management problems arise because an individual just does not want to do the job. This lack of motivation may be due to the mismatch between the individual's skills, needs, or abilities and intensified by the IT change.

Another technique is related to the use and analysis of daily log activities. An individual may be an ineffective time manager but in only certain situations. In the analysis of the daily log of activities, attention should be given to the situations that can be regarded as particularly ineffective and effective. The effective situations may reveal use of effective time management practices, which can then be applied to other situations.

Nutrition

Dietary factors are of great importance in the development of disorder of the cardiovascular system. Tuchweber, Nadeau, and Perea (1987) state that malignant hypertension with hyalinizing cardiovascular and renal disease is easily elicited by stress on high-sodium diets. Chronic partial starvation produces stress (pseudohypthysectomy) accompanied by adrenal atrophy. The response of adrenal cortex is curtailed or may even break down because of malnutrition. Although more research is needed, we can conclude that the type and quality of food ingested "has definite effects upon the development of stress manifestations" (Tuchweber et al., 1987). A balanced diet is therefore an essential ingredient of a stress management strategy (Albrecht, 1979).

Physical Activity

The concern for physical activity is based on the recognized value of exercise, as both a stress reduction technique and a wellness technique for sustaining positive health. There is enough research evidence to validate this belief (Jette, 1984). Jette (1984: 220) explains:

Exercise protects the individual by enhancing the state of resistance to any stimulus so that the individual is less susceptible to the effects of stress. A higher degree of health and physical fitness will provide the individual with an "armor plating" that can repulse and absorb, with less physiological intensity, the effects of a stressful situation.

Meditation

Meditation can be used as a coping strategy. It can help increase awareness of stress and clarify perceptions about stress so that distress can be tackled with a renewed and clearer perspective.

Meditation is defined as a noncalculating mood. This mood, which may happen with the aid of a technique or spontaneously, indicates an altered state of consciousness, which is free of anxiety, tension, and distress. Meditation increases the sense of having control over one's life, and as Frankenhaeuser (1980) has found, controllability is a critical variable in moderating type A behavior in technostress management.

The recent scientific investigation of meditation has emphasized the somatic effects of meditation. Research conducted by Wallace and Benson (1972) suggests that persons in meditation experiments reveal "reductions in oxygen consumption, carbon dioxide elimination, and the rate and volume of respiration; a slight increase in the acidity of arterial blood; a marked decrease in the blood-lactate level; a slowing of the heartbeat; a considerable increase in skin resistance; and an electroencephalogram pattern of intensification of slow alpha waves with occasional theta-wave activity." According to Wallace and Benson (1972: 86–87) meditation helps to control an involuntary mechanism in the body, presumably the autonomic nervous system. "The reduction of carbon dioxide elimination might have been accounted for by a recognizable voluntary action of the subject—slowing the breathing—but such an action should not markedly affect the uptake of oxygen by the body tissues. Consequently, it was a reasonable supposition that the drop in oxygen consumption, reflecting a decrease in the need for inhaled oxygen, must be due to modification of a process not subject to manipulation in the usual sense."

Meditation can help to moderate type A behavior. Friedman and Rosenman (1974) showed that individuals with an aggressive and competitive personality profile (type A) are more than twice as prone to cardiovascular disease as those who are not so preoccupied with achievement and are less competitive (type B). These findings have been supported in Canada by studies conducted by Howard, Rechnitzer, and Cunningham (1978). The A-type person has a "coronary-prone behavior pattern" characterized by:

1. Intense, sustained achievement orientation toward self-directed but usually ill-defined objectives, to achieve more and more in less and less time (Friedman and Rosenman, 1974)
2. Strong tendency to compete and persistent desire for recognition
3. Persistent rumination about multiphasic activities
4. Extraordinary mental and physical alertness used for "activities for becoming" rather than enjoying the "joys of being"

Yoga

Yoga offers a powerful set of options for technostress management. This includes work on developing awareness and control of the physical body, emotions, mind, and interpersonal relations. Yoga is an art of mental modification and is concerned with freedom from mental disturbances. The word *yoga* means union; it implies union with the ultimate where the process of desiring has come to an end and where stress is nonexistent (Rama, Ballentine, and Ajaya, 1976; Stearn, 1965; Sethi, 1984).

Biofeedback

In biofeedback a variety of modalities can be used: EMG muscle activity and skin temperature for stress reduction; skin temperature, blood flow, pulse volume, heart rate, and blood pressure; motor unit activity used in muscle rehabilitation; and EEG components. Two types of biofeedback procedures are used: operant conditioning and augmented biofeedback. In the former, the biofeedback information is used as a reinforcement signal, and physiological changes (e.g., in heart rate or muscle tension or EEG alpha) are accumulated and averaged. In the second procedure, biofeedback information is provided on a continuous basis; it reinforces performance and has the added benefit of operating on a time scale more closely associated with physiological changes.

Biofeedback is capable of evoking fundamental normal mechanisms of the body (Brown, 1984) and is a useful technique in reducing anxiety, depression, phobias, tension headaches, drug abuse, alcoholism, and learning and perceptual problems. It can be used in conjunction with other techniques, such as progressive relaxation, autogenic training, and meditation.

NEW TECHNOLOGY-BASED STRATEGIES: IMPLICATIONS FOR SHRM

Although intuition and pragmatism should guide the health administrator in managing time and communications, there are some newly emerging techniques that he or she can use for effective performance. Current and future forms of automation and artificial intelligence systems have begun to alter the structure and process of office systems, leading to a new concept of the office of the future:

1. Teleconferencing: Teleconferencing gives the leader the ability to arrange an electronic meeting between two groups of people in distant cities. The visual and audio capabilities are supported by a computer-based information system that can receive and reproduce graphic information (Davis, 1985).

2. Networking: Although there has been phenomenal growth in the use of personal computers, managers have found some limitations in their usage (Chevreau, 1985). The focus has thus shifted to networking personal computers (PCs) as well as the bigger minicomputers, mainframes, and other devices. IBM has developed local area networks (LAN) (followed by other major computer companies) linking PCs to voice systems, telephone sets, and video devices. A further trend is toward wide area networks (WANs), which make intercity communications possible. Managers can plan their communications around a central computer system. Networking is thus the strategic tool of the future, helpful in planning time strategy and communications. This is an example of using information technology to cope and manage the impact of IT change throughout the organization.

3. Electronic mail: There is a rapidly increasing use of electronic mail, along with long-distance blackboards, computer bulletin boards, and instant transferable data (Kiesler, Siegel, and McGuire, 1984). When a manager can receive electronic mail from 10,000 employees, it changes the nature of controls, participation, and conflict resolution. It is crucial to examine the "behavioral, social and organizational processes that surround computer-mediated communication" (ibid.: 1124).

4. Integrating time management with IT change: There are several principles that can be used in effective integration of time and IT change. First, the direction and timing of IT change can be anticipated and planned. Second, leaders could ensure that time strategies are integrated in the light of criteria for successful management of IT change. "Technology priorities should dictate investment thrust. An effective use of technology leverage should avoid mismatches among strategic objectives and technology investments" (Pappas, 1984: 31).

5. Using a strategic management approach: The effectiveness of an organization depends more on the quality of time and communication strategies than on the rate of making changes. IT change can be a factor of success only if it is part of a well-defined time and communication strategy that will exploit and orient it, not only within the health care organization but also in relation to the external technological environment. Psychosociological elements of time and communications thus affect the process of technological management.

SOCIOPSYCHOLOGICAL ASPECTS OF TIME MANAGEMENT AND COMMUNICATIONS AND IMPLICATIONS FOR SHRM

The use of electronic mail and computer-mediated communication can help health administrators in planning their time resource as well as reorder the communication process. A number of research questions are raised in regard to the appropriate use of electronic devices in time and information management. Kiesler et al. (1984: 1124–26) have posed five key questions with regard to psychological and social aspects of computer-mediated communication insofar as SHRM is concerned:

1. Does rapid electronic communication alter the quantity, distribution, or timing of information exchanged?

2. Does computer communication reduce coordination of communication and weaken social influence by the absence of nonverbal cues, such as head nods, eye contact, touching, and gesturing?

3. Does computer communication reduce the influence of charismatic and high-status people by allowing organizational members to participate equally by ignoring vertical hierarchy in social relationships?

4. Does electronic communication encourage depersonalization?

5. How do people develop communication network social norms and etiquettes governing its use?

According to Kiesler et al. (1984: 1126) computer-mediated communication has at least two interesting characteristics: a paucity of social context information and few widely shared norms governing its use. They explain how communication may be affected in at least three areas:

First, the lack of social feedback and unpredictable style of messages might make it difficult to coordinate and comprehend messages.... Second, social influence among communicators might become more equal because so much hierarchical dominance and power information is hidden.... Third, social standards will be less important and communication will be more impersonal and more free because the rapid exchange of text, the lack of social feedback, and the absence of norms governing the social interaction redirect attention away from others and toward the message itself. Indeed, computer-mediated communication seems to comprise some of the same conditions that are important for the reindividuation anonymity, reduced self-regulation, and reduced self-awareness. (1126)

The results of experiments conducted by Kiesler et al. (1984: 1131) suggest that "the lack of nonverbal involvement is a critical dimension of electronic communication." Another important finding is that electronic communication encourages uninhibited behavior. Group decisions may also be affected as persons tend to participate more openly and equally. Future research is needed to explore many of the implications for SHRM to assist the administrator in using modern technology in increasing organizational efficiency and effectiveness. It might be possible to turn computer networks into socially supportive human resource networks.

GUIDELINES FOR ADMINISTRATORS AND PROFESSIONALS

Technostress refers to the inability to adapt and to cope with anxiety resulting from demands and pressures from information systems technology. The proposition is that based on strategic planning strategies of the corporation, health care executives may develop a vision of the future to create a cultural climate in their environments in which technological change can take place smoothly and effectively.

The assumption of this proposition is that progressive executives are able to define strategy and develop culture at the individual employee and organizational levels; they have a vision of the future for their corporation and are able to integrate strategy with culture in order to forge the change process effectively. The following guidelines are recommended:

1. *Plan technostress strategy and culture.* During the early period of computer introduction, strategy and culture tend to be separate unless they are coordinated by key

leaders of the corporation. Administrators and professionals should develop creative insight, sensitivity, and vision.

2. *Monitor technostress strategy and culture as an integrated process.* New computers demand a new culture. Any growth-oriented organization whose goal is to innovate and cater to changing health needs of the population needs to weigh the consequences for its culture carefully. Time and money will be needed to develop the new culture based on new value orientations. Vision and patience are needed.

3. *Alter technostress strategy and culture.* In order to prevent negative impacts of IT, a strategic approach is needed by changing values underlying culture and strategy, "but too much or too little will destroy the organization" (Hickman and Silva, 1984: 38). Insight, versatility, and focus are important.

4. *Adjust technostress strategy and culture.* In order for health care organizations to implement information technologies successfully, they need to employ strategies of adaptation on an ongoing basis within their environmental contexts. Hickman and Silva (1984: 39) report: "Perennially excellent organizations feed off common purpose, satisfied customers, distinctive competence at delivering products and services, dominance over competitors, and consistency in hiring and keeping good people—but they must constantly withstand the threats of a changing environment. Strategy must assume a reinforcing role to bolster the culture and adapt it to the changing environment."

Flexibility and adaptation to change thus become important elements of a hospital environment.

Utilize Technostress Coping Skills

Key skills can be developed to enable health administrators to increase their ability to develop culture to manage technostress. Skills to be promoted include cultural sensitivity, a vision of the future, and the development of executive commitment and patience to organizational ethos. These skills are needed to develop and integrate technostrategy and culture for successful management of technological change in health care.

Implementing new technological changes successfully in the health care organization requires not only strategic decision making but also monitoring and evaluating skills to ensure that technological strategies are implemented in a productive manner that presents uncertainties in a technological implementation process. An effective monitoring system would assess both negative and positive impacts of new technology on the worker as well as on the patient. The "quality monitoring organization" thus becomes an essential part of the overall planning of new technology (Toffler, 1985: 143–44).

THE FUTURE CHALLENGE OF INFORMATION TECHNOLOGY FOR SHRM

Information system technological innovations and their introduction in hospitals and health care systems require vision and reflection. The change is astonishingly rapid, causing value shifts and value conflicts among administrators and professionals in the organization. Toffler (1985: 101) states:

The new technology is driving us not toward an Orwellian world of robotized, standardized, monotonic societies, but toward the most highly differentiated social structures in history, each of which produces its own transient subsystems of values within the larger framework of society. Corporations will have to accommodate themselves to small, short-lived sub-cultural groupings, each busily expressing, propagating and attempting to effectuate its unique value set. Overlapping, conflicting, and randomly reinforcing one another, these value sets will face corporate personnel with enormous difficulties of choice and will impose extreme pressure on the integration of both personal and corporate identity and roles.

The health care executive measures his or her vision through reflections on the role and vision of new technology and how to develop the ability to cope with the impacts of technology in an emerging integrated health care system. SHRM needs to take these impacts into account.

SUMMARY

Health care organizations that can continually adapt and implement change on a strategic basis (forward looking with a long-term perspective, exhibiting patience and sensitivity to the cultures of their organizational environments) will have a competitive edge through effective management of technostress and technodistress in introducing new information technology. Technostress management is an integral part of strategic HRM.

The future health care executive will need insight skills to adapt to technological impacts. This insight, as Toffler (1985) points out, will require an imaginative and thinking reorientation, toward "the creation of fully integrated planning machinery from the supra-corporate to the sub-corporate level; the addition of socio-cultural information and models to the present economic data base; and the development of new methods involving a shift from aggregate toward more sub-aggregate planning, from linear toward more non-linear projection, and from quantitative toward more qualitative materials" (Toffler, 1985: 166). The future health care executive will need insights to unify strategy and culture in coping with the tremendous impacts of information technology (Bennis, 1968; Zaleznik, 1977). SHRM will be needed to adapt to this technological imperative.

NOTE

1. Portions of this chapter originally appeared in A. S. Sethi, D. Caro, and R. S. Schuler (Eds.), *Strategic Management of Technostress in an Information Society.* © 1987 by C. J. Hogrefe Publishers, Inc., Toronto. Reproduced by permission of the publisher.

REFERENCES

Alcalay, R., and Pasick, R. J. (1983). Psychsocial factors and the technologies of work. *Social Science Medicine* 17 (16): 1075–84.

Albrecht, K. (1979). *Stress and the Manager*. Englewood Cliffs, N.J.: Prentice-Hall.

Anderson, C. R., and Paine, F. R. (1975, December). Managerial perceptions and strategic behavior. *Academy of Management Journal* 18: 811–23.

Applebaum, S. H. (1984, January–February). Organizational climate audit. *Hospital and Health Services Administration*, 51–70.

Atkinson, J. W. (1964). *An Introduction to Motivation*. Princeton, N.J.: D. Van Nostrand Co.

Attewell, P., and Rule, J. (1984). Computing and organizations: What we know and what we don't know. *Communications of the ACM* 17 (12): 1184–92.

Bain, J. S. (1968). *Industrial Organization*. New York: John Wiley.

Baum, A., Singer, J. E., and Baum, C. S. (1981). Stress and the environment. *Journal of Social Issues* 37 (1): 4–35.

Beehr, T. A. (1984). Stress coping research: Methodological issues. In A. S. Sethi and R. S. Schuler (Eds.), *Handbook of Organizational Stress Coping Strategies*, 277–300. Cambridge, Mass.: Ballinger.

Beehr, T. A., and Newman, J. E. (1978). Job stress, employees health and organizational effectiveness: A facet analysis, model and literature review. *Personnel Psychology* 31 (4): 665–99.

Beer, M. (1980). *Organization Change and Development: A Systems View*. Santa Monica, Calif.: Goodyear Publishing Co.

Benjamin, R., Rockart, J. F., Morton, M. S., and Wyman, J. (1984). Information technology: A strategic opportunity. *Sloan Management Review*, 3: 10.

Bennis, W. (1968). *The Temporary Society*. New York: Harper & Row.

Blumberg, M., and Gerwin, D. (1984). Coping with advanced manufacturing technology. *Journal of Occupational Behavior* 5: 113–30.

Braybrooke, O., and Lindblom, C. E. (1970). *A Strategy of Decision*. New York: Free Press.

Brief, A. P., Schuler, R. S., and Van Sell, M. (1980). *Managing Job Stress*. Boston: Little, Brown.

Brod, C. (1982, October). Managing technostress: Optimizing the use of computer technology. *Personnel Journal*, 753–56.

——— (1984). *Technostress: The Human Cost of the Computer Revolution*. Reading, Mass.: Addison-Wesley.

Brown, B. B. (1984). Stress coping through biofeedback. In A. S. Sethi and R. S. Schuler (Eds.), *Handbook of Organizational Stress Coping Strategies*. Cambridge, Mass.: Ballinger.

Burke, R. J., and Weir, T. (1980). Coping with the stress of managerial occupations. In C. L. Cooper and R. L. Payne (Eds.), *Current Concerns in Occupational Stress*, 299–335. Chichester: John Wiley.

Canada Tomorrow Conference (1983, November 6–9) (1984). *Summary*. Ottawa: Supply and Services.

Caro, D., and Sethi, A. S. (1985). The strategic management of technostress: The chaining of Prometheus. *Journal of Medical Systems* 9 (5–6): 291–304.

Chevreau, J. (1985, March 1). Personal computer is driving the trend toward networking. *Globe and Mail*.
Child, J. (1972, January). Organizational structure, environment and performance: The role of strategic choice. *Sociology* 6: 1–22.
Crozier, M. (1964). *The Bureaucratic Phenomenon*. Chicago: University of Chicago Press.
Cyert, R. M., and March, J. G. (1963). *A Behavioral Theory of the Firm*. Englewood Cliffs, N.J.: Prentice-Hall.
Davis, Ted (1985, March 1). Teleconferencing services still growing in Canada. *Globe and Mail*.
Deal, T. E., and Kennedy, A. A. (1982). *Corporate Cultures: The Rites and Rituals of Corporate Life*. Reading, Mass.: Addison- Wesley.
Dunham, R. B. (1984). *Organizational Behavior*. Homewood, Ill.: Richard D. Irwin.
Feeney, D. (1986). Introduction: Health care technology. In D. Feeney, G. Gisyatt, and P. Tugwell (Eds.), *Health Care Technology: Effectiveness, Efficiency, and Public Policy*, 1–4. Halifax: Institute for Research on Public Policy.
Feigenbaum, E., and McCorduck, P. (1983). *The Fifth Generation*. Reading, Mass.: Addison-Wesley.
Festinger, L., Pepitone, A., and Newcomb, T. (1952). Some consequences of deindividuation in a group. *Journal of Abnormal and Social Psychology* 47: 382–89.
Folkman, S., and Lazarus, R. S. (1980). An analysis of coping in a middle aged community sample. *Journal of Health and Social Behavior* 21: 219–39.
Forsyth, D. R. (1983). *An Introduction to Group Dynamics*. Monterey, Calif.: Brooks/Cole.
Frankenhaeuser, M. (1979). *Living in a Technified Society: Stress Tolerance and Cost of Adaptation*. (In Swedish.) Psychological Institute, University of Stockholm.
Frankenhaeuser, M., and Johansson, G. (1981). On the psychophysiological consequence of understimulation and overstimulation. In L. Levi (Ed.), *Society, Stress and Disease*, vol. 4: *Working Life*. Oxford: Oxford University Press.
——— (1980). Psychoneuroendocrine approaches to the study of stressful person-environment transactions. In H. Selye (Ed.), *Selye's Guide to Stress Research*, 46–70. New York: Van Nostrand Reinhold.
Fraser, T. M. (1983). *Human Stress, Work and Job Satisfaction*. Geneva: ILO.
French, W. L, and Bell, C. H., Jr. (1983). A definition of organizational development. In W. L. French, C. H. Bell, Jr., and R. B. Zawack (Eds.), *Organizational Development*, 27–30. Plano, Tex.: Business Publications.
French, W. L., Bell, C. H., Jr., and Zawack, R. B. (Eds.) (1983). *Organizational Development*. Plano, Tex.: Business Publications.
Friedman, M., and Rosenman, R. H. (1974). *Type A Behavior and Your Heart*. New York: Knopf.
Gibson, J. L., Ivancevich, J. M., and Donnelly, J. M. (1985). *Organization*. Plano, Tex.: Business Publications.
Glueck, W. F., and Snyder, N. (1982). *Readings in Business Policy and Strategy*. New York: McGraw-Hill.
Goh, S. C. (1985). Uncertainty, power and organizational decision making: A constructive replication and some extensions. *Canadian Journal of Administrative Sciences* 2 (1): 177–91.
Hacker, W., Plath, H. E., Richter, P., and Zimmer, K. (1978). Internal representation

of task structure and mental load of work: Approaches and methods of assessment. *Ergonomics* 21: 187-94.
Hickman, C. R., and Silva, M. A. (1984). *Creating Excellence*. New York: New American Library.
Hinings, C. R., Hickson, D. J., Pennings, J. M., and Schneck, R. E. (1974). Structural conditions of intraorganizational power. *Administrative Science Quarterly* 19: 22-44.
Holmes, T. H., and Rahe, R. H. (1967). The social readjustment rating scale. *Journal of Psychosomatic Research* 11: 213-18.
Howard, J., Rechnitzer, P. A., and Cunningham, D. A. (1978). *Rusting Out, Burning Out and Bowing Out*. Toronto: Macmillan.
Hubbard, J. (1984, December 8). More firms learn the value of corporate culture. *Globe and Mail*.
International Labour Organization (1984). *Automation, Work Organization and Occupational Stress*. Geneva: ILO.
Ivancevich, J. M., and Mattison, M. T. (1980). *Stress and Work: A Managerial Perspective*. Glenview, Ill.: Scott Foresman.
Jelinek, M., Smircich, L., and Hirsch, P. (1983). Introduction: A Code of Many Colors. *Administrative Science Quarterly* 28: 331-38.
Jette, M. (1984). Stress coping through physical activity. In A. S. Sethi and R. S. Schuler (Eds.), *Handbook of Organizational Stress Coping Strategies*, 215-31. Cambridge, Mass.: Ballinger.
Johansson, G., and Aronsson, G. (1984, July). Stress reactions in computerized administrative work. *Journal of Occupational Behavior* 5 (3): 159-81.
Johansson, G., Aronsson, G., and Ludström, B. O. (1979). Social psychological and neuroendocrine stress reactions in highly mechanized work. *Ergonomics* 21: 583.
Jones, G. R. (1983). Transaction costs, property rights, and organizational culture: An exchange. *Administrative Science Quarterly* 28: 454-67.
Kets de Vries, M.F.R. (1979, Fall). Organizational stress: A call for management action. *Sloan Management Review* 1.
——— (1984). Organizational stress management strategies: The stress audit. In A. S. Sethi and R. S. Schuler (Eds.), *Handbook of Organizational Stress Coping Strategies*, 251-75. Cambridge, Mass.: Ballinger.
Kiesler, S., Siegel, J., and McGuire, T. W. (1984). Social aspects of computer-mediated communication. *American Psychologist* 39 (10): 1123-34.
Kluckhohn, C. et al. (1951). Value and value-orientations in the theory of action: An exploration in definition and classification. In T. Parsons and E. Shils (Eds.), *Toward a General Theory of Action*. Cambridge, Mass.: Harvard University Press.
Kochan, T. A., McKersie, R. B., and Capelli, P. (1984). Strategic choice and industrial relations theory. *Industrial Relations* 23 (1): 16-39.
Landes, D. S. (1969). *The Unbored Prometheus: Technological Change and Industrial Development in Western Europe from 1750 to the Present*. Cambridge: Cambridge University Press.
Lazarus, R. S. (1974). Psychological stress and coping in adaptation and illness. *International Journal of Psychiatry in Medicine* 5: 321-33.
——— (1978a, November 3-6). *The stress and coping paradigm*. Paper presented to The Critical Evaluation of Behavioral Paradigms for Psychiatric Science, Conference, Glendon Beach, Oregon.

——— (1978b). *The Stress and the Coping Process.* New York: McGraw-Hill.
Levi, L. (1984). *Stress in Industry.* Geneva: ILO.
Lippitt, G. L. (1982). *Organizational Renewal.* Englewood Cliffs, N.J.: Prentice-Hall.
McClelland, D. (1953). *The Achievement Motive.* New York: Appleton-Century-Crofts.
McDonald, T. F. (1983, September). Technostress links inside every manager. *Data Management*, 10–14.
McLean, A. A. (1979). *Work Stress.* Reading, Mass.: Addison-Wesley.
Mann, F. C., and Williams, L. K. (1960). Observations in the dynamics of a change to electronic data processing equipment. *Administrative Science Quarterly* 5: 217–76.
Meichenbaum, D. (1977). *Cognitive Behavior Modification: An Integrative Approach.* New York: Plenum.
Miles, R. E., and Snow, C. C. (1978). *Organizational Strategy, Structure and Process.* New York: McGraw-Hill.
Mintzberg, H. (1983). *Power in and around Organizations.* Englewood Cliffs, N.J.: Prentice-Hall.
Mumford, E. (1981). *Values Technology and Work.* The Hague: Martinies Nijhoff Publishers.
Naylor, J. C., Pritchard, R. D., and Ilgen, D. R. (1980). *A Theory of Behavior in Organizations*, 251–68. New York: Academic Press.
Newell, A., and Simon, H. A. (1972) *Human Problem Solving.* Englewood Cliffs, N.J.: Prentice-Hall.
Organization for Economic Cooperation and Development (1983). *The Impact of Industrial Robots on the Manufacturing Industries of Member Countries.* Paris: OECD.
Pappas, C. (1984). Strategic management of technology. *Journal of Productivity Innovation Management* 1: 30–35.
Pettigrew, A. M. (1973). *The Politics of Organizational Decision Making.* London: Tavistock.
Pfeffer, J., Salancik, G. R, and Leblebeci, H. (1976). The effect of uncertainty on the use of social influence in organizational decision making. *Administrative Science Quarterly* 21: 227–45.
Porter, M. (1980). *Competitive Strategy.* New York: Free Press.
Pratt, J. W., Raiffa, H., and Schlaifer, R. O. (1976). The foundation of decisions under uncertainty: An elementary exposition. In V.M.R. Tummala and R. C. Henshaw (Eds.), *Concepts and Applications of Modern Decision Models.* East Lansing: Michigan State University.
Rada, J. (1980). *The Impact of Micro-Electronics.* Geneva: ILO.
Raiffa, H. (1970). *Decision Analysis.* Reading, Mass.: Addison-Wesley.
Rama, S., Ballentine, R., and Ajaya, S. (1976). *Yoga and Psychotherapy.* Honesdale, Pa.: Himalayan International Institute of Yoga Science and Philosophy.
Ray, C., Lindop, J., and Gibson, S. (1982). The concept of coping. *Psychological Medicine* 12: 385–95.
Rumelt, R. P. (1979). Evaluation of strategy: Theory and models. In D. E. Schendel and C. W. Hofer (Eds.), *Strategic Management*, 196–215. Boston: Little, Brown.
Schlaifer, R. O. (1967). *Analysis of Decisions under Uncertainty.* New York: McGraw-Hill.
Schönpflug, W. (1983). Coping efficiency and situational demands. In R. Hockey (Ed.), *Stress and Fatigue in Human Performance*, 299–326. New York: John Wiley.

Schuler, R. S. (1984). *Personnel and Human Resource Management*. 2d ed. St. Paul, Minn.: West Publishing Company.

Schwartz, H., and Davis S. (1981, Summer). Matching corporate culture and business strategy. *Organizational Dynamics*, 30–48.

Selye, H. (1974). *Stress without Distress*. Philadelphia: J. B. Lippincott.

────── (1976). *The Stress of Life*. New York: McGraw-Hill.

Sethi, A. S. (1982, July–August). Stress coping. *Canadian Journal of Public Health* 734: 267–71.

────── (1983). Stress coping strategies: The role of meditation. In H. Selye (Ed.), *Selye's Guide to Stress Research*, 164–81. New York: Van Nostrand Reinhold.

────── (1984). Yoga for coping with organizational stress. In A. S. Sethi and R. S. Schuler (Eds.), *Handbook of Organizational Stress Coping Strategies*, 167–83. Cambridge, Mass.: Ballinger.

Sethi, A. S., and Caro, D. (1987). Organizational culture in technostress management. In A. S. Sethi, D. Caro, and R. S. Schuler (Eds.), *Strategic Management of Technostress in an Information Society*, 200–212. Toronto: Hogrefe International Inc.

Sethi, A. S., and Schuler, R. S. (1984). Organizational stress coping: Research issues and future directions. In A. S. Sethi and R. S. Schuler (Eds.), *Handbook of Organizational Stress Coping Strategies*, 301–7. Cambridge, Mass.: Ballinger.

Sethi, A. S., Caro, D., and Schuler, R. S. (Eds.) (1987). *Strategic Management of Technostress in an Information Society*. Toronto: Hogrefe International Inc.

Simon, H. A. (1957). *Administrative Behavior*. New York: Free Press.

Smircich, L. (1983, September). Concepts of culture and organization analysis. *Administrative Science Quarterly* 28 (3): 339–58.

Stearn, J. (1964). *Yoga, Youth and Reincarnation*. New York: Bantam Books.

Tapscott, D., Henderson, D., and Greenberg, M. (1984). *Planning for Integrated Office Systems*. Toronto: Holt, Rinehart & Winston.

Toffler, A. (1985). *The Adaptive Corporation*. New York: McGraw-Hill.

Tuchweber, B., Nadeau, M., and Perea, A. (1987). Nutritional strategies for technostress management. In A. S. Sethi, D. Caro, and R. S. Schuler (Eds.), *Strategic Management of Technostress in an Information Society*, 229–50. Toronto: Hogrefe International.

Turner, J. (1987). Integrated information systems: Work design and ergonomic strategies. In A. S. Sethi, D. Caro, and R. S. Schuler (Eds.), *Strategic Management of Technostress in an Information Society*. Toronto: Hogrefe International.

Turner, J. A., and Karasek, R. A. (1984). Software ergonomics: Effects of computer application, design parameters on operator task performance and health. *Ergonomics* 27 (6): 663–90.

Ulrich, W. L. (1984, Summer). HRM and culture: History, ritual, and myth. *Human Resource Management* 23 (2): 117–28.

Von Neuman, J., and Morgenstern, O. (1947). *Theory of Games and Economic Behavior*. Princeton, N.J.: Princeton University Press.

Wallace, R., and H. Benson (1972, February). The physiology of meditation. *Scientific American*, 84–90.

Weizenbaum, J. (1976). *Computer Power and Human Reason*. New York: W. H. Freeman.

Wereneke, D. (1983). *Microelectronics and Office Jobs*. Geneva: ILO.

Wilkins, A. (1983, Autumn). Looking at organizational cultures. *Organizational Dynamics*.
Wilkins, A. L., and Ouchi, W. G. (1983). Efficient cultures: Exploring the relationship between culture and organizational performance. *Administrative Science Quarterly* 28: 468–81.
Winner, L. (1977). *Autonomous Technology*. Cambridge, Mass.: MIT Press.
Wolf, C. P. (1983, September-October), What is social impact assessment. *Social Impact Assessment Newsletter* 11: 83–84.
Zaleznik, A. (1977, May–June). Managers and leaders: Are they different? *Harvard Business Review* 3: 67–68.

Index

Ability requirements scales, 70
Acceptance, cooperative, 262
Accreditation, recruiting efforts and, 87
Accrediting Commission on Education for Health Services Administration (ACEHSA), 87
Acquired immune deficiency syndrome (AIDS), 236–37; as employment handicap, 243; refusal to work with victim of, 242
Action-research model, 226
Adaptability, 230
Administrative control, performance appraisal as means of, 100
Administrator(s): employee rights and, 265–69; job analysis and design and, 72; managerial competence of, 228; occupational safety and health and, 244–46; organizational development and, 231–33; technostress management and, 327–28. *See also* Management; Manager(s)
Advancement opportunities for home aides, 205
Advertisements, employment, 81–85
AET, 70–71
Affirmative action: effect on goal development and planning, 34; federal funding and, 269n5; for handicapped, 250–51, 260–61; legal status of, 259–60, 264; practical effect of, 259; quota approach to, 259, 271n39; recruitment and, 77, 79, 88, 92; theory behind, 250
Age: job satisfaction and, 188; labor force distribution according to, 9
Age Discrimination in Employment Act (ADEA) of 1967, 76, 250, 260
Agencies: employment and outplacement, 86; home care service, 216
Aides. *See* Home care industry
AIDS. *See* Acquired immune deficiency syndrome (AIDS)
Aid to Families of Dependent Children, 86
Albermarle Paper Company v. *Moody*, 47
Alcohol testing, preemployment, 261–62
Alienation, work, 178–80
American Compensation Association, 133
American Federation of State, County, and Municipal Employees, 277
American Hospital Association, 134
American Medical Association (AMA), 121
American Nurses Association (ANA), 166, 238, 277

American Productivity Center, 133
American Society of Hospital Marketing and Public Relations, 85
Analysis, job. *See* Job analysis
Antidiscrimination laws, state, 244, 250
Anti-kickback rule, 121
Antitrust laws and lawsuits, 150, 160
Applicant log, 91
Applicants, walk-in, 88, 92
Appraisal forms, 105–6
Arbitration, 249, 276, 295
Arline case, 242–43
Arrest records, racial discrimination and, 273*n*63
Asbestos, 236
Assembly line production techniques, 48
Assessment, 3, 4–5
Attitude, 230
Attorneys, contingency fee arrangements for, 272*n*58
Audit, stress, 314–16
Augmented biofeedback, 325
Autonomous work group, 50, 190
Autonomy, employee, 49
Average length of stay (ALOS) for circulatory diseases, 200
Awareness, time management and, 322

Bargaining, good faith, 277–78. *See also* Collective bargaining
Barnes Hospital, 134–35
Base salary rate, 136, 151
Behavior economics, 316
Belief, degree of, 306
Benchmark jobs, 155
Benefits for home aides, 204
Biofeedback, 325
Blind advertisements, 83–84
Blueprint planning, 16
Board of trustees, 139
Bona-fide occupational qualifications (BFOQs), 257
Bonuses, 128, 141
Bonus plans, 132
Breach of employment contract: implied in fact, 252; implied in law, 253
Briggs v. *City of Madison*, 166
Brito v. *Zia Company*, 47

Bureaucratic orientation, 59
Bureau of Labor Statistics, 160
Burnson, Robert, 90

Cable Employment Network, 82
Canada, 48; recruitment laws in, 76; technological revolution in, 312
Canada Labor Code, 48
Canadian Human Rights Code, 48
Career counseling, 189
Career development, quality of worklife and, 188–90
Career pathing, 189
Career performance planning, 3, 4
Career planning programs, 79–80
Career stages, 188
Center for Disease Control (CDC), 237
Change(s): operational, 30–32; organizational, 191–93. *See also* Organizational development (OD)
Chart, replacement, 30, 31
Charter of Rights, 48
Chicago Hearing Society, 89
Chicago Lighthouse for the Blind, 88–89
Chicago Tribune, 82
Chief executive officer (CEO), 138
Chief financial officer, 139
Chief operating officer, 139
Chief planning officer, 139
Child care, recruitment and, 89
Child labor, 249, 256
Choice, strategic, 6–8
Circuit breakers, 144
Circulatory diseases, average length of stay for, 200
Civil Rights Act (1964), 166; Title VII of, 76, 241–42, 244, 250, 256–59
Civil rights movement, 276
Civil Service Reform Act of 1978, 278
CODAP, 68
Cognitive job elements, 52
Collective bargaining, xii, 193, 275–99; in changing economic environment, 295–96; collective bargaining agreement, 275; conduct of negotiations, 290–93; development of, 276–77; effects on planning, 33; emergence of, 249; guidelines for practitioners, 296–

Index

99; implications of, 275–76; labor organizations and, 277; legal framework for, 277–83, 293–95; preparation for, 283–88; safety issues in, 238; stages of, 288–90; unrealistic expectations in, 291
College recruiting programs, 87
Communicable diseases as employment handicap, 242–43
Communication: career development programs and, 189–90; computer-mediated, sociopsychological aspects of, 326–27; organizational change and, 192; performance-based pay system and, 130, 137; quality of worklife and, 177, 194
Comparable worth, 165–68, 267; Equal Pay Act and, 256
Comparable Worth Task Force, 150
Compensation, x-xi, 8, 34–35; deferred, 121, 132; executive, 163–64; human resource planning and, 17; incentive, 120–22, 163; job analysis and, 46; physician, 163; time to fill vacancies and, 81. *See also* Pay systems, performance-based
Compensation system design, 147–75; assessing effectiveness of, 162–63; comparable worth and, 165–68; corporate and regional office mandates and, 149; employee involvement in acceptance of, 164, 170; government control of wage rates and, 149–51; growing vs. mature business and, 157; guidelines for administrators, 168–71; implementation of, 171; job hierarchy vs. separate groupings and, 157–58; maintenance program for, 162; objectives of, 151; pay equity and, 158–61, 165–68; paying individuals, 161–62; pay philosophy establishment, 168–69; pay satisfaction and, 164–65; quality control and, 149; scope of, 157–58; secrecy and, 164; shortages of professional workers and, 148–49; unskilled workers and, 149. *See also* Job evaluation
Competition: among health care organizations, 2; in home care industry, 206; performance-based pay systems and, 128–29
Complaints, safety, 243–44
Comprehensive Employment and Training Act (CETA), 86
Compressed workweek, 191
Conditioning, operant, 325
Confidentiality, disciplinary action and, 267
Conrail v. *Darrone*, 271n47
Consultants, outside, 139
Consumer acceptance, 181
Consumer Credit Protection Act, 261
Contingency fee arrangements for attorneys, 272n58
Contract(s): breach of, 252, 253; express, 252; federal, 46; management preparation for bargaining and, 284; no-strike clause in, 280; performance appraisal as, 96; theories, 252–53; wage, 164
Control systems, job design and redesign strategies, 59, 60
Cooperative Home Care Associates (CHCA), 213–14, 216
Cooperative systems, 262–63
Corporate culture, 318–19
Corporate office, influence on pay decisions, 149
Cost(s), health: home care industry and, 198–200; of hospitalization, 200–201; regulation of, 150
Cost containment, 120–21, 180; occupational safety and health concerns of employees and, 237–38
Counsel, general, 139
Counseling, career, 189
County of Washington, Oregon v. *Gunther*, 166
Couples, dual career, 90
Critical incident technique (CIT), 69–70
Cultural analysis, technostress and, 319–20
Cultural matrix, 319–20
Cultural network, 318
Culture, organizational, 8, 317–21
Cybernetics, 6

Daily log activities, 323
Data collection phase of OD, 226
Data preparation for collective bargaining, 283–85
Decision making, participative, 33–34, 178. *See also* Participative management
Defamation, 254–55, 266
Deferred compensation, 121, 132
Delphi approach, 26
Demographics, 8–10; examination of, 33; home care industry and, 198–201
Design, job. *See* Job design
Deutsch, Shea & Evans (advertising firm), 84
Diagnostic phase of OD process, 226, 229
Diagnostic related groups (DRGs), reimbursement by, 150, 227, 237
Dictionary of Occupational Titles, 67
Discharge from employment, 268; wrongful, 255
Discipline, employee, 267; to maintain safety, 244–45
Discrimination, 264–65; age, 76, 250, 260; handicap, 76; in performance appraisal, 96; pregnancy, 76, 251, 260, 263, 271n45; race and national origin, 257–58, 273n63; religious, 259; sex, 166, 258–59, 263
Discriminatory effect, intent vs., 257–58
Diseases, communicable, in workplace, 236–37, 242–43
Dissatisfaction, work, 179
Distress, intentional infliction of emotional, 254, 270n15
Documentation: disciplinary action and, 267; for performance appraisal, 111
Domain sampling approach, 70
DRGs, 150, 227, 237
Drug screening, preemployment, 261–62, 266
Dual career couples, 90

Economic conditions, 11
Economics, behavior, 316
Economic variables, preparation for collective bargaining and, 285

Economy: collective bargaining and, 295–96; effects of changes in, 34
Education, continuing, 229
Educational institutions, recruitment through, 87
Electronic mail, 326
Emergency response protocols, 240
Employee(s): control over performance, 138; handicapped, 46; minority, underrepresentation of, 259; models of behavior of, 164–65; occupational safety and health concerns of, 237–38; participation in managerial decisions, 33–34, 88, 106–7, 164, 170; protection for filing safety complaints, 243–44; reaction to jobs, 50–53; records of, privacy laws affecting, 261; reduction in force and relations with, 36; self-development strategies, 321–25; transitions, 27–29. *See also* Labor force; Personnel; Rights, employee
Employee health service (EHS), 239–40
Employment agencies, private, 86
Employment-at-will doctrine, 248–49, 251
Employment demand, forecasting, 20–26; long-term, 23–26; short-term, 20–23
Employment Equity Act of 1986, 48, 76
Employment leasing, 90–91
Employment services, state, 86
Ends goals, 35
Entrepreneurial approach, performance-based pay systems and, 129
Environment, external, 8–13; assessment of, 32–34; demographics, 8–10; economic conditions, 11; government regulations, 13; information technology, 11–13; job preference, 10–11; OD efforts on, 229; perception of, 8; value systems, 13
Environment, internal, 8
Environmental Protection Administration (EPA), 237
Environmental scanning, 33
Equal employment opportunity: internal recruitment and, 79; litigation, 264–65
Equal Employment Opportunity Act of 1972, 76

Index

Equal Employment Opportunity Commission, 166
Equal opportunity laws, recruitment methods and, 88
Equal Pay Act (1963), 249, 256
Equifinality, concept of, 16
Ergonomic approach to job design and redesign, 56
ERISA, 253
Executive compensation, 163–64
Executive Order 11246, 269n6
Executive Order 11375, 166
Executive search firms, 86
Express contract, 252
Extended CIT, 69–70
External equity, 160–61
External supply, staffing needs and, 35

Face saving, in negotiations, 292
Fact finding, 295
Factor comparison, 152, 154–55, 159
"Failure to exhaust internal remedies" defense, 268
Fair Employment Standards Act of 1938, 249
Fair Labor Standards Act, 151, 255–56
Federal contracts, 46
Federal factor evaluation system, 172n3
Federal Mediation and Conciliation Service (FMCS), 280–81
Federal Privacy Act of 1974, 261
Federal-State Employment Service, 86
Feedback, 49; employee motivation and, 111; performance appraisal and, 107, 111, 114–15
Fee-for-service basis (FFS), 163
Fetal protection policies, 241–42
Fifth Report to the President and Congress on the Status of Health Personnel in the United States, 33
Finances, personal employee, 261
Financing of home care industry, 206–7, 217
Flextime, 91, 190
Ford Foundation Home Care Project, 212–13, 216
Forecasting employment demand, 20–26; long-term, 23–26; short-term, 20–23

Forms, appraisal, 105–6
Functional job analysis (FJA), 67
Future demand, internal supply and, 35

Gain sharing, 131–32
Galstad, Robin, 89
Gender model of worker behavior, 164–65
General counsel, 139
Gilbert v. *General Elec.*, 269n7
Goal(s), health care: determining, 228; job design and, 44; performance measure and, 140–41; planning and, 34–36; setting, 35
Good faith bargaining, 277–78; strikes and, 281
"Good old boys" network, 87
Government: control of wage rates, 149–51; regulations, 13
Grade creep, 154
Grading (position) classification system of job evaluation, 152–54
Grievance procedures, 268–69, 276
Griggs v. *Duke Power and Light*, 257
Growth need strength, 50
Guidelines-oriented job analysis (GOJA), 70

Half, Robert, 81, 84
Handicap, communicable diseases as, 242–43
Handicapped employee, 46; affirmative action for, 250–51, 260–61; discrimination protection for, 76; facilities for, 90; reasonable accommodation of, 260–61; recruitment of, 88, 89; referrals for, 88–89
Harassment, sexual, 258–59, 271n34
Hay Guide Chart Profile Method, 155–57
Hay Plan Compensable Factors, 67–68, 152, 153, 155–57
Hazard Communication Standard (1983), 143
Hazardous materials, 243
Hazardous waste storage and disposal, 237
Hazardous waste technicians, 238–39
Hazards identification, 236

Head hunters, 86
Health, occupational. *See* Occupational safety and health
Healthcare Financial Management, 83
Health Care Financing Administration (HCFA), 121, 122, 149–50
Health systems, values toward, 13
Hepatitis-B (HBV), 236–37
Heroes, corporate, 318
Hierarchy of need theory, 165
High-Tech Training Module, 211
Hiring: employee rights in, 265–66; of veterans, 76. *See also* Recruitment
Hiring attitude study, 81
Hiring halls, 86
Home care industry, xi, 197–220; agency capacity and, 216; competition in, 206; Cooperative Home Care Associates, 213–14; demographics and, 198–201; financing and, 206–7, 217; Ford Foundation Home Care Project, 212–13; for-profitization in, 206; fragmentation of, 205–6, 217; gender and race issues in, 217; guidelines for managers, 217–18; health care costs and, 198–200; as high-growth industry, 203; high-tech care, 207–8; High-Tech Training Module, 211; Homemaker/Home Health Aide Service, 214; market conditions and, 215; narrow margins and declining profits in primary services sector of, 206–7; quality of service, 210; quality of worklife and, 203–5, 208–11; regulatory and reimbursement condition and, 215–16; women in workforce and, 201–3; workforce characteristics and, 216–17
Homemaker-Home Health Aide Services in Support of High-Tech Patients and Their Families, 211, 214
Horizontal mobility, 189
Hospitalization costs, 200–201
Hospitals (trade publication), 83
Hourly pay rate, 131
Human nature, performance appraisal problems and, 102
Human relations school of management, 108

Human resource system, viability and control maintenance in, 6

Identity, defined, 230
Immigration and Naturalization Service, 88
Immigration Reform and Control Act (IRCA) of 1986, 88, 257–58
Impasse rule, 278
Implementation, strategy, 316
Incentive, individual vs. group, 141
Incentive compensation, 120–22, 163
"Incentive Compensation in the Health Care Industry," 134
Incentive pay, 128, 131. *See also* Pay systems, performance-based
Incrementalism, 15–16
Individual contemporary approach to job design and redesign, 54–56
Individual development, performance appraisal and, 100
Industrial relations, 8
Infection control committee, 240
Information: job-related, gathering, 66; preparation of, for collective bargaining, 283–85; as roadblock to human resources planning, 37; on wages, sharing of, 150
Information system, development of, 38
Information technology (IT), xii, 2, 11–13; defined, 302–4; developments in, 3; functions and applications, 12; future challenge of, 328–29; operational definition, 301–2; prospective planning in managing, 309; technostress and, 11–13; time management and, 326; working patterns and, 9. *See also* Technostress
Instrumentality, job, 52
Intent, discriminatory effect vs., 257–58
Interdisciplinary safety committee, 245
Internal environment, perception of, 8
Internal Revenue Service, 122, 150
Internal supply, future demand and, 35
Intervention, redesign, 53–54
Interviews, applicant, 57, 184
Intrinsic-extrinsic motivation theory, 165

Index

Inventory, skills, 32
Inventory buildup, 288

Job analysis, x, 3, 4, 8, 41–73, 190; compensation and, 46; contemporary challenges in, 41–43; defined, 43; guidelines for administrators and professionals, 72; importance of, 41; information gathering, 66; job descriptions and, 64–66; job design and, 44–46; job specifications and, 66; legal considerations in, 46–48; promotion and, 46; as strategic choice, 43; techniques for, 66–72; training and, 46
Job assistance, spousal, 90
Job banks, 85
Job boards, 85
Job books, 85
Job characteristics approach to job design, 48–50
Job classification system, 20
Job component method, 52, 70, 152
Job description(s), 43, 64–66, 70; job evaluation and, 158; occupational safety and health and, 244; performance appraisal standards and, 105
Job Description Index (JDI), 186
Job design, x, 3, 4, 8, 41–73; approaches to, 54–61; contemporary challenges in, 41–43; defined, 43; employee reaction to, 50–53; goals and, 44; guidelines for administrators and professionals, 72; importance of, 41; job analysis and, 44–46; job matching and, 61–64; job qualities and, 52; legal considerations in, 46–48; performance appraisal and, 44; recruitment and, 44; selection and, 44; as strategic choice, 43; technology and, 44, 59–61; theoretical perspectives on, 48–50; union-management relations and, 44
Job duties, 52
Job enlargement, 55
Job enrichment, 13, 55–56, 190; union opposition to, 193
Job evaluation, 15–57; factor comparison, 152, 154–55, 159; goal of, 152; grading or positioning classification, 152–54; Hay Plan Compensable Factors, 152, 153, 155–57; internal, 159; job-component method, 152; job description and, 158; objections to, 157; point rating, 152, 154, 158–62, 170; whole-job ranking, 152
Job inventory approach, 68
Job matching, 61–64
Job model of worker behavior, 164–65
Job postings, 79, 189
Job preference, 10–11
Job qualities, 52
Job redesign, 13, 43, 53–54, 190; approaches to, 54–61; Stamps-Piedmonte Index and, 187; supervisors and, 50; technology and, 59–61
Job referral services, 85
Job rotation, 54–55
Job satisfaction: age and, 188; Herzberg's theory of, 178; quality of worklife and, 185–88
Job sharing, 91
Job simplification, 55
Jobs Now Program, 88
Job specialization, 55
Job specification(s), 43, 66, 158
Job stability of home aides, 204
Job Training Partnership Act (JTPA) of 1984, 86
Joint Commission on the Accreditation of Hospitals (JCAH), 240
Journals, job advertisements in, 82–83
"Just cause" standard of discharge, 268

Kirkland v. *New York Department of Correctional Services*, 47

Labor force: age group distribution percentages, 9; external supply, 32–33; in home care industry, characteristics of, 216–17; reduction in, 36. *See also* Employee(s); Personnel
Labor-Management Relations Act of 1935 (Taft-Hartley), 193, 249, 251; 1947 amendments, 193, 276
Labor-Management Reporting and Disclosure Act (Landrum-Griffin Act), 193
Labor markets of OECD countries, 201–3

Labor organizations. *See* Union(s)
Law(s): antidiscrimination, state, 244, 250; antitrust, 150; comparable worth activity in, 166; effects of changes on, 33; equal opportunity, 88; ERISA, 253; incentive compensation and, 163; job analysis and design and, 46–48; "master-servant," 248; occupational safety and health, 240–44, 246; performance appraisal and, 96–99; performance-based pay systems and, 144; quality of worklife and, 193; recruitment and, 76; regulating health care costs, 150. *See also* Rights, employee
Lawsuits: antitrust, 150, 160; equal employment opportunity, 264–65; individual, 264; malpractice, 239
Leasing, employment, 90–91
Lemons v. *City and County of Denver*, 166
Lewin, Kurt, 192
Libel, 254
Life expectancies in OECD nations, 198, 199
Life-time employment relationships, 178
Line managers, 46
Line training, 230
Lockouts, 281–82, 283, 294

McDonald's Corporation, 89
Mail, electronic, 326
Malice, action in, 254
Malpractice action, 239
Management: attention to performance-based pay system, 138; classic style of, 179; hierarchical structure of, 227; human relations school of, 108; job design and relationship with union, 44; operation through strike, 281; organizational changes and, 191–93; participative, 33–34, 54, 178, 182, 191, 195; positive discipline applied to maintain safety, 244–45; quality of worklife and, 178, 182, 191, 194, 195, 208–10, 217–18; resistance to human resources planning, 37, 38; responsibility for employee rights, 263; risk, 239; salaries, 163; scientific, 48, 54; strategic approach, 326; support for occupational safety and health, 245; Theories X, Y, and Z of, 178; time, 322–23; trust in performance-based pay system and, 136–37; of turnover, 29–30. *See also* Collective bargaining
Management development, 230–31
Management education programs, quantitative orientation of, 107–8
Management Position Description Questionnaire (MPDQ), 67
Management rights clause, 279
Manager(s), 139; concern for job satisfaction, 186; critical skills needed by, 6; democratically oriented, 107–8, 109; home care industry and, 217–18; incentive payments for, 120–21; line, 46; selection of job analysis techniques by, 71
Mandatory issues of bargaining, 279, 281
Markov analysis, 27, 28, 32
Marxist view of alienation, 179
Massachusetts Rate Setting Commission, 214, 215
"Master-servant" law, 248
Material safety data sheets (MSDS), 243
Matrix, cultural, 319–20
Means goals, 35
Mechanistic approach, 5–6, 16, 57
Mediation, 280–81, 290, 295
Medicare, 121, 269n5; reimbursement policies, 207
Meditation, 323–24
Merit award, 141
Merit pay, 128, 131
Methods analysis, 68
Microcomputers, impact of, 311. *See also* Technostress
Minimum wage, 249, 255
Minority workers, underrepresentation of, 259
Mission, HCO, 8
Mobility: horizontal, 189; values toward, 13
"Mothers in the Workplace," 89
Motion study, 68
Motivation, employee: feedback and,

Index

111; intrinsic, 52; Job Characteristics Model of, 48–50; theories of, 165
Multihospital systems, 150
Multiple Sclerosis Society, Northern Illinois chapter of, 89
Multisystem development among health care organizations, 2
Multivariate quantitative approach, 25

National Business Employment Weekly, 83
National Institute for Occupational Safety and Health (NIOSH), 236
National Labor Act, 276
National Labor Relations Act (NLRA) of 1935, 47, 193, 242, 277, 278
National Labor Relations Board, 47, 282
National origin discrimination, 257–58
National Union of Hospital and Health Care Employees, 277
Negligence, 254, 255
Network: computer, 325; cultural, 318
Neutral board of inquiry (BOI), 280–81
"New pay." *See* Pay systems, performance-based
Newspaper job advertisements, 82–83
New York City Transit Authority v. *Beazer*, 172n55
No-lockout clause, 281–82
Nonmandatory issues of bargaining, 279, 281
No-spouse rule, 270n31
No-strike clause, 280
Nurse(s): alternative work patterns for, 190; exposure to reproductive hazards, 236; job satisfaction among, 186–87; pay satisfaction among, 165; salaried, 148–49; shortage of, 87–88, 148–49; wages of federally employed, 150–51
Nursing administration, 76
Nutrition, stress management and, 323

Objectives, performance-based pay systems and, 129. *See also* Goal(s), health care
Observation technique, 108
Occupational safety and health, xi, 8, 235–46; communicable diseases in workplace, 236–37, 242–43; emergency responses, 240; employee concerns, 237–38; guidelines for administrators and professionals, 244–45; hazardous waste storage and disposal, 237; hazards idenification, 236; interdisciplinary safety committee and, 245; job descriptions and, 244; legal issues, 240–44, 246; positive discipline and, 244–45; preemployment physicals and, 244; safety surveillance department, 238–40; senior management support for, 245; training and, 245; workplace exposures, 236
Occupational Safety and Health Act, general duty clause of, 243
Office of Federal Contract Compliance Programs, 264
On-call personnel, 91
Operant conditioning, 325
Operating structure, reduction in force and, 36
Organic approach to organization, 57
Organizational assessment phase of OD, 226
Organizational change, 191–93; organizational development and, 231–33
Organizational culture, 8, 317–21
Organizational design: job design and redesign strategies and, 57–59; mechanistic vs. organic technology and, 59–61
Organizational development (OD), xi, 8, 221–34; definitions of, 222–23; external environment focus of, 229; guidelines for administrators and professionals, 231–33; in health sector, 227–29; the individual and, 223–24; limitations to, 227–28; open systems perspective of, 229; process and techniques of, 226; theoretical perspectives on, 222–26; training and, 229–31; value-based focus of, 224–25
Organization for Economic Cooperation and Development (OECD) countries, 198, 199, 201–2
Organization Readiness Questionnaire, 142

Organizations, health care: alienation and nature of, 179; multisystem development among, 2; nature of, 224; political nature of, 228–29
Organization-task fit, model for, 58–59
Orientation program, employee, 184–85
OSHA, 237
Outplacement agencies, 86
Output, measurability of, 138
Overload, quantitative and qualitative job, 52
Overtime, 249, 255–56

Participative decision making, 178
Participative management, 33–34, 54, 178, 182, 191, 195
Part-time employment: growth of, 201; permanent, 190; women on, 202
Pay equity, 165–68; impact on job analysis, 48
Pay Equity Act, 48
Pay-for-knowledge systems, 132–33
Pay grades, 159, 161
Pay philosophy, 168–69
Pay satisfaction, 164–65
Pay system(s): base rate establishment, 151; internally equitable, 136; ratchet, 148. *See also* Compensation
Pay systems, performance-based, x, 127–45; advantages of, 129–30; in Barnes Hospital, 134–35; bonus plans, 132; competitiveness and, 128–29; definitions, 127–28; development in health care of, 128–29; disadvantages of, 130; entrepreneurial approach and, 129; gain sharing, 131–32; guidelines for administrators, 136–44; job-component method of job evaluation and, 152; key players in, 138–39; level of inclusion in, 139–40; merit pay systems, 131; objectives of, 128; in Planned Parenthood (Schenectady), 135–36; potential for high earnings in, 137; profit sharing, 132; in San Pedro Peninsula Hospital, 135; Scanlon plan, 132; simple incentive plans, 131; skill-based pay, 132–33; training and, 138
Performance, 230; defined, 97–100; employee control over, 138; measurability of, 138; measures of, 140–41
Performance appraisal, x, 3–5, 8, 95–125; compensation-driven, 105; criteria-based, 136; defined, 128; democratically oriented manager and, 107–8, 109; designing, 97; dissatisfaction with, 103–5; effectiveness of, 100–102; employee involvement in, 106–7; employee rights and, 267; establishing standards for, 105–8; feedback and, 111, 114–15; frequency of, 103; growing concern for, 95–96; incentive compensation and, 120–22; interview phase, 114; job design and, 44; legal considerations in, 96–99; need for documentation for, 111; preview phase, 108–13; problems with, 102–3; reasons for, 100; review phase, 115; self-appraisal and, 109–10
Performance-based pay systems. *See* Pay systems, performance-based
Performance share system, 135–36
Personnel: internal supply of, 27–32; on-call, 91; requisition for, 77, 78; supervision of, 178; temporary, 91. *See also* Employee(s); Labor force
Personnel department, 46, 76
Physical abilities analysis (PAA), 69
Physical activity, stress management and, 323
Physical job elements, 52
Physicals, preemployment, 244
Physicians: compensation of, 163; incentive payments for, 120–21
Picketing, 281, 294
Piece-rate system, 131
Planned Parenthood of Schenectady, 135–36, 141
Planning, career, 3, 4, 79–80
Planning, human resource, 15–40; assessment of internal supply, 27–32; business planning and, 17–19; collective bargaining and, 33; concept of, 15–16; defined, 16–17; determination of future employment demand, 20–26; implementation, monitoring, and evaluation, 36–37; information from job classifi-

cation system and, 20; model of, 17–19; "muddling through" approach to, 15–16; operating and strategic levels of, 17; participants in, 19; phases of, 20–37; policies, goals, and programs establishment, 34–36; rational (mechanistic), 16; reconciliation of external environment, 32–34; roadblocks to, 8, 37; systemic view of, 16
Planning, succession, 3, 4
Planning, technological, 312–14
Point-factor systems, 170
Point rating evaluation, 152, 154, 158–62, 170
Policy, organizational, 34–35; constraints on recruitment from, 77; defined, 34; effect on internal supply of personnel, 28–29; job design and redesign strategies and, 59
Policy, public, employer retaliation and, 253
Politics, effects of changes on, 33
Polygraph examinations, 261–62, 266
Position Analysis Questionnaire (PAQ), 69, 172n3
Position control systems, 77
Postings, job, 79, 80, 189
Pregnancy discrimination, 76, 251, 260, 263, 271n45
Pregnancy Discrimination Act of 1978, 76, 251, 260
Privacy, right to, 261–62
Privilege, qualified, 254
Problem-solving cycle, 61, 64
Productivity: defined, 180; estimation of future, 22–23; improvement in, 36; input and output measurements of, 180–81; job matching and, 61; performance-based pay systems and, 129; quality of worklife and, 180–82, 191, 209–10; work satisfaction and, 185–86
Professional(s): employee rights and, 265–69; job analysis and design and, 72; occupational safety and health and, 244–46; organizational development and, 231–33; relationships among, 262–63; technostress management, 327–28

Profit sharing, 132
Program implementation, 36–37
Programming, 35–36
Prohibited issues of bargaining, 280
Promissory estoppel, 252
Promotion(s), 79; bottlenecks in paths to, 9; job analysis and, 46; job design and redesign as alternatives to, 43
Prospective planning, 309
Prudent buyer rule, 121
Publicity as collective bargaining pressure, 294–95
Punitive damages, 254

Qualified privilege, 254
Quality circles, 178, 181–82, 191, 229
Quality control, 149, 181
Quality of home care service, 210
Quality of worklife (QWL), xi, 8, 177–220; advancement opportunities and, 205; alternative work patterns and, 190–91; benefits and, 204; career development and, 188–90; communication and, 177, 194; demographics and, 9; goals of, 182–83; industry structure and financing and, 205–8; job matching and, 61; job satisfaction and, 185–88; job stability and, 204; legal system and, 193; management and, 178, 182, 191, 194, 195, 208–10, 217–18; productivity and, 180–82, 191, 209–10; program adoption and implementation, 192, 214–17; quality circles and, 178, 181–82; recruitment and, 183–85, 194, 208–9; responsibility for, 191–92, 193; retention and, 183–85, 188; selection and, 183–85, 194; service quality and, 210; Theory X and Y and, 178; training and support and, 204, 211; turnover and, 209; unions and, 193, 210; wage levels and, 203; wage parity and, 204; work alienation and, 178–80
Questionnaire(s), 57; Management Position Description Questionnaire (MPDQ), 67; Organization Readiness, 142; Position Analysis Questionnaire (PAQ), 69, 172n3

Quota approach to affirmative action, 259, 271n39

Racial discrimination, 257–58, 273n63
Radio advertising for job openings, 82
Ratchet pay adjustment system, 148
Rational planning, 16
Reasonable accommodation of handicap, 260–61
Reassignments, 79
"Receipt of federal funds," defined, 269n5
Recruitment, x, 3, 4, 8, 36, 75–93; advertising and, 81–85; affirmative action and, 77, 79, 88, 92; alternatives to, 90–91; child care and, 89; constraints on, 77–79, 87; defined, 75; dual career couples and, 90; in educational institutions, 87; employee involvement in, 88, 92; employment agencies and, 86; evaluating methods of, 91–92; executive search firms and, 86; external, 81–89; guidelines for administrators and professionals, 92; handicap facilities and, 90; of handicapped, 88, 89; human resource planning and, 17, 33; initiating, 77; internal, 74–81; job design and, 44; law and, 76; outplacement agencies and, 86; overseas, 87–88; performance-based pay system and, 130; quality of worklife and, 183–85, 194, 208–9; responsibility for, 76–79; retention goals of, 183–84; of retirees, 89; timing of, 75; walk-in applicants, 88, 92
References, employment, 88, 92, 184; defamation in, 254, 266; of handicapped worker, 88–89
Referrals, 88–89, 92
Referral services, 86
Refreezing, 192–93
Regional office, influence on pay decisions, 149
Regression projections of long-term staffing demand, 23–25
Rehabilitation Act of 1973, 76, 242, 243
Reinstatement rights of strikers, 282–83
Related party rule, 121

Reliability of home aide, 210
Religious discrimination, 259
Replacement chart, 30, 31
Replacement planning, 30
Reproductive hazards, 236, 241–42
Requisition, personnel, 77, 78
Research, technostress, 317
Resignations, employee, 27
Retaliation by employer, public policy and, 253
Retention, employee, 183–85, 188
Retirees, recruitment of, 89
Reward-penalty system, 114
Rewards, organizational: allocation of, 228; desired behaviors and, 101–2
Rights, employee, xii, 8, 247–73; Age Discrimination in Employment Act (ADEA), 76, 250, 260; child labor, 249, 256; civil rights movement and, 250; collective bargaining emergence of, 249; comparable worth, 256; contract theories and, 252–53; discharge from employment, 268; discrimination and, 166, 257–59, 263–65, 273n63; employee discipline and, 267; employment-at-will doctrine and, 248–49, 251; equal pay for equal work, 249, 256; everyday employee relations and, 266–67; Fair Labor Standards Act, 255–56; future trends in, 263–64; grievance procedures, 268–69, 276; guidelines for administrators and professionals, 265–69; handicaps and, 260–61; health care amendments to National Labor Relations Act, 251; in hiring, 265–66; individual litigation, 264; minimum wages, 249, 255; overtime, 249, 255–56; performance appraisal and wage administration, 267; predominance of women in health occupations and, 263; Pregnancy Discrimination Act, 76, 251, 260; privacy rights, 261–62; relationships among health care professionals and, 262–63; responsibility for, 263; retaliation and public policy, 253; Title VII of Civil Rights Act (1964), 256–59; torts in, 254–55; Vocational Rehabilitation Act,

Index

46, 250–51, 260–61; work hours, 255–56. *See also* Affirmative action; Law(s)
Right-to-know laws, 243
Risk management, 239
Rites and rituals, corporate, 318
Role underload, 52
ROPEP (results-oriented performance evaluation program), 152
Rope theory, 225
Rotation, job, 54–55
Rowe v. *General Motors*, 47

Safety. *See* Occupational safety and health
Safety complaints, 243–44
Safety specialists, 238
Safety surveillance department: administrative structure of, 238–39; as organizational liaison, 239–40
Salary: based, 136, 151; defined, 128; surveys, 160–61
Sampling, work, 68
Sanders, Frank, 89
San Pedro Peninsula Hospital, 135
Scanlon plan, 132
Scanning, environment, 33
Schedule(s) and scheduling, 266; part-time, permanent, 190; religious discrimination and, 259
Scientific management, 48, 54
Screening, preemployment, 261–62, 265–66, 270n26
Secrecy, compensation system design and, 164
Selection: human resource planning and, 17; job design and, 44; quality of worklife and, 183–85, 194
Self-appraisal, 109–10
Self-development strategies, employee, 321–25
Service(s): alternative sources of, 288; diversification of, 30; expected levels of, 20–23
Service Employees International Union, 277
Services sector, growth of, 201–2
Sex discrimination, 166, 258–59, 263
Sexual harassment, 258–59, 271n34

Simplification, job, 55
Skill-based pay, 132–33
Skills, job matching to, 61
Skills inventory, 32
Skill variety, 49–50
Slander, 254
Sociotechnological approach to job design, 50
Sore-thumbing, 157
Specialization, job, 55; alienation and, 179–80
Spokesperson of bargaining team, 287
Spousal job assistance, 90
"Squaring of the pyramid" phenomenon, 198, 200
Staff: external supply and, 35; reconciliation of supply of and demand for, 32; surpluses, 36; training of, 230. *See also* Employee(s); Labor force; Personnel
Stamps-Piedmonte Index, 187
State employment services, 86
State rate commissions, 150
Sterilizer, surgical instrument, malfunction of, 240
Strategic choice, 6–8
Strategic human resource management (SHRM), ix, 1–14; changes influencing, 2; defined, 1; for integrated human resource system, 3–5; internal and external environment, 8–13; overall outcomes, 13; purposes of, 2–3; strategy and strategic choices, 6–8; theoretical perspectives, 5–6
Strategic management approach, 326
Strategic technological planning, 312–14
Strategy: implementation of, 316; operational definition of, 6
Stress: audit, 314–16; worker, 210. *See also* Technostress
Strike(s), 280–83, 293–95; economic vs. unfair labor practice, 282–83; good faith bargaining and, 281; incentive role of, 293; management planning for, 287–88; mandatory issues of bargaining and, 281; unions' right to, 280, 281. *See also* Collective bargaining
Struck work, 282

Structure, organizational, 8
Succession planning, 3, 4
Supervisor(s): collective bargaining preparation and, 283–84; internal recruitment and, 80–81; job redesign and, 50
Supreme Court, 265
Surgical instrument sterilizer, malfunction of, 240
Surveys, salary, 160–61
Systemic view of planning, 16
Systems model of human resources management, 5–6
Systems planning, ix-x

Taft-Hartley Act of 1935, 193, 249, 251; 1947 amendments, 193, 276
Task force, redesign, 53
Task identification, 49–50
Task Inventory CODAP, 68
Task-organization fit, model for, 58–59
Task significance, 49–50
Tax code, two-income families and, 150
Tax-exempt status, 144
Team, collective bargaining, 286–87
Team building, 229
Team contemporary approach to job design and redesign, 56
Technicians, hazardous waste, 238–39
Technological planning, strategic, 312–14
Technology: alienation and, 179–80; effect on human resources, 34; in home care, 207–8; job design and, 44, 59–61; job redesign and, 59–61; negative and positive impacts of, 309, 310–11; organizational design and, 59–61. See also Information technology (IT)
Techostress, xii, 2, 8, 301–35; adaptation and, 304; concept of, 302–5; cultural analysis and, 319–20; employee self-development strategies, 321–25; factors of, 302; guidelines for administrators and professionals, 327–28; information technology and, 11–13; moderating variables, 305; new technology-based strategies and, 325–26; operational definitions, 301–2; organizational culture and, 317–21; sociopsychological aspects of time management and communications, 326–27; strategic choice model of, 305–11; technoeustress and technodistress components of, 304–5, 314; technology strategy for managing, 311–17. See also Information technology (IT)
Teleconferencing, 325
Television advertising for job openings, 82
Temporary personnel, 91
Terminations, employee, 27
Tests, employee, written, 57
Tests, preemployment, 261–62, 265–66, 270n26
Theories X, Y, and Z, 178
Thompson, James, 88
Threshold traits analysis, 68
Time, as roadblock to human resources planning, 37
Time management, 322–23; information technology change and, 326; sociopsychological aspects of, 326–27
Time-series projections of long-term staffing demand, 23–25
Time span of discretion, 172n3
Title VII of Civil Rights Act of 1964, 76, 244, 250, 256–59; fetal protection policies and, 241–42
Torts, 254–55
Trade unions, 86
Training, 3, 4–5, 8; for home aides, 204; job analysis and, 46; line, 230; occupational safety and health and, 245; organizational development and, 229–39; performance-based pay system and, 138; quality of worklife and, 204, 211; of staff, 230
Training programs, 188–89; design of, 230
Transfer policy, 189
Trend evaluation, 29–30
Trustees, board of, 139
Trust in management, performance-based pay system and, 136–37
Turnover, 183; controllable vs. uncontrollable, 30; evaluation and management of, 29–30; functional vs.

dysfunctional, 29–30; among home aides, 209; rate of, 27, 188
Two-income families, tax code and, 150

Uncertainty, technological. *See* Technostress
Underload, role, 52
Unfair labor practice strike, 282–83
"Unfreezing," 192
Uniform Guidelines (1978), 47
Union(s), 249, 277; home care workers and, 2, 210; labor practice strike, 282–83; impact on wage scales, 151; job design and relations with management, 44; opposition to job enrichment, 193; quality of worklife and, 193, 210; right to strike, 280, 281; trade, 86. *See also* Collective bargaining
Unionization, 33, 276
Union movement, 178
U.S.A. v. City of Chicago, 47
U.S. Department of Labor, 88
U.S. Employment Service, 86
Unskilled workers, 149
Unwed motherhood, 260
Utilization rate, 20–21

Vacancies, compensation and time to fill, 81
Valences, job, 52
Values, organizational, 318
Value systems, 13
Vancouver (B.C.) Sun, 82
Vertical loading, 55
Veterans, hiring of, 76
Vietnam Era Veterans Readjustment Act of 1974, 76
Visiting nurse associations (VNAs), 205, 206
Vocational Rehabilitation Act of 1973, 45, 250–51, 260–61

Wage(s): competitive, 160–61; contract, 164; employee rights and, 267; government control of, 149–51; minimum, 249, 255; quality of worklife and, 203, 204; sharing information on, 150
Wagner Act. *See* National Labor Relations Act (NLRA) of 1935
Walk-in applicants, 92
Wall Street Journal, 83
What-if approach, 26
Whistle-blowing, 253
Whole-job ranking, 152
Women in health occupations: home care industry and, 201–3; part-time employment, 202; predominance of, 263. *See also* Nurse(s)
Women's movement, 276
Work: alienation from, 178–80; dissatisfaction with, 179; hours of, 255–56; measurement of, 68; models of, 164–65; patterns of, 9, 190–91; values toward, 13
Worker reliability, 210
Workforce. *See* Labor force
Work groups, autonomous, 50, 190
Work Incentive (WIN) Program, 86
Worklife, quality of. *See* Quality of worklife (QWL)
Workloads: estimation of, long-term staffing demand and, 23; service level measures and, 21–22
Workplace: communicable diseases in, 236–37, 242–43; exposure to hazards, 236
Work sampling, 68
Work stoppage, 290. *See also* Lockouts; Strike(s)
Work-study programs, 87
Work teams, autonomous, 56
Work time, regular, 151
Workweek, compressed, 191
Written tests, 57
Wrongful discharge, 255

Yoga, 324

About the Editors and Contributors

EDITORS

AMARJIT S. SETHI is Associate Professor at the Faculty of Administration, University of Ottawa. He specializes in Industrial Relations and Human Resource Management in the health care sector. He received his M.S. (Industrial Relations) from the University of Wisconsin and his Ph.D. (Social Administration) from Manchester University. He has worked as a consultant in health care and international development projects in India, Afghanistan, the United Kingdom, the United States, and Canada. He is the author, coauthor, and editor of many books including *Industrial Relations and Health Services* (1982); *Handbook of Organizational Stress Coping Strategies* (1984); *Strategic Management of Technostress in an Information Society* (1987); *Collective Bargaining in Canada* (1989); *Collective Bargaining in the Public Sector in the United States: A Time of Change* (in press); *Mediation as an Intervention in Stress Reactivity*; and *Industrial Relations in the Public Services in the United Kingdom* (in press).

RANDALL S. SCHULER is Research Professor, Stern School of Business, New York University. His interests are international human resource management, organizational uncertainty, personnel and human resource management, entrepreneurship, and the interface of competitive strategy and human resource management. He received his M.B.A. and Ph.D. degrees from Michigan State

University. He has authored and edited twenty books including *Personnel and Human Resource Management*, 4th ed.; *Case Problems in Management*, 3rd ed.; *Effective Personnel Management*, 3rd ed.; *Book of Readings in Personnel and Human Resource Management*, 3rd ed.; *Human Resource Management in the 1980s*; *Personal Computer Projects for PHRM*; and *Managing Job Stress*. In addition, he has contributed over twenty chapters to reading books and has published over seventy articles in professional journals and academic proceedings. Presently, he is on the editorial boards of *Academy of Management Executive*, *Human Resource Management*, *Journal of Management*, and *Organization Science*. He is Editor of the *Human Resource Planning Journal* and is on the Board of Directors of the Human Resource Planning Society.

CONTRIBUTORS

JOHN BERNAT is an Assistant Professor of Health Systems Management at Rush University and also an instructor at De Paul University College of Law. He received a B.S. and an M.B.A. degree from Illinois Institute of Technology and a J.D. from IIT/Chicago–Kent College of Law. He is Director of Personnel at Rush–Presbyterian–St. Luke's Medical Center in Chicago and President of Neighborhood Justice of Chicago, a Chicago Bar Association project for alternative dispute resolution.

PATRICIA L. BIRKWOOD holds B.Sc. and M.Sc. degrees in biochemistry from McMaster University and an M.H.A. degree from the University of Ottawa. She is currently Project Coordinator for the Special Projects Office of the Bureau of Radiation and Medical Devices, Health and Welfare Canada, and works in the area of medical device risk management.

ROBERT BOISSONEAU, Ph.D., is a Professor in the Center for Health Services Administration and Policy at Arizona State University, in Tempe, Arizona. He has authored two books, *Health Care Organizations and Development* and *Continuing Education in the Health Professions*, and has written several articles in the field of management development. He is a member of the editorial board of *Journal of the Association of Human Resource Management* and *Organizational Behavior*, 1985 to the present.

EUGENE P. BUCCINI, Ph.D., is a Professor of Management at Western Connecticut State University. He is also the president of Human Resource Systems, a management consulting company specializing in human resource management in the health services industry. Among his publications is *Personnel Policies and Procedures for Health Care Facilities* (Greenwood Press, 1989), coauthored with Charles P. Mullaney. His current projects involve developing human resource charge-back systems and organizational effectiveness indicators for health care facilities.

About the Editors and Contributors

DAVID N. CALVERT, M.B.A., is a freelance consultant in Tempe, Arizona.

DENIS H.J. CARO holds an M.H.A. from the University of Montreal, an M.B.A. from the universities of McGill and Minnesota, and a Ph.D. from the University of Minnesota. He is an Associate Professor and Director, Master's Programme in Health Administration at the Faculty of Administration, University of Ottawa. He works as a consultant in health care finance, planning and evaluation, and health care information systems and has also written extensively. His work includes contributions to *Dimensions in Health Service*, and he is coauthor with Amarjit S. Sethi of a book entitled *Strategic Management of Technostress in an Information Society*.

THOMAS E. DUSTON is Associate Professor of Economics at Keene State College of the University System of New Hampshire. His field is health economics, and he has publications on moral hazard, patient payment behavior, and health resource education. His current research interest concerns the assessment of reproductive technology.

PENNY HOLLANDER FELDMAN is a Political Scientist on the faculty of the Department of Health Policy and Management at the Harvard School of Public Health. Her research is on health policy, regulation, and organizational behavior. She is the author of several articles on health care regulation, Medicaid, and medical technology. Feldman has recently completed a three-year Ford Foundation funded study of quality of worklife in the U.S. home care industry.

LOIS FRISS is Associate Professor in Health Services Administration at the University of Southern California School of Public Administration. She has authored several articles on nursing turnover and comparable worth. Her book, *The Basis for the Strategic Management of Nurses*, which is in press, provides a focused synthesis of the research in nursing work and employment.

DEBRAH J. GAULDING, R.D.H., is a practice management consultant in Scottsdale, Arizona. She was working for G.E. Dantona and Associates, a consulting firm in Scottsdale, Arizona, when the article was written.

DONNA L. GELLATLY, M.B.A., C.P.A., is a University Professor of Health Administration at Governors State University, University Park, Illinois. She is the course developer and instructor of a elecourse in management accounting for health care organizations. Gellatly was among those awarded a grant to develop a long-term care administration module in human resource management by the Association of University Programs in Health Administration (AUPHA).

KIRK C. HARLOW is Assistant Professor of Administrative Sciences at the University of Houston–Clear Lake. He has written on a variety of topics including employee assistance programs and financial analysis of local government projects. He is currently working on research examining the application of strategic planning methods in a public health agency.

JAMES HILL has worked as a human resources professional in health care since 1983. He holds a B.A. degree from St. John's College in Annapolis, Maryland, and a Master's degree in industrial relations from Loyola University. He received a J.D. from the John Marshall Law School in 1988. He is presently Director of Human Resources at Rush–North Shore Medical Center of Rush–Presbyterian–St. Luke's Medical Center in Chicago and an instructor in Rush University's graduate program in Health Systems Management.

HOWARD M. LEFTWICH is an Associate Professor of Economics and Coordinator of Labor and Employment Relations Studies at the University of Cincinnati. He is the author of a number of articles on labor relations and human resource issues. His primary current research interest is dispute resolution systems in public sector labor relations. Leftwich has taught numerous courses in labor and employment relations and labor economics.

ALICE M. SAPIENZA is Assistant Professor of Management at Harvard School of Public Health's Department of Health Policy and Management. She teaches graduate courses in strategic planning and organizational design, as well as executive courses in organizational behavior. A former general manager in a Harvard University teaching hospital, Sapienza has more than a dozen years of practical management experience in a range of organizations.

PAULA L. STAMPS is Associate Professor in the Health Policy and Management Program of the School of Health Sciences at the University of Massachusetts in Amherst, Massachusetts. Her research has concentrated on program evaluation as well as occupational satisfaction. In 1986 she published a book describing ten years of research that led to the statistical validation of an attitude scale to measure occupational satisfaction of nurses. This work has led her to the broader issues regarding the quality of work life.

JOSEPH K. TAYLOR is Associate Professor and Director of the Center for Administration of Health Services at the University of Houston–Clear Lake. He has written on a variety of topics in the field of health care administration,. He spent twenty years as a hospital chief executive officer prior to teaching and academic administration. His research interests concern productivity in health care facilities.

RUTH B. WELBORN is Associate Professor and Chair of the Departments of Allied Health Sciences and Health Administration at Southwest Texas State University. Her research has focused on the relationship of learning styles and teaching styles of health professional students and their instructors as it relates to achievement levels. Welborn is currently working on a project relating the human resource developer's teaching style to employee performance in a variety of health care settings.